Sources
of
Contemporary Radicalism

Studies of the Research Institute on
International Change, Columbia University
Zbigniew Brzezinski, series editor

Zbigniew Brzezinski is Herbert Lehman Professor of Government and director of the Research Institute on International Change at Columbia University, where he has taught since 1960. Dr. Brzezinski serves also in the Carter administration as assistant to the president for national security affairs.

Radicalism in the Contemporary Age
Seweryn Bialer and Sophia Sluzar, editors
Vol. 1—Sources of Contemporary Radicalism

To understand contemporary society, it has become more and more essential to understand the phenomenon of radicalism—the aspirations of radical movements, the strategies and tactics of radicalism, and the impact of radicalism on contemporary society. *Radicalism in the Contemporary Age* grew out of the recognition of this need. A study in three volumes, it is based on original papers that were prepared for a series of workshops held in 1975 at the Research Institute on International Change, Columbia University, and then revised in light of the workshop discussions.

This volume, *Sources of Contemporary Radicalism,* begins with Seweryn Bialer's examination of the definitional aspects of radicalism, as well as with the identification of specific contemporary sources of the radical impulse and the social groups that are the carriers of radicalism within society. In the next two chapters, Seymour Lipset and Stanley Rothman consider the case of the United States. Lipset asks anew the question posed by Werner Sombart at the beginning of this century: "Why is there no socialism in the United States?" From the perspective of a century of literature addressed to this question, he provides his own critique and explanation. Rothman considers the relatively new phenomenon of student radicalism in the United States, and, on the basis of interviews with student activists and results of tests they agreed to take, he offers hypotheses concerning their psychological motivation. Sidney Tarrow's chapter presents a comparison and contrast of the societal sources contributing to the growth of radical movements in post–World War II France and Italy. Henry Landsberger, in his chapter, concentrates on one societal group, the peasantry. Landsberger addresses the methodological issue that arises in defining peasant discontent as radicalism, and examines what it is that provides a "new" dimension to peasant discontent in modern times. In the final chapter, William Overholt presents a valuable interpretive survey of the literature on radicalism.

Radical Visions of the Future, the second volume of this study, treats the visionary component of radicalism, the component that encompasses an image of the "good society" and that provides inspiration and possibly even direction to a radical movement in its combat with the existing order.

The third volume, *Strategies and Impact of Contemporary Radicalism,* deals principally with three themes: the models and strategies of revolutionary change adopted by diverse radical movements; the impact of radicalism on the societies where it exists; and the prospects of radical success in the political arena.

* * *

Seweryn Bialer, an expert on comparative communism and revolutionary change, teaches in the Department of Political Science at Columbia University and is director of programs at the Research Institute on International Change.

Sophia Sluzar is assistant director of the Research Institute on International Change. A doctoral candidate in Columbia University's Department of History, she has taught modern European history at Pace College for four years.

Other Titles in This Series

Radicalism
in the
Contemporary Age

Seweryn Bialer, editor
Sophia Sluzar, associate editor

Volume 1
Sources
of
Contemporary Radicalism

CONTRIBUTORS

SEWERYN BIALER   HENRY A. LANDSBERGER
SEYMOUR MARTIN LIPSET   WILLIAM H. OVERHOLT
STANLEY ROTHMAN   SIDNEY TARROW

PREFACE BY ZBIGNIEW BRZEZINSKI

WESTVIEW PRESS
BOULDER, COLORADO

A Westview Special Study

Copyright © 1977 by the Research Institute on International Change, Columbia University

Published 1977 in the United States of America by
  Westview Press, Inc.
  1898 Flatiron Court
  Boulder, Colorado 80301
  Frederick A. Praeger, Publisher and Editorial Director

Library of Congress Cataloging in Publication Data

Main entry under title:

Sources of contemporary radicalism.

  (Radicalism in the contemporary age; v. 1)
(Studies of the Research Institute on International Change, Columbia University)
  1. Radicalism—History—Addresses, essays, lectures. I. Bialer, Seweryn. II. Series. III. Series: Columbia University. Research Institute on International Change, Columbia University.
HX15.R25 vol. 1 [HX36]   320.5'3s [320.5'3]   76-39891
ISBN 0-89158-217-7

Printed and bound in the United States of America

Contents

320.53
2084B

Preface

The three volumes composing *Radicalism in the Contemporary Age* are the outcome of a series of workshops held at the Research Institute on International Change between February and May 1975. Four workshops were organized to examine the sources of radicalism; the aspirations of radical movements; the strategies and tactics of radicalism; and the conditions of success and the impact of radicalism on contemporary societies.

The first workshop was designed to explore whether and to what extent the explanations given in past studies for the development of radicalism—explanations such as rapid changes in the stratification system, rising expectations, the characteristics of marginality in individuals, and so forth—still held true. It seemed possible that contemporary conditions required a different explanatory framework for radical behavior. The second workshop, dealing with the aspirations of radical movements, was organized because it seemed important to examine not only the much neglected "visionary" aspect of radical movements, but also the function of this vision in the formation, development, or decline of radical movements. By developing and linking new revolutionary theories with new forms of revolutionary warfare—for example, in the perception of the relation of forces underlying the revolutionary process, in the selection of methods, and in the expectations of success—radical movements since World War II have demonstrated distinctive characteristics.

Thus, the third workshop was devoted to a partial examination of these aspects of radicalism. The final workshop dealt not only with questions regarding the kinds of revolutions possible in the contemporary world, but also with conditions of stability in industrialized democracies in an era of rapid global change. It should be noted that the focus of the workshops was on radicalism in the United States and Western Europe; developing and communist societies entered only marginally into the discussions.

We attempted to assure continuity in the workshops by inviting to all four a core group of the same participants. We also tried to assure that the participants would be heterogeneous in terms of age as well as in their political and methodological orientations. The papers for the workshops were distributed to the participants in advance so that each session would be devoted entirely to discussion led off by a principal commentator.

It had been our original intention to publish not only the papers from each workshop, but also the remarks of the principal commentators as well as the discussions. The constraints of publication have necessitated the abandonment of this ambitious scheme and, we regret, the elimination of some papers. Nevertheless, complete transcripts of the discussions and the original papers, as well as summaries, are available and can be consulted at the institute's library.

An enterprise of this nature involves the efforts of many persons. First of all, I would like to thank the principal commentators and the authors of the papers for the workshops. Seymour Martin Lipset (then at Harvard University, now at Stanford University) spoke at the first workshop, Februrary 5, 1975, on "Sources of Radicalism in the United States"; Juan Linz (Yale University) wrote a paper on "The Sources of Radicalism in the Iberian Peninsula"; and Sidney Tarrow (Cornell University) wrote on "Sources of French Radicalism: Archaic Protest, Antibureaucratic Rebellion, and Anticapitalist Revolt." The principal commentator was Mark Kesselman (Columbia University). The paper by Stanley

Rothman (Smith College) et al., "Ethnic Variations in Student Radicalism: Some New Perspectives," was discussed by Dr. David Gutmann (Center of Psycho-Social Studies, Chicago). The principal commentator for Henry Landsberger's (University of North Carolina at Chapel Hill) paper, "The Sources of Rural Radicalism," was Donald Zagoria (Hunter College, City University of New York). William H. Overholt (Hudson Institute) contributed a paper on "Sources of Radicalism and Revolution: A Survey of Literature."

At the workshop on March 5, the discussion of a paper by Robert Nisbet (Columbia University), "The Function of the Vision of the Future in Radical Movements," was initiated by Leszek Kolakowski (Oxford University). William Griffith (Massachusetts Institute of Technology) and Ira Katznelson (University of Chicago) discussed papers by Bertell Ollman (New York University), "Marx's Vision of Communism: A Reconstruction"; Maurice Meisner (University of Wisconsin), "Utopian and Dystopian Elements in the Maoist Vision of the Future"; and Dick Howard (State University of New York, Stony Brook), "The Future as Present: Political and Theoretical Implications." Marcus Raskin (Institute of Policy Studies) spoke on "Futurology and Its Radical Critique."

At the April 2 workshop the principal commentator on Alexander Dallin's (Stanford University) paper, "Retreat from Optimism: On Marxian Models of Revolution," was Michel Oksenberg (University of Michigan). Bogdan Denitch (Queens College, City University of New York) introduced the discussion of Henry Bienen's (Princeton University) paper, "New Theories of Revolution," and Sidney Tarrow led off the discussion on Peter Lange's (Harvard University) paper, "The French and Italian Communist Parties: Postwar Strategy and Domestic Society." Klaus Mehnert (*Osteuropa*) gave the initial comments on Massimo Teodori's (Rome) paper, "The New Lefts in Europe."

At the fourth workshop the discussions were initiated by Lewis Coser (State University of New York, Stony Brook), on John Dunn's (Cambridge University) "The Success and

Failure of Modern Revolutions"; Douglas Chalmers (Columbia University), on Alfred Stepan's (Yale University) "Inclusionary and Exclusionary Military Responses to Radicalism with Special Attention to Peru"; and Seweryn Bialer (Columbia University), on Charles Maier's (Harvard University, now at Duke University) "Beyond Revolution? Resistance and Vulnerability to Radicalism in Advanced Western Societies." Samuel Huntington (Harvard University) spoke on "The Meanings of Stability in the Modern Era."

In addition to the authors of papers and the principal commentators, the participants in the discussions at the workshops were Isaac Balbus (York, City University of New York), Thomas Bernstein (Yale University, now at Columbia University), Bernard Brown (Graduate Center, City University of New York), Mauro Calamandrei (*L'Espresso*), Alexander Erlich (Columbia University), Stuart Fagan (Columbia University), Oleh Fedyshyn (Richmond, City University of New York), Clifford Geertz (Institute for Advanced Study, Princeton University), Charles Issawi (Columbia University, now at Princeton University), Joachim Kondziela (University of Lublin, Poland), Irving Kristol (Graduate Center, City University of New York, and *Public Interest*), Robbin Laird (Columbia University), Robert Lane (Yale University), S. Robert Lichter (Harvard University), Egon Neuberger (State University of New York, Stony Brook), William Odom (U.S. Military Academy, West Point), Harvey Picker (Columbia University), Carl Riskin (Columbia University), Joseph Rothschild (Columbia University), James Schmidt (Columbia University, now at University of Texas), Bhabani Sen Gupta (Nehru University, New Delhi), Allan Silver (Columbia University), Bruce Smith (Columbia University), Fritz Stern (Columbia University), and Ronald Tiersky (Amherst College).

It gives me pleasure to acknowledge the important contribution rendered by the staff of the institute. Mitchell Brody was helpful in the early planning stages of the workshops. Richard Royal helped not only with the organizational aspects but also in the preparation of summaries of the discussions. Richard Snyder and Robert Nurick were invaluable in contributing their technical and substantive expertise during the revision and preparation of the papers for publication. The institute owes a special debt to Reet Varnik, to whom the preparation of the transcripts was entrusted. Subsequently she prepared summaries of the discussions and had the responsibility of making many of the initial revisions on the papers. Her considerable editorial talents are deeply appreciated.

A central role in our efforts was played by the institute's director of programs, Seweryn Bialer, who designed the broad intellectual structure of the enterprise and provided the intellectual impetus for it, and by the assistant director of the institute, Sophia Sluzar, who contributed creatively to the intellectual format and also supplied the indispensable organizational leadership. Without them, this series would not have been realized.

The institute also wishes to acknowledge and to thank the National Endowment for the Humanities for providing partial funding for the workshops.

Zbigniew Brzezinski

Sources
of
Contemporary Radicalism

Seweryn Bialer, an expert on comparative communism and revolutionary change, teaches in the Department of Political Science at Columbia University and is director of programs at the Research Institute on International Change. He is author of Stalin and His Generals, *which deals with Soviet World War II memoirs, as well as of numerous articles on Soviet and Eastern European affairs and on radicalism. His most recent publication is "The Soviet Political Elite and Internal Developments in the USSR," chapter 2 in* The Soviet Empire: Expansion and Detente, *edited by William E. Griffith (volume 9 of* Critical Choices for Americans, *published by Lexington Press). Professor Bialer is currently working on a monograph on Leninism and the peasantry in the Russian revolutions.*

1

On the Meanings, Sources, and Carriers of Radicalism in Contemporary Industrialized Societies: Introductory Remarks

Seweryn Bialer

This volume needs no elaborate introduction. Five papers address its subject—the sources of contemporary radicalism. Two are studies of particular countries—the United States by Professor Lipset, France and Italy by Professor Tarrow. The third, by Professor Landsberger, concentrates on a specific dimension of the problem—rural radicalism. Professor Rothman's paper is an initial report on an imaginative study of American student radicals which relates their ethnic background to the psychological sources of their radical commitment.[1] The final essay, by Dr. Overholt, contributes a comprehensive and critical review of the literature on the subject.[2] Still other dimensions of the problem might have been explored, both on the conceptual level and on the concrete level of historical analysis;[3] but the scope of the issues presented seemed quite sufficient for a single volume.

These introductory remarks will focus less on the specific issues raised in these five papers than on several broad themes elaborated in their vigorous discussion at the workshop on the Sources of Radicalism, chaired by Professor Zbigniew Brzezinski. The ideas expressed here will draw on both papers and discussion, but they of course reflect solely the opinions of the author. They treat two main themes: the meaning of radicalism and the sources and carriers of contemporary radicalism.

We all know how fruitless discussions of definition can be, how often the choice of a definition follows the rule "to each axe-grinder his own." As social scientists we have to seek clarity in the use of terms and concepts, especially since these terms and concepts carry highly emotive connotations not only within the academic community but beyond it as well. It might be useful to begin the attempt, therefore, with a few words about the function and purpose of definition.

First, as Stanislaw Ossowski reminds us, the procedure of defining may perform different functions: either *terminological,* when one seeks to select a term for an already established concept, or *conceptual,* when one seeks to establish the extension of the concept to be designated by a given term. Clearly, the second function more properly relates to the discussion of radicalism. And this being the case, one should remember that

> to fix the boundaries of the application of the concepts in a particular way can be the result of a passive submission to tradition, but it can also be the result of choice. Disputes over the boundaries of concepts are—provided one does not assume a prelogical standpoint—disputes about the relative importance of particular boundaries.[4]

Secondly, in the quest for a degree of definitional clarity we should not forget that

> the ambiguous or multiple meanings of words, as they are ordinarily used, are an important part of the evidence. Social scientists should consider this evidence with clear heads, but should not clarify it out of existence. The scientist's legitimate quest for clarity can subtly distort such evidence by supposing that, once the confusions of a term are cleared up, the problems to which it refers have disappeared also.[5]

Third, we must appreciate that central to any quest for understanding social reality is a statement of propositions which can be tested for truth and not auxiliary definitions which provide merely the scaffolding of social discourse.

In light of these observations, I will limit my discussion of the meaning of radicalism to the essential minimum, even though the participants in the workshop developed on this subject an extended and often provocative exchange.

The term "radicalism" as a political phenomenon is most commonly used to describe the advocacy of and action toward sweeping, fundamental, and rapid change of laws and methods of governing.[6] Yet, as Professor Lipset remarks at the beginning of his essay, the basic definition "still leaves the empirical problem of filling in the concept with indicators of actual events and movements." Empirical considerations suggest that the phenomenon of radicalism has both structural and historical dimensions. Probably the most rapid and direct access to the structural dimension is through defining its *genus proximum,* the attributes which it shares with a larger class, as well as its *differentia specifica,* the attributes which are peculiar to the category defined. This approach yields more useful results than the more common but less precise form of nominal definition which enumerates ostensible component factors.[7] Let me introduce a number of postulates that may help to define radicalism. Some of them are readily accepted and elicit little controversy. Others, as the discussions of the term revealed, involve major differences of opinion that reflect divergent political and ideological premises.

Some of the most sweeping changes in the sociopolitical arena have occurred as unintended consequences of individual and mass actions, where the participants were not interested in sociopolitical change, were not motivated by a desire for such change, or were not conscious of the transformative potential of their efforts. Since it is generally accepted, however, that radicalism involves an orientation toward the change of existing conditions, the initial postulate should be that such orientation is intentional, conscious.[8]

This is not to say that the consequences of "radical" actions will necessarily reflect the intended radical goals. In some cases where the actions are manifestly unsuccessful, the consequences may yield the opposite of what radicals intended. The observation that nineteenth century bomb-throwing anarchists were the best friends of policemen applies frequently to the second half of the twentieth century as well. And, in those instances where radical actions were so successful that they resulted in a victorious political revolution, it seems fair to say that not one contemporary example has as yet implemented or is moving toward implementing its proclaimed key goals.

This situation, however, does not alter the fact that we understand radicalism to mean movements, groups, and individuals who desire change and openly proclaim as their goal the transformation of the existing order—those motivated on the conscious level by an orientation against the status quo.

One can suggest further that perceptions of radicalism tend to stress not its ends but its means. Both in the popular mind and very often in the social sciences as well, radicalism is most commonly associated with subversion, unrest, militancy, uncompromising stance, direct action, extremism, and violence. As a matter of fact some definitions focus entirely on the means of radicalism. The official Marxian-Leninist definition of radicalism in the Soviet *Political Dictionary* reads: "a tendency, propensity for forceful drastic measures."[9]

It seems to me, as it did to many participants in the workshop, that such a stress is false and may be highly misleading. No doubt there exists the propensity among radical movements, groups, and individuals to engage in extraparliamentary, nonconstitutional, and confrontational, often violent forms of action. It would be surprising indeed if extralegal methods of action were shunned by movements which object so strenuously to an existing system, which question its historical and actual legitimacy in part or entirely, which are intensely committed to its change, and for one reason or another deeply believe in the righteousness of their cause. In this sense, militancy, direct action,[10] violence are actually in many cases structural components of radicalism and are always present as a latent tendency.

Yet I would argue that the presence of militancy, direct action, and violence, far from being a sufficient condition in the definition of radicalism, is not even a necessary condition. It is not a sufficient condition because the instruments of militancy and violence, let alone those of nonparliamentary actions, are not confined to what can be called, by any stretch of the term, radical movements and groups, even within democratic societies. Moreover, if one remembers the fact that an overwhelming majority of contemporary nation-states is authoritarian, and that authoritarian tendencies are strong even in democratic systems, the main source of violence rests today in the established orders themselves and is generated primarily by defense of the status quo.[11] Such means do not constitute a necessary condition because, in many cases, movements and groups that are committed to a struggle for basic changes choose nonviolent methods; and, even more frequently, the question of means, far from being a structural component of the radical identity, is entirely a question of tactics, a situational component.

It seems to me, therefore, that the question of ends or goals rather than means of radicalism constitutes both structurally and historically the center of its specific identity. The goal of significantly changing the order is the minimal common denominator of radical movements and groups. Yet the question of what changes are significant, let alone fundamental, is obviously open to various interpretations, ranging from narrow to broad, from those focused on a specific aspect or dimension of an existing order to an all-embracing program of transformation.

The question of which desired changes can be considered a radical orientation leads, both within the social sciences and within the political community, to a number of positions, one of which, probably the most prevalent and influential, invites comment. It posits that the only meaningful and

far-reaching changes which can be deemed radical are those
which concern the central characteristics of an existing order,
especially its fundamental systemic inequities. One participant in the workshop forcefully presented this point of view
with regard to industrialized societies.

> We need to spend some time simply to find out whether there is a
> phenomenon that we can call radicalism in general. I would sug-
> gest that there is, but the definition I would offer implies a cer-
> tain stance toward the study of radicalism and social change. The
> task that we face is trying to isolate radicalism from the infinite
> blur of things happening in the society—change going on, pro-
> tests occuring, inequalities which exist, different means used by
> different groups to attain their ends— . . . and to sort out those
> which have something in common and which we call radicalism.
> I would suggest that the way to do this would be to focus on
> what could be called core inequalities in the society. Societies
> vary as to what those core inequalities might be; they vary in re-
> gard to the degree to which inequalities exist. Again, there are
> many problems in this definition, but one can at least simplify
> by saying that radicalism as an impulse, as a movement, takes its
> stand vis-à-vis whatever the core inequalities, the systemic struc-
> turally rooted inequalities are in society. Its stance vis-à-vis these
> inequalities is to confront them openly and totally in an attempt
> to transcend them, or reduce them, to overcome them, or to
> eliminate them. . . . the central political dialectic or dynamic of
> society is precisely the conflict between those who defend and
> benefit from and wish to protect core inequalities, and those who
> are disadvantaged by and wish to challenge core inequalities.[12]

In my opinion, the above statement is open to at least
three objections. First, restricting the term radicalism to
opposition to core inequities of a given system implies a
notion of true and false radicalism. That is to say, it implies
that the identification of such core inequities is a matter of
objective standards rather than of the specific views and judgments of particular groups, movements, and individuals. It
means in practice that for groups or movements applying
a Marxian critique to the existing order, only their own

description of what is wrong with the society and their own prescription of what is to be done about it represents true radicalism, while, let us say, a populist critique and strategy can be termed false or unauthentic radicalism. Moreover, given the increasing fragmentation of the corpus of radical criticism derived from the Marxian tradition into separate organizational and ideological entities, for which there is abundant evidence at present, each of these entities becomes convinced of its own true radicalism and of the fallacy of the others.[13]

A second objection is closely related to the first. The identification of radicalism with the core inequities of the social order, especially as understood in the Marxian tradition which stresses the primacy of the economic roots of all inequities, negates or ignores the importance of the self-consciousness of the various radical impulses or movements themselves. That is to say, it ignores or at least minimizes the fact that what are perceived as core inequities may and do differ drastically from different vantage points in society; and, after all, the radical actions of groups and movements derive from their own particular perceptions. For nineteenth and twentieth century peasant populists, the perceived core inequity was not the existence or principle of the private ownership of the means of production, especially property in land, but its unequal distribution; for the Basque separatists it is not the social structure of their own region, but the dominance of the central Spanish government; for the Black Muslims in the United States it is not the American socio-economic system, but the racial barriers to their full participation in it. Does this make their goals and actions any the less radical?

Third, and most important, the identification of radicalism with an orientation toward the change of alleged core inequities is highly restrictive in two crucial interrelated respects. It necessarily associates true radicalism with the quest for freedom from injustice and inequality; and, moreover, it limits radicalism to orientations and movements of the left. This procedure is open to many objections. To start with, it attaches too much importance to the professed, explicit, and ultimate aims of left radical movements and ignores the actual consequences of such movements. After all, every *successful* left radical movement in the twentieth century which addressed inequities in the status quo brought about inequities at least as great as those which it had opposed. If one agrees with Barrington Moore, Jr., that success for a radical movement means to make some lasting contribution to human freedom, one should admit, it seems, another of his views:

> So far, I think it is fair to assert that no radical revolutionary movements have made such contributions on their own, at least not yet. They have made them only as part of the "bourgeois" or "liberal" revolutionary movements—the great surges of the Puritan and French revolutions and our own Civil War, which belong to an historical epoch that is now drawing to a close. The first revolution that took power mainly as the result of a radical thrust, the Bolshevik revolution, turned into a vicious form of oppression that has yet to be shaken off. In China the issue is still doubtful. I believe very firmly that unless future radical movements can somehow synthesize the achievement of liberalism with those of revolutionary radicalism, the results for humanity will be tragic.[14]

Obviously the violent or nonviolent defense of a status quo is the opposite of radicalism. But the exclusive identification of radicalism with the quest for expansion of freedom and with the left goals of transformation not only provides a blank check for left radical movements by assuming, against the record of past performance, that their stated goals will be realized; it also entails the application of different standards to left and right radicalism and their quests for power as well as to the various radical movements which have acquired power. Those who would exclude the association of right with radicalism understate, in my opinion, the role of the political, symbolic, and cultural spheres of social life and contribute a strong dose of economic determinism to the consideration of the nature of privileges and the importance of the distributive sphere. In this sense right-wing radical-ism—e.g., fascism or whatever one wishes to call it—may to a very large extent defend the fundamental elements of the status quo in the economic sphere; but right-wing radicalism is not limited to an economic program. With regard to politics and culture its goals are profoundly at variance with the status quo of liberal industrialized democracies. It behooves us to remember the catastrophic consequences of the left's failure to recognize this truth in the interwar period. That the lesson was not learned may be seen in the careless use by the New Left in the sixties of the fascist label to brand its oppo-nents and the system.

The identification of radicalism with professed left goals of transformation also leads to confusion and misunderstanding as regards radical movements which gain power. Whether one agrees with Trotsky that the Stalinist party of the Soviet Union in the late twenties and thirties betrayed and reversed the goals of the Leninist revolution, or whether one considers Stalinism a logical, though extreme, outgrowth of Leninism, Stalin and his party in the pre–Second World War period were a radical, revolutionary force in the deepest sense of the word —it wrought changes much more fundamental and lasting than the Leninist political revolution in 1917. It is only in considering a later period that one can view Stalin's party and especially Stalin's successors as defenders of the status quo, who have sought to perpetuate the existing order and condition.

In attempting to formulate a useful and comprehensive definition of modern radicalism, it is essential to ascertain what all movements which can be described as radical share in common; what main characteristic distinguishes them from other forms of group political behavior. It seems clear from the preceding discussion that the common denominator of radicalism, the trait which distinguishes it from other types of political behavior, is not the means, methods, and forms of struggle actually chosen and applied, however visible and important these may be in their consequences for the society and for the radical movements themselves. The common denominator and distinguishing trait, in my opinion, consists of the combination of three attributes.

The first relates to methods of political action. It involves the principled refusal by the movement to confine itself to activity within the existing political structure and consonant with established political processes. Basic here is not the form of action chosen at a specific time but an openness in the matter of choosing methods that can be applied at different times.[15]

The second and crucial attribute of radicalism is rejection of the existing order and the commitment to its structural change. More precisely, it is a commitment not only to alter existing policies which can lead to amelioration of perceived inequities but to change the framework, the political and social setting in which the political process occurs. The possible range of such radical commitments can be conceived very broadly, from concentration on a single issue like land reform or ethnic autonomy to total transformation. Here one may look for major differences among radical movements with regard to the range and focus of their goals of transformation.[16]

Third, it is not only rejection of the existing order and orientation toward its transformation that characterizes radicalism. Its most marked distinction from other types of protest is its effort to project its goals into the future, to establish for its participants what they consider a coherent vision of a better order. This vision, however broadly or narrowly focused, forms part of the culture of radicalism and both inspires and nourishes its commitment to change and action. In the words of one author, the radicals' "negation of what exists proceeds from an underlying affirmation, an idealized image of the world that ought to be."[17]

The presence of these attributes in combination is what separates radicalism from various forms of conflict behavior within society, diverse forms of protest against inequities, expressions of social or class conscience, and the innumerable instances of rebelliousness or actual rebellion against particular features of the existing order or against the generalized "evil" of a society.

Viewing radicalism from this perspective, we not only gain insight into its structural dimension but also directly approach its historical dimension, at the very center of which is the association with ideology in general and with ideologies of change and reconstruction in particular. Reinhard Bendix suggests a common element in all diverse uses of ideology by which one cultural epoch can be distinguished from another. The term ideology, he asserts,

> is not properly applicable in Western civilization prior to the seventeenth or eighteenth centuries, somewhat in the way that terms like "economy" or "society" or "intellectuals" do not fit the "premodern" period either. It is when human reason and the ends of action are questioned that ideology comes into its own.[18]

Inequalities and radical protests and rebellions against them have existed throughout history; radicalism is indigenous to the modern world. Its development accompanied the shaping of a belief that man can reconstruct society through the application of his reason. Radicalism is associated with ideologies that are directly responsive to such beliefs or with ideologies that emerged to a large extent in passionate opposition to such beliefs and to the social praxis they justify.

This exploration of the meaning of radicalism on the foregoing pages was an effort to grasp and interpret an experience, not a word. It is fitting to recall here Jacques Ellul's elaboration of the two images of radicalism encountered by all observers and participants in radical politics, one "hot," the other "cold."[19] The "hot" image centers on emotions and conveys the sense of tragedy and the romance of radical impulse; it is blurred and vague. The "cold" image centers on the premeditation and planning of radicalism and conveys its determination and discipline; it is sharp and uncompromising. While the "cold" image tends to dominate in the discussion of definition, it is the first image which emerges more clearly in some of the essays in this volume and which we expect to stress more as we move from definitional discussion to consideration of certain sources and manifestations of radicalism as they appear in the contemporary world.

The literature on radicalism and revolution, as the closing essay of this volume shows, provides a prodigious assortment of general approaches and particular answers to the question of the sources of contemporary radicalism. The radical community itself, however, shares almost universally a most general, all-embracing answer to the question. It is the traditional Marxian view that modern capitalism as a mode of production and as a specific social formation is the fundamental and irreducible source of both the inequities in society and the radical responses to them. This central argument remains a major axis on which debate concerning the sources of contemporary radicalism revolves. The workshop was no exception.

A number of participants expounded this view and stressed three major propositions. First, the notion that to identify an immediate target of radical attack is tantamount to discovering the root cause of that attack must be rejected. Second, the variegated institutions, dimensions, and aspects of societal organization under capitalism (e.g., state, bureaucracy, ethnicity, science) are not autonomous but are rather determined, shaped, and colored by the mode of production within which they exist. Third, from acceptance of the second proposition it would follow that ostensibly similar institutions will differ in fundamental respects when present in different social formations.[20]

There are a number of doubts, some of them expressed in the discussion at the workshop, that come to mind in response to the proposition that capitalism is actually the underlying root of contemporary left radicalism—or for that matter of right radicalism, which in this light can be construed as a logical culmination of capitalist tendencies in the superstructure and as the defense mechanism against threats to the capitalist system posed by the growth of left radicalism. This point of view, I would argue, is basically an exercise in reductionism and has to be questioned first and foremost with regard to its utility in contributing to our understanding of the contemporary world and particularly the sources of contemporary radicalism. It is precisely with regard to utility that the most convincing objections to this approach can be advanced.

It is doubtless true that one cannot infer the root causes of radicalism from looking simply at its immediate and specific targets; such a procedure would be very superficial. But having accepted this premise, one does not have to follow the rest of the analysis which reduces these causes to capitalism. One participant made the astute observation, moreover, that even if we were to assume that the capitalist form of production provides the ultimate key to understanding, which we should not of course do a priori,

> we still have the question of why in one capitalist society one thing happens while in another something else happens. Then the variable of capitalism seems in the end to be very unimportant for our work. . . . We then have to start asking ourselves what it is about different capitalist societies that some have dictatorships, some of them have democratic regimes, some have powerful states and bureaucracies, some have intelligentsias while others do not have them. . . . So even if we assume this term "capitalism" as a global term, it does not help us to go any further unless one is willing to start analyzing types of capitalism.

This argument can be carried still further. If one wishes to press at any cost the link of the present to the past or to stress the minimal common denominator of many societies rather than their variety and most important specific characteristics, one can arrive at the kind of analysis which reduces the phenomena of divisions, grievances, and protests in some societies to capitalism. The value of this kind of analysis as a general procedure becomes even more questionable, however, when one considers that the generalization about capitalism as the basis for explaining reality has not been limited in the writings of radicals to industrialized or industrializing societies where private ownership of the means of production and a market economy prevail. In most Marxian analyses independent of the Soviet line, the communist systems in Europe (and most recently in Cuba as well) are most often described as "state capitalist," "bureaucratic collectivist capitalist," etc. Yugoslavia, for example, is in the opinion of Paul Sweezy well along the "road to capitalism."[21] The Soviet Union figures as a state capitalist society in the first extended analysis of Soviet society published in France by the Marxist Charles Bettelheim.[22] A volume of essays on ruling communist parties composed by the luminaries of the European New Left comes to the conclusion that

> the socialist society remains still a transitional society in a very specific meaning of the word: a social formation in which the capitalist method of production is intertwined with new elements and exercising a decisive pressure on the political sphere, on the relations between people, and on the relations between the rulers and the ruled.[23]

How helpful, then, is the reiterated generalization of the term "capitalism" when it has become so inclusive as to encompass *all industrial societies* despite enormous differences of origin, organization, and developmental tendencies?

Yet it is undeniable that most of the radical (and even not so radical) left in the West—almost all varieties, from large movements to splinters of splinter groups, from the most authoritarian in terms of organization, behavior, and goals for the future to the most antiauthoritarian—subscribes almost uniformly to the same rhetoric and has the deep-seated belief that capitalism is the fundamental source of all evil and the underlying target of all struggle.

The reason most readily discernable for this is so immediately obvious that one is almost compelled to look for deeper sources. I would like to suggest, however, that in this case it is exactly the reasons on the surface that bear principal responsibility for the phenomenon: in the twentieth century the expression, the vernacular, the symbolic framework of left radical protest in almost all its variations has become consciously and explicitly Marxian, even in such cases when Marxian tradition and symbolism, let alone Marxian theory, is nothing but a thin veneer coating a wide variety of beliefs, aspirations, and actions that have little to do with "original" Marxism.

It is the acceptance by a part of the intelligentsia in modern (and modernizing) societies of at least the symbols, language, and concepts of the Marxian heritage that infuses radical anticapitalist rhetoric and beliefs into so many protest movements. That is to say, it is not so much the practice of capitalism which has made the Marxian symbolism and framework of thought so dominant today in radical movements, but rather the dominance of Marxian symbolism which has made an ideal-type capitalism the root target of radicalism.

Rejection of the leftist tendency to consider capitalism the ultimate source of contemporary radicalism does not exclude the possibility, probability, and in many cases the virtual certainty that the capitalist form of economic organization is indeed at the root of radicalism. (Professor Tarrow argues persuasively that the question of capitalism is very much a genuinely central issue in France.) No less serious difficulties undermine the perspective of those who approach the subject from a loosely defined "right" position and, while making broad generalizations about the inevitability of inequality, reduce radicalism to the "politics of fantasy" and "political pathology."[24] The sole way to bridge, or at least to attempt to escape, the disadvantages of these different analytical orientations concerning the sources of contemporary radicalism is to examine specific dimensions of the problem at a less grand level of generalization.

We shall be closer to understanding the roots of contemporary radicalism if we eschew the elaboration of generalizations that seek to provide ultimate answers. More useful is an approach which isolates and describes the particular elements which distinguish the sources, targets, and carriers of today's radicalism in industrialized democracies from those of the past. To my mind, such an approach calls for serious attention to three themes which disclose the most striking differences with the past: the general setting in which the social and political evolution of industrial democracies occurs, the consequences of the changed functions of the state, and the specific characteristics of the contemporary intelligentsia.

What is new about contemporary radicalism, both left and right, both authoritarian and antiauthoritarian, derives less from novelty in the content of radicalism than novelty in the social and political setting in which it operates. This setting should affect our discussion of radicalism more profoundly than what happens within radicalism itself or what happens because of radicalism. As one workshop participant said,

> I feel uncomfortable with the very term "radicalism" as suggesting the most important movement of the present time. I think even more important than a recurrent radicalism is a degree of disaffection in our respective countries which is far wider than radicalism and may in its qualitative form be far greater than anything we have seen in a very, very long time. That, it seems to me, is really the deepest problem that we have.

First and most crucial in the new setting are the doubts, disenchantment, loss of illusions, and uncertainties, not only about the answers to the ills besetting developed societies, but even about which questions might lead to the source of the malady. These doubts are shared by both the general population and the traditional elites in modern Western society. It is as if the continuity of Western civilization has been disrupted and, in the words of J. H. Plumb, we are witnessing "the death of the past."[25] It is as if what haunted Tocqueville more than a century ago when he looked at the new postrevolutionary world has come to haunt us in turn; in his memorable phrase, "since the past has ceased to throw its light on the future, the mind of man wanders in obscurity."[26]

The crisis is political in origin and nature and until recent decades it was most strikingly expressed in the political arena. Yet as we now see it clearly, the crisis far transcends the political dimension. It goes beyond the faults of economic and social organization to the very core culture of modern civilization. A general disaffection proceeds from and in turn deepens a crisis of values, not simply capitalist values. It erodes the very foundation of all systems of belief that emerged with the advance of Western civilization.[27]

Alvin Gouldner captures the dilemma of ideology in this new situation:

> Ideologies are project-centered moralities tacitly seeking to reconstruct a frayed, fragmented whole, or, in any event, a totality taken to be defective. Ideologies are defocalized efforts to integrate formally separated parts, to reknit the unravelled, to extend the boundaries and to reconstruct the moral grounding of human solidarity. . . . All ideologies are pursuing a *latent* project: the reconstruction of a social whole weakened by the emergence of privatizing interests. It is precisely for this reason that the attenuation of ideologies in the modern world . . . constitutes not simply the de-authorization of political authority per se but undermines the legitimacy of the total social order of everyday life in the modern world.[28]

All the principal modern ideologies have expounded the rationalization and justification of the progress, growth, and achievement of the new technological and democratic society, as did liberalism, or the possibility of shattering impediments inherent in the capitalist form to effect the limitless extension of the progress, growth, and achievement of the technological and democratic society, as did Marxism. When the doubts and disaffection of today attack not simply the form but the basic values of the technological-democratic society, they express the general failure of all modern ideologies and the decay of the basic assumptions on which they have till now rested.[29]

The failure of the old ideologies, measurable in the magnitude of popular disaffection, in the uncertainties and doubts afflicting the elites, has not been accompanied, however, by the elaboration of new ideologies which could or do assure "the reconstruction of the social whole." The fads which periodically seize fragmented social groups, especially the youth, afford at most a cultural escape or inner-directed, short-term gratification. The replacement of ideologues by technologues on which the futurologists postulate their visions of the new knowledge-dominated society remains as yet an unrealized and perhaps unrealizable promise.[30]

Had one to isolate the single element which contributes most to illuminating what is new in contemporary radicalism, both with regard to its major target and its key source, the choice, it would seem, probably rests with the modern state and its bureaucracy. This would be true even were one to accept, with the majority of left radicals, the theoretical premise that the root cause of radicalism invariably derives from the mode of production or the specific social formation. Even given this premise, it cannot be denied that the modern bureaucratic state has become a central element in the relations of the population with the social formation and that, therefore, the set of relations between the state and its "clients" must constitute the focal point of all considerations of core inequalities in society.

The state has significantly expanded its role in the economic sphere as regulator, consumer, and employer. It has assured the growing burden of social welfare and dominates the educational and scientific sector. In so doing it has produced new divisions in society and attendant new sets of grievances which do not overlap the traditional divisions of class but cut across and often supersede them.

The French student revolt of May-June 1968 serves to illustrate both the nature of the new situation and the consequences of failing to recognize and act upon it. The clients of the state include in the first rank the educational sector of society. The grievances of French students were those of clients; yet the consciousness of their movement lacked ideological consistency, homogeneity, and clarity about the precise objects of their attack. The grievances of French workers focused on the expression of traditional claims of class and division of labor. The inability of the old radical element within French society, specifically the French communists, to reconcile the two positions led to their split and precipitated the collapse of the combined revolt. What happened in 1968, one may argue, was that those organizations capable of transforming this revolt of the clients into a broader political conflict either intervened against the clients or engaged in a simultaneous but separate struggle. That is to say, the old class parties could not or would not deal with the problems presented by the state-client relationship in general or with specific aspects of the relationship that escaped the sphere of their immediate, familiar concerns.[31]

Comparing the events in France with those in other industrialized democracies, Professor Tarrow sees as exceptional the fusion of the French student revolt with a working class uprising. What is exceptional in my opinion is the temporal coincidence of the two rather than their fusion. It is doubtful whether one can speak about a shared common source of the two revolts, let alone about the fusion of the consciousness of the two movements. (These doubts do not, of course, lead me to question Professor Tarrow's point concerning the impact of the combined events of 1968 on the subsequent organized and institutionalized growth of the left in Europe.)

The importance of bureaucratic state-client relations as a core source and target of contemporary radicalism does not lie only in their impact on the actual struggle of radical movements, especially those which are consciously linked with the Marxian tradition. These relations bear as well on the major problem which confronts any serious radical movement of the old or new left (or revitalized old left like the Italian communists): the program for reconstructing the existing reality, their vision of the future, their model of the "good society." It would seem that serious and intellectually courageous radicals will have to draw consequences from the fact that past revolutionary experience and Marxian theory do not prepare them to deal with contemporary reality. The posing of the question may be seen, for example, in the recent work of the Marxist Perry Anderson:

The Russian Revolution was not made against a capitalist State at all. . . . The Bolsheviks made a *socialist revolution,* but from beginning to end they never confronted the *central enemy* of the workers' movement in the West. Gramsci's deepest intuition was in this sense correct: the modern capitalist State of Western Europe remained—after the October Revolution—a *new* political object for Marxist theory, and revolutionary practice. . . . The failure of the November Revolution in Germany, as momentous for the history of Europe as the success of the October Revolution in Russia, was grounded in the differential nature of the State machine with which each was confronted. The mechanisms of socialist victory and defeat in these years go to the bottom of the deepest problems of bourgeois and proletarian democracy, which have still to be theoretically and practically solved in the second half of the 20th century.[32]

A large and very crucial part of state-client relations extends well beyond specific grievances and can best be understood through its general cultural consequences. The importance, and in some cases, the dominance, of the cultural dimension in contemporary radical criticism is quite striking. Themes such as the evils of constraint, the poverty of experience, the sense of powerlessness tend to crowd out institutional reforms, distribution of wealth, the inequities of the market system, and other traditional anticapitalist themes. As Michael Walzer writes:

The increasing size of the state, the growing power of administration, the decline of political life: all these turn politics from a concrete activity into what Marx once called the fantasy of everyday life. The state becomes an arena in which men do not act but watch the action, and, like all the audiences, are acted upon. . . . When the modern state moves beyond welfare, it does not bring us the satisfactions of citizenship, but only vicarious participation, the illusion of a common life. We find ouselves as if in a dream, living once again in a world which is morally dense and opaque, mystified by ideologies, dominated by leaders whose purposes are not obvious. . . . It is difficult not to conclude, as the liberals do, that with provision of individual material needs, the state reaches or ought to reach its limits. That is the end of its history, the culmination of its legitimacy. There is no state beyond the welfare state.[33]

The cultural dimension of contemporary radicalism brings us directly to the question of the intelligentsia as the principal carrier of this new type of discontent in industrialized democracies. Participants in the workshop advanced a number of propositions concerning the nature of the contemporary intelligentsia, four of which can be summarized as a basis for further discussion.[34]

First, one phenomenon we are witnessing today in the United States and other industrialized democracies is the rise of an intelligentsia which recalls nineteenth and early twentieth century Russia—that is, "a revival of the phenomenon of educated oppositionists within the larger framework of the privileged elites," at the core of which are creative talents, scholars, and the wider intellectual community, as well as some members of the media and bureaucracy.

Second, whereas in the past the correlation between left and right political forces was essentially a class correlation, today it cuts across class lines, at least with regard to the educated strata. In both the university and media communities one finds an interesting pattern of correlation:

> As you move from low to high, for example, from low income to high income, low prestige to high prestige, provincial to metropolitan, less important to more important, you go from right to left. In the academic community and in the newspaper and media world, the more well-to-do, the more important, the more prestigious, the more related to the center of the community, the greater the strength of the left intelligentsia.

Third, "in the old industrial complex you get the traditional class relationship; in the new intelligentsia or intellectually-related culture, media, or welfare complex you get the opposite." Therefore a conflict develops between two elite strata: the intellectual elite and the old economic managerial elite.

Fourth, what is therefore new and distinct from earlier leftist radicalism in industrialized democracies is the emergence of a kind of upper-class intelligentsia which protests against the producers.

> Of course there is a lot of recurrent glamorization of the working class and the poor, but it stems from imposing the values and feelings of this privileged stratum onto the lower stratum. What we have today is a new revolt of the privileged or a new split within the elites, one which uses the language and ideologies of Marxism, socialism and revolution. But this is not fundamentally a class split, although the class is again invoked.

With these propositions as a starting point I should now like to consider whether the phenomena they describe are true and, if true, are really new; and, second, whether this present-day intelligentsia to which they refer is more properly related to radicalism or to a reform movement within the system.

The term "intelligentsia," if it is to be applied, has to be used in its specific and precise meaning, not as a synonym either for "intellectuals" or "educated people" or as a classificatory term for members of certain occupations, e.g., professionals. Historically, in its specific meaning, the term has been applied primarily to a social stratum in tsarist Russia in the nineteenth and early twentieth century and reflects a social position as well as a cluster of social attitudes, a cultural mood as well as a propensity for a specific political behavior. It denotes a stratum estranged by its cultural values from the elites that govern and at the same time isolated by its social position from the working classes. The stratum aspires to advance the interests of society as a whole, not simply its own material interests. In its political attitudes it opposes the status quo by definition, while differing widely in its perception of how to alter or replace the status quo.[35]

Important in assessing the estrangement of the intelligentsia in tsarist Russia and its radicalization is the simple fact that only through its radicalization could it participate meaningfully in politics. For the intelligentsia in autocratic Russia to accept established values and its own social position meant to accept powerlessness, marginality, and stifling limits on freedom of expression. The existing political framework and political process did not offer any institutionalized means or any leverage for action toward change apart from incremental pressures exerted from within the bureaucracy or ardent hope for a tsar-reformer. For these reasons the existence of the sociopolitical phenomenon of the intelligentsia has usually been associated with economic underdevelopment, backwardness of the social order, and authoritarianism of the political process. It was not hitherto linked with industrial democracies.

The phenomenon of the intelligentsia, however, or something very closely resembling it, was also associated with one set of circumstances that was not confined to any single country, system, or century, namely, with the symptoms of a prerevolutionary situation. Starting with Crane Brinton's analysis, a number of students of revolutionary change have described one set of mutations occurring within the dominant social strata prior to the outbreak of serious revolutionary violence as the "desertion of the intellectuals," that is to say, the estrangement of intellectuals from the establishment and its traditional values.[36] How relevant is this analysis for understanding the place of estranged intellectuals in industrialized democracies today?

Clearly the phenomenon of estranged intellectuals does exist today in industrialized democracies. But just as clearly the phenomenon of such estrangement in itself is not at all new either in West European countries or, for that matter, in the United States.[37] Indeed the participation of part of the intelligentsia in radical movements or the presence of an estranged intelligentsia alongside the radical or protest movements of the lower classes is the rule rather than the exception in the history of modern radicalism and protest movements. The estrangement and opposition of intellectuals to the established order is obviously a question of degree, ranging from total rejection, as was the case with an overwhelming majority of the intelligentsia in tsarist Russia before the turn of the century, to reform-minded criticism, which was not at all unusual in the history of the United States. What is clearly important in assessing today's situation is the evaluation of the intensity of estrangement and the extent of its spread within the educated stratum. Some degree of estrangement and oppositional spirit, far from symbolizing Brinton's "desertion of the intellectuals" and heralding revolutionary upheaval, is, as Samuel Huntington suggests, a component part of political development.

> Criticism from intellectuals is the hallmark of any established political system including a one-party system. The stability of the system, in turn, depends upon the capacity of the political elite to mobilize the support of the masses against the intellectual elite.[38]

If the estrangement of intellectuals from the established order and traditional values has long existed to some degree, just which elements of the present phenomenon can be identified as new? In my judgment there are several, particularly with regard to the United States. First, we are not witnessing today a single tendency within the intellectual elite but rather divergent tendencies that may be said to represent opposite poles. No doubt a part of the elite displays characteristics of estrangement, challenges the prevailing modes of thought, exhibits cultural discontent, and engages in political opposition. Its discontent is especially visible within the educational establishment and especially intense among the young generation. Yet at the same time a part of the actual and potential intellectual elite, that is both old and young, is engaged, more closely than ever before, in serving the established power and participating in the existing political process. It is difficult to determine which of the two tendencies—the union or the divorce of intellect and power—is stronger when assessing secular tendencies rather than short-term trends. Without doubt both are present. Therefore, to compare the present situation with that of the past when the old intelligentsia dominated the educated stratum is problematical.

I am not minimizing in the least the importance of the

estrangement which undoubtedly exists and the potential for the radicalization of a part of the intellectual elite in industrialized democracies. On the contrary, what strikes me as another new element in the present situation, one which the two tendencies of estrangement and participation both illustrate, is exactly the extraordinary potential influence of the intellectual stratum today when compared to the past. The estrangement of part of the stratum may have influence more powerful and more destructive for the existing order in terms of its *long-range* effects than ever before. This potential is connected precisely with the strategic location of the intellectual stratum in relation to the exercise and especially the legitimization of power, never enjoyed by its predecessors. What is new, in other words, is what the new intelligentsia has at its disposal when compared to the old intelligentsia. The immensely expanded educational establishment constitutes today the chief socializing agency for the new elite and subelite generations. The revolution in communications has made the media, and especially television, the key source of ideas, information, and opinion for the majority of the nation. In such a situation the mediating role of intellectuals within the political order and between political institutions and society is more crucial than ever for the stability and continuity of the existing system.[39]

Yet another striking new element is the transnational character—one can even say the internationally synchronized nature—of the discontent and disaffection exhibited within the educated strata, especially among the youth. Partly a reflection of the greater technological, economic, and cultural leveling of conditions in industrialized democracies, the phenomenon is also partly the result of the communications revolution which enhances the possibility of viewing one's own society in the light of events and moods from other societies.

In the past the desertion by intellectuals never served as the cause or catalyst of lower-class radicalism and very seldom even influenced its expansion. Where radical organizations or protest movements did exist among the lower classes, the main function of estranged intellectuals was to provide direction for the movement or to appropriate its energies.

What is striking and new in the contemporary situation in industrialized democracies is the degree of isolation within society of the carriers of the radical intellectual current. What is remarkable is, on the one hand, the degree of separation of the radical intellectual current from organized lower-class radicalism to which it can provide no sense of direction and, on the other hand, the inability of radical intellectuals in the absence of organized lower-class radicalism to translate, to catalyze the general social disaffection and disillusionment with existing institutions into a protest movement. Disenchanted intellectuals are able to associate with mass movements only at the cost of sacrificing their own independence and taking part in established traditional radical organizations where they exist. What we are seeing, therefore, especially in countries like the United States which has no organized lower-class, mass radical movements, is an important contribution of the "deserter-intellectuals" to the undermining of the legitimacy of the existing order, to the widespread feeling of cultural discontinuity. The long-range effects of such a contribution may be very significant. But at the same time these intellectuals are not providing leadership or purpose nor are they even being accepted by those organized or amorphous groups at the bottom of the social ladder who express their own grievances against the existing order. The prevailing mood in such circumstances is not of a social order under siege or endangered by revolutionary change, but rather a state of chaos, uncertainty, and drift.

The question remains whether what we are witnessing with regard to a large part of the educated stratum in industrialized democracies is the process of radicalization, which invites comparison to the phenomenon of the "intelligentsia," or whether we are seeing instead a symptom of the crisis of liberalism out of which there is evolving a reform movement within the system. Since there is as yet no persuasive evidence, I feel that this question cannot now be answered. Some factors suggest the possibility, however slight, that the latter may be the case.

The first factor that inclines me to believe this is the assimilation of yesteryear's radicals—at least in America—into the mainstream of the political process and their attempts to ameliorate inequities through legitimate political actions. The second factor is the disappearance of certainty among the radical intelligentsia that it knows the solutions not only for specific ills but also for the root causes of perceived systemic evil, that is, the retreat from totalism. The total solutions, indeed the messianism, of earlier intelligentsias were derived either from foreign practices or from abstract ideas. Today the mood is different; there are no foreign models, and there are very few answers among intellectuals, let alone certainty that the answers are right.

So far, those who reject what exists have failed to provide any intellectual schemes which offer an alternative to the traditional perception of the social hierarchy and social organization. Can one consider seriously the clusters of ideas which advocate deindustrialization, the back-to-nature movement, and other panaceas which could arise only in the wake of the affluence brought by industrialization and which prefer virtually to ignore the existence of sovereign nation-states, worldwide poverty, and the conflict-ridden international system? It is frivolous to expect that this kind of change in the realm of thought alone "can carry the political freight that its optimistic advocates hope will be possible. As a new locomotive of history under changed circumstances it just won't do."[40]

It is still possible that an intellectual movement to restore and revitalize the existing order may evolve with the system itself and attempt to adapt it to changing internal and international circumstances. On the other hand, should such revitalization within the system fail to materialize, there will remain and increase the possibility in democracies of a different kind of ideological revitalization. Carried by groups which are marginal today or which as yet still accept existing political arrangements, it would be an antidemocratic revitalization from the right, an outcome to which contemporary democracies remain vulnerable even today, as they were in other times of drift and breakdown of established values.

Seymour Martin Lipset, formerly George Markham Pro-
fessor of Government and Sociology at Harvard University,
is currently professor of political science and sociology and
senior fellow at the Hoover Institution, Stanford University.
He is author and coauthor of numerous outstanding books,
including Agrarian Socialism, Union Democracy, The First
New Nation, Political Man, Rebellion in the University, *and*
The Divided Academy. *A distinguished scholar, Professor*
Lipset has held fellowships from the Social Science Research
Council, the Ford Foundation, the Guggenheim Foundation,
and the Center for Advanced Study in the Behavioral
Sciences. He is vice-president for the social sciences at the
American Academy of Arts and Sciences and is a member of
the National Academy of Sciences.

2

Why No Socialism in the United States?
Seymour Martin Lipset

The larger subject of this volume, the sources of radicalism in the modern world, raises the question of what is meant by radicalism, particularly in the United States where the very existence of a radical movement can be a matter for debate. The basic definition of the word—fundamental change—is as good as any, but still leaves the empirical problem of filling in the concept with indicators of actual events and movements.

In discussing radicalism in the United States, the key question remains that of Werner Sombart, "why is there no socialism in the United States?"[1] However one defines radicalism of the left, the movements which call themselves socialist were and are still extremely weak in the American body politic. The number of Americans who identify themselves as socialists or radicals remains extremely small. According to national polls, there were only 2 to 3 percent self-identified radicals or socialists at the height of activism in the 1960s. The largest national vote which the Socialist Party and the socialist movement ever received in the United States was in the 1912 elections, when approximately 6 percent of the votes were cast for Eugene Debs, the presidential candidate of the Socialist Party.

Yet while socialist and other radical movements remain weak in the United States, parties calling themselves Socialist, Social-Democratic, Labor, or Communist are major forces in every other democratic country in the world. Why America, the most developed capitalist industrial society, should constitute the great exception has interested socialist and other intellectuals since the late nineteenth century. Reading the abundant literature on the subject suggests that little new may be said on the issue. Therefore, I have chosen to contribute to the discussion by bringing together the main interpretations that have been advanced, beginning with the writings of Marx and Engels and continuing through the recent discussions by contemporary historians and social scientists.

The purpose of this essay is not to evaluate the validity of different approaches to the topic, but rather to treat the analyses themselves as the raw material. These writings tell us much about what people, and in particular radicals and students of radicalism, have seen as the sources of strength and weakness, of stability and tension in the United States. A wise sociologist, W. I. Thomas, once said, "That which men believe is real, is real in its consequences." As we shall see, Marxists and others who have pondered the question "why no socialism in the United States?" have approached a surprising degree of consensus on what is real in the United States.

Marx and Engels

The continued weakness of socialism in the United States has been a major embarrassment to Marxist theorists who assumed that the cultural superstructure, including political behavior, is a function of the underlying economic and technological structure. The class relationships inherent in capitalism as a social system should inevitably eventuate in a working class which forms the majority of the population and comes to political consciousness organized in a revolutionary socialist party. The most developed society should have the most advanced set of class and political relationships. "The country that is more developed industrially only shows, to the less developed, the image of its own future," is how Marx put it in the preface to *Capital*.[2]

Karl Marx and Friedrich Engels constantly looked for signs of class consciousness in the United States. Marx himself was initially confident that the workers would form class parties because of the Workingmen's parties, which secured sizable numbers of votes in several eastern cities in the late 1820s and early 1830s.[3] Marx's views on these parties, as Lewis Feuer and Maximillian Rubel have documented, were strongly influenced by a book, *Men and Manners in America*, written by Thomas Hamilton, a British Tory, who visited the United States in 1830.[4] Marx's notebooks reveal that he had copied out a number of Hamilton's statements, describing the emergence of class consciousness in New York in 1830. From his reading of "the first story of an organized political party of labor in the world's history,"[5] Marx anticipated that the American working class would inevitably develop class-conscious politics and lead the world on the road to socialism. Given the importance of Hamilton's work in convincing Marx of the political role of the working class, passages from Hamilton, which Marx copied in his notebooks, are worth quoting extensively:

> Thomas Hamilton had conversations with "enlightened Americans" on the social prospects of the American Constitution and he gained the conviction that there was no will to "counterpoise . . . the rashness of democracy by the caution and wisdom of an aristocracy of intelligence and wisdom." Then he gives the following illustration of what he calls the "progress and tendency of opinion among the people of New York":
>
> > "In that city a separation is rapidly taking place between the different orders of society under the name of 'THE WORKERS,' in direct opposition to those who, favored by nature or fortune, enjoy the luxuries of life without the necessities of manual labor. These people make no secret of their demands, which to do them justice, are few and emphatic. . . . Their first postulate is 'EQUAL AND UNIVERSAL EDUCATION.'. . .

"But those who limit their views to the mental degradation of their country, are in fact the MODERATES of the party. There are others who go still farther, and boldly advocate the introduction of an AGRARIAN LAW, and a periodical division of property. These unquestionably constitute the EXTREME GAUCHE of the WORKY parliament, but still they only follow out the principles of their less violent neighbors, and eloquently dilate on the justice and propriety of every individual being equally supplied with food and clothing."

Dealing with the labor policy of the American government and the vast internal resources of the United States, Thomas Hamilton has no doubt "that the Americans are destined to become a great manufacturing nation." And then he makes the following prognostication:

"Huge manufacturing cities will spring up in various quarters of the Union, the population will congregate in masses, and all the vices incident to such a condition of society will attain speedy maturity. Millions of men will depend for subsistence on the demand for a particular manufacture, and yet this demand will of necessity be liable to perpetual fluctuation. When the pendulum vibrates in one direction, there will be an influx of wealth and prosperity; when it vibrates in the other, misery, discontent and turbulence will spread through the land. A change of fashion, a war, the glut of a foreign market, a thousand unforeseen and inevitable accidents are liable to produce this, and deprive multitudes of bread, who but a month before were enjoying all the comforts of life."

And now Thomas Hamilton enunciates a prophecy in the purest "Marxian" style:

"Let it be remembered that in the suffering class will be practically deposited the whole political power of the state; that there can be no military force to maintain civil order, and protect property: and to what quarter, I should be glad to know, is the rich man to look for security, either of person or fortune?"

Not one of the "eminent" Americans with whom Thomas Hamilton conversed on the future prospects of his country denied that a period of trial such as he had ventured to describe, was inevitable. But the general answer was that this period was very distant and that people feel very little concern about evils which may afflict their posterity. At this, the Scottish visitor notes:

"I cannot help believing, however, that the period of trial is somewhat less distant than such reasoners comfort themselves by imagining; but if the question be conceded that democracy necessarily leads to anarchy and spoliation, it does not seem that the mere length of road to be travelled is a point of much importance. This, of course, would vary according to the peculiar circumstances of every country in which the experiment might be tried. In England, the journey would be performed with railway velocity. In the United States, with the great advantages they possess, it may continue a generation or two longer, but the termination is the same. The doubt regards time, not destination."

In becoming a communist, Marx had only to substitute the word "communism" for Hamilton's words "anarchy and spoliation." And in becoming an economist, Marx will give to Thomas Hamilton's premonitory warnings the theoretical coating in the famous chapter of *Capital* entitled "Historical tendency of capitalist accumulation."[6]

Although the Workingmen's Party disappeared in the 1830s, Marx and Engels were to emphasize to deprecators of the potential for American socialism that Americans "have had, since 1829, their own social democratic school."[7]

America as a New Society

In analyzing the prospects for socialism in America, Marx and Engels did not limit themselves to economic factors. Like many latter-day analysts they focused on various unique sociological aspects of the United States, as compared to Europe, namely, that it was a new nation and society, that it lacked many of the institutions and traditions of previously feudal society, as a result of which it had the most "modern" and purely bourgeois culture, and that it was the most democratic country. But as Michael Harrington has noted: "Marx and Engels could never decide whether the exceptional characteristics of American society boded good or evil for the socialist movement."[8] In their early writings, Marx and Engels perceived these qualities as encouraging the emergence of proletarian consciousness, since the workers would not have to cast off the old "baggage of backward feudal Europe" or to struggle to gain the franchise and political rights. But, when the movement failed to develop, they reversed their analysis to stress the ways in which many of these attributes operated as obstacles. Their latter writings presaged the analyses of more contemporary scholars, such as Leon Samson and Louis Hartz.

The young Marx agreed with foreign travelers Alexis de Tocqueville and Thomas Hamilton that political democracy, as first developed in the United States, had inevitable egalitarian, that is, socialist implications. He expected in 1847 that the "social question" would emerge more rapidly in the United States than in Europe, precisely because the United States was more democratic politically. He noted that political equality would foster conscious resentment of economic inequality,

> in a constitutional monarchy more glaringly than in an absolute one, in a republic more glaringly than in a constitutional monarchy.... Nowhere does social inequality appear more harshly than in the eastern states of North America, because nowhere else is it less whitewashed by political inequality.[9]

American democracy seemingly gave politicians greater independence from class domination by the bourgeoisie than in Europe. As Engels put it: "Nowhere do 'politicians' form a more separate, powerful section of the nation than precisely in

North America. . . . It is in America that we see best how there takes place this process of the state power making itself independent in relation to society."[10]

The absence of a feudal past in the United States was seen at times by the Marxist fathers, particularly Engels, as providing a greater potentiality for a quick transition to socialism than in the socially more backward European countries, and at other times as a source of the political backwardness of the American working class. As positive factors conducive to the emergence of trade unions and labor political consciousness in America Engels cited, for example, "the more favored soil of America, where no medieval ruins bar the way, where history begins with the elements of modern bourgeois society, as evolved in the seventeenth century."[11] In discussing Britain, Engels emphasized the negative political effects of a feudal past, the way in which the more explicit status stratification derived from its history inhibited class consciousness and produced a deferential working class: "The division of society into innumerable strata, each recognized without question, each with its own pride but also its inborn respect for its 'betters' and 'superiors' is so old and firmly established that the bourgeois still find it fairly easy to have their bait accepted."[12]

Yet the reality was that in the United States socialist movements did not emerge on a mass scale as compared to the European continent. In seeking to explain this phenomenon, Engels attributed the political backwardness of the American workers to the absence of a feudal past as well. Thus, he wrote that Americans "are born conservatives—just *because* America is so purely bourgeois, so entirely without a feudal past and therefore proud of its purely bourgeois organization."[13] Again he noted: "It is . . . quite natural, that in such a young country, which has never known feudalism and has grown up on a bourgeois basis from the first, bourgeois prejudices should also be so strongly rooted in the working class. Out of his very opposition to the mother country—which is still clothed in its feudal disguise—the

American worker also imagines that the bourgeois regime as traditionally inherited is something progressive and superior by nature and for all time a *ne plus ultra*."[14]

Sectarianism

One of the special features of American society which adversely affected the character of working class politics was the propensity of radicals for sectarianism, for treating Marxism or other radical doctrines as absolute dogmas to be applied in all situations. Engels referred to "that sectarian land, America," where purists could always count on support.[15] Marx "confessed to a certain suspicion of 'Yankee socialists' as 'crotchety and sectarian.' "[16]

Engels repeatedly criticized the first major American socialist party, the Socialist Labor Party (S.L.P.), for treating Marxist theory in a "doctrinaire and dogmatic way as something which has got to be learnt by heart and which will then supply all needs without more ado. To them it is a *credo* and not a guide to action."[17]

In 1894 he criticized the American S.L.P. and the British Social Democratic Federation for being "the only parties that have managed to reduce the Marxian theory of development to a rigid orthodoxy, which the workers are not to reach themselves by their own class feeling, but which they have to gulp down as an article of faith at once and without development. That is why both of them remain mere sects and come, as Hegel says, from nothing through nothing to nothing."[18]

Why were American radicals so sectarian? One frequently enunciated reason was that many of them were German-born immigrants who were isolated from the American reality. On a more general sociological level, the sources of political sectarianism may be linked to Marx's and Engels' discussion of America's religiosity, and to the strength of Protestant sectarianism which also affected the English movement. Engels noted that the United States had taken over from England "common law, religion, and sectarianism."[19]

Marx was particularly impressed with the role of religion in American life. Like Tocqueville, he saw its vitality as a consequence of secular political institutions, the absence of an established church:

> North America is pre-eminently the country of religiosity, as Beaumont, Tocqueville and the Englishman Hamilton unanimously assure us. . . . We find that religion not only *exists,* but displays a *fresh and vigorous vitality.*[20]

In a society which has disestablished religion, "banishing it from the sphere of public law to that of private law," religion becomes

> the spirit of *civil society,* of the sphere of egoism, of *bellum omnium contra omnes* [war of each against all]. It is no longer the essence of *community,* but the essence of *difference.* . . . It is . . . the abstract avowal of specific perversity, *private whimsy,* and arbitrariness. The endless fragmentation of religion in North America, for example, gives it even *externally* the form of a purely individual affair.[21]

As a result, religious and political sectarianism is certain to abound.

Resistance to Theoretical Thinking

Curiously, while the Marxist fathers identified the sectarian character of the young American socialist movement as one of the sources of its weakness, they also emphasized the special propensity of the English-speaking peoples to reject abstract and theoretical ways of thought, to be "slow" in grasping ideas, as a reason for the failure of Marxism to have as broad an appeal as it did on the European continent.

In 1833, Engels contended that "if American energy and vitality were backed by European theoretical clarity, the business would be finished over there in ten years."[22] In 1887, he concluded that the Communist Manifesto, "like almost all the shorter works of Marx and myself, is far too difficult for America at the present time. The workers over there . . . are still quite crude, tremendously backward theoretically, in particular, as a result of their general Anglo-Saxon and special American nature and previous training."[23]

In the nineties, he continued to complain that "the Anglo-Saxon race—those damned Schleswig-Holsteiners, as Marx always called them—is slow witted anyhow."[24] He explained the weakness of the American movement as in part flowing from "the tenacity of the Yankees, . . . a result of their theoretical backwardness and their Anglo-Saxon contempt for all theory." He contended that a nation "so conceited about its 'practice' and so frightfully dense theoretically as the Americans are, gets thoroughly rid of . . . a fixed idea only through its own sufferings."[25]

Engels' very limited efforts to explain the incapacity for theory and the pragmatic orientations of Anglo-Saxons generally and of Americans in particular are not very satisfactory. Thus in 1886, he stressed that for "good historical reasons, the Americans are worlds behind in all theoretical things," but does not explain these.[26] On another occasion in the same year he noted that "theoretical ignorance is a characteristic of all young peoples." He generalized that "in a country as primitive as America . . . the exigencies of practical labor and the concentrating of capital have produced a contempt for all theory."[27] But the English also exhibited this failing and, in 1892, he commented that the history of the Anglo-Saxons "both in Europe and America (economic success and predominantly peaceful political development)" has encouraged their "backwardness of thought."[28]

Concern over the twin American propensities, sectarianism and reluctance to accept general theoretical explanations, led Engels to advise American Marxists on a number of occasions not to press their theory and conceptions on the American workers. Leave the workers alone to form their own movement and learn from their own mistakes. In 1886 he stressed:

> But above all give the movement time to consolidate, do not make the inevitable confusion of the first start worse confounded by forcing down people's throats things which at present they cannot properly understand, but which they will soon learn. A million or two of workingmen's votes next November for a *bona*

fide workingmen's party is worth infinitely more at present than a hundred thousand votes for a doctrinally perfect platform.[29]

Stratification Factors

The factors contributing to the failures of the workers' movement discussed by Marx and Engels were, of course, not limited to cultural and political variables. Among "the special American conditions" inhibiting the emergence of a workers' movement stressed by Engels in 1851 were "the ease with which the surplus population is drained off to the farms, the necessarily rapid and rapidly growing prosperity of the country, which makes bourgeois conditions look like a *beau idéal* to them, and so forth."[30]

America's situation as an underpopulated overseas settler colony produced an economy and class system far different from Europe. In the Old World, peasants had been driven off the land to the cities by expropriation to become lowly paid workers. In the United States, Marx believed, the proletarians retained opportunities to become independent producers.

> The wage-worker of to-day is to-morrow an independent peasant, or artisan, working for himself. He vanishes from the labour-market, but not into the workhouse. This constant transformation of the wage-labourers into independent producers, who work for themselves instead of for capital, and enrich themselves instead of the capitalist gentry, reacts in its turn very perversely on the conditions of the labour-market. Not only does the degree of exploitation of the wage-labourer remain indecently low. The wage-labourer loses into the bargain, along with the relation of dependence, also the sentiment of dependence on the abstemious capitalist.[31]

This situation in which labor scarcity kept wages high in America as compared to Europe had to end ultimately as a result of waves of immigration. Marx noted, however, that even with the industrial expansion during and after the Civil War, the "lowering of wages and the dependence of the wage-worker are yet far from being brought down to the normal European level."[32] Harvey Klehr has pointed out that elsewhere in *Capital*, "Marx maintained that needs were culturally determined, so that the wages paid to workers would vary from area to area, depending on historical factors. Unlike the price of other commodities, the price of labor-power had a historical component." Klehr also notes that Marx's discussion of the relevance of such factors "suggests that American wages might always remain higher and satisfy more needs than those paid in Europe."[33]

It is, therefore, not surprising that in the 1890s Engels again cited among the "very great and peculiar difficulties for a continuous development of a workers' party" in the United States, the economic growth and prosperity of the country. In contrasting the situation in the two great English-speaking nations, he noted:

> The native American workingman's standard of living is considerably higher than even that of the British, and that alone suffices to place him in the rear [politically] for some time to come.[34]

Two years later, he emphasized again that "through . . . the steadily growing domestic market the workers must be exposed to a prosperity no trace of which has been seen here in Europe for years now," and he noted that in America, prosperity actually reached the workers, not merely the coffers of the bourgeoisie as in Russia, which was also experiencing growth.[35]

Economic and population growth and an open land frontier also produced high rates of social mobility, a factor stressed by Marx in the early 1850s when writing about America. He noted that "though classes, indeed, already exist, they have not yet become fixed, but continually change and interchange their elements in a constant state of flux."[36] Similarly, Engels reported that the ideal of America is a nation "without a permanent and hereditary proletariat. Here everyone could become if not a capitalist, at all events an independent man, producing or trading, with his own means, for his own account."[37]

The open land frontier to which the ambitious who sought

independence could go had to vanish before class politics could emerge. Engels presented this "safety-valve" theory in 1892:

> Only when the land—the public lands—is completely in the hands of speculators, and settlement on the land thus becomes more and more difficult or falls prey to gouging—only then, I think, will the time come, with *peaceful* development, for a third party. . . . Only when there is a generation of native-born workers that cannot expect *anything* from speculation *any more* will we have a solid foothold in America.[38]

It is interesting to note that almost half a century earlier, in 1846, Marx noted that the political efforts of Americans to extend the opportunity to settle on free land and become farmers represented a leftist demand, an effort to gain equal opportunity. He saw

> the freeland movement . . . as the first form of the proletarian movement made necessary under certain specific conditions, as a movement based upon the living conditions of a class which necessarily must become communist. . . . Communist tendencies in America must originally appear in this seemingly anti-communist agrarian form.[39]

This conclusion by Marx is particularly noteworthy since he seems to be saying that the desire of ordinary Americans for individual upward mobility and for the ownership of their own plot of productive land reflected basically the same motivation as found in support for communism. The mass of Americans who believed that the American system assured them such opportunity also believed that they were living in an equalitarian society, that is, a society that socially resembled communism. This argument, like many others by Marx, was destined to reappear again and again down through the 1970s.

Ethnic and Racial Conflict

Racial differences and mass immigration also undermined class consciousness by giving the native-born white workers a privileged position and thus enabling the bourgeoisie to divide the workers of different racial and ethnic backgrounds against one another.

In a letter written in 1870 to two friends in New York, Marx compared the situation in America to that in Britain where the "working class is *split* into two *hostile* camps, English proletarians and Irish proletarians. The ordinary English worker hates the Irish worker as a competitor who lowers his *standard* of life. . . . His attitude toward him is much the same as that of the *poor white* to the *niggers*" in America. He pointed out to his correspondents that just as socialists in Britain must break down the cleavage between the Irish and English workers, in America they should also "do this kind of work," pressing for a "coalition among workers of different ethnic backgrounds."[40]

Engels, commenting on the same problem in America two decades later in 1892, noted:

> Your great obstacle in America, it seems to me, lies in the exceptional position of the native workers. . . . Now a working class has developed and has also to a great extent organized itself on trade union lines. But it still takes up an aristocratic attitude and wherever possible leaves the ordinary badly paid occupations to the immigrants, of whom only a small section enter the aristocratic trade unions. But these immigrants are divided into different nationalities and understand neither one another nor, for the most part, the language of the country. And your bourgeoisie knows much better even than the Austrian Government how to play off one nationality against the other: Jews, Italians, Bohemians, etc., against Germans and Irish and each against the other, so that differences in the standard of life of different workers exist, I believe, in New York to an extent unheard of elsewhere.[41]

Two years later, he again stressed, as a major obstacle for the workers' movement,

> immigration, which divides the workers into two groups: the native-born and the foreigners, and the latter in turn into (1) the Irish, (2) the Germans, (3) the many small groups, each of which

understands only itself: Czechs, Poles, Italians, Scandinavians, etc. And then the Negroes. To form a single party out of these requires quite unusually powerful incentives. Often there is a sudden violent *élan*, but the bourgeois need only wait passively, and the dissimilar elements of the working class fall apart again.[42]

Political Factors

America's special political conditions also contributed to the weakness of organized radicalism, according to Engels. In 1893, in a list of factors preventing the growth of a third, workers', party, he laid great stress on "the Constitution . . . which causes every vote for any candidate not put up by one of the two governing parties to appear to be *lost*. And the American . . . wants to influence his state; he does not throw his vote away."[43] He also concluded during the period of the greatest strength of the Populists that "there is no place yet in America for a *third* party" because of the size, complexity, and heterogeneity of the country. "The divergence of interests even *in the same* class group is so great in that tremendous area that wholly different groups and interests are represented in each of the two big parties, depending on the locality."[44]

Although democracies offer an opportunity for the masses to form their own party and to seek political power by peaceful means, they inhibit independent and original thought. Engels in 1844 argued that public opinion in a democracy is repressive, intolerant of independent views, following much the same logic as Tocqueville's discussion of the tyranny of the multitude in his *Democracy in America*. Engels was mainly writing about England but, as he himself noted, the analysis applied even more strongly to the United States.[45]

The Inadequacy of Marxian Explanations

Marx and Engels clearly had no coherent explanation for the failures of socialism in America during their lifetimes. As the purest example of a bourgeois industrializing society, they expected America to provide a political model for the rest of the capitalist world. When it became obvious that this anticipation of a powerful socialist movement in the most advanced bourgeois nation was not being fulfilled, they resorted to a variety of ad hoc explanations, including reversing the presumed consequences of the absence of a feudal past. In Engels' most comprehensive discussion of the problem, written in 1893, he cited three sets of factors: (1) political—those inhibiting third parties; (2) ethnic and racial diversity among workers, which negate common action, and (3) economic wealth which affected the workers' situation.[46] If the question is turned around and we ask what Marx and Engels thought would have to occur to stimulate a socialist movement, the emphasis throughout their writings falls much more on economic factors, that is, a decline of growth and rates of profits and consequent increased unemployment and lower real wages.

In one of his earliest commentaries on America, written in 1847, Marx applied a basic proposition of historical materialism, in words which were reiterated in *Capital*, two decades later: "The more developed a society, . . . the more glaringly does the social question emerge," and he went on to predict that an inevitable increase in poverty in the United States will intensify the conflict, noting that "pauperism is making the most gratifying progress."[47] Five years later, in a letter to Engels, he anticipated an economic crisis in America as a result of "frantic speculation," and wrote "the revolution may come sooner than we wish."[48]

Engels continued to see economic crisis and depression, and consequent impoverishment of the American working class, as the catalytic agent. He wrote in 1886:

> the present chronic depression . . . will tell its tale in America as well as in England. . . . even in America the condition of the working class must gradually sink lower and lower . . . I believe it [the depression] will mark an epoch in the mental and political history of the American and English working classes.[49]

The reluctance of American workers to accept a general theoretical interpretation of their situation could only be changed by economic pressures. "With the Anglo-Saxon mind, and especially with the eminently practical development it has taken in America, theory counts for nothing until it is imposed by dire necessity."[50] The inevitable end of opportunity following upon the closing of the open frontier would create a favorable political situation.

On a different level, Engels identified rapid economic development, or industrialization, as the basis for the formation of working class consciousness. In England and Germany, *"the period of development* of large scale industry" coincided with intense class struggle in the former and "with the rise of the Socialist movement [in the latter], and it will be no different, probably, in America. It is the revolutionizing of all established conditions by industry *as it develops* that also revolutionizes people's minds."[51]

Thus in spite of their sophisticated awareness of the way in which a variety of superstructural elements in the cultural, status, and political systems served to inhibit the emergence of socialism in America, Marx and Engels remained faithful in the last analysis to their basic commitment to the centrality of economic factors. The American workers would come to true consciousness when the economic contradictions of capitalism would undermine their favorable position. "Dire necessity" would be the mother of American socialism.

A Note on Bakunin

Michael Bakunin, the famous Russian anarchist leader and principal rival of Marx and Engels for control of the First International, also paid considerable attention to America from his visit there in 1861 to his death in 1876. Much of his descriptive analysis and interpretive commentary coincided with that of his socialist rivals. Writing in the late 1860s, he pointed to the higher standards of living and wider distribution of educational opportunities among the masses in America as compared to Europe, as a result of which class conflict was almost nonexistent. Bakunin also emphasized the fact that America was a "new world" uninfluenced by the "obsessions of the past." Like Marx and Engels, he saw a safety

valve in the vast acres of unsettled western lands, since the
poorly paid could always move to the Far West.

> Offering a freedom which does not exist anywhere else, it [Amer-
> ica] attracts every year hundreds of thousands of energetic, in-
> dustrious and intelligent settlers whom it is in a position to admit
> because of this [territorial] wealth. It thereby keeps poverty
> away and at the same time staves off the moment when the social
> question will arise. A worker who finds no work or is dissatisfied
> with the wages which capital offers him can in the last resort al-
> ways make his way to the Far West and set about clearing a patch
> of land in the wilderness.[52]

As an anarchist, Bakunin placed more stress than his socialist opponents on the importance in America of decentralized
political institutions—federalism, in the context of the English libertarian tradition. The United States was "the classic
land of political liberty." There, "liberty and political action
directly exercised by the masses have attained the highest
degree of development known in history up to now."[53]

America was, of course, far from being a utopia. The
masses were oppressed and exploited economically. In spite
of universal suffrage, the bourgeoisie held power effectively.
Politicians were able to manipulate the electorate. Ultimately, America would be unable to sustain a high wage structure,
since its manufacturers would be unable to compete with
Europeans. The "social question" would emerge as "masses
of workers . . . gradually begin to find themselves in a situation analogous to that of workers in the great manufacturing
states of Europe."[54]

Bakunin was much more optimistic than Marx and Engels
about the revolutionary potential of the American working
class, perhaps because he did not believe in the need for a
workers' political party, and possibly because the National
Labor Union, the American affiliate of the First International, followed Bakunin.

Foreign and Domestic Socialists

From the death of Engels until World War I, a variety of
leading European Marxists and other radicals emulated his

example of paying close attention to American events. They continued to believe that the most developed capitalist country had to lead the world into socialism. The British Marxist H. M. Hyndman noted in 1904 that "just as North America is today the most advanced country economically and socially, so it will be the first in which Socialism will find open and legal expression."[55]

Karl Kautsky, considered the leading Marxist theoretician in the German Social Democratic Party, enunciated in 1902 that "America shows us our future, in so far as one country can reveal it at all to another." He reiterated this view in 1910, anticipating the "overdue sharpening of class conflict more strongly" there than anywhere else.[56] Eduard Bernstein, the future leader of Marxist "revisionism," noted in the 1890s, while still an orthodox Marxist: "We see modern socialism enter and take root in the United States in direct relation to the spreading of capitalism and the appearance of a modern proletariat."[57] August Bebel, the political leader of the German Social Democrats, in an interview in the American socialist paper, *Appeal to Reason*, stated unequivocally in 1907: "You Americans will be the first to usher in a Socialist Republic." His belief, at a time when his party was already a mass movement with many elected members of the Reichstag and the American Socialist Party secured less than 2 percent of the vote, was based on the fact that "your country is far ahead of Germany in industrial development." He reiterated this opinion in a second interview in 1912, when the discrepancy in the strength of the two movements was even greater, saying that America will "be the first nation to declare a Co-operative Commonwealth."[58] The French socialist Paul Lefargue, who was also Marx's son-in-law, paraphrased Marx on the flyleaf of his book on America: "The most industrially advanced country shows to those who follow it on the industrial ladder the image of their own future."[59]

The desire to see their theoretical anticipations confirmed led various European Marxists repeatedly to draw enthusiastic, but inevitably exaggerated, conclusions on the basis of limited events to the effect that the American workers were finally awakening and that a mass socialist movement was on its way. Yet, these expectations repeatedly came to naught. Max Beer, whose fifty-year career in international socialism included participation in the Austrian, German, and British parties, toward the end of his life described the anxiety and embarrassment created by the weakness of socialism in America.

> The attitude of American Labour appeared to stand out as a living contradiction of the Marxian theory that the concentration of capitalist production, and attendant proletarization of the masses, was necessarily bound to lead to class struggles and to the formation of an independent Labour movement with Socialist aims and ends. . . . Was the generalization faulty, or were there forces in operation that neutralized it?[60]

The Class System

A number of socialist observers who sought to explain the lack of class consciousness in America as compared to Europe suggested it was due to differences in their origin and history. Max Beer, who spent three years around the turn of the century in the United States, put forth a rather sophisticated set of hypotheses concerning the source of the differences between the workers of America and Europe.

1. The class of "craftsmen, and artisans, and small masters . . . displaced in Europe by the factory system," which had provided the leadership base for various early socialist and labor movements, "did not exist in the United States, since the latter had no Middle Ages."

2. "In the United States, with the limitless opportunities for agricultural, industrial, and commercial expansion, the factory system dispossessed nobody and bred no despair; if the worker disliked factory discipline, there was ample room for him in the Middle States, in the North and West, where jobs were running after him, while even in the populous Eastern states there was room for shopkeeping, salesmanship and professional careers." Those who see opportunity available are not interested in upsetting the existing order.

3. "Even when the time is ripe for a Socialist movement, it can only produce one when the working people form a certain cultural unity, that is, when they have a common language, a common history, a common mode of life. This is the case in Europe, but not in the United States. . . . The solid middle-class civilization . . . absorbs the best elements of the immigrants, turning them into middle-class Americans. . . . And middle-class civilization meant private property as the basis of material life."[61]

The foreign-born American socialist leaders Victor Berger and Morris Hillquit emphasized the enduring historic character of class consciousness in Europe. It had long predated the rise of socialist consciousness. As Berger put it in 1903:

> The feeling of class distinction in America, at least among native workingmen, has not the same historic foundation that it has in Germany, France, or England. There the people were accustomed for over a thousand years to have distinct classes and castes fixed by law.[62]

Not so with the American workingmen. Their existence as a class was of too recent date to have developed decided class feelings in them. Hillquit noted also that "the ethnic conditions of the country [are not] very favorable to the growth of socialism. . . . The Socialist Party . . . is compelled to address the workers of the country in more than twenty languages. . . . The presence of about nine millions of Negroes, mostly workers, with special racial and social conditions, raises another very serious problem for the socialist movement."[63]

H. G. Wells related the unique history and resultant class structure of the United States not only to the fact that it lacked a socialist party, but also to the absence of a Tory, a true conservative, party. As he presented the case, two major European classes—the subservient land-bound peasants and the aristocracy—were missing from the American social structure. The absence of the former implied no "servile tradition" while that of the latter meant that the sense of "state responsibility, which in the old European theory of society was supposed to give significance to the whole," was also missing. "The American community, one cannot too clearly insist, does not correspond to an entire European community at all, but only to the middle masses of it. . . . This community was, as it were, taken off its roots, clipped of its branches and brought hither. . . . Essentially America is a middle-class become a community and so its essential problems are the problems of a modern individualistic society, stark and clear, unhampered and unilluminated by any feudal traditions either at its crest or at its base."[64]

The theory of America as a liberal society—put forth again a half-century later by Louis Hartz—was enunciated in 1906 by the socialist Wells:

> It is not difficult to show for example, that the two great political parties in America represent only one English party, the middle-class Liberal party. . . . The new world [was left] to the Whigs and Nonconformists and to those less constructive, less logical, more popular and liberating thinkers who became Radicals in England, and Jeffersonians and then Democrats in America. All Americans are, from the English point of view, Liberals of one sort or another. . . .
>
> My chief argument . . . is that the Americans started almost clear of the medieval heritage, and developed in the utmost . . . the modern type of social organization. They took the economic conventions that were modern and progressive at the end of the eighteenth century.
>
> The liberalism of the eighteenth century was essentially the rebellion of the modern industrial organization against the monarchical and aristocratic state—against hereditary privilege, against restrictions on bargains. Its spirit was essentially Anarchistic—the antithesis of Socialism. It was the anti-State.[65]

The System of Rewards

The explanations for the weakness of socialism in America were not restricted simply to historical factors. Many foreign

socialists contended that American workers in the late nineteenth and early twentieth century had more opportunity to
advance themselves, were better off economically, and were
accorded more respect in cross-class interpersonal relations
than their European counterparts. Vera MacGahan, a Russian
radical married to an American, writing in a Russian populist
magazine in 1886, compared the static "social system of
castes, orders and estates" of Europe with the more fluid
stratification system of America:

> The European worker, who is excluded at birth from any contact
> with the so-called upper classes, has no chance to become a man
> of standing.

> The United States, on the contrary, represents another extreme.
> Here every boy grows up with the confidence that all ways are
> open to him, that it is up to him alone to get riches and achieve
> the highest honors of the country. . . . However low a family may
> be in its social level, you will always hear from its members that
> one or another relative became socially outstanding in the past, or
> that at present occupies a most important place.[66]

Much of the discussion about social stratification in America in the decade preceding World War I was based on Werner
Sombart's detailed study *Warum gibt es in den Vereinigten
Staaten keinen Sozialismus?* Given the comprehensive character and the importance of this work in structuring subsequent
discussion in Europe, a detailed specification of Sombart's
analysis seems in order:

1. The American workers have much higher incomes and
   real standards of living than Germans.

> The diet of the American worker is much closer to that of
> our better-off middle-class circles than to that of our class of
> wage laborers. . . . The fact that the American worker ranks
> much more nearly with our bourgeois middle class than
> with our working class as far as standard of living is con-
> cerned is shown perhaps most clearly in his *clothing*. This
> strikes everyone who comes to America for the first time.

2. America is a freer and more egalitarian society than
   Europe.

> [The worker's] relationship to other people and to social
> institutions . . . is also advantageous compared to the situa-
> tion in Europe. For him "freedom" and "equality" . . . are
> not empty concepts, or vague dreams, as they are for the
> proletariat in Europe. . . .
>
> In his external appearance, the worker does not bear those
> signs of belonging to a separate class which almost all Euro-
> pean workers have. . . . He seems neither oppressed, nor
> submissive.
>
> Cringing and crawling before the "upper classes," which
> makes such an unpleasant impression in Europe, is absolute-
> ly unknown.
>
> The workingman *feels* differently than his counterpart does
> in a country where "man" first begins if not with the bar-
> on, then with the reserve officer, the doctor or the govern-
> ment official. Due to the factors described above, social dis-
> tance . . . becomes even smaller in the minds of the various
> classes than it actually is.
>
> This tone of "equal treatment," to which social and public
> life in the United States is attuned, is also dominant within
> the capitalist enterprise itself. Here, too, the employer does
> not treat the worker as if he [the employer] were a "lord"
> who demands obedience, as the employer did, and still gen-
> erally does, in "old" Europe with its feudal traditions. . . .
> Even today, even English workers are astonished at the re-
> spectful tone which [American] employers and foremen
> adopt toward their workers.

3. These first two sets of factors would not suffice to prevent the growth of "a spirit of opposition" to capitalism, were it not for the fact that workers can see "an
   avenue of escape" through opportunities for social and
   geographical mobility.

> Anglo-Saxon purposefulness, the newness of the society and
> its democratic character, the smaller class barriers between
> employers and employees . . . all these and many other fac-
> tors not infrequently operated to allow the ordinary worker
> to climb the ladder of capitalism. . . . [In addition] millions
> of workers have striven for and reached in the course of the
> past century . . . a free homestead in the unsettled west. . . .
> Internal migration takes on greater dimensions in the
> United States than it does in any other country.[67]

At the same time, Sombart emphasized the sharply exploitative character of American capitalism. "Objectively,"
he noted, "in no other country in the world is the worker so
exploited by capitalism as in the United States—in no other
country is he 'rubbed so bloody by the harness of capitalism,'
or works himself to death as quickly there." But the American capitalist "understands how to keep the worker in a con-
tented mood in spite of all the actual exploitation . . . [by]
being generous in little things. . . ."[68] Sombart felt obligated
to conclude, however, that the factors which inhibited socialism in the United States would decline, that "socialism will in
all likelihood come to fullest bloom in the New World."[69]
Yet, he also raised the spectre that if socialism did not
emerge under conditions of the most advanced capitalism,
perhaps it would grow weaker in Europe as European countries reached the economic heights attained by the United
States. As he noted, "we have a land without socialism in
spite of the highest capitalist development. The doctrine of
the inevitable future is disproved by the facts."[70]

Sombart's analysis was subjected to merciless attacks in
German Marxist publications. It was also rejected as a distor-
tion of the American reality by the *International Socialist
Review*, which had begun publishing an English language
translation of Sombart's work, a task it suspended after the
first chapter with this explanation: "When we came to the
nonsense on the condition of the American worker we
stopped further publication."[71]

The Marxist critics looked for other explanations which would pose less of a challenge to their basic theory. Karl Kautsky argued that class consciousness was weak in America because of the absence of a native working class. Through an examination of the 1900 Census, he calculated that 60 percent of the industrial workers were foreign-born whites, children of the foreign-born or Negroes. He revived the contention of Marx and Engels that the ethnic and racial heterogeneity of the American workers prevented them from class-oriented political action.[72] Franz Mehring, author of the major biography of Marx, saw a source of the socialist failure in the still overwhelmingly agricultural character of the United States.[73]

Others offered a special American variant of the thesis then being developed by Kautsky, Rosa Luxemburg, and Lenin to the effect that the economic wealth gained by imperialist countries at the expense of their colonies enabled the capitalists in the metropolis to pay high salaries and thus buy off protest for a period. The theory, as applied to America, was that the United States, as a continent-wide nation, had domestic colonies, as well as having a larger internal market than other countries.[74]

Some Marxists turned the thesis about the greater development around to urge that precisely because American capitalism, particularly in the form of the trusts, was the most powerful in the world, it was better able to repress socialist tendencies than elsewhere.[75]

All European Marxists, however, did not reject Sombart's arguments. George Plekhanov, the father of Russian Marxism, who in 1890 emphasized that America's exceptional conditions stem from its "never having known feudal or patriarchal relations," praised Sombart for applying "Marx's method of explaining social phenomena quite successfully." He spoke approvingly of Sombart's explanation which focused on the "democratic character of North American political institutions; . . . the extremely favorable economic position of the North American worker compared to that of the European, and . . . a multitude of free lands which made it possible for the proletariat 'to escape to freedom' from capitalism." Plekhanov, however, also stressed that the favorable economic factors have "diminished over the course of time," and that socialism would finally take root in the United States.[76]

Various "revisionist" socialists were more willing than the orthodox Marxists to accept the proposition that workers were doing well in advanced capitalism. Emile Vandervelde, the Belgian socialist leader, reported after a trip to America in 1904 that "no one seriously disputes that, all in all, American workers have a position very superior to that of the European worker." J. Keir Hardie, leader of the British Labour Party, commented in similar terms after his visit across the Atlantic in 1908. The German revisionist, Ludwig Quessel, in 1909 countered Kautsky's arguments that the real wages of Americans were declining, with statistical evidence that they were increasing, a development he credited to the power of labor unions.[77] Fabian socialist H. G. Wells emphasized the fact that while "a growing proportion of the wealth of the community is passing into the hands of a small minority of successful getters, this is masked . . . by the enormous increase of the total wealth." And he concluded that "the great mass of the population is not consciously defeated in the economic game. It is only failing to get a large share in the increment of wealth."[78] (No "evolutionary" socialist, Leon Trotsky, in an autobiography written at the start of his final exile in 1929, which contains almost no mention of personal matters in adult life, still described, almost in awe, the material level available in "an apartment in a workers' district" in New York where he and his family lived for two months in 1917.[79])

Morris Hillquit, writing the first major history of American socialism, also laid stress, in explaining its weakness, on the fact that "the American working men still enjoyed some actual [economic] advantages over their brethren on the other side of the ocean. . . . They were still inclined to consider wage labor as a mere transitory condition."[80]

Although social and political class-consciousness were inhibited by more egalitarian social relationships, a high standard of living and belief in the existence of widespread opportunities to advance, these did not make for a docile working class in America. Foreign visitors to the United States around the turn of the century commented on the greater "frequency and bitterness of industrial conflict" in comparison to Europe. They analyzed such behavior as another consequence of the peculiar American social system. One analyst of the foreign traveller literature has aptly summarized these conclusions:

> Most of the European visitors explained industrial conflict as a result rather than a contradiction of the material and social democracy which typified the life of the American worker. The abundance of his life, they pointed out, added to the strength of his ambition for more. His self-reliance made him sensitive to his rights. Industrial conflict in America was a man-to-man fight, with no quarter asked or given, unmitigated by the tradition of subordination on the one hand, or of benevolence and responsibility on the other.[81]

The Political System

Many of the explanations for the failure of socialism in America published in the late 1890s and the early years of the twentieth century continued to emphasize the unique elements stemming from America's lack of a feudal past and its consequent early democratic political institutions which inhibited workers from recognizing their class situation. In much of Europe, socialist parties had gained strength fighting for elementary political rights, particularly for suffrage, which the Americans had prior to industrialization. As Karl Kautsky put it in 1904, "the struggle for freedom is very much superior to the effortless possession of a freedom that others have won before."[82]

Writing in 1907, Lenin emphasized that the weakness of socialism in America stemmed from "the absence of any at all big, nation-wide *democratic* tasks facing the proletariat."[83] Political freedom in America has produced "the complete subjection of the proletariat to bourgeois politics; the sectarian isolation of the [socialist] groups, . . . not the slightest success of the Socialists among the working masses in the elections, etc." American socialism was weak precisely because it was dealing with "the most firmly established democratic system, which confronts the proletariat with purely socialist tasks."[84] To reverse Lenin's words, European socialism was much stronger because it could appeal to the workers for support, not on "purely socialist," but on democratic issues. As he emphasized, the German Social Democrats were powerful because they worked in "a country where the bourgeois-democratic revolution was still incomplete, where 'military despotism, embellished with parliamentary forms' (Marx's expression in his *Critique of the Gotha Programme*) prevailed, and still prevails."[85] Generally, socialists were strong in countries "where the proletariat has formed its party before the liberal bourgeois have formed theirs."[86]

Morris Hillquit elaborated on the argument that political freedom undermines class consciousness, noting that "paradoxical as it may seem, our very democracy has militated against the immediate success of socialism."

> Another check to the progress of the socialist movement in the United States was to be found in the political institutions of the country: the working classes of the European countries were, as a rule, deprived of some political rights enjoyed by other classes of citizens, and the common struggle for the acquisition of those rights was frequently the first cause to draw them together in a political union.
>
> In the United States, however, the working men enjoyed full political equality at all times, and thus had one less motive to organize politically on a class basis.[87]

Max Beer emphasized the absence of a middle-class revolutionary history which had involved an effort to mobilize the working class for reforms. In the Old World "the rise and effervescence of Socialist Labour movements at various periods were, as a rule, the concomitant phenomena of middle-class upheavals, which directly or indirectly mobilized some strata of the working class" and which "were accompanied by an inrush of Socialist ideas." These included the Reform Bill struggles in Britain, the nineteenth century revolutions in France and Germany, the 1905 Revolution in Russia, etc. "In the United States middle class movements against a privileged upper class or personal monarchy could not arise, for these phenomena did not exist, and there was no need to mobilize the working classes for the fight."[88]

The sheer fact that bourgeois democracy and universal suffrage in America predated the emergence of a large-scale proletariat would not, in and of itself, prevent class political organization. But as Sombart emphasized, the American electoral system encourages two parties which "are essentially only indefinite unions [for electoral purposes] . . . so it is easy for even the 'class conscious' laborer to unite with one of the two parties." The politicians

> must constantly use systematic methods in order to retain the good favor of the masses. Success in elections depends primarily upon the votes of the great masses. As a result the proletariat with all the lower classes of the people is in the fortunate situation that the two great parties are in competition for its favor.[89]

The electoral system and the two coalition parties which it produced were seen by many as a major obstacle in the path of the Socialist Party. Hillquit, in portraying the supposedly special conditions which resulted in an unexpectedly small socialist vote in 1908, unwittingly described the general conditions which prevail whenever a third party threatens to accumulate a large vote.

> The Democratic party . . . revived all the slogans of its old time middle-class radicalism and re-instated the prophet of that brand of radicalism, William J. Bryan, in the leadership of the party. . . . The direct and public endorsement of the Democratic Party by the officials of the American Federation of Labor and their appeal to organized labor for active support of the candidates of that party, could not but be detrimental to the socialist campaign.[90]

Philipp Rappaport, who wrote often on American conditions in the German socialist magazine *Die Neue Zeit*, was moved by the small vote obtained by the socialists in presidential elections to declare that socialism in America must await the conversion of the Democratic Party.[91]

This recommendation accorded with the earlier history of efforts to create left third parties. The Workingmen's parties of the 1830s which so impressed Marx had been absorbed by the Jacksonian Democrats who had modified their politics to appeal in the cities where the third party had strength. Orestes Brownson, one of Workingmen's party's leaders, had urged the same strategy suggested by Rappaport. He was the first, but definitely not the last, to suggest that radicals should work to make the Democrats a party of social as distinguished from political democracy.[92] In 1872, the Presidential nomination by the Democrats of Horace Greeley, social reformer and member of the pre–Civil War Fourierist socialist movement, undermined the effort of the American affiliate of the First International, the National Labor Union, to run David Davis for the presidency as a labor candidate. A quarter of a century later, the most sustained and successful effort to build a left third party which appealed to farmers and workers, the People's Party, failed when the Democrats absorbed it, accepting much of the populist program, and nominating a militant advocate of agrarianism, William Jennings Bryan, for the presidency.

The ability of major parties, particularly the Democrats, to absorb radical protest within their electoral coalition was not simply a function of the special sophistication of American politicians or the weak sense of solidarity of prospective American leftist voters. Rather, Hillquit noted, it was inherent in the special electoral system of the United States. In other parliamentary countries,

the elections are by district and the ticket of each party is, as a rule, limited to one candidate for each district. Each electoral campaign is thus conducted on the merits of the given district, and is in no way dependent upon conditions in other districts. In an electoral district largely made up of radicals the voters may, therefore, enter the contest with the expectation of victory regardless of the more conservative sentiments in other districts or in the country at large. In the United States . . . the ticket handed to the voter . . . contains the names not only of candidates for the state legislature or congress, but also for all local and state officers and even for President of the United States. And since a new party rarely seems to have the chance or prospect of electing its candidate for governor of a state or president of the country, the voter is inclined in advance to consider its entire ticket as hopeless. The fear of "throwing away" the vote is thus a peculiar product of American politics, and it requires a voter of exceptional strength of conviction to overcome it.[93]

Sombart emphasized other factors which reduced potential support for third parties. He suggested that the "over-valuation of success" inherent in America's pure bourgeois culture made "Who won?" the only question of interest in sports and in economic life.[94]

This emphasis on success, on winning every race in which one participates "predestinates 'majority' politics."

It is an unbearable feeling for an American to belong to a party that always and forever comes out of the election with small figures, and which can apparently attain no visible success within an immediate period, and which because of this is subject to the stigma of ridicule. A member of a minority party finds himself on election day, when the ecstasy of the statistical success of the great party reaches its highest point, when all the newspapers are displaying the electoral success of their candidates in giant letters, when the figures of the presidential election are thrown upon gigantic transparencies, compelled to stand at one side with martyrlike resignation—something which in no way accords with the American temperament.[95]

European observers also stressed the causal role of other special American cultural and political conditions in affecting socialist prospects and deplored the sectarianism of American socialists. R. L. Moore writes about the complaints from the members of England's Independent Labour Party that

American socialists "refuse to make the necessary overtures to American trade unionists who alone could give strength to the cause."[96] Such comments came even from English socialists who were at times criticized for similar shortcomings. In 1907, Lenin wrote: "What Marx and Engels criticize in British and American socialism is its isolation from the labour movement. The burden of all their numerous comments on . . . the American Socialists is the accusation that they have reduced Marxism to a dogma, to a 'rigid orthodoxy' . . . that they are incapable of adapting themselves to the theoretically helpless but living and powerful mass labour movement that is marching alongside them."[97]

In discussing differences between European and American socialism in 1906, Marx's grandson, Jean Longuet, noted that orthodox Marxism was stronger within the American socialist movement than anywhere else except in Russia.[98] H. G. Wells noted the difference between British and American socialism. The latter "is a fierce form of socialist teaching that speaks throughout these regions, far more closely akin to the revolutionary socialism of the continent of Europe than to the constructive and evolutionary Socialism of Great Britain. . . . It is a Socialism reeking with class feeling and class hatred and altogether anarchistic in spirit. . . ."[99] The British socialists were disturbed that their American comrades refused to follow their lead in joining with the unions in a mass-based labor party and repeated the advice Engels had given a quarter of a century earlier that it was more important to have a large, independent labor movement than an ideologically correct small socialist party.

Yet the basic factors which European socialists identified as inhibiting their movement in America were its freedom and economic wealth. Lenin summed up the case in 1912:

> The principal historical cause of the particular prominence and (temporary) strength of bourgeois labor policy in . . . America is the long-standing political liberty and the exceptionally favourable conditions, in comparison with other countries, for the deepgoing and widespread development of capitalism.[100]

Most writings dealing with the weakness of socialism and

of class consciousness in the United States in the late nineteenth and early twentieth century came from socialist intellectuals. However, a nonsocialist academic school on institutional labor economics and history developed at the University of Wisconsin under John R. Commons and then Selig Perlman. Both advocated for American workers the limited antipolitical job-consciousness approach of the American Federation of Labor. Their lifelong study of organized workers led them to a rejection of socialism as inappropriate to American conditions. Socialism seemed to them a dysfunctional ideology brought to the workers by intellectuals who were imposing their own anticapitalist resentments onto the working class. Like the socialists, Commons and Perlman sought to explain the differences between Europe and America. Their explanation included also many of the same factors brought out by the socialists, in spite of the basic differences in economic assumptions and political goals.[101]

Communist Interpretations

The most important event affecting radicalism in the world and America was the Russian Revolution. In 1917, a Marxist party took and retained power for the first time in history. That party, renamed Communist, became the center of a new International, the Third, and insisted that its followers in other countries break with existing socialist parties and form communist parties. This, of course, occurred in the United States and, from 1919 on, the United States has had three or more parties, each claiming to represent authentic socialism, namely, the old Socialist Labor Party, composed of followers of Daniel DeLeon, the Socialist Party, a shadow of the pre–World War I organization, and the Communist Party.[102]

The victory of communism in Russia had as one minor consequence the end of intense discussions of American socialism which had begun with the Marxist assumption that the most advanced capitalist country should be the first one to become socialist. A Marxist party had triumphed first in an industrially backward, predominantly rural society. The Russian Bolsheviks, as good Marxists, initially believed that their victory was an historic anomaly, that socialism could only be meaningful in an industrial society. In their early years in power, they assumed that the revolution was imminent in the industrialized West, and that Western socialist governments would come to their aid economically and absorb the less developed Russian economy into their own.

The Communist International's manifesto on May Day 1919 proclaimed: "The great International Soviet Republic will be born in the year 1920." Lenin in July 1919 guaranteed that "the victory of the International Soviet Republic . . . will be complete and irrevocable" by July 1920. Lenin, Zinoviev, and other Bolshevik leaders eagerly inquired of American visitors when a revolution in America could be expected.[103]

By 1920, the Russian communists recognized that the world revolution was not on the immediate agenda of the West and they turned to building their own country. Whatever faith they might retain in the European Revolution, they, of course, knew better about America. In 1920, Zinoviev, the head of the Comintern, mocked the American communists who boasted they would lead a successful revolution soon, but who were pessimistic about their ability to make headway within the trade-union movement.[104] The incongruity between communist power in backward Russia and the weak radicalism in the highly developed United States created a major paradox for the communist movement and for Marxist theory. As Theodore Draper put it:

> The Americans represented the most advanced capitalist country in the world. Both the American economy and the American working class were developed to a point that backward Russia could hope to reach only in decades. . . . Politically, however, the Americans came to them as novices.

> This was the paradox, the contradiction, which took root in the Comintern at the very start and became progressively more acute as time went on. From the Communist point of view, history had played a cruel joke on the development of the revolution: Russia had to learn from America technically, and America had to learn from Russia politically. The material basis of the Russian

Revolution was in America; and the political fulfillment of the
American economy was in Russia. This was not at all what anyone had expected, least of all the Marxists, who had taught for
decades that politics and economics move together.[105]

Some communists tried to understand America. Why was
it so backward politically when it was so advanced economically? The answer, insofar as one could be given, lay in
America's economic affluence, in the fact that its great
wealth gave the masses a high standard of living, and in the
fact stressed by Lenin before World War I, that it was the
purest example of bourgeois society. It was a society in
which bourgeois values dominated the thinking of all its inhabitants, including the workers, in ways that had never developed in European countries, torn between precapitalist
and capitalist values and interests.

The example of their own revolution, occurring in an economically backward society, led the Bolsheviks to an emphasis on economic and social breakdown as the catalytic agent
for class consciousness and revolution. Following from this
conception, they now anticipated that the United States
would be the last country to become socialist because its economy was in better shape than those of Europe or the underdeveloped world. As they saw the situation, North America
was in a position, because of its superior wealth, resources
and industrial technique, to take away markets from Britain
and continental European countries, and to maintain its economic strength, while the economies of the Old World would
go into a steady decline that would lead to the revolution
triumphing there.

The greater wealth and economic power of the United
States produced a relatively conservative working class which
thought in bourgeois categories. This situation would continue
as long as America remained wealthy and stable. The communists, both in Russia and the United States, therefore, constantly looked for signs that American capitalism was finally
about to break down, that its material postwar prosperity
was ending.

By 1926, however, Zinoviev, as leader of the Communist International, enunciated a new formula forecasting that the United States, Japan and some of the overseas British Dominions were still "on the upgrade." Bukharin proclaimed: "Our party in America is still quite small. American capitalism is the stronghold of the entire capitalist system, the most powerful capitalism in the world. Our tasks in this country are for the present still very modest."[106]

The American communists echoed their Russian comrades. W. Z. Foster, the party's leading trade-unionist, emphasized the extent to which American wealth had created a self-satisfied "labor aristocracy." Jay Lovestone, the General Secretary, pointed out that the American workers had been "bourgeoified" ideologically, that "objective conditions prevailing today in the United States are not favorable for the development of a mass Communist Party.[107] John Pepper, who had been sent to the American party by the Comintern in 1922, published an article in the American party's theoretical organ *The Communist,* early in 1928, in which he laid down five "fundamental differences" between the United States and Europe: "American capitalism was still on the upgrade; American imperialism was still increasing in power; the American working class was more privileged than the European; it did not have its own mass [labor] political party; and it showed no marked tendency of a left trend on a national scale."[108]

Such opinions ceased being official doctrine in the Russian and American parties later in 1928. Stalin proclaimed that worldwide and American capitalism were on the verge of economic collapse and that communists everywhere should make a sharp turn to the left, preparatory to coming to power on their own.[109] In reaction to initial limited objections by American communists to this policy, Stalin in May 1929 laid down the dictum that the United States must be treated like all other countries. He accused the leaders of the American Communist Party of the heresy of believing in "American exceptionalism," and of exaggerating the unique features of American capitalism. Stalin, in a sense, returned to the view that America, as the foremost and most developed capitalist country, must play a leading role in the worldwide move towards socialism. He stated, "The Communist Party of America is one of the few communist parties in the world upon which history has placed tasks of decisive importance from the point of view of the international revolutionary movement. . . . Many seem to think that the general crisis of capitalism will not affect America. This, of course, is wrong. . . . I think that the moment is not far off when a revolutionary crisis will be unleashed in America, when that revolutionary crisis comes in the United States, it will mark the beginning of the end of world capitalism."[110]

Stalin, of course, recognized that the United States, like all countries, had some "special peculiarities," but he did not bother to enunciate them and indicated that it would be a mistake to emphasize them.

> The Communist Party must reckon with them in its work. But it would be even more incorrect to base the activities of the Communist Party on these specific features, since the basis of any Communist Party, including the Communist Party of America, are the general features of capitalism, features which in the main are the same in all countries and are not the specific characteristics of the given country. . . . Specific features merely supplement the general features. The mistake of both groups [the factions in the American party] is that they exaggerate the importance of the specific features of American capitalism.[111]

Therefore, both factions were committing mistakes of a right-wing character.

Stalin and his colleagues in the leadership of the world movement also laid stress on the special propensity of the American communist to engage in sectarian factional struggles, putting the victory of each particular faction ahead of efforts to build a mass movement.[112] They did not, however, try to specify the nature of the unique American conditions which caused communists there to engage in factional sectarianism and to overestimate their weakness.

Other communists, particularly "the great heretic" Leon Trotsky, as long as he was close to power in the Soviet Union, and Antonio Gramsci, an Italian party leader who, sitting in Mussolini's prisons, was free to use his intelligence and ignore the party line, treated the American situation in a more sophisticated fashion than Stalin and his colleagues. Each stressed the special nonfeudal origins of American society which gave it a value system sharply differentiated from that of Europe and acted both to stimulate economic growth and to retard working-class consciousness.

Trotsky, who paid particular attention to problems of the World revolution, discussed the United States in a number of articles and talks in the early twenties. In 1922 he reported to the Tenth Congress of the Soviet party:

> Certainly, considering its economic and social power, the American working class is ready to take power, but given its political and organizational traditions, it is less prepared than the European workers. . . . If you ask me which will come first, the victory of the proletarian revolution in Europe or the creation of a powerful Communist party in America, . . . the chances are much greater [for the former]. . . . The triumph of the workers in the principal countries of Europe is a necessary condition for the rapid development of the revolutionary movement in America.[113]

In a discussion in 1926 Trotsky elaborated on the American situation and anticipated a continuing brilliant economic future for the United States as it absorbed much of Western Europe, Canada, Australia, Latin America, and the colonial world of Africa and Asia into its economic orbit. This economic wealth enables America "to apply the traditional method of the British bourgeoisie to fatten the labor aristocracy in order to keep the workers in shackles."[114]

Yet, the argument that the American expansion, combined with economic recovery in postwar Europe, meant a revival of capitalism was perceived by Trotsky as a fundamental challenge to the assumptions underlying the existence of the Soviet Union.

If it is true that capitalism is still capable of playing a progressive role, of increasing wealth, of making labor more productive, this means that, we, the Communist party of the U.S.S.R., were mistaken in singing *de profundis*, in other words that we took power too soon in order to build socialism. Because, as Marx explained, no social system disappears before having exhausted all its latent possibilities. . . . Has capitalism exhausted itself or can it still hope for more progress?[115]

The largest developed area controlled by capitalism, Europe, was finished, it was on the decline:

European capitalism has become reactionary in an absolute sense. Not being able to lead the nations into the future, it is not even able to maintain its present standard of living.

Certainly American capitalism is incomparably stronger and more solid than European capitalism, it can look forward to the future with considerable optimism. But it can not only base itself on domestic conditions. It must face world conditions. Europe relies increasingly on America, but as a result, America, in its turn, must rely more and more on Europe.[116]

The United States with its increasing productivity must export goods and capital. It invests its surplus in Europe and the less developed world, but by so doing it becomes more vulnerable. The revolution in Europe will bring down Wall Street.

This means that the revolution will come to America later. It will begin in Europe and the Orient. . . . Certainly it would be advantageous to begin the nationalization of the means of production in a country as extremely rich as America, then continue it in the rest of the world. But our own experience shows that this is impossible. . . . Russia, poor and economically backward, has had the first proletarian revolution. Now it is the turn of the other European countries.[117]

The United States will not be able to defeat the united power of socialist Europe and Asia. Meanwhile, however,

American workers, who live well because the United States exploits the peoples of the world, continue to support the class collaborationist unions of the American Federation of Labor and reject the small American Communist Party.

In 1939, after a decade of the worst depression to affect the United States and the world, Trotsky repeated much of his analysis of America made thirteen years earlier.[118] Like Engels, Plekhanov, and Lenin, Trotsky also found it necessary to add to his materialistic explanation about the continued strength of bourgeois democracy, the sectarian character of the "three strange types" of Marxists in America: "the emigrés cast out of Europe . . .; isolated American groups, like the DeLeonists, who in the course of events, and because of their own mistakes, turned themselves into sects; . . . [and] dilettantes attracted by the October Revolution and sympathetic to Marxism as an exotic teaching that had little to do with the United States."[119]

Similar historical and structural analyses were presented by one of the most gifted non-Russian communist theoreticians, Antonio Gramsci, in a series of essays written in prison during the early 1930s. Like Trotsky, he emphasized America's unique origins and resultant value system as a source of its sophisticated modern industrial system. Gramsci placed more emphasis on the role of values in producing economic development and affluence in the United States than on its natural wealth.

The Anglo-Saxon immigrants are themselves an intellectual, but more especially a moral, *élite.* I am talking, naturally, of the first immigrants, the pioneers, protagonists of the political and religious struggles in England, defeated but not humiliated or laid low in their country of origin. They import into America, . . . apart from moral energy and energy of will, a certain level of civilization, a certain stage of European historical evolution, which, when transplanted by such men into the virgin soil of America, continues to develop the forces implicit in its nature but with an incomparably more rapid rhythm than in Old Europe, where there exists a whole series of checks (moral, intellectual, political, economic, incorporated in specific sections of the population, relics of past regimes which refuse to die out) which generate opposition to speedy progress and give to every initiative the equilibrium of mediocrity, diluting it in time and in space.

There has been a massive development, on top of an industrial base, of the whole range of modern superstructure. . . . the lack of a vast sedimentation of traditional intellectuals such as one finds in countries of ancient civilization explains, at least in part, both the existence of only two major political parties, which could in fact easily be reduced to only one . . . , and at the opposite extreme the enormous proliferation of religious sects.[120]

Gramsci stressed that America's unique sociological background has resulted in a general value system, a conception of life, which he dubbed "Americanism." The essence of Americanism is rationalism, "economicity," the logic of a pure bourgeois society, uninhibited by the existence of classes and values derived from a feudal past. Americanism is not simply a way of life, it is an ideology. Unlike other nations, America is characterized by the complete ideological "hegemony" of capitalist values.[121]

Americanism, in its most developed form, requires a preliminary condition. . . . the fact that there do not exist numerous classes with no essential function in the world of production. . . . European "tradition," European "civilization," is, conversely, characterized precisely by the existence of such classes, created by the "richness" and "complexity" of past history.

America does not have "great historical and cultural traditions"; but neither does it have this leaden burden to support. . . . The non-existence of vicious parasitic sedimentations left behind by past phases of history has allowed industry, and commerce in particular, to develop on a sound basis. . . . Since these preliminary conditions existed, already rendered rational by historical evolution, it was relatively easy to rationalize production and labour by a skillful combination of force (destruction of working-class unionism on a territorial basis) and persuasion (high wages, various social benefits, extremely subtle ideological and political propaganda) and thus succeed in making the whole life of the nation revolve around production.

The "vocation of work" was not a trait inherent only in the working class but it was a specific quality of the ruling classes as well. The fact that a millionaire continued to be practically active until forced to retire by age or illness and that his activity occupied a very considerable part of his day is a typically American phenomenon. This, for the average European, is the weirdest American extravagance. . . . In Europe, it is the passive residues that resist Americanism (they "represent quality," etc.) because they have the instinctive feeling that the new forms of production and work would sweep them away implacably.[122]

Americanism came to full fruition in what Gramsci called "Fordism," the total rationalization of economic production, derived from the necessity to achieve the advantages "of a planned economy" under capitalism. It has produced a new psychological "type of man suited to the new type of work," whose values are in harmony with the economic system. As a result "there has not been, except perhaps sporadically, any flowering of the 'superstructure.' In other words the fundamental question of [class] hegemony has not yet been posed. . . . The absence of the European historical phase . . . has left the American masses in a backward state. To this should be added the absence of national homogeneity, the mixture of race-cultures, the Negro question."[123]

The communist movement, though claiming to be orthodox Marxist, was forced, as we have seen, to "revise" Marx with respect to the assumption that the most developed country "only shows to the less developed the image of its own future." Trotsky explicitly faced up to the issue, quoted Marx, and then wrote: "Under no circumstances can this thought be taken literally."[124] The United States had shifted from the first to the last in the line to enter socialism.

Yet the explanations which the communist theoreticians offered for American political "backwardness" had not changed much from those presented by Marxists and others before World War I. They focused on the effects of affluence

in avoiding tension and—in the case of Trotsky and Gramsci—
on elaborations of the way in which America's unique nonfeudal, immigrant settler history resulted in a unique social
structure and value system, accepted by the working class as
offering what it sought for itself. Like Marx, the communists
saw class consciousness and revolution arising when American
affluence based on its world market position would decline.
Such an event occurred in 1929, but a decade later the American proletariat had still not turned to socialism.

Americanism as Surrogate Socialism

The conception suggested by Gramsci that Americanism
represents a distinct ideological alternative to socialism, one
that is accepted by American workers, was independently developed and elaborated at about the same time by two quite
different individuals: Hermann Keyserling, a conservative
German aristocrat, and Leon Samson, an American socialist.
Keyserling in 1929 and Samson in 1933, suggested that
Americanism is surrogate socialism. Each contended that socialism has not been accepted in the United States because
the ideological content of Americanism is so similar to socialism that Americans believe they already have most of what
socialism promises. As Keyserling put it:

> The Americans are the only socialists I know of in the true sense
> of the term in the Western World. . . . The spirit of the revolu-
> tions of the eighteenth century, the essence of which was revolt
> against all hierarchy of values still rules [there] . . . . Owing to the
> peculiar opportunities offered by a New World overwhelmingly
> rich in natural resources and the absence of counteracting tradi-
> tions, it was able to expand and develop in intensity as it could
> have done nowhere else. . . . The United States must obviously be
> immune to Socialism in the European sense *because of the fact,*
> *unheard of in Europe, that the very problem which the reformers*
> *undertake to solve appears solved from the outset.*[125]

Keyserling was not a naive believer in America as a classless
utopia. He stressed that mobility was in fact limited, that
American life was based on competition, that it offered more

risk than security, that the differences in position, wealth and social standing were very great, and that "there are probably more 'pirates' of society in America than in any European country."[126] Nevertheless, what made Americanism a surrogate for socialism was its emphasis on the idea that individual action should serve community welfare objectives.

> American millionaires pride themselves on making gifts to the community. . . . Private munificence has made a great many educational institutions rich. . . . There can be no doubt that the proclaimed belief in the ideal of service is genuine.

> [Socialism] teaches that only he who works has a right to live; usefulness for the community provides the only basis of individual rights. This is the very belief of all typical Americans. However rich one may be, one *must* continue working. . . .

> Why does the idea that the workmen should profit not as little but as much as possible from the works, that they should be paid the highest possible wages . . . strike the American as essentially sound and the European as Utopian?

> Socialism demands a unified standard of living for each and all. This actually exists in the United States. However great the differences in income and fortune—all Americans live very much in the same way. . . . The difference between the facts of Bolshevik Russia and America, in this connexion, only amounts to the difference in prosperity.

> It is one of the most instructive things I have ever come across, this extraordinary likeness between Bolshevik Russia and America. . . . The spirit is the same, whatever the causes which in each case brought it into empiric existence.[127]

Leon Samson reached similar conclusions from an examination of Americanism as ideology.

> When we examine the meaning of Americanism, we discover that Americanism is to the American not a tradition or a territory, not what France is to a Frenchman or England is to an Englishman, but a doctrine—what socialism is to a socialist. Like socialism,

> Americanism is looked upon . . . as a highly attenuated, conceptu-
> alized, platonic, impersonal attraction toward a system of ideas, a
> solemn assent to a handful of final notions—democracy, liberty,
> opportunity, to all of which the American adheres rationalisti-
> cally much as a socialist adheres to his socialism—because it does
> him good, because it gives him work, because, so he thinks, it
> guarantees him happiness. Americanism has thus served as a sub-
> stitute for socialism. Every concept in socialism has its substitu-
> tive counter-concept in Americanism, and that is why the socialist
> argument falls so fruitlessly on the American ear. . . . The Ameri-
> can does not want to listen to socialism, since he thinks he al-
> ready has it.[128]

Samson, who was a radical socialist, emphasized the exploitative and imperialist character of American capitalism as a
social system. But he contended that to its inhabitants, "in
their manner, their rhythm, their style of life, the American
civilization appears to be in no sense capitalistic, appears, on
the contrary, socialistic, proletarian, 'human,' at any rate far
from imperialistic." America, of course, emphasized individualism rather than collectivism. Samson argued, however,
that the American "ideal of universal individualism is a socialist conception of individualism," one available for everyone,
not just businessmen. Equality of opportunity, as stressed in
America, is a "socialist conception of capitalism."[129] "Only
under socialism does system take precedence over class. Socialism is a system minus a class. This minus the Americans
assume."[130] America represents in the minds of its citizens a
rejection of the class-bound European society from which
they or their ancestors escaped. America "is still under classes,
but its mind has leaped forward toward classlessness."[131]
   Samson noted that conservatives, Republicans, and businessmen, whom he preferred to quote to illustrate his own
assumptions, use language, concepts, and goals for American
society which in Europe are only voiced by socialists. Thus,
he emphasized that Herbert Hoover took Europe as a negative model, saying that in America, "we resent class distinction because there can be no rise for the individual through

the frozen strata of classes." Hoover emphasized the abolition of poverty as a goal of the American system. But, argued
Samson, "Hoover may not know it but when he talks this
way he is simply talking socialism. To 'abolish poverty' is a
time-honored socialist aim. Who has ever heard of a responsible spokesman of European capitalism announce that it is the
aim of, let us say the French or the English 'system' to 'abolish poverty'?"[132]

Samson pointed out that the emphasis on what Gramsci
conceptualized as "Fordism" produces one of the conditions
for socialism. Samson noted that American Republicans emphasized "the right to work," a phrase first used by revolutionary workers in Europe and never proclaimed by states-
men in Europe. The same unconscious use of socialist concepts may be seen in an American's attitude towards politics
and the state.

> With the class line blurred and blotted out from his mind, the
> American is blind to the real meaning of the state. The state is in
> the American mind not the dominion of class over class, but the
> (perfectly human) administration of the perfectly classless mass.
> . . . It is noteworthy that what in other countries is known as
> "The Government" . . . is here called "The Administration." Our
> political scribes may not be aware of it, but when thus they speak
> of the "administration" instead of the "government" they are re-
> citing socialist phraseology straight from Engels. The idiom of a
> people, like the *lapsus linguae* of an individual, is, when consid-
> ered socio-analytically, expressive of its deepest unconscious
> wishes and longings. To the American socialism is an unconscious
> wish.[133]

Like Marx, Tocqueville, and Gramsci, Samson was impressed by the special character of American religion, by the
predominantly Protestant denominations which had never
been state churches and which called on parishioners to follow their own conscience. American political idealism and
radical sectarianism are linked to the country's religious heritage.[134] Following up on Marx and Samson, the socialist leader Michael Harrington writes:

Americanism, the official ideology of the society, became a kind
of "substitutive socialism." The European ruling classes, which
derived from, or aped, the aristocracy, were open in their contempt for the proletariat. But in the United States equality, and
even classlessness, the creation of wealth for all and political liberty were extolled in the public schools. It is, of course, true that
this was sincere verbiage which concealed an ugly reality, but
nonetheless it had a profound impact upon the national consciousness.

So it was America's receptivity to utopia, not its hostility, that
was a major factor inhibiting the development of a socialist movement. The free gift of the ballot and the early emergence of working-class parties were portents of assimilation, not revolution. . . .
The country's image of itself contained so many socialist elements
that one did not have to go to a separate movement opposed to
the status quo in order to give vent to socialist emotions.[135]

In his analysis of socialism's weakness in America, Harrington argues that socialist sentiments recurrently have been expressed in nonsocialist economic terms, for example, in the
effort to create an independent labor party in the late nineteenth century during Henry George's campaign in 1886.
Harrington suggests that this process has continued to the
present, particularly in the activities and ideologies of the
organized labor movement, which has emphasized socialist
values without socialist economic content.

Gramsci's emphasis on Fordism as a major aspect of the
contemporary content of Americanism was extended a quarter of a century later by a French visitor to the United States,
the Dominican, R. L. Bruckberger. Like Gramsci, he argued
that the emphasis on standardized mass production in America could not be explained as a simple or direct response to
America's natural economic conditions and that the answer
lay in the unique national value system, one that differed
sharply from the elitist aristocratic ones of Europe. Lending
support to his argument, Bruckberger points out that in 1915
Ford was taken to court by major stockholders for sharply
cutting dividends in order to expand production by building

a larger and more mechanized plant, while continuing to pay high wages. The Dodge brothers, the plaintiffs, argued that the main purpose of business is to maximize profits, and that Ford's policies placed increased productivity at lower prices ahead of profits.[136]

Bruckberger's intention in emphasizing Ford's ideology as prototypically American was not to suggest that Ford was some sort of socialist. He was aware that Ford was an authoritarian in his labor relations, that he sought to impose a puritanical morality on his workers and that he strongly resisted unionization. But like Trotsky and Gramsci before him, Bruckberger recognized in Ford's emphasis on mass production and mass markets a uniquely American phenomenon, stemming from the differences between its social structure and the elitist one of Europe.

Gramsci acknowledged that his interest in Americanism and Fordism was derived in part from Trotsky's proposition that the American organizational model was that of the Ford organization which the Soviet Union must adopt. Continuing Trotsky's argument, Gramsci wrote, "the new methods of work are inseparable from a specific mode of living and of thinking and feeling life. One cannot have success in one field without tangible results in the other. . . . [It is necessary to understand] the importance, significance and objective import of the American phenomenon, which is *also* the biggest collective effort to date to create . . . a new type of worker and of man."[137]

Post–World War II Critiques

American capitalism emerged out of World War II seemingly in extremely good condition. The United States was the most powerful country, militarily and economically. Europe, both communist and noncommunist, had been devastated by the war, and the United States was in a position to supply it with goods and capital. Domestically, the predictions by many leftist and liberal economists and political figures that depression conditions would reemerge proved to be in error. The economy took off on its longest boom of prosperity in

history. The strength of radical groups declined. The Socialist
Party, securing presidential votes of under 100,000 in 1952,
decided to abandon electoral action. Membership and support of the communists, which had grown considerably during the wartime alliance with the Soviet Union, almost van-
ished under the impact of revelations of overt anti-Semitism
in the Soviet Union, Russian-directed seizure of power in
Czechoslovakia in 1948, the emergence of the "cold war"
and repressive American governmental actions during the
Korean War, the revelations of Stalin's crimes in the Khrush-
chev speech at the Twentieth Party Congress of the CPSU,
and the crushing of the Hungarian Revolution in 1956.

More than a full century after the Communist Manifesto
and a half century after the Russian Revolution, efforts to
foster Marxism and socialism appeared to be a closed chapter
in American life. A variety of political scientists and sociologists took up the challenge to explain "why is there no socialism in the United States?" The analyses written in the 1950s
for the most part assumed that Marxism and revolutionary
movements in American society were historical tendencies
which would not recur in any significant fashion. With the
beginnings in the 1960s of the so-called New Left group of
radical scholars, largely recruited from students and young
faculty, this assumption came to an end. The New Left produced its own school of historians and social scientists, some
of whom concerned themselves with the study both of explaining its past failures and of learning lessons from it which
would enable contemporary radicals finally to build an important mass movement in America. The New Left scholars
have tended to criticize the writings which emphasized the
unique attributes of America's historical social structure and
which minimized the extent to which class consciousness and
struggle have characterized the American past. They felt that
the academic writers had exaggerated or misinterpreted the
extent to which the economy and social structure had fostered greater equality of status, opportunity, or a higher
standard of living for the masses. The radical critics have
tended to emphasize the *power* of American capitalism to

weaken socialist prospects by elaborating a bourgeois value system, or by directly repressing radical activities as with the Wobblies before World War I, the socialists and communists during and immediately after that war, and assorted radicals and communists during the Korean War. Some have also contended that various American left groups failed, in part, because they pursued opportunistic policies—in the case of the Socialist Party—or slavishly followed shifts in the Soviet international position—in the case of the communists.

Given these different perspectives, the post-World War II literature contains some sharp differences in interpretation of the facts, both of American life and of the history of radical movements. There is, however, a considerable overlap in the hypotheses explaining the weakness of socialism.

Americanism as Liberalism

The most influential interpretation from the 1950s of the American experience, bearing directly on the issue of "why no socialism" is Louis Hartz's *The Liberal Tradition in America*. In many ways it is an extensive elaboration of the thesis advanced by H. G. Wells in 1906 that the United States is a society whose dominant ideology stems from eighteenth century Lockean liberalism or Whiggery, and which lacks a feudal past and an aristocratic tradition; as a result, it has no Tory *or* Socialist Party. Hartz began his book by noting the curious failure of American historians who repeated endlessly that America was grounded in an escape from the European past but neglected to follow through when interpreting its history.[138] Yet, as we have seen, this emphasis on the absence of a feudal past has been an almost constant theme of Marxist and labor-oriented writers from Marx and Engels through Sombart, Hillquit, Lenin, Trotsky, Gramsci, and Samson. Hartz stated:

> It is not accidental that America which has uniquely lacked a feudal tradition has uniquely lacked also a socialist tradition. The hidden origin of socialist thought everywhere in the West is to be found in the feudal ethos.

Everywhere in Europe, in MacDonald's England hardly less than
in Kautsky's Germany, socialism was inspired considerably by the
class spirit that hung over not from capitalism but from the feudal system itself.[139]

Hartz, like Samson, argued that American socialist parties
failed because they did not understand America, and insisted
on "persistent use of the European concepts of Marxism"
formed in response to a different social structure.[140] "Moreover the instinctive tendency of all Marxists to discredit ideological factors as such blinded them to many of the consequences, purely psychological in nature, flowing from the
nonfeudal issue. Was not the whole complex of 'Americanism' an ideological question? . . . Wasn't the whole meaning
of 'Americanism' that America was a peculiar land of freedom, equality, and opportunity?"[141]

The sectarian character of American socialism, the weakness of "reformism," the refusal to compromise and work
with progressive nonsocialist elements to build a third party,
is linked by Hartz to the fact that nothing remained in the
United States to be reformed, to be changed, except capitalism itself—exactly the same point made by Lenin a half
century earlier.

The antitheoretical orientation of Americans, which so
disturbed Marx and Engels, is seen by Hartz as an inevitable
outgrowth of the consensus within the country on a liberal
conception of Americanism. Americans could and did divide
sharply over questions of implementation, but they did not
divide over the goals, so that "all problems emerge as problems of technique." And "pragmatism . . . America's great
contribution to the philosophic tradition" permitted political
leaders and parties to be extraordinarily flexible in changing
policies, in appealing to groups with diverse interests, since
they were not bound by any commitment to an ideological
purpose other than Americanism.[142]

Americanism was not only egalitarian, but individualistic
and antistatist; yet the United States has moved in a statist
direction in reaction to the problems posed by the Great

Depression. Hartz stresses, however, that this was done under the banner of liberal objectives, of proposing individual reforms to enhance equality of opportunity. "If the New Deal assembled all of its specific measures into a pattern of 'collectivism,' . . . the question of 'Americanism' would be bound to arise. . . ." But it did not do so, Horatio Alger "could remain intact, and a succession of ideologically dehydrated 'problems' could be solved. . . . One can call this pragmatism, or one can call it obscurantism, but it was the basic formula by which the . . . [United States] handled the inescapable exigencies of state action in the economic sphere."[143]

The Ideology of the Labor Movement

The thesis that America was formed as a liberal society was further amplified with specific reference to the behavior of the American labor movement by the historian, Marc Karson. He also discussed the existence of a "central creed," which emphasized individualism and fear of strong central government. Karson reiterated the now traditional explanation that the "absence of a feudal tradition with its accompanying class stratification" led to the general acceptance by workers of what he describes as "middle-class psychology." But the defeat of the socialists within the labor movement before World War I was not simply a consequence of structural conditions and a persistent value system. He emphasized that the sophisticated ideological leadership provided by Samuel Gompers played a major role in elaborating a proletarian version of Americanism and in defeating the socialists within the American Federation of Labor.[144]

A more recent analysis by another historian of labor, William Dick, also credits Gompers with a major role in preserving a belief in values derivative from "Louis Hartz's 'irrational Lockean Liberalism . . . [among] American workers.' " Gompers provided an alternative ideology which emphasized class militancy to attain increased power and economic gains through strong unions, skillful use of electoral influence in bargaining with politicians who had a realistic chance of election, and a syndicalist philosophy of distrust of the state, which fitted into the American value system. Dick notes:

> Gompers had a surprisingly sophisticated conception of the place of democratic socialism in western countries. As far as he was concerned, its accomplishments would be political, not social. Socialism would raise the working class to full citizenship. . . . In short socialism was procuring what Americans already achieved through the Revolution. Gompers maintained that if he had lived in Germany he would be a socialist.

> But in the American context, he saw no need for increased power of the state. All [that] labor expected was the guarantee of the right to pursue its aims independently. And as a labor editor pointed out in 1920 Gompers described himself as a "Jeffersonian Democrat . . . that is three-quarters anarchist."[145]

The unwillingness of Marxists and most social scientists to credit long-term consequences, such as the specific ideology of the American labor movement, to the manipulative talents of one man, may be responsible for the relative paucity of attention paid to Samuel Gompers. Lenin was one of the few Europeans to emphasize his role. Historian Norman Ware singled out Gompers' "great abilities as an agitator . . . [and] his even greater abilities . . . as an official" in providing an ideology, "voluntarism," and building a machine "consisting of a group of general organizers appointed by himself all over the country and not under the authority of the officers of the national unions, [which] kept him in close touch with what was going on and in control of conventions."[146]

Although the historians who stress the importance of Gompers in fostering a highly individualistic, antistatist liberal ideology on the labor movement undoubtedly have a point, it is significant to note that the revolutionary alternative union to the AFL during Gompers' lifetime, the Industrial Workers of the World (IWW), also was antistatist, and emphasized individual's rights against large scale public and private bureaucracies. Yet the IWW failed and the AFL succeeded.

Analyses of the history and ultimate failure of the AFL's

chief rival for trade-union hegemony in Gompers' lifetime, the revolutionary syndicalist IWW, pointed to factors in the external environment which inhibited the Wobblies (as the IWW members were called), particularly to the willingness of American elites to accept reforms when pressured. Melvyn Dubofsky ends his major study of the Wobblies by saying that the dynamics of American history unquestionably upset them.

> Unlike radicals in other societies who contended with established orders unresponsive to change from within, the Wobblies struggled against flexible and sophisticated adversaries. . . . Whatever success the Wobblies achieved only stimulated the reform process, for employers who were threatened by the IWW paid greater attention to labor relations, and government agencies, initially called upon to repress labor strife, encouraged employers to improve working conditions. . . . Reform finally proved a better method than repression for weakening the IWW's appeal to workers.[147]

Another historian of the IWW, Robert Tyler, notes that "any explanation of failure and decline specific to the IWW must be but a variant or special case for the explanation for the failure of Socialism in general."

> It seems . . . —however against the grain of the newest revisionism it may seem—that such "consensus" historians as Louis Hartz may have proposed the most persuasive explanation of this indubitable hostility of America toward socialism and all its class conscious relatives. . . . Even radicals, themselves, late or soon, come to be overpowered by the reality of this bourgeois consensus at the heart of the American culture.

> Dubofsky has cited . . . a recurring IWW protestation of its essential "Americanism". . . . The New Left, of more contemporary experience, can be observed doing the same thing, as in Staughton Lynd's recent quest of a usable American past. . . . [In so doing] the radical assumes the role of suppliant, a petitioning outsider. . . . The radical is proffering a wistful code word which seems to say, "Look I am a real American too. And, moreover, I am not *really* dangerous because my people are your people."[148]

Gus Tyler, former Socialist Party leader, trade union official and author of a number of scholarly analyses, traces the orientation of the American labor movement, both the AFL and the IWW, and the ideology of the AFL's most important leader to the antiauthoritarian components of the American value system. He explains this, not in Lockean terms but as a consequence of the fact that the "continent was peopled by runaways from authority." And this antiauthoritarianism was expressed in individualism and in "an innate, even if unspoken, disestablishmentarianism, a visceral kind of anarchism."

> In the United States, the bent of the worker has been toward individualism rather than collectivism. Add militancy and violence to this individualism and the result was the IWW—the first important anarcho-syndicalist movement anywhere in the world.
>
> The sense of Samuel Gompers, ironically, was much closer to that of the anarchists than to that of the socialists. . . . Gompers caught the spirit of the American proletarian—a spirit that in its more desperate and angry phase was the syndicalism of the IWW and in its more measured phase was the pure-and-simplism of the AFL. In neither case was it socialism.[149]

In *The First New Nation* and a series of related essays, written in the 1950s and 60s, I elaborated on some of the themes discussed by Samson and Hartz. My analysis agreed with theirs that the emphasis in Americanism has been on two values—equality and achievement—derived from its nonfeudal past and the conceptions incorporated in the American Creed, as elaborated in the Declaration of Independence, an ideological document justifying the very existence of the nation. In succeeding decades, in preindustrial America, under Jefferson and Jackson, these conceptions informed an expansion of democratic rights. "The very success of the American revolution and its leftist political aftermath, which gave the lower strata a place in society superior to that of lower classes in any other nation, also meant that there was less they would want in the future. The subsequent moderation of American class politics is related to the fact that egalitarianism and democracy triumphed *before* the workers were a politically relevant force. Unlike the workers in Europe, they did not have to fight their way into the polity; the door was already open. Hence, they had little use for socialist revolutionary theories, for approaches which argued the class domination of the society."[150]

The value system also serves to explain some of the other unique features of the labor movement, such as its militancy, its greater propensity to strike and use illegal tactics, which flow in part from the American emphasis on winning at all costs, stressed by Werner Sombart half a century earlier. As I put it some time ago:

> The American labor movement has been less class conscious and more militant than those in European countries where there is less emphasis on individual achievement and equality. Since the American emphasis has been on individual responsibility for success or failure, the American worker has not seen himself as a member of a class. He has felt his lower status as a personal affront, while he has felt that his attempts to better himself, collectively as well as individually, were legitimate. As a result, there have been pressures, unchecked by traditional deference relations between classes, to support aggressive union action.
>
> While the principle of equality has thus extended pressures to succeed to all members of the society, regardless of class, the stress on achievement has created inequalities. The difference between the income and status of union leaders and the union rank and file [much higher in the United States than in Europe] is but one example of the way in which the stress on both equality and achievement may bring about institutional features that appear contradictory to one another.[151]

Like Hartz, I also trace the weakness of socialism in America to the absence of an elitist conservatism, a philosophy rejected by the Declaration of Independence and subsequent political events.

In a real sense, the more conservative the adjustment which a nation made to facing the problems of industrialization, that is, the
more it preserved aspects of traditional pre-industrial values, particularly ascription and elitism, the greater the strength of radical
lower-class movements within it. The United States, which retained fewer of these values than did any industrialized European
country, has consequently been able to adjust to the structural
changes imposed by economic and population growth with much
less intense class conflict. Since progress is part of America's national self-image, progressive movements have been able to induce
change without becoming radical.[152]

As indicated by the citation above from *The First New Nation,* I do not assert that the continued weakness of socialism
or working-class consciousness in America may be explained
by the creation and elaboration of an egalitarian-achievement
value system in the eighteenth and early nineteenth centuries,
but rather by a combination of factors: (1) the development
of an extraordinarily successful capitalist industrial system,
which in spite of sustaining enormous economic inequalities,
has increased opportunities and brought a higher standard of
living to the less privileged; (2) certain other special American
factors, particularly the heterogeneity of its working class,
first created by mass immigration from Europe and more recently by a migration from other parts of America, blacks
from the South, Spanish-speaking persons from Mexico and
Puerto Rico; and (3) the fact that the dominant political ideology, Americanism, legitimated and encouraged the efforts
of the more liberal, progressive or left sectors to extend and
deepen the content of egalitarianism through giving them an
advantage in the political conflicts over two centuries. Since I
have elaborated on these elsewhere, I will not repeat the doc-
umentary material here.[153]

The radical historian, Gabriel Kolko, has criticized the
"consensus" interpretations of American history, which focus
on a unique value system, for ignoring the class nature of the
society. Nevertheless, he states that class conflict and opposition to the dominant value system were never sufficiently

pronounced to generate a viable alternative, that "the prime values of the society . . . [have been] accepted by those segments of the society without an objective stake in the constituted order."[154]

The most recent effort to deal with the absence of socialism in America, a forthcoming history of American socialism by John Laslett, takes off from Gramsci's concept of "ideological hegemony." Laslett agrees with Gramsci that in the United States "the ideals of bourgeois civilization—individualism, the sanctity of private property, antipathy towards state interference in the economy, as well as a whole host of other factors—have become diffused throughout society in all its institutional and private manifestations, informing with its spirit all taste, morality, customs, religions and political principles, particularly in their intellectual and moral connotations."[155]

Laslett notes that although Gramsci and Hartz both emphasize the impact of an ideological system in helping to provide the basis for a "unified capitalist system of economics, politics and culture," they differ greatly because Hartz sees a country "frozen" in the mode set by its special formative conditions, while for Gramsci "bourgeois hegemony is seen as an instrument of class rule, a technique or series of devices by which one class, having achieved dominance in society at one particular 'historical moment,' imposes its will temporarily upon the rest."[156] Such hegemony can and will be challenged from below.

The questions for Laslett become, first, "why has bourgeois hegemony been allowed to remain relatively unchallenged throughout most of American history . . .; and second, why has the American working class found it so extraordinarily difficult, compared to a number of its European or other counterparts, to develop a counter-hegemonic ideology of its own?"[157] The answer to these questions lies in three main features and four secondary ones which enabled the ideology "to remain dominant long after the structural changes have occurred which undermine the purely objective conditions upon which classical liberalism [stressed by Hartz] rests." These are:

First, the institution of slavery, which was even more brutal and dehumanising in Anglo-Saxon culture than it was in others and which, unlike that of Latin America, meant the territorial separation of Blacks into plantation ghettoes in the deep South. After abolition this meant that most Blacks, although the most obviously exploited segment of the working class, remained segregated in the South during the most critical decades of industrialisation, and had only minimal contact with the more advanced sections of the northern working class until after the First World War. As a result their traditions of revolt even after they moved into the industrial sector, have continued to be based more on a consciousness of race than they have on a consciousness of class. Secondly, the legacy of the frontier, seen not so much as a safety-valve but as the creator of a tradition of rapid geographical mobility among American working people which enabled more of them to "vote with their feet" than they could elsewhere, and which endowed the agrarian radical movement with elements of a predominantly individualistic, entrepreneurial, single-family farm tradition which has prevented the rise of a successful socialist-labor-farmer alliance. And thirdly, the massive influx of immigrants both from Europe and the Orient who when they first came here, like the Blacks were frequently divided up and manipulated to their advantage by the employers, and who to some extent even now put ethnic loyalties above those of class. . . .[158]

Some of these conditions have also appeared in other overseas countries settled by Europeans, i.e., Canada, Latin America, and Australia, which have produced larger socialist or labor parties than the United States. But Laslett notes, there are four other "secondary features of American society, some structural and some ideological, which taken together with the legacy provided by slavery, the frontier, and by mass immigration, have so far proved fatal to revolutionary movements in the United States."

These four secondary features, in order of chronological appearance are as follows. The order itself is a matter of considerable significance, because of the establishment of precedents which have proved extremely hard to break. First, there came the fusing of American nationalism which had its origins in the patriotic ardor engendered by the American Revolution, with loyalty to the bourgeois values of the liberal state. Beginning with the pro-French revolutionary sympathies of the Jeffersonian party which resulted in the Alien and Sedition Acts of 1798 and 1799, this has led to the growth of a "red scare" syndrome which has been used repeatedly throughout American history to uphold the hegemony of bourgeois rule. Secondly came the early spread of the franchise and the development of a two-party system in the Jacksonian period, which encouraged the growth of broadly-based liberal coalition-oriented political parties and inhibited the growth of successful third parties which could challenge bourgeois hegemony, either from the left or the right. Third, we have the absence in America of a revolutionary intelligentsia which is in any sense comparable to those in most European countries, and which has been willing and able to devote itself to cooperate in the development of a genuinely 'American' form of socialism. And fourthly, there has been the enormous and continuing success of American capitalism as a mechanism for generating wealth. Even though wealth may often have been distributed *even more unjustly than in Europe*, those in power have never allowed any potentially powerful element in the society to go for so long unrewarded that it can generate a successful movement for revolutionary change. Most of the problems of the American left, both Old and New, have been connected in one way or another with these primary and secondary features.[159]

These seven factors are not the only historical elements of the American situation to which Laslett calls attention. Thus, he notes that the American "distrust of state and power leads in the direction of anarchism or anarcho-syndicalism," not socialism; that the American Puritan religious tradition "helps account for the continued importance in the American social system of the individual's *own* efforts at social and economic salvation"; that "in Germany, France and to some extent in Great Britain working class parties came into being *before* the spread of the franchise"; that "the growth of a coalitionist two-party system . . . gave large numbers of work-ingmen a stake in the ongoing operation of society"; that the factors affecting labor militancy and political class conscious-ness are not the same, since in the late nineteenth and early twentieth centuries, the level of strike activity in the United States was "greater than that of many industrializing coun-tries" in Europe; that in the United States "the absence of an Established Church and the much greater fragmentation of Protestant sects meant that there could be no such clear iden-tification of religous [or anti-religious] sentiments with class loyalties" as occurred in Britain and other European coun-tries; that "anti-socialist lay Catholic organizations . . . came to exert an extremely powerful influence over American Catholic workingmen"; that the failure of efforts to establish a linkage between Marxist intellectuals and the labor move-ment was in part a consequence of the "general climate of anti-intellectualism with materialist values bred in America"; that the much greater "ratio of full-time officials to union members" in America than in Europe and the higher salaries paid to them has served as a check on rank-and-file protest movements led by unpaid local officials or shop stewards; and that the "crusading zeal" of Americans, absent in Eu-rope, led to more systematic waves of antiradical repression in periods in which that zeal was awakened.[160]

Given the number of major, secondary, and minor factors which Laslett finds sustaining bourgeois ideological hege-mony, to use Gramsci's term, in America, it is not surprising that he concludes that "the American working class perma-nently missed the socialist boat." Many of the factors are clearly still operative, and economic and political develop-ments continue to sustain liberalism as "the dominant ideol-ogy of most Americans."[161]

Individualism and the Left

The continued vitality of American emphasis on individ-ualism and antistatism may be seen in the orientations and behavior of the most recent effort to build a mass radical movement, the New Left of the 1960s. Their ideology stressed decentralization and community control.

There are clearly strong links between the orientations of the IWW and the early New Left, both extremely American movements. The reliance on confrontationist tactics and other forms of civil disobedience by the New Left also follows well the traditions of the American labor movement and the Wobblies. One of the most influential professorial influences on the early New Left, the historian William Appleman Williams, whose students started *Studies on the Left*, reflects this orientation in his strong preference for Herbert Hoover rather than Franklin Roosevelt as embodying the best in the American capitalist tradition. Hoover is to be preferred since his solution for the crisis of capitalism lay not in strengthening the power of the central state, but rather in the proposal "that American capitalism should cope with its economic problems by voluntaristic but nevertheless organized cooperation within and between each major sector of the economy."[162] The ideological congruence between academic spokesmen of the extreme left and right may be found in an anthology of articles from *Studies on the Left*. In introducing an essay by laissez-faire economist Murray Rothbard, the New Left editors comment: "He is a free-Market conservative and individualist whose anti-imperialism and proscriptions of bureaucracy and the corporist state coincide with those of the New Left."[163]

Another early academic stimulator of the student New Left, C. Wright Mills, also exhibited a strong admiration for the competitive, free yeoman tradition of American free enterprise and decentralized politics. There is perhaps no more favorable portrait of the operation and consequences of the pre–Civil War American economy and polity than is presented by Mills. He describes early nineteenth century America as having been an almost perfect utopia, with property widely and equitably distributed, with rapid and continuing social mobility, so that few remained propertyless for long, with property ownership providing security against the business cycle, and protection against tyranny.[164] Mills saw the early United States as close to a libertarian society. "Political authority, the traditional mode of social integration, became a loose framework of protection rather than a centralized engine of domination; it too was largely unseen and for long periods very slight."[165] Mills's strong preferences for a decentralized society went along with a lifelong opposition to Stalinism, orientations which a practicing hard-line communist like Che Guevara would describe as reflecting typical impractical North American naiveté.

More recently, the individualist proclivities of the American left have been reflected in the special role played by anarchist and decentralist socialist intellectuals such as Noam Chomsky, David Dellinger, and Staughton Lynd. Such men have been influential in strengthening the antistatist components of New Left ideology.

The American New Left even found a common ground with some whose penchant for individualism first led them to right-wing politics. What was once the "libertarian" faction of the Goldwater-Buckley–oriented Young Americans for Freedom has cooperated with the decentralizers of the New Left. Both groups found a common cause in their rejection of the welfare state, of the Vietnam war, and of large bureaucratic organizations. Karl Hess, Senator Goldwater's main speechwriter in the 1964 presidential campaign, became a "card-carrying" member of the New Left and even served as an editor of the New Left organ, *Ramparts*, while insisting that he had not changed his political beliefs in any substantial manner. Indicative of the congruence of ideological concerns was the composition of the Board of the National Taxpayers' Union, an organization formed largely by conservatives and dedicated to "individual liberty and financial security for the American taxpayer," which actively lobbies against high taxes and the big bureaucratic welfare state. The Board not only has included eminent conservatives such as Ludwig von Mises, Henry Lazlitt, and Felix Morley, but also Noam Chomsky, Marcus Raskin—the head of the New Left think tank, the Institute for Policy Studies, and codefendant with Dr.

Benjamin Spock in the Boston draft conspiracy trial—and Karl Hess.[166] In commenting on the National Taxpayers' Union, New Left columnist David Deitch pointed out some of the sources of agreement between the ideological extremes in America.

> If the decentralization of government is a key place where New Left and Old Right have touched bases, taxation, the handmaiden of big government, is the arch enemy of libertarians everywhere. . . . Its [the National Taxpayers' Union] board of directors is a left-right alliance of strange bedfellows made comfortable by a single-minded devotion to tax cutting and the social possibilities that might accrue from a less elephantine government. . . . There is overwhelming agreement [among them] that whether known as the "corporate State" or "big government" the growth of institutions has resulted in a significant loss of freedom.[167]

According to Deitch, the group is concerned that its tax cuts do not hurt "needy recipients such as welfare people." The solution to the problem is "a proposal for a system of tax credits for any individual or group that provides private support for welfare recipients," whether they be other individuals or incorporated communities. "The law now permits charitable contributions to be deducted from gross income, but the new proposal would make it even more attractive to make private support contributions by granting an outright cut." It is difficult to realize that this proposal was made by an organization whose leaders included some of the leading left-wing radicals in America. To find anything resembling it, one must go back at least to the literature in opposition to federal welfare programs presented by the Liberty League in the 1930s.

New Left writers found to their surprise that much of what is said by extreme right-wingers exposing the interlocking activities of the Establishment forces strongly resembles their own outlook. This first became apparent on a wide scale during the 1968 presidential campaign, when many New Leftists found much with which to identify in the campaign utterances of George Wallace. Clark Kissinger, a correspondent for the national New Left weekly *The Guardian*, noted Wallace's strong populist sentiments (power to the people, local control), and said that Wallace, by sometimes making "a comment worthy of any New Leftist," has been able "to mobilize the very real force of class consciousness in America."[168] More recently William Domhoff, a New Left faculty member at the University of California at Santa Cruz, who has written a widely used radically oriented textbook, *Who Rules America*, has recommended in a political pamphlet, *How to Commit Revolution in Corporate America*, that left wing radical students read the Dan Smoot Report, as a "right-on" guide to the activities of the establishment. Smoot, who lives in Dallas and was supported by ultrarightist millionaire H. L. Hunt, put out a Birchite-oriented newsweekly which in the words of another New Left writer, Charles Fager, "looks exactly like a right-wing take-off on I. F. Stone's *Bi-Weekly*."[169]

The antistatist, strongly individualist views of the New Left and much of the extreme Right in America today offer a sharp contrast of substance to those of the ideological extremes in Europe. There, the fascist right and the communist left have coincided in their support for a strongly centralized government. Both extremes attack the democratic center for its inefficiency, its inability to control the society. Similarly, the democratic socialist left and conservative right have often shared a belief in the welfare state. European conservatism with its origins in the interests and values of aristocracy and monarchy supported the collectivity assumptions inherent in the *noblesse oblige* concept of the role of the privileged classes and the state. Socialist and welfare-state concepts have in fact been closer to the basic morality of aristocratic conservatism than either is to the laissez-faire, rugged individualist assumptions of bourgeois Manchester liberalism. In the United States, on the other hand, the national ethos with its emphasis on equality and liberty has basically gloried in the image of a free decentralized society of yeoman property holders, the one which C. Wright Mills found so appealing.

The strong appeal of liberty, populism, and decentralization to Americans may explain, in part, the lack of popular support for traditional European-oriented Marxist socialist efforts. The stress on the part of the American Socialist Party on the need to expand the role of government, to widen public ownership on the municipal, state, and federal level, was never appealing in the American social context. Americans had rejected the all-powerful monarchical state in 1776, and reiterated their objections to it whenever they commemorated their revolutionary origins. They saw the state as an enemy of equality and liberty, not as a force to enhance them. They would support radical populist movements which denounced great wealth and economic power, but in the name of widening the base of property ownership or the strength of nonstatist popular institutions, the trade unions and the cooperatives. The long-term opposition of the AFL to socialist movements and its antagonism until the New Deal period to various welfare state proposals may also reflect the comparative strength of individualist and decentralist values in America, as contrasted to the strong collectivity orientations of Europe.

Some may want to counter this argument by pointing to the obvious fact that the United States, like all other nations, has experienced a steady increase in state power, that it is committed to the welfare state, that the Populist, Progressive, Socialist, and more recently the Democratic parties have each in different ways secured electoral strength for programs which advocated a moderate or considerable enlargement of the functions and power of the central state. Yet these policies in the American context have been presented largely as a way of making the American objective of equality of opportunity, of the competitive race for success, more meaningful, as distinct from the greater stress in Europe on raising the level of the less privileged as a class.

The first party in the world to appeal to workers as a class, the Workingmen's parties of New York and other eastern states which arose in the 1820s and which greatly influenced Marx, initiated this pattern. The New York party called attention to the fact that the children of the poor were less able to compete with those from well-to-do families because they suffered from what we, today, call cultural deprivation and from inadequate education. One solution proposed by the Workingmen's Party was that *all* children be required to attend state boarding schools, that they be taken from their unequal family backgrounds and placed in a common total school environment.[170] This radical proposal, of course, was not stressed or widely backed, but the extension of education was at the heart of their concerns, for many believed "that a sound system of educating the young was not only the surest guarantee that society would be changed but, in itself, the central feature of the good society."[171] Yet this radical party adhered in the main to a "laissez-faire philosophy," and believed in the competitive race for economic success.[172]

The latter-day agrarian, Populist, and Progressive parties which attained considerable success as third parties between the Civil War and World War I, although advocates of increased state power and nationalization of various utilities and industries, also emphasized the preservation of private property and the extension of opportunity to succeed. They attacked the banks, the railroads, and the "trusts" for undercutting the free enterprise system. But unlike European socialist movements, or even Tory radicals like Disraeli and Bismarck, they rarely stressed the need to use state power to transfer wealth from the rich to the poor. Essentially, like the early Workingmen's parties, they sought to protect individualism and the opportunity to succeed as an independent entrepreneur against the restrictions imposed by large concentrations of economic power.

The pre–World War I Socialist Party, which reached a membership of over 125,000, cannot be described in the same terms as these other movements. Whatever criticisms may be made of its policies at any given time, there can be little doubt that it was able to attract the support of a significant minority of Americans for a statist program. Yet, Daniel Bell has pointed to a curious characteristic of the party at its height, the attraction which "get-rich-quick fantasies" had for its supporters.

One can find regularly in the pages of the *International Socialist Review*—which labeled itself "the fighting magazine of the working-class," and of which William D. Haywood was an editor—a large number of advertisements which promised quick returns through land speculation. In the June 1912 issue, a full-page advertisement proclaimed: "DOUBLING OR TRIPLING YOUR MONEY THROUGH CLEAN HONEST INVESTMENT." It stated (shades of Henry George): "Getting in Ahead of the railroad and the resulting rise in real estate values is the way thousands of people have made fortunes, especially in Western Canada. The wise real estate buyers of yesterday are wealthy people today." And in the text following: "Lots in the Fort Fraser B.C.—destined to be the hub of the Canadian West." Nor were these isolated instances. Similar advertisements kept appearing in the *International Socialist Review* for many years, indicating their "pulling power." (The cover of the January 1916 issue is a painting of a hungry man in the snow, the inside half-page has an ad stating that a salesman could make $300 a month selling a cream separator.)

But this type of get-rich-quick appeal was not limited to the *International Socialist Review*. It was a mania throughout the party.[173]

The various native American radical movements such as the Populist Party, the Socialist Party, the Industrial Workers of the World (IWW), or the early New Left also emphasized in their organizational structure the American concern for individualism and local control. Unlike the European movements, which Robert Michels rightly described as highly centralized and bureaucratic, these American ones resembled the major parties in being decentralized, reflecting the federal pattern of party power being located at the local city, county, and state level, rather than at the national center. Some of the leftist movements went much further than the major groups, in part perhaps because they had less resources, in rejecting tendencies toward bureaucratization, i.e., "machines."

The factors which inhibited support for centralization and strong leadership in much of the American left must also be added to the list of factors involved in the repeated failure of efforts to build radical movements in America. For however praiseworthy resistance to bureaucratic domination and strong personal direction may be, it would seem true that even protest movements require institutionalization and competent experienced leadership for survival and growth. The IWW failed, in part, because its anarcho-syndicalist antibureaucratic ideology dictated reliance on inexperienced leadership, since it required frequent turnover in office (officials could only serve for a year and received the same pay as workers in the trade). It had an unstable organization, because it refused to sign contracts with employers which would have ensured continuity of membership and of dues income.

In different ways, many of the original New Left groupings which emerged in the 1964-68 period also followed organizational practices which limited institutional stability and encouraged factionalism. The national office of SDS, for example, was little more than a mail drop which also published *New Left Notes*. Most members of local chapters did not contribute a cent to the upkeep of the national organization. Organizers, as in the case of the IWW, usually were dependent upon local contributions for a bare sustenance. The enormous funds generated by the movement largely went to support the myriad of underground newspapers and magazines. Following traditional American political practice (accepted by the Socialist Party) and movement ideology, the hundreds of papers remained the private property of their owners, who were free to adopt any political line they wished, and not infrequently to use some of the worst methods of yellow journalism, particularly pornography, to promote circulation and advertising revenue. Yet almost no one within the American New Left of the 1906s saw any incongruity or problem in these practices; the few who argued the need to convert the chaotic movement into a revolutionary organization met with little response.

The analyses of Samson, Hartz, and myself which emphasize the impact of Americanism, the American value system, in preventing the rise of socialism as a separate movement of the working class, have been criticized by various socialist scholars for assuming that there is some enduring element, rooted in the nation's formative period, which has served steadily to dampen efforts to build a socialist movement.[174]

One persistent critic of the value emphasis interpretation has been a Canadian socialist historian, Kenneth McNaught. He argues that those, like Hartz, who emphasize the import of the absence of feudalism in America exaggerate its presence in Britain and other countries; that the nineteenth and early twentieth century social systems in which socialists tried to make headway were not that different; that there were major issues of democratic rights in America; and that conservatism did exist among the American elite in forms similar to Britain and Europe. The defeat of socialism in America, therefore, was not inevitable but flowed from the specific results of policies followed by different forces in America.[175]

But in seeking to explain the failure of the American socialists, McNaught himself comes up with intriguing hypotheses derived from assumptions about differences between the European and American social structures. Thus he explains the greater propensity of critical American intellectuals to be absorbed into the "liberal establishment" stressed by labor historian Selig Perlman, and the "extinction of party-based dissent" before the first World War, "not because American society was essentially liberal but because that society broke an aristocratic tradition of eccentricity and intellectual discipline." Although the weakness of socialism in America "was by no means inevitable," the American failure to sustain an independent social-democratic party was rendered more likely in the absence of an aristocratic tradition, of nonconformity. McNaught basically has reiterated Tocqueville's analysis of the "tyranny of the multitude," the extent to which an egalitarian society produces "other-directed" individuals concerned with what is thought of them, as contrasted to the importance, in a society which rests on hereditary status and aristocracy, of standing up against the multitude. McNaught argues that the "intellectual and social independence that characterized the Fabian Society" in contrast to the greater conformity exhibited by their American peers reflected the difference between a "political-social milieu" still affected by "an aristocratic tradition" and that existing in America.[176]

Thus, McNaught concludes that the absence of aristocratic values weakened the propensity for elitist dissent by the intellectuals, and led to the socialist failure. There really is not too much distance between his "non-inevitabilistic" analysis and those who argue that the absence of traditional aristocratic values of *noblesse oblige* and community responsibility for welfare negated the socialist appeal in America.

Some historians of American socialism, fewer than might be expected, cite government repression as a source of socialism's failure. Thus Gabriel Kolko notes that immediately after World War I, "at the very moment American socialism appeared on the verge of significant organization and success, it was attacked by the combined resources of the Federal and various state governments," who denied socialists the positions to which they were elected, deported foreign-born leaders, jailed others, and "generally harrassed the party." He does not give such repression major significance, however, believing that other events "would have destroyed it in any case."[177]

John Laslett also emphasizes "the long history of repressive acts undertaken against radicals and Marxists" from the Haymarket Red Scare of 1886 down to McCarthyism in the 1950s. He notes, however, that "in America repression of radical movements has not taken the form of deliberate murder or destruction as often as it has in a number of European countries." But he argues that repression has been more successful in inhibiting radical movements here than abroad because of the different stratification systems.

I would suggest that part of the explanation is to be found in the fact that where you have a highly stratified society in which crucial elements of either the peasantry or the proletariat are already predisposed against constituted authority and at a time of crisis are willing to follow class leaders or otherwise to act in a class way, then repression simply drives the movement underground, from where it will reemerge, strengthened, at a suitable moment. On the other hand, if you have a society in which either the agrarian element or the urban working class lacks any coherent sense of class loyalty and is predisposed toward acculturation or assimilation, as in the United States, then repression will have the opposite effect. Instead of nourishing rebellion, in other words, it will induce its followers to draw back from any fundamental challenge to the society, and to accept their place instead in what may continue to be an unjust social system.[178]

Thus with the variable of repression, as with the lesser influence of the radical intellectual, the analyst is forced back on the influence of America's unique stratification system.

The Distribution of Opportunity and Rewards: Social Mobility

Many of the efforts to account for the lower level of working-class consciousness in America as compared with much of Europe, from Marx down to various sociologists writing in the post–World War II period of economic expansion and prosperity, have stressed the supposed effect of a high American rate of social mobility in defusing class resentments. The emergence of a class political culture is presumably related to generational class continuity, i.e., limited opportunity to move up the occupational ladder. The argument was and still is made that socialist and other efforts at working-class politics have suffered from the fact that American workers could realistically hope and work to improve their circumstances, while European workers living in societies which offered much less opportunity were more likely to support socialist efforts to change the distribution of reward and opportunity. Socialists, from Marx on, who made these assumptions anticipated the emergence of working-class consciousness and radical political movements in a future period when changes in the economic system would sharply reduce upward mobility.

These interpretations have been subject to two kinds of

empirical challenge. First, a number of students of social mobility in comparative perspective (Sorokin, Glass, Lipset and Bendix, Miller, Blau and Duncan, and Boudon) have concluded from an examination of mobility data collected in various countries that the American rate of mass social mobility is not uniquely high, that a number of European countries have had comparable rates; and second, that with increasing industrialization and urbanization, rates of social mobility have not declined.

Such efforts at comparability are, of course, inadequate since they are often dependent on quite forced comparisons; many restrict their definition to shifts between manual and non-manual categories of occupations.[179] It may be noted, however, that the earliest such effort at broad international comparisons, that of Sorokin in 1927, reported on literally hundreds of limited studies of social mobility in various countries, some dating back to the late nineteenth century. While these data did not permit any systematic statistical evaluation of variations in rates, they did suggest that none of the societies or structures reported on could be described as "closed" or "non-mobile" systems. That is, all studies located substantial minorities who rose or fell in occupational status as contrasted with that of their fathers or their first jobs.[180]

These findings detailed by Sorokin, as well as the many subsequent results from national surveys in many countries, do not imply identical rates of social mobility. There are a number of relatively minor differences among the various countries, with the United States having a "slightly higher" rate, according to Blau and Duncan, the authors of the most comprehensive extant survey in the United States. They conclude, however, that "there is indeed little difference among various industrialized nations in the rates of occupational mobility between the blue-collar and the white-collar class."[181] A more recent effort at a systematic quantitative comparison of data from thirteen countries by Philips Cutright does suggest that countries with a higher industrial level (and lower proportion of the work force in agriculture) do have higher rates of social mobility for the population as a whole. The differences, however, are considerably reduced when comparisons are limited to the non-farm population.[182] In any case, the variations are not great, and still serve to confirm Joseph Schumpeter's insistence that "class barriers are always, without exception, surmountable, and are in fact surmounted."[183]

If, in fact, the United States is not a more open society than much of Europe, to what extent can the observations about opportunity and the "mythology of the open-class society" advanced by so many sophisticated observers in the nineteenth and twentieth centuries have played a role in affecting the prospects for socialism?[184] It may be, as Stephan Thernstrom has emphasized, that "it is by no means evident that we may safely extrapolate these findings backward to the time, probably somewhere in the nineteenth century, at which the political rule of the working class was initially defined." And Thernstrom points to data from nineteenth century Marseille, which indicate a lower rate of social mobility than in Boston at the time.[185] This issue is unresolved, however, since data from Copenhagen from 1850-1950 suggest comparable rates to the American. Both Danish and American cities had an extremely high rate, one which corresponded to 80 percent of the maximum possible in a society with total equality of opportunity.[186]

But if the strong possibility exists that nineteenth century Europe and America had comparably high rates of social mobility, why then the agreement among many who knew both societies that the American was much more open and that this fact explained some of the variations in the political reactions of their lower strata? Reinhard Bendix and I suggested an explanation when we first became cognizant of these similarities in rates in the 1950s, which is related to America's basic value system. "Cultural traditions . . . may result in a massive difference between the values that two different societies assign to social mobility. . . . Ideological equalitarianism has played . . . an important role in facilitating . . . beliefs about opportunity in the United States."[187]

But whether the belief in the *unique* character of the American opportunity system was actually due more to

variations in its status system and level of affluence than to
real differences in mobility rates, there was general agreement
among many nineteenth and early twentieth century socialist
and nonsocialist interpreters of the American political culture
that working-class consciousness and socialism would develop
here and intensify in Europe as a result of the growing "rigidification" which would occur with the increase in large-scale
factories and the need for more factory workers. The growth
of monopoly capitalism and powerful corporations and the
decline in the importance of small independently owned busi-
nesses would also sharply reduce chances for upward mobility. But a number of analyses of the pattern of opportunity
in American society clearly indicate that there has been no
decline in social mobility; in fact, in some respects American
society today is less rigid in terms of social advancement than
it was in the past. A *Scientific American* survey of the backgrounds of big-business executives (presidents, chairmen, and
principal vice-presidents of the 600 largest U.S. nonfinancial
corporations) found that as of 1964 the business elite was
composed to a larger degree than ever before of individuals
from lower status groups.

> Only 10.5 percent of the current generation of big business exec-
> utives . . . are sons of wealthy families; as recently as 1950 the
> corresponding figure was 36.1 percent, and at the turn of the cen-
> tury, 45.6 percent . . . Two-thirds of the 1900 generation had
> fathers who were heads of the same corporation or who were in-
> dependent businessmen; less than half of the current generation
> had fathers so placed in American society. On the other hand, less
> than 10 percent of the 1900 generation had fathers who were
> employees; by 1964 this percentage had increased to nearly 30
> percent.[188]

Surprisingly both to scholars in the field and to those radicals convinced that a mature capitalism would become increasingly immobile, particularly with respect to sharp jumps
into the elite, the evidence indicates that the post–World War
II period brought the greatest increase in the percentage of
those from economically poor backgrounds who entered the

top echelons of American business. (The proportion rose from 12.1 percent in 1950 to 23.3 percent in 1964.) A number of the underlying structural trends that were expected to limit mobility appear to be responsible for opposite developments: the replacement of the family-owned enterprise by the public corporation; the bureaucratization of American corporate life; the recruitment of management personnel from the ranks of college graduates; and the awarding of higher posts on the basis of a competitive promotion process similar to that which operates in government bureaucracy. Because of the spread of higher education to the children of the working classes (almost one-third of whom now attend college), the ladder of bureaucratic success is increasingly open to those from poorer circumstances. Privileged family and class backgrounds continue to be enormous advantages in the quest for corporate success, but training and talent can increasingly make up for them. These findings, drawn from observations of the backgrounds of the big-business elite, are reinforced by national surveys which indicate that opportunities "to enter high-status occupations appear to have improved in successive cohorts of U.S. men for at least the last 40 years, irrespective of those men's occupational origins."[189]

Other, more broadly focused studies provide further evidence that there has been no hardening of class lines in American society. According to Thernstrom (who has played the leading role among historians both in doing research and in stimulating work on the part of others), there has been a continuation of a high rate of social mobility over a 90-year period. In Boston, which Thernstrom studied in detail, there was "impressive consistency" in career patterns between 1880 and 1968: "About a quarter of all the men who first entered the labor market as manual workers ended their careers in a middle-class calling; approximately one in six of those who first worked in a white-collar job later skidded to a blue-collar post." Patterns almost identical to Boston's have been reported in a "dozen samples [from various American cities] for the period from 1850 to World War I"; about 30 to 35 percent of those from working-class backgrounds moved into middle-class positions in various surveys. Rates of downward mobility also did not vary a great deal; the large majority of those from middle-class backgrounds (between 70 and 80 percent) maintained middle-class status.[190]

Thernstrom notes that these findings challenge the often voiced belief that changes in American capitalism have created a permanent and growing class of the poor. In fact, all the available evidence points in the opposite direction. Statistical data from Poughkeepsie, New York, in the 1840s; Boston in five different samples from the 1880s to recent years; and Indianapolis in 1910; as well as from various after–World War II local and national surveys indicate that most of the sons of unskilled workers either moved up into the ranks of the skilled or found middle-class jobs of various kinds.

These conclusions are reinforced by the most comprehensive and methodologically sophisticated analysis by Blau and Duncan of a national sample survey of the American population that was conducted in 1962. Analyzing the mobility patterns of American families over several generations by relating family occupational background to first job (thus permitting a comparison of the very young still on their first job with the experience of the very old when they were young), they found that "the influence of social origins has remained constant since before World War I. There is absolutely no evidence of 'rigidification.'"[191]

A recent effort by a group of sociologists at the University of Wisconsin to update the Blau-Duncan research reports similar findings. They suggest that "the dependence of sons on father's occupation has been remarkably stable for more than half a century."[192] In evaluating the social implications of these findings, it should be noted that they were obtained by holding constant changes over time in the occupational structure. Since the proportion of higher-status, higher-paying positions requiring more education and skill has been increasing steadily, there has in fact been an increase in the proportion of those securing a more rewarded position than their fathers. Hence, though relative opportunity has not increased, the absolute levels have, and this may affect the popular feeling about opportunity.

Speaking more generally to the issue of equality of opportunity, another set of studies by a group of Harvard sociologists and economists, led by Christopher Jencks, reanalyzed the data from a number of sources, seeking to specify the factors involved in occupational choice and earning capacity. These scholars, many of whom happen to be socialists politically, found that the results contradicted their anticipations:

> Poverty is not primarily hereditary. While children born into poverty have a higher-than-average chance of ending up poor, there is still an enormous amount of economic mobility from one generation to the next. Indeed, there is nearly as much economic inequality among brothers raised in the same homes as in the general population. This means that inequality is recreated anew in each generation, even among people who start life in essentially identical circumstances.[193]

These researchers came to these conclusions by comparing the occupational status scores on the "Duncan scale" (which ranks occupations from 96 points to 0) of fathers and sons and of brothers with a random sample of unrelated individuals. They found that random individuals differed in occupational status by an average of 28 points, while brothers differed from each other by 23 points, and fathers from sons by 20 points. As they note, "there is nearly as much variation in status between brothers as in the larger population. Family background is not, then, the primary determinant of status." These findings imply that "when people have had relatively equal opportunity, as brothers usually have, they still end up with very unequal incomes."[194]

These results, of course, do not mean that a father's status has no effect on the occupational achievements of his offspring. Rather, as Jencks and his collaborators note:

> [The] role of a father's family background in determining his sons' status is surprisingly small, at least compared to most people's

preconception. The correlation [indicator of association] between
a father's occupational status and his sons' is less than 0.50. If two
fathers' statuses differ by, say 20 points [on the Duncan scale],
their sons' statuses will differ by an average of 10 points.[195]

Immigration

These data which point up the continued, even enhanced,
role of social mobility apply to white males. As noted by
many commenting on American stratification, the fact that
in America occupational position has been differentially distributed along ethnic, racial and, it should be added, sexual
lines, has given an enormously privileged position with respect to opportunity and income for those who have belonged to the dominant group. Analyses of census data in the
late nineteenth and early twentieth centuries demonstrate
that immigrants have generally taken the most lowly positions, while their children and other native-born were able to
rise, in part because of the immigrants below them. This pattern continued into the 1920s.[196]

Michael Harrington has reemphasized the importance of
mass immigration in producing a working class which rejected
socialist appeals. "For it is true that many of the immigrants,
even though living under objectively degrading conditions,
saw their lot as improved compared to the old country. They
thus had an impression of relative betterment, not relative
deprivation."[197]

But independent of the role immigration played in producing opportunity for native-born workers, it is also important
to note that late nineteenth and early twentieth century immigration resulted in a working class which was disproportionately Catholic. The extensive anti-Socialist activities of
powerful lay Catholic groups backed by the Church helped to
prevent the development of socialist sympathies among the
large mass of Catholic workers.[198] Before World War I, Catholics made up close to half the membership of the AFL and
furnished at times a majority portion of the officers of the
unions and delegates to AFL conventions. Philip Foner
estimates that socialists were able to gain the support of two-
thirds of the non-Catholics, Jews and Protestants, at AFL

conventions.[199] Hence beyond the impact of immigration on the opportunity structure, the fact that so much of it was Catholic placed another major obstacle in the socialist path in the crucial years before World War I.

Since the passage of restrictive immigration legislation in 1924, European immigration has been sharply reduced. But, in recent years, particularly since the economy began a prolonged period of relatively full employment in the 1940s, migrant groups from various parts of North America—blacks, Puerto Ricans, and Mexicans—have furnished a large segment of the less skilled labor force.

The contribution of minorities to the higher occupational status of those belonging to dominant social groups is not limited to racial and ethnic factors. Women have disproportionately filled the lower-paid, lower-status and less interesting jobs in American and other societies. Over the years, as the nonmanual professional, executive, technical, white-collar and service sectors of the occupational structure have expanded, and as the proportion of less skilled, manual jobs has declined, women have filled the bulk of the low-status, nonmanual positions. By so doing women have enabled men, often their fathers, husbands, and sons, to secure better positions, and to continue to see America as a land of opportunity.[200] Thus, though blacks, Hispanics, and women have organized to improve their economic and social position, white males have on the whole remained outside of these struggles. And minority organization does not lead to radical political action, since the political system retains its ability to respond to pressure and to co-opt new organized groupings. Both blacks and women, particularly the better educated among them, made considerable gains in the sixties and early seventies. Some of these gains, however, were reduced during the massive recession in 1973-75.

Income Distribution

The concern for greater equality does not mean only equal opportunity; it also means reward. No complex society, other than perhaps the kibbutzim (collective settlements) in Israel, which encompasses over 100,000 people has ever come close to approximating this objective. Although the mobility data reported by Blau and Duncan, and by Jencks and his associates, suggest the United States is beginning to approximate equal opportunity for white males, it is clear that such a situation continues together with sharp inequalities in income, and Jencks notes:

> This implies that even if America could reduce inequalities in income to the point where they were no greater than those that now arise between one brother and another, the best-paid fifth of all male workers would still be making 500 percent more than the worst-paid fifth. We cannot, then, hope to eliminate, or even substantially reduce income inequality in America simply by providing children from all walks of life with equal opportunity. When people have had relatively equal opportunity, as brothers usually have, they still end up with very unequal incomes.[201]

The only solution Jencks sees to the problem of gaining greater income equality is government politics which "establish floors beneath which nobody's income is allowed to fall and ceilings above which it is not allowed to rise." Although this proposal by socialists such as Jencks may appear quite radical, it is interesting to note that leading Republicans now assert that "there is much in the new doctrine of equality of results that is solid"—to use the words of Paul McCracken, a member of President Eisenhower's Council of Economic Advisers from 1956 to 1959 and chairman of the same body for President Nixon from 1969 to 1972. McCracken, speaking to the American Business Council, noted that American society is concerned with finding an optimum balance between its traditional ideal of equality of opportunity and its growing commitment to greater equality of result:

> For economic policy we need to have a more explicit and coherent income maintenance policy. Powerful intellectual impetus for this, as for so much of the current economic policy landscape, came from Milton Friedman in his writings on the negative income tax. It was given programmatic expression four years ago in the President's Family Assistance Plan. Ours is now a rich econo-

my, and we can well afford it. And all of us here would have to
admit that there is a substantial element of random luck in success. . . . Moreover, we need a more explicit and coherent income-
sharing plan to win more leeway for using the pricing system.

The optimum toward which society is trying to feel its way here
will be neither pure "equality of results" nor just "equality of
opportunity." A society organized solely on the principle of
equality of opportunity is not acceptable, and one organized solely around the principle of equality of results would not be
operational.[202]

Once again, we see a familiar American pattern recurring.
As events and the "emerging conscience" of the society bring
new issues and more radical proposals to the fore, spokesmen
for the establishment move with the times and acknowledge
the new objectives, much as Johnson and Kennedy proposed
a "war on poverty."

Government policy has seemingly been committed to
equalizing incomes beyond what would occur through the
natural workings of the market economy. Various policies
have been used, ranging from the graduated income tax,
which increases the tax percentage on higher income, to assorted income-transfer welfare programs, which give income
directly to the less privileged. Such welfare policies, stimulated by the New Deal programs initiated in the 1930s,
should have the effect of reducing the pattern of gross
inequalities. While these policies attest to the continued significance of equality as a national value, more important in
the long run in affecting income distribution are changes in
the occupational structure which serve to reduce the proportion of unskilled and low-paid jobs and to increase the proportion of jobs requiring higher education in the upper ranges
of income distribution. The spread of higher education to the
point where close to half of all Americans of college age continue their education beyond high school attests to the ex-
tensiveness of this process.

Recent historical research has not only challenged the conventional wisdom about mobility rates, which assumed that
the growth of large corporations would mean movement

from greater to lesser equality of opportunity; it has also upset long-cherished notions about the direction of change in the distribution of income from the early nineteenth century on. The tentative conclusion which may be reached from a number of studies is that Jacksonian America—described by Tocqueville and others as an egalitarian social system (which, compared to Europe, it undoubtedly was)—was characterized by much more severe forms of social and economic inequality than the society of the 1970s. As historian Edward Pessen points out:

> The explanation, popular since Karl Marx's time, that it was industrialization that pauperized the masses, in the process transforming a relatively egalitarian social order, appears wanting. Vast disparities between urban rich and poor antedated industrialization [in America]. . . . Even Michael Harrington and Gabriel Kolko, whose estimates reveal the greatest amounts of [present-day] inequality, attribute percentages of income to the upper brackets that are far smaller than the upper one percent of New York City controlled in income in 1863 or in wealth in 1845.[203]

Most other pre-Civil War American cities resembled New York in these respects, and even in rural areas the pattern of property distribution was extremely unequal.[204]

Detailed analysis of the distribution of total personal income since 1929 by the foremost authority on the subject, Simon Kuznets, indicates that the proportion of the income going to the bottom sections of the population (the lower fifth and lower 5 percent) increased during the 1930s and 1940s, while the portion going to the upper groups (the top fifth and top 5 percent) dropped considerably. Thus the proportion of the total family income received by the upper fifth fell from 54 percent in 1929 to 42.7 percent in 1951; the corresponding change for the top 5 percent was from 29.5 percent to 18.4 percent.[205]

Since 1950, however, total family income distribution data suggest that the process has slowed down although a recent review of a number of American studies of the subject by the Organization for Economic Cooperation and Development

(OECD) concludes that there "has been a slight but percepti-
ble tendency, over 1950-1970 period, towards greater equality in family income distribution." Thus in 1970 the proportion received by the top 5 percent had fallen to 14.4
percent.[206]

Nevertheless, it is far from certain that the egalitarian
trend with respect to income is declining. Government
welfare agencies, combined with the American emphasis on
individualism and the nuclear family, has led to a continuing
increase in the number of separate households headed by
those under 25, those 65 and older, and women—people who
in many other societies would not be living apart from rela-
tives and would not be counted as independent family units in
the income statistics. These three groups form a very large
proportion of the lowest 20 percent of the income distribution. As Kuznets pointed out in 1962:

> Splitting up [family units] would, all other conditions being
> equal, widen the inequality in the distribution among consumer
> units—as measured, for it would create an increasingly large group
> of units at the lower end of the distribution. . . . The point to be
> stressed is that insofar as splitting up began in the 1930s [as a
> result of old-age pensions and other welfare policies] and con-
> tinued thereafter, inequality in the distribution of income among
> consumer units declined until 1947 and was constant thereafter
> *despite* the underlying trend in the structure of consuming
> units.[207]

More recently, Kuznets has analyzed the impact of these
changes on income distribution for the period 1947-1968. He
finds that family units headed by women, persons over 65, or
persons under 25 increased by 17.4 percent during this
period. Since old people constituted half of this group, a
large proportion of them were not in the labor force.

Families with young, old, and female heads make up an
increasing proportion of low-income units, fully two-thirds of
the lowest fifth by 1968. When these three groups are
excluded from the income distribution, "the general level of
the shares of the lowest fifth, and to a lesser extent of the

second fifth, are raised perceptibly, while those of the [upper] 80-95 percent, and particularly of the top 5 percent group, are lowered—thus narrowing inequality significantly." Thus the share received by the bottom fifth rose from 5.8 percent after the war to 7.3 percent in 1968, while that of the upper 5 percent fell from 16 percent to 12.8 percent. In short, while the total income distribution among all families has been relatively stable, the distribution "among families with male heads aged 25-64 (what might be called 'standard' family units), showed a sustained movement of some magnitude through almost the whole period." Further, since "the young and old family head units are characterized by much smaller families than the average . . . an adjustment for these differences in *average* size of family would also yield an income distribution with a more sustained and larger movement toward equality over the period."[208] Controlling for the age factor, economist Morton Paglin also finds a significant decline (of 23 percent) in income equality from 1947-1972. In addition, Paglin calculated the impact of transfer payments such as "public housing, rent supplements, food stamps and food assistance, Medicaid, and social services" on the income distribution. Including these as income and controlling for age, he estimates that the poorest 20 percent of the population in fact receive about 54 percent of what they would get if there were complete equality, as contrasted with the previously accepted estimate of 27 percent, using traditional methods which do not control for age and do not include transfer payments as income.[209]

With respect to the way in which people *perceive* the distribution of income, and react politically, it may be argued that the distribution of different kinds of *consumer goods*, those people use for immediate gratification, is more important in affecting their feelings about equity than the actual distribution of income as such. In this connection, it would appear that the distribution of consumer goods has been commented on by the Swedish socialist economist Gunnar Myrdal: "It is, indeed, a regular occurrence that the poorer the country, the greater the difference between poor and rich." In the United States the average per capita income has increased almost eightfold during the course of this century, and this dramatic growth has brought about a wide distribution of various social and economic benefits, greater than that in almost all other countries. Thus, in America a much larger proportion of the population graduates from high school (over 80 percent) or enters college (close to 45 percent) than in any other nation. The greater wealth of the United States also means that consumer goods such as automobiles and telephones are more evenly distributed than elsewhere. As historian David Potter stressed: "If the American class structure is in reality very unlike the formalized class societies of former times . . . the factor of abundance has . . . constantly operated to equalize the overt differences between the various classes. . . . "[210] An evaluation by *The* (London) *Economist* using twelve social indicators to assess the relative advantages of different countries as places to live for the broad mass of the population placed the United States far in the lead over eight other noncommunist industrialized states.[211]

Political Consequences

Sociologist Gideon Sjoberg has traced historically the implications of such developments in America. He suggests that the emergence of mass production during the twentieth century has caused such a redistribution of highly valued prestige symbols that the distinctions between social classes are much less immediately visible than they were in nineteenth-century America, or in most other affluent countries. Sjoberg argues that the status differences between many blue-collar workers and middle-class professionals have become less well-defined, since working-class families, like middle-class ones, have been able to buy goods that confer prestige on the purchaser—clothing, cars, television sets, and so on. Such improvements in style of life help to preserve the belief in the reality of the promise of equality. A person who can buy his own house, or a new car, may feel that he has moved up in the world even if he has not changed his occupational or relative income position.[212]

Beyond consideration of the levels of opportunity, the availability of consumers' goods, and distribution of income, Thernstrom suggests that the especially high level of "geographical mobility, or population turnover . . . may retard the development of class consciousness." Noting the evidence that workers in isolated occupational communities, e.g., miners, loggers, shipboard workers, are especially strike-prone and militant, Thernstrom points out that studies of behavior for over 100 years point to a highly volatile urban population. He reports that "in no American city has there been a lower-class element with continuity of membership. More or less continuously lower-class *areas* can be identified, but *the same individuals do not live in them very long.*" Although European data on the subject are less developed than the American, the available evidence suggests that the absence of an itinerant pattern in some communities was related to a "high degree of solidarity."[213]

The discussion of rates of social and geographic mobility, of income trends, and of the distribution of status-enhancing consumer goods is pertinent to the suggestion repeated here that such attributes affect the extent to which the country is likely to experience intense class conflict, or polarized politics. A detailed effort to test some of the implications of these assumptions, particularly in the context of evaluating the political effects of social mobility, indicates that mobile individuals (up or down) are less likely to take strong class positions than the nonmobile. The political scientist James Barber concludes his study with the assertion: "The influence of mobility on the political system would seem . . . to be a moderating one: lending flexibility to the electoral process, reducing the stakes involved in elections, and diluting the class content of politics."[214]

Empirical studies by sociologists and economists made in recent years clearly indicate that the preconditions for increased working-class consciousness in America anticipated by Marx and subsequent socialists, i.e., greater rigidification of the class structure and increased income inequality, simply have not occurred. If anything the reverse has happened. There is more opportunity and greater equality, within what is still a highly inegalitarian society, than ever before. Mass production continues to expand the spread of consumers' goods which reinforce the mythology of classlessness.

Poverty, of course, continues to exist within the rich society, but as John Kenneth Galbraith pointed out in his book, *The Affluent Society*, what was once the situation of the large majority now characterizes a minority of the population: the politically weakest and least participant groups, that is, the ethnic and racial minorities. And, among the dominant group, there are the aged, the uneducated and unskilled, migrant farm laborers, families without male heads, and that large group with individual handicaps (those with low IQs, physical deformities, mental illness, or other chronic ailments.)

The growth of material abundance which permits the spread of consumers' goods, education, and opportunity among the less privileged in the post–World War II period convinced a number of leftist writers that the chances for the development of an organized radical alternative based on the underprivileged had come close to vanishing. Thus, Barrington Moore, Jr., wrote in the 1950s:

> As we reduce economic inequalities and privileges, we may also eliminate the sources of contrast and discontent that put drive into genuine political alternatives. In the Unites States today, with the exception of the Negro, it is difficult to perceive any section of the population that has a vested material interest on behalf of freedom.[215]

Herbert Marcuse argued in the early 1960s in a discussion of "The Paralysis of Criticism: Society Without Opposition" that increased affluence in advanced industrial society has modified "the consciousness and . . . political action of the two great classes which faced each other in the society: the bourgeoisie and the proletariat" in Europe as well as America.

> In the capitalist world, they are still the basic classes. However,
> the capitalist development has altered the structure and function
> of these two classes. . . . An overriding interest in the preservation
> and improvement of the institutional status quo unites the former
> antagonists in the most advanced areas of contemporary society.
> . . . Even the most empirical analysis of historical alternatives ap-
> pears to be unrealistic speculation, and commitment to them a
> matter of personal (or group) preference.[216]

In effect, Marx's dictum, "The country that is more developed industrially only shows, to the less developed, the image
of its own future," may lead to a reversal of Marxist expectations about the future of capitalist society. The political culture of the United States, the most economically developed
society, should be the most appropriate to an affluent, technologically advanced society. A consistent Marxist sociology
would expect the social class relationships of the United
States to present an image of the future of other societies
that are moving in the same economic direction. Characteristic of such a social system is a decline in emphasis on social
class, that is, a decline of distinct visible strata with a "felt
consciousness of kind." Beyond the effect of purely economic and technological factors one may argue that the
United States, precisely because it lacks a feudal past, has
evolved in purest form the institutions of a highly developed
industrial society.

Moralistic Protest Movements, Not Third Parties

Although most of the critics of efforts to explain the failure of radicalism by emphasizing the continuing impact of
formative social structures and basic values contend that
these versions of "consensus" history ignore the fact that
there have been major conflicts and tensions, they pay little
attention to the fact that the United States has been the
country, *par excellence*, of moralistic, often tactically extremist social movements, some of which have also been parties. The issue is not simply why no socialism, the question
must be raised, why social movements?

A focus on the role and tactics of movements, as distinct from parties, must produce the conclusion that reliance on methods outside of the normal political game has played a major role in affecting change throughout much of American history. While most of the movements have not engaged in violence as such, some of the major changes in American society have been a product of violent tactics resulting from the willingness of those who felt that they had a morally righteous cause to take the law into their own hands in order to advance their cause. By extreme actions, whether violent or not, the moralistic radical minorities have often secured the support or acquiescence of some of the more moderate elements, who came to accept the fact that change was necessary in order to gain a measure of peace and stability. To some extent, also, the extremists on a given side of an issue have lent credence to the arguments presented by the moderates on that issue. Extremists, whether of the right or left, have often helped the moderates to press through reforms.

The most striking example of this sort of behavior in American history was the successful movement to abolish slavery. The radical abolitionists were willing to violate Congressional law and Supreme Court decisions to make their case before the public and to help Negro slaves escape to Canada. Some of them were even ready to fight with arms in order to guarantee that the Western territories would remain free of slavery. John Brown's armed raid on Harper's Ferry played a major role in convincing both Southerners and Northerners that the slavery debate had to be ended either by secession or by some form of emancipation. Conversely, the violence of the first Ku Klux Klan after the Civil War helped convince the North that it had to desist in its effort to prevent white domination of the South. The guerrilla actions of the Klansmen played a major role in reestablishing white Bourbon power and securing the end of Reconstruction.

As noted earlier, the American labor movement has been more militant, more prone to use violent and illegal methods to gain its ends than the more explicitly socialist and politically class conscious ones in Britain and Europe. Michael

Harrington points out that in the course of the organization
of the labor movement from the 1880s to World War I, "the
class struggle in America was more fierce than in any European country."[217] Labor Historian Selig Perlman concluded
as well that the *nonsocialist* "union leaders in this country
have, on the whole, always been more aggressive against the
employers . . . than have their radical rivals."[218] The historian of the IWW, Melvyn Dubofsky, notes that one former
Wobbly, Rudolf Katz, "was perhaps close to the truth when
he informed federal investigators: 'The American Federation
of Labor does not preach sabotage, but it practices sabotage;
and the IWW preaches sabotage, but does not practice it.'"[219]

The women's suffrage movement, as it gained strength,
similarly displayed the depth of its commitment through various forms of civil disobedience: illegal demonstrations to
disrupt the orderly operation of government, chaining themselves to buildings, and so forth. Some prohibitionists showed
the intensity of their feelings against liquor by ridiculing and
ostracizing those who patronized saloons, and on occasion
even by violently attempting to prevent dispensers of liquor
from doing business.

During the Great Depression, illegal actions were also important. Agrarian movements brought about moratoriums on
mortgage-debt collection and changes in various banking laws
by their armed actions to prevent the sale of farms for non-
payment of debt. In the cities, the labor movement won its
right to collective bargaining in industries that had traditionally opposed it by illegal sit-ins in factories in Akron, Detroit,
and other places. State governments found themselves unable
to remove workers from factories, and antiunion employers
quite often were forced by these actions to accept unions in
their plants.

Moralistic politics and movement politics clearly continue
today. Each wave of moralistic protest and reform is necessarily followed by a period of institutionalization in which
the inspired utopian hopes become the daily work of bureaucrats, and thus the passion which aroused them is left unsatis-
fied. Further, it becomes obvious that the problems are much

more complex than assumed in the simple solutions proposed by protest movements, whether for emancipation, civil service reform, prohibition, conservation, women's suffrage, control of trusts and monopolies, or intervention for economic and welfare purposes. What is often worse is the realization that what Robert Merton has termed the "unintended consequences of purposive social action" have brought new evils.

Even when the reforms accomplish their manifest purpose, they still leave a society which is highly immoral from the vantage point of those who take seriously the constantly redefined and enlarged ideals of equality, democracy, and liberty. Corruption is perhaps endemic in a competitive meritocratic society, whether capitalist or communist, and periods of prolonged prosperity in which many become visibly wealthy generally witness the spread and institutionalization of corruption. Privilege, too, always seeks to entrench itself, and is generally able to do so in such times. Thus it is not surprising that new generations of Americans recurrently respond to some event or crisis which points anew to the gap between the American ideal and reality by supporting a new protest wave on the assumption that a corrupt and morally sick America must be drastically reformed.

The United States has been in such a period since the mid-1960s. As in the past, the moralistic reformers have thrown a wide net of criticism over American institutions and behavior. Not surprisingly, those most motivated to support these criticisms place them in a traditional Protestant context—of good versus evil, God versus Satan, progress against reaction—and define American society as totally evil in much the same terms as abolitionist William Lloyd Garrison did when he tore up the Constitution as a compact with the Devil. The rhetoric of American politics normally goes far beyond the substantive content of the issues.

Moralism is an orientation Americans have inherited from their Protestant past. This is the *one* country in the world dominated by the religious traditions of Protestant "dissent"—the Methodists, Baptists, and other sects. The teachings of these denominations called on men to follow their conscience, with an unequivocal emphasis not to be found in those denominations which evolved from state churches (Catholics, Lutherans, Anglicans, and Orthodox Christians). The American Protestant religious ethos has assumed, in practice if not in theology, the perfectibility of man and his obligation to avoid sin, while the churches whose followers predominate in Europe, Canada, and Australia have accepted the inherent weakness of man, his inability to escape sinning and error, and the need for the church to be forgiving and protecting. This basic observation was made by Edmund Burke two centuries ago:

> The People are Protestants; and of that kind most averse to all implicit submission of mind and opinion. . . . Everyone knows that the Roman Catholic religion is at least coeval with most of the governments, where it prevails; that it had generally gone hand in hand with them. . . . The Church of England too was formed from her cradle under the nursing care of regular government. But the dissenting interests have sprung up in direct opposition to all the ordinary powers of the world. All Protestantism, even the most cold and passive, is a sort of dissent. But the religion most prevalent in our northern colonies is a refinement of the principles of resistance; it is the dissidence of dissent, and the Protestantism of the Protestant religion.[220]

The fact of disestablishment—that is, the absence of a state church in America—meant, as Tocqueville and Marx noted, that a new structure of moral authority had to be created to replace the link between Church and State. The absence of government support made the American form of Protestantism unique in the Christian world. Ideological and institutional changes which flowed from the Revolution led to forms of church organization analogous to popularly-based institutions: the United States became the first nation in which religious groups were viewed as purely voluntary organizations, which served to strengthen the introduction of religious morality into politics. Many ministers and laymen consciously recognized that they had to establish voluntary organization to safeguard morality in a democratic society which lacked an established church. Associations for domestic missionary work, for temperance, for abolition, for widespread education, for peace, for the reduction of the influence of the Masons or the Catholics, and more recently for the elimination of Communists, were organized by people who felt these were the only ways they could preserve and extend a moral society.

The need to assuage a sense of personal responsibility has made Americans particularly inclined to support movements for the elimination of evil—by illegal and even violent means, if necessary. A key element in the conflicts that culminated in the Civil War was the tendency of both sides to view the other as essentially sinful—as an agent of the Devil. And more recently, the resisters to the Vietnam War reenacted a two-century-old American scenario in which a Protestant sense of personal responsibility led the intensely committed to violate the "rules of the game." This moralistic tendency in a more secular America has been generalized far beyond its denominational or even specifically religious base. During the McCarthy era, a French Dominican, R. L. Bruckberger, criticized American Catholics for having absorbed the American Protestant view of religion and morality. He noted that American Catholics resemble American Baptists and Presbyterians more than European or Latin American Catholics.[221] Presumably the emergence of a Catholic left, and the behavior of the Berrigans and others, adds weight to this observation. But agnostic and atheistic reformers in America also tend to be utopian moralists who believe in the perfectibility of man and of civil society and in the immorality, if not specifically sinful character, of the opposition.

But the American propensity to moralistic and extreme politics has never resulted in the institutionalization of protest in third parties. This is not only true for socialist and labor movements; all others, including right wing and single-issue movements, have been stopped by the unique American electoral and political system. As I noted some time ago:

We have had major extremist social movements in this country, of which the Know Nothing Party and the Ku Klux Klan are perhaps the most extreme, but among which must be included Abolitionism, Populism, Prohibitionism and the like. Although some of these movements have become organized into political parties, they have never been able to sustain themselves, and their programs have been dependent upon endorsement by one of the major political parties for influence in the national power arena. To a considerable degree one must recognize that the failure of these and other movements, such as the Socialist, to create viable third parties which would change the political system is as much a consequence of the legal structure of the polity as it is of elements in the value system or of the distribution of wealth.[222]

Efforts to institutionalize protest in third parties have been effectively countered by the compromise coalition parties characteristic of the America party system. The need to construct coalitions, often involving groups with sharply opposed interests and values, and the development of party ideologies and rhetoric appropriate to keeping such coalitions together repeatedly undercuts the moralistic passion of social movements. If the country is to be governed, party leaders must find ways of encapsulating and incorporating indignation.

In a two-party system, both parties aim at securing a majority. Elections become occasions for the two parties to seek the broadest base of support by convincing divergent groups of their common interests. In contrast to much of Europe, where divergent *parties* join coalitions *after* elections to form cabinets, in the United States divergent *factions* come together *before* elections to elect presidents or governors. The system thus encourages compromise and the incorporation into party values of those general elements of consensus upon which the polity rests. The normal lack of emphasis on ideological differences inherent in two-party systems has the further consequence of reducing intense concern with particular issues and sharpening the focus on party leaders.

The structural factor which has made this balancing act possible in America is the electoral system, which is almost required by the Constitutional separation of executive and legislative powers. The presidential system, virtually alone in the democratic world until DeGaulle attempted to imitate it in France, dictates a two-party system. Unlike the situation in parliamentary countries, where new and/or small, ideologically committed parties may establish a core of elected representatives (easier if a system of proportional representation is used, more difficult but possible with single-member districts if the parties have local strength in distinct regions or political units), the effective constituency for electing an American President is the entire country, and for a governor the whole state. This has had the effect of preventing American third parties from building up local constituency strength as labor, agarian, religious, or ethnic parties have done in most single-member constituency systems. Evidence for this interpretation is the fact that third parties in the United States have gained their greatest support in municipal, and occasionally, state contests, and in Congressional elections held in non-presidential election years, but have almost invariably lost strength in subsequent presidential elections. Essentially, the division into two parties is maintained by those factors which lead people to see a third-party vote as "wasted." Thus, since opinion surveys began in the 1930s, polls have indicated a steady decline in support, as election day nears, for third-party candidates.

Another factor which contributes to the stability of the American two-party system is the decentralized structure of the major parties, stemming from both the federal system and the separation of powers. Since a setback in Congress does not affect the executive's tenure in office as it does in parliamentary systems, party discipline in Congress is weak, and allows for cross-party alignments on particular issues. Congressmen who represent minority orientations within one party can vote against the party leadership and the president in order to please their constitutents. Further, primary elections give minority interests an opportunity to express opposition to those in office from their own party, and thus help to keep these minorities within the party.

During the 1920s and 1930s a variety of former socialists formed factions with the major parties, mainly the Democrats, in a number of states. They succeeded in winning nominations for high state office, the House of Representatives, and the Senate in a number of states, including California, Minnesota, North Dakota, Oklahoma, Oregon, South Dakota, Washington, and Wisconsin.

The construction of electoral coalitions on a national level is an extremely delicate task, and often requires that party leaders deemphasize ideological (moralistic) appeals and focus on either "throwing the rascals out" or keeping them out. Critical change periods—e.g., the slavery issue and the Civil War, the rise of agrarian populism in tandem with the industrialization at the end of the 19th century, the Great Depression—have witnessed realignments of party supporters into new coalition systems, and such periods of realignment have usually produced coalitions that have persisted for some decades. They break down, however, as groups find themselves out of step with their party on specific new issues, while the alternative party is not prepared to make their causes its own.

Thus, extra-party "movements" arise for moralistic causes, which are initially not electorally palatable. These extra-major-party movements have taken various forms, most often emphasizing a single special issue, but sometimes cohering around a broader ideology. Such movements are not doomed to isolation and inefficacy. If mainstream political leaders recognize that a significant segment of the electorate feels alienated from the body politic, they will readapt one of the major party coalitions. But in so doing, they temper much of the extremist moralistic fervor. Sometimes this may be done by accommodations in rhetoric, but the results are often actual changes in policy. The protestors are absorbed into a major party coalition but, like the abolitionists who joined the Republicans, the Populists who merged with the Democrats, or the radicals who backed the New Deal, they contribute to the policy orientation of the newly formed coalition.

The breakdown of parties and the political disorganization

which appears to characterize the contemporary scene are far from unique. In the past, dislocations of the great party coalitions have also been accompanied by the process of "polarization," a term generally used to describe the condition whereby significant sections of the population move to the left and right of normal two-party politics. In the 1820s and 1830s the rise of the bigoted Anti-Masons was paralleled by the Workingmen's parties; the nativists of the 1840s and 1850s by the Free Soilers, Liberty Party, and Abolitionists; the anti-Catholic American Protective Association of the 1890s by the Populists; the massive Klan of the 1920s by the Progressive and Farmer-Labor movements; the Coughlinites of the 1930s by significant, active, leftist radical movements; and in the last decade, George Wallace and his followers by the movement encompassing the New Left, the New Politics, the Black Revolution, and the opposition intelligentsia.

This polarization process always involves two forces which react not only to specific issues but to each other. As this occurs, politics increasingly comes to be perceived in purely moralistic terms, as involving a struggle between good and evil forces rather than as a series of collective bargaining issues. Yet each time this happens, the dynamics of the American electoral system, the requirement that the electorate vote for one person for president or governor, forces the diverse tendencies which in a parliamentary country would assemble into separate parties to unite into two broad preelectoral coalitions, much as diverse parties in Europe, including socialists and communists, have joined together with ideological opponents in postelection coalitions. And this uniquely American system produces the image of moderate nonideological parties. James MacGregor Burns has noted:

> Majority rule in a big, diverse nation must be moderate. No majority party can cater to the demands of any extremist group because to do so would antagonize the great "middle groups" that hold the political balance of power and hence could rob the governing party of its majority at the election. A democratic people embodies [a] . . . great variety of sections and groups and classes

and opinions stitched into the fabric of society and thus into the majority's coalition. . . . Moreover, the majority party—and the opposition that hopes to supplant it—must be competitive; if either one forsakes victory in order to stick to principle, as the Federalists did after the turn of the century, it threatens the whole mechanism of majority rule. Majoritarian strategy assumes that in the end politicians will rise above principle in order to win an election.[223]

The two most recent leaders of the Socialist Party, Norman Thomas and Michael Harrington, in the last years of the party's electoral history in the 1950s came to accept this explanation of the "general failure of 'third' parties." As Thomas put it "had we had a centralized parliamentary government rather than a federal presidential government, we should have had, under some name or other, a moderately strong socialist party." He placed particular emphasis on the fact that third party supporters in America are always faced with the dilemma that they are casting a "wasted vote" which may help elect the major party candidate they most dislike.[224]

In 1938 and then from the 1950s on, Thomas became convinced that the socialists only hurt their cause by running candidates for president. He reluctantly came to the conclusion that the party's experience demonstrated the futility of third parties in America, a view a majority of the party came to accept by 1960.[225]

Socialist Strategy and Tactics

Although this essay has focused on structural factors rooted in American society, economy, and polity, which have been cited as sources for the failure of socialism in America, many of the chroniclers of the history of the movement have emphasized the failings of American socialists, themselves. That is, some argue that if American socialists had pursued other strategies, they could have been more successful, that they might have even built a mass socialist movement.

Ironically, but naturally, such criticism takes two quite

opposite though related forms. Most writers follow the lead of Engels in stressing the persistent sectarian character of American socialism, that is, its reluctance to work with non-socialist groups, its concern for doctrinal purity, as a source of its failure to win a mass following. Others contend the precise opposite, particularly in attempting to explain the decline of the relatively large pre–World War I Socialist Party. This alternative view suggests that the Socialist Party collapsed because of its opportunism, its inclusion of nonsocialist elements, which made its support base vulnerable to seduction from nonsocialist progressive forces.

The interpretations of those who stress the sectarian character of the movement, such as Daniel Bell, Martin Diamond, Michael Harrington, Bernard Johnpoll, Laurence Moore, and David Shannon, seem to me to correspond more with the historical facts than do the analyses of scholars like Philip Foner and Ira Kipnis, who criticize the Socialist Party for its lack of militancy, its repression of far-left or syndicalist tendencies within it, its lack of concern for Negroes and immigrants.[226] Related to the sectarian explanation is the seemingly special propensity of American radicals to engage in factional fights and splits. As Daniel Bell has noted, "the Socialist Party has never, even for a single year, been without some issue which threatened to split the party and which forced it to spend much of its time on the problem of reconciliation or rupture. In this fact lies the chief clue to the impotence of American socialism as a political movement."[227] As Shannon puts it, the Socialist Party, by striving "to become homogeneous, to cast all its members in the same mold, violated one of the basic principles of American political parties. . . . Over the years the Socialist Party became increasingly homogeneous. . . . It is almost a political axiom *that any party* that is 'pure,' . . . is a weak party."[228]

Various writers over the years have pointed to different policies and tactics which supposedly have had an adverse effect on the efforts to build a socialist party. The earliest example given is the role of the sectarian opposition to the AFL in its early years by both the Socialist Labor Party and important segments of the Socialist Party "in creating an antisocialist sentiment in key elements of the AFL."[229] The insistence by Daniel DeLeon and the Socialist Labor Party in 1890 that unless the young AFL would admit the party to affiliate, a proposal which Engels thought wrong, that it must be rejected and attacked by all socialists, clearly helped to alienate Samuel Gompers and other union leaders, and intensified Gompers' conviction that socialists must be prevented from dominating the unions. As Henry Pelling notes: "This conflict was an important one partly because it threw Gompers, who was as yet by no means a anti-Socialist, into a defensive attitude against the Socialist movement. . . ."[230] A few years later, DeLeon set up a parallel union, the Socialist Trades and Labor Alliance. It is conceivable that had the American Marxists cooperated with the AFL from the start, a symbiotic relationship could have eventuated. Many in the somewhat less sectarian Socialist Party, including its most prominent leader, Eugene Debs, also rejected the AFL. Debs and other socialists backed the syndicalist Industrial Workers of the World (IWW) when it was established in 1905 as an alternative union competing with the AFL. In an article in the *International Socialist Review* in 1911, Debs, the party's principal spokesman, reiterated his contempt for the AFL.

> Not for all the vote of the American Federation of Labor and its labor-dividing-and-corruption-breeding craft unions should we compromise one jot of our revolutionary principles; and if we do we shall be visited with the contempt we deserve by all real Socialists, who will scorn to remain in a party professing to be a revolutionary party of the working class.[231]

The second major thesis relates to the consistent opposition of the Socialist Party from its formation in 1900 until 1922 to all efforts to form a labor party, on the model of the one in Britain, which would include socialists and unionists. At various times in the first three decades of this century, nonsocialists in the union movement sought to create such a party. The socialists always resisted such efforts, insisting that the Socialist Party was the labor party.[232] In resisting these proposals, the socialists ignored Engels' advice that the first step in America should be to mobilize workers into their own unions and party, regardless of ideology.

Finally, the third general policy which has been attacked by Bell and others as a basic error, as a misreading of the American scene, is the effort to build a third party, rather than working as an organized faction within the regular party coalitions. The critics point to the difficulties involved in creating a third party in the United States, difficulties which American and foreign socialists have repeatedly noticed, and the success on a state level achieved in primaries at various times by Progressive and near-socialist groups, such as the Non-Partisan Leagues of North Dakota and Oklahoma, Upton Sinclair's EPIC (End Poverty in California) movement, and the Cooperative Commonwealth Federations in Oregon and Washington.

It is argued that the socialists did not understand that American parties differ fundamentally from those of Europe, that basically they are not parties, but mechanisms for selecting candidates for the final contest. By participating in the electoral coalition system as one of the factions, the socialists could have mobilized their maximum strength, and have cooperated with unionists in groups such as the Labor Representation Committees which were established by the AFL before World War I to elect prolabor people to Congress.

Critics note that the ultimate isolation of the Socialist Party from the mainstream of labor, progressive, and prosocialist sentiment occurred during the worst economic depression in the 1930s. Norman Thomas' explanation for this failure of socialism to grow at a time when socialist predictions about capitalism were seemingly validated was "Roosevelt in a word."[233] The word subsumed the fact that the Democratic-New Deal administration had enacted much of the "immediate demands" advocated by the socialists in the welfare and economic planning areas and had supported trade-union organization. As a result, it incorporated into its coalition almost all of the labor movement, including many labor leaders who had belonged to the Socialist Party, and many others who had been active socialists or communists. By insisting on running candidates against Roosevelt and other liberal Democratic candidates, in the 1930s and 40s, the Socialist Party lost almost all the support and membership it had gained in the early years of the Depression. Will Herberg notes:

> The New Deal had brought vast ideological confusion in socialist ranks. Almost overnight, socialists, who had been proclaiming for years that any government under capitalism must be a capitalist government fundamentally inimical to the workers and that nothing good could be hoped for from the old capitalist parties, became enthusiastic supporters of the Roosevelt regime, many—yes, many "militant" socialists—even accepted appointive office under it in some of the New Deal agencies that were springing up in Washington. No more shattering blow to socialist morale—based as it was on the *mystique* of intransigent class struggle—could be imagined. It left socialist principles in a state of utter chaos.[234]

The communists, from the mid-thirties on, under orders from Moscow to cooperate with all left-of-center elements to build an antifascist Popular Front, joined the New Deal coalition, a fact which enabled their trade union leaders and followers to back Roosevelt and the now prolabor Democratic Party, while remaining communists. Socialist unionists, by contrast, were faced with the choice of opposing the New Deal or leaving the Socialist Party. Earl Browder, the leader of the Communist Party at the time, points out that the socialists refused to learn that they could participate as a organized group in the Democratic coalition, that they refused to learn any lesson "from the spectacular capture of the [California] Democratic party primary [in 1934] by [former Socialist Party leader] Upton Sinclair's EPIC Movement."

> The Communist party, on the other hand, rapidly moved out of its extreme leftist sectarianism of 1930 toward the broadest united front tactics of reformism for strictly limited immediate aims. It relegated its revolutionary socialist goals to the ritual of chapel and Sundays on the pattern long followed by the Christian Church. On weekdays it became the most single-minded practical

reformist party that America ever produced. Thus the Socialist party, despite its initial advantages over the Communists, lost ground steadily to them. By the middle of the thirties the positions of the two parties were reversed, the Communists had the upper hand in all circles that considered themselves left of the New Deal.[235]

The considerable strength the communists built up within the labor movement and the Democratic Party was, of course, destroyed by their need to follow the changes in the international communist line dictated by the Russians. Thus in 1939, the Stalin-Hitler pact isolated the party from much of the support and membership it had won from 1935 on. Again, in 1948, renewed hard line tactics dictated by the emerging "cold war," broke the party's links to the Democrats and forced many communist union leaders to choose between their union posts and their party membership.

The socialists have also been criticized for not adapting to the American political games in other ways. Bell notes the "rigidity of rules imposed on Socialist office-holders, which proved quite irksome for many." Elected officials were attacked for making compromises and concession. "As a result, many who wanted to 'get things done' soon left the party."[236] Shannon emphasizes that "most Socialists never saw the value of political organization: they regarded the building of local machines as 'ward heeling,' sordid truckling for votes beneath the ideals of Socialism." Although the socialists had a number of local electoral successes, on the whole they ignored local and regional issues, focusing on "national and international matters. This lack of interest in local matters was a disregard of one of the basic features of American politics."[237]

Those who reject the view that the socialists contributed to their own failure by sectarian policies argue that the American party, particularly in its heyday before America's entry into World War I, was not that different from the European parties, that it was in fact a heterogeneous coalition party with left, center, and right factions. There can be no doubt that the party was divided, but it is also true that its right and center were considerably to the left of comparable factions in Europe and Britain. As noted earlier, Jean Longuet in 1906 placed the American party ideologically in the same category as the Russian party, both considerably to the left of European parties. John Spargo, who had been active on the left of the British socialist movement, and "was consequently regarded as one of the intransigents, after emigrating to America took his place among the moderates of the Socialist Party without *any noticeable change in his views*."[238] The rigidly Marxist British Social Democratic Federation (S.D.F.), led by Henry Hyndman, denounced by Engels for arch sectarianism, regarded itself "as the British counterpart of the Socialist Party of America." The leaders of the more moderate Independent Labour Party (I.L.P.) were annoyed by the tendency of American socialists to identify with the S.D.F. "British socialists in the Labour party . . . felt a kinship with very few of the American socialist leaders. From their point of view, the insistence by the latter on strict socialist independence thwarted in advance the attempts to win over American labor."[239]

Laurence Moore points out that leaders of the right wing of the American party, such as Victor Berger and Robert Hunter, rejected the "revisionist" views of Eduard Bernstein. Berger, attacked by his left critics as the "American Bernstein," remained "much closer to [the Marxists] Bebel and Kautsky than to any of the German revisionists." British socialists considered moderate to right American leader Morris Hillquit "foolishly sectarian." In general, European socialist visitors to America before World War I "were impressed and quickly conceded the radical cast of the American Socialist party."[240]

The basic cast of the American Socialist Party can be seen in the personalities of the two men, Eugene Debs and Norman Thomas, who led the party for almost the entire period of its history. The two were, of course, different in origin and style. Debs was a worker and former union leader; Thomas was a graduate of Princeton, an ordained minister and the author of many books. Yet each was a dogmatic moralist. Debs always sought to stand on the left of the party, to describe himself as a revolutionary, to oppose reforms. Although party leader and presidential candidate for many years, he was a lonely prophetic figure who remained outside of all party factions and cliques. James Weinstein notes that Debs' approach was close to that of the moralistic *Christian Socialist* group which saw socialism as an extension of Protestant moralism. "Although an atheist, Debs' moral tone was close to that of these Protestants."[241] Daniel Bell describes Debs in similar terms:

> It was perhaps because in a final sense he was the true protestant. Debs stood at the end of the long road of the reformation. He had an almost mystical—at times omniscient—faith in the dictates of his inner self. Like the Anabaptists of old, all issues were resolved by private conscience. From the priesthood of all believers he had become the solitary individual, carrying on his shoulders the burdens of humanity. That sense of loneliness—and grandeur—touched others who were equally afflicted with the terrible sense of isolation. By his standing alone, he emphasized the individual and his rights.[242]

Norman Thomas had even closer ties to Protestant moralism than Debs, coming from an orthodox Calvinist home, with a father and grandfather who were Presbyterian ministers. Although he left the ministry after becoming an active socialist, Thomas continued throughout his life to emphasize being morally right rather than seeking to be politically effective. Bell described him well: "As a man whose instincts are primarily ethical, Thomas had been the genuine moral man in the immoral society."[243]

Ira Kipnis, who blamed the failure of American socialism on its opportunism, ended his history of *The American Socialist Movement* in 1912, a year in which the socialists received the highest percentage of the presidential vote they were to ever achieve, and in which the national convention amended the Socialist Party's constitution to provide for the expulsion of anyone "who opposes political action or advocates crime against the person or other methods of violence."[244] This motion, of course, was directed against members and supporters of the anarcho-syndicalist IWW. In January 1913, William Haywood, who was both a leader of the IWW and a left-wing member of the National Executive Committee of the Socialist Party, was recalled from the Committee by a referendum vote of 22,000 to 11,000.[245] As Kipnis interprets the party's history, these events led to "the disaffection of left-wing members," and a precipitous decline in party membership and electoral support which mean the effective end of the party as a political force.[246]

Laurence Moore points out that by voting this resolution and expelling Haywood, the party was only reinforcing the repeated efforts of Marxists to draw a line "between themselves and anarchists." But he goes on to note that these actions were another example of the insistence on principle and lack of political expediency of American socialists. Most European socialist parties were able to house much more widely divergent reformist and revolutionary views than the American party did. "American socialists, had they been less stubborn, might well have profited from the example."[247]

James Weinstein, in his history of the Socialist Party from 1912-25, counters Kipnis, pointing to the continued vitality of the party through World War I, as reflected in its membership of over 100,000 in 1919 and its large vote in elections in 1917 and 1918. Weinstein ascribes the subsequent decline of the party to the splits induced by the formation of the Communist International, and the insistence by the Russians that a communist party be formed in the United States, even though the bulk of the leaders and members of the Socialist Party strongly supported the Russian Revolution.[248]

Finally, it may be noted that two scholars, Martin Diamond and Frank Warren, who agree that the tactical errors of the Socialist Party were irrelevant to a consideration of its failure, since no strategy would have worked, disagree sharply as to the validity of the socialist approach to American politics and society. Diamond concludes that "it is clear that no change in strategy would have altered the bankruptcy of historic socialism," that neither a right-wing opportunistic policy or a revolutionary one could have worked.

> Whatever the specific issue or circumstances, the fundamental left-wing case was always this: you right-wingers (usually in the leadership) are diluting and betraying socialism with your "opportunism" and your compromises. The right-wing case always was: you left-wingers are insane fanatics, "impossibilists," you alienate the masses and keep socialism from gaining power. The tragedy of socialism is that both arguments were right. Right-wing successes did not advance *socialism;* left-wing policies *were* incapable of bringing socialism to pass (one good proof being that the left-wingers but rarely could even win the party over, let alone the masses). Cleverness of strategy was purchaseable only at cost to the essential nature of socialism, intransigent purity only at cost to effectiveness.[249]

Frank Warren, on the other hand, defends the policies of Norman Thomas and the Socialist Party in the 1930s as correct, even though the party declined greatly in membership, votes, and influence during this period. His basic arguments are first that the Socialist Party's criticisms of the ultimate consequences of Roosevelt and the New Deal were right, that capitalism, inequality, and class-rule were strengthened, and second, that those former socialists and communists who joined the Democratic Party and the Roosevelt administration were absorbed into status quo politics.

Without going further into the issue of strategy and tactics, it would appear evident that the American socialist movement has been more sectarian, more intransigent than those of other developed countries. But reaching such a conclusion, as most historians of the movement have done, begs the question why sectarianism has been more prevalent in the United States than elsewhere. Is it simply an outgrowth of specific events, is it chance that two such men as Eugene Debs and Norman Thomas led the Socialist Party?

It is possible to give a negative answer to this question. As has been implied earlier in this paper, the Protestant character of American society, whose political consequences were first noted by Burke over two centuries ago, has fostered a variety of moralistic responses. The propensity to pietistic moralism, however, has been countered in major party politics by the need to compromise in order to form one of two electorally viable coalitions. Thus both the Democratic and Republican parties restrain moralistic tendencies and present a relatively nonideological face. But social movements, including third parties, have been relatively unrestrained in giving vent to moralistic sectarian impulses. The very strength of voluntaristic denominational religion which so impressed Tocqueville and Marx has made for secular as well as religious sectarianism. The Socialist Party, as well as other movements, has reflected this aspect of the American social system. It has been more sectarian, has chosen more chiliastic leaders than socialist parties in other industrialized nations, and in so doing has reduced its chances of becoming a mass party. Thus it may be argued that the tactical errors of the American Socialist Party constitute another example of American exceptionalism, of a unique response flowing from the nation's special circumstances.

Concluding Remarks

After this long look at the different efforts to account for the failure of socialism in America, it may come as a shock to the reader to find that a number of writers, including this author, have suggested that America is not so different, that social democratic movements resembling in content and function, if not in exterior form, the social democratic parties of Europe have existed in the United States.

Historian George Mowry suggests that the problem of "why no socialism" during the period of industrial growth is a semantic one, that between 1902 and 1918, "the progressive years, most parties advocating widespread social reforms, including proposals for government ownership and operation of various enterprises, have been described as 'progressive'" when in fact they were "social democratic." He argues that "if one looks at the record instead of the rhetoric, one finds, surprisingly, an almost simultaneous development of social democracy in the United States and Europe despite the differences in material conditions, relations between the social classes, and political traditions."[250]

Mowry points to the enactment of an extensive set of reforms on the municipal, state and national levels, which extended popular electoral power, restricted the freedom of business, protected labor, increased support for higher education, provided for progressive income taxation on individuals and corporations, conserved natural resources, and extended the rights of labor unions. As he sees it, Progressivism was the American functional equivalent to the rise of powerful Social Democratic and Labor parties in Europe and should be understood in comparative terms. But obviously it also differed from the European movements, particularly in its emphasis on "attaining basic economic security for all, whether on the land or in the factory, and at the same time preserving a large element of individual freedom to compete, and thus to maintain the traditional element of mobility in society."

> In summary, while the major factors stemming from advanced industrialization and urbanization produced demands for social democracy in the United States at about the same time they did in Europe, many idosyncratic factors in American society gave it a somewhat different character from its European counterparts. Because of its roots in both the farm and the city, American social democracy was far less labor oriented than most such movements. Because of its ponderable support from the middle class, it was also far less motivated by ideology from the traditional European left.[251]

In analyzing more recent events, Michael Harrington, David Shannon, J. David Greenstone, and I have suggested the welfare-state-planning prolabor politics fostered by the New Deal Democratic Party since the 1930s constitute an American political equivalent to the mass social democratic and labor parties of the British Commonwealth and northern Europe. As Shannon puts it:

The British and Scandinavian political arms of labor pay homage to socialism in the abstract, but they in fact have put their main emphasis on welfare state features such as unemployment insurance, old-age pensions, and national health plans. American labor, with only a few exceptions, has failed to pay homage to socialism in the abstract, but it has in fact put a major political emphasis on gaining welfare state objectives. One can even make too much of the absence of an American labor party such as Great Britain's. . . . In the heavily industrialized states, particularly those with basic industries that the CIO unions organized in the 1930's and 1940's, such as Michigan, the Democratic party's strongest element is organized labor.[252]

Another historian of labor, J. David Greenstone, has also emphasized the comparabilities, noting that "in their support of the Democrats as a mass, pro-welfare state party, American trade unions have forged a political coalition with important—although hardly complete—structural and behavioral similarities to the Socialist Party-trade union alliances of western Europe."[253]

Michael Harrington has described social democracy as America's "invisible mass movement."

There is in the United States today a class political movement of workers which seeks to democratize many of the specific economic powers of capital but does not denounce capitalism itself. . . . And its impact upon the society is roughly analogous to that of the social democratic parties of Europe.[254]

He argues that by identifying social democracy with the Socialist Party, observers have failed to notice that "the movement in this country followed the English, not the German pattern."[255] The turning point in the emergence of this movement was the alliance of the New Deal with labor, which in Richard Hofstadter's words, "gave the New Deal a social democratic tinge that had never been present in American reform movements."[256] Since the 1930s this alliance between labor and the Democrats has grown, the Democratic Party has become a firm supporter of state intervention and planning in economic affairs, and the AFL-CIO officially calls for government policies which resemble those advocated by the Socialist Party which the AFL rejected at the turn of the century. Labor through its political action committees has "created a social democratic party, with its own apparatus and program, within the Democratic Party." George Meany, the president of the Federation, has on a number of occasions accepted the description of the AFL's political program as "socialist."[257]

Harrington is careful to distinguish between social democracy, perceived as an independent, class-based political movement with a ranging program for the democratization of the economy and the society, and socialism, involving the total overthrow of private capitalism. As he sees it, a powerful social democracy now exists in America comparable to those in other industrialized countries, but not a socialist party.

I have made a somewhat similar argument to those of Shannon, Greenstone, and Harrington, adding the point that since the 1940s, not only have the American labor movement and the Democratic Party behaved more like unions and social democratic parties in northern Europe and Australia, but that the latter have increasingly acted like the American organizations, placing more emphasis on serving the popular interest and being multiclass parties seeking to extend the welfare state than on representing working-class interests and securing socialism. They have come increasingly to resemble each other in policy terms. The Democrats have "become committed to the welfare state and trade unions, whereas conversely, the European social democratic parties have moved in the direction of becoming Democratic-type parties."[258]

These conclusions do not satisfy many contemporary new or old American leftists who argue that the Social Democrats or Labourites are not really socialists, in terms of a conception of socialism which involves eliminating private ownership. But by such "criteria it can be argued that there is no truly socialist movement of any significance in any advanced industrial country. That is to say, if it is true that the policies of the American Democratic Party are similar to those of the Swedish, British, or German Labour or Social Democratic parties, and one says that these parties are not socialist, then there is no mass socialist party in any advanced industrial country, unless the communists are counted as 'real' socialists and the Latin countries of Europe are considered as fully industrialized. But leaving these issues aside, the question becomes not 'why no socialism in the United States and yet socialism in Europe?' but 'why has the form of labor representation taken on an explicitly class form in northern Europe, and a populist multi-class one in the United States?' "[259]

Sombart implied over seven decades ago that the Marxian maxim that the most industrialized nation shows to the less developed ones the image of their own future suggested that there would be less revolutionary socialism in the future of Europe, rather than more, and the European industrial systems became, in Gramsci's terms, more Americanized, less feudal and traditional. This anticipation that European societies would become more American in their cultural and political superstructure may turn out to have been a valid insight. From a very different contemporary, neo-Marxist perspective, Herbert Marcuse also has noted the decline of revolutionary, class-conscious, working-class-based movements in all advanced industrial societies flowing from relative abundance and the ability of the welfare state to avoid major depressions through planning.[260]

It is significant to note that the greatest similarities in the approach of left parties are among the English-speaking ones, whose antitheoretical (read anti-Marxist) proclivities so troubled Marx and Engels. Mass trade-union-based Labour parties, frequently in control of government, exist in Australia, Britain, and New Zealand. In Canada, since the early 1930s, the social democratic New Democratic Party (formerly the Cooperative Commonwealth Federation) backed by the labor movement has secured between 10 and 20 percent of the national vote, has been the third party in Parliament, generally with less than 10 percent of the seats, and has on occasion captured the government of three western provinces. Yet Marxism has always been weak in each of these parties. They have always been social democratic, rather than socialist, parties in Harrington's sense, and programmatically resemble the liberal and labor wings of the Democratic Party.

Why, Then, No Socialism in the United States?

One thing is clear, the United States remains unique in not having socialist representation in its legislative bodies. Why is this so? It should be obvious by now that no one can give a simple response to this question. But the very fact that it still must be asked close to a century after Marx's death indicates that American exceptionalism still lives.

Reading through the many efforts to answer Sombart's question points to the many ways in which America is different. The various explanations fall into two main categories: attributes of American society—sociological, economic, and political—and factors internal to the various radical movements. To a considerable degree, almost all point to conditions which are unique, separately or together, to the United States, and which serve to weaken class consciousness and socialist politics.

America has been a new nation, a new society, a frontier society. It lacks a feudal, well-stratified past; it emphasizes equality in social relations; it defines itself in liberal, egalitarian, antistatist ideological terms; it stresses individualism in its secular and religious traditions; and it is the only country where the majority of the inhabitants adhere to the Protestant sects. It has been formed out of diverse ethnic and racial immigrant stocks, emphasizes equality of opportunity and the pursuit of success as supreme values, and presses people, organizations, and parties to win by any means.

America is the most productive, technologically developed society in the world. It has steadily expanded economically and geographically. This has permitted economic goods, including education, housing, and many others to be more widely distributed throughout the population than elsewhere. Technological growth has shifted its class structure upward, that is, fewer unskilled positions, more requiring training and education, and therefore more upward mobility. Economic growth has encouraged people to move geographically as well.

The unique presidential system has produced a need for two broad electoral coalitions undercutting all efforts to build and institutionalize third parties. Early manhood suffrage eliminated the struggle for the ballot as a stimulant for class organization by the less privileged. Democratic innovations, such as the primary system and initiative and referendum, have further weakened the possibilities for creating mass "third parties." The responsiveness of the electoral coalitions to protest has repeatedly led to the decline, or cooptation, of social movements expressing the concerns of "out" groups. This process has occurred with leftist movements from the Workingmen's Party of the 1820s through the New Left of the 1960s. Orestes Brownson walked down a road to the Democratic Party which became well worn during the following century and a half. The most recent travelers have included Sam Brown, Michael Harrington, and Tom Hayden.

Even when looking at the history of American radicalism in a comparative context, it is impossible to determine which of the many factors has been most important, how much each explains, even whether some of them are valid to any extent. It should be clear that the complex characteristics of a total system, such as this essay deals with, are multivariate in causation. By asking "why no socialism in the United States?", all those who have tried to answer the question from Marx to the present day have been forced to think in comparative terms, to suggest possible ways in which the United States differs from other countries. As we have seen, the variations in the answers linked to different ideological orientations have been relatively minimal, even though some contemporary radical scholars have tried to emphasize the distance which separates their particular explanation from others. Ironically, many of the hypotheses which they reject as exaggerating American virtues were presented earlier by Marx, Engels, Lenin, Gramsci, and other radical theorists.

In recent times, a new dimension has been added to the discussion, because a significant social democratic party, the New Democrats (formerly the Cooperative Commonwealth Federation), has become a major third party in English-speaking Canada. Before the formation of this party in 1933, Canadian politics also lacked an electorally viable socialist movement. One may now ask why Canada and the United States are different. Answers may be provided on a number of levels: differences in historical origins and consequent social structures, variations in governmental systems which affected electoral systems and opportunities for third parties, and finally, the different responses to the depression of the 1930s.

Many efforts to account for variations in the political life of the two North American democracies have assumed that Canada has been a much more conservative, traditional, and hierarchically elitist society than the United States. This phenomenon presumably stems from the fact that Canada's existence as a nation is an outgrowth of the defeat of the American Revolution in the north, while the United States is the result of the triumph of the Revolution in the thirteen more southern colonies. The United States took pride in being born of a revolution, and emphasized egalitarian and populist elements in its self-image. Canada, however, had to legitimate itself and take pride in the fact that it was not like the populist United States; its English-speaking leaders, including the intellectuals, long emphasized the value of its ties with Britain, its monarchical institutions, its elitist character. Following the American Revolution, Tories migrated north of the new border, supporters of the revolution moved south. The established Anglican church was strengthened in the north; the "nonconformist" sects were reinforced by the migrations south.[261]

These differences tended to inform later events in both countries. American political parties following the rise of

Jacksonian democracy emphasized their role as popular parties. Both major American parties stressed their links to the Jeffersonian Democratic-Republicans and were anti-statist. Canada was formed as a continental nation in 1867 under Conservative leadership. Unlike the United States, it has had a Conservative as well as a Liberal Party. Canadian conservatism resembled British conservatism in supporting a strong state which assumed the responsibility for national needs, partly to maintain nationally needed, governmentally funded institutions which private enterprise was able to provide in the more populous United States. Thus Canadians, both on the left and the right, have had much more respect for central state authority and a greater willingness to call on the government for assistance than have Americans. The very strength of hierarchical status, traditional religion, and governmental authority in Canada has meant that in a variety of ways, which I have documented elsewhere, Canadian values and practices fall somewhere between those of Britain and the United States.[262]

The presidential electoral system of the United States undercuts third parties, while the single-member parliamentary district system of Canada permits third parties to develop constituency strength. These variations in electoral systems mean that the northernmost nation has had a much greater propensity for significant third parties than its southern neighbor, particularly since 1921. The absence of the primary system of nominations in Canada, and the need for the governing party's members in Parliament to always vote for the government's measures, has encouraged Canadian factions to form new third parties more often than in the United States.

Canada also has differed from the United States economically. As a smaller market traditionally less developed, its average income level, while generally higher than in European countries, has been until recently considerably less than that in the United States. Canadians, below the level of the upper classes, have lived less well than Americans. Fewer of them have graduated from high school or gone on to higher education.

All of these factors differentiated the two North American

nations before 1930, but Canada, like the United States, lacked a significant socialist party. Seemingly the factors they had in common were more significant than those which divided them with respect to the potential for socialist politics. During the 1930s, however, Canadian socialists were able to form an electorally viable party, the Cooperative Commonwealth Federation (CCF); labor unions have moved increasingly to working with the socialists. If, as Norman Thomas put it, the answer to the decline of the American Socialist Party in the 1930s was "Roosevelt in a word," it was the absence of a comparably charismatic reform leader in Canada which permitted Canadian socialists to grow during the Depression. Mackenzie King, the leader of Canada's Liberal Party, though in many ways the nation's most successful politician, did not respond to the depression with anything resembling the extensive welfare-state-planning pro-trade-union program identified with Roosevelt and the New Deal.

Looking at the differences between Canada and the United States helps to clarify some of the issues discussed in this essay, but the fact remains that organized social democratic politics in Canada are much weaker than in the British or continental European nations. The New Democratic Party is still a "third party" with no immediate prospects for improving its status. It received 16 percent of the vote in 1974, the same percentage it obtained in 1945. Some of the North American factors which have inhibited socialism in the United States apparently are also operative in Canada.

If we accept the view presented earlier by Harrington, Greenstone, and others that a social democratic force now exists in the United States, based largely on the labor unions (and, one may add, the emerging intelligentsia), and that this force operates within the Democratic Party, then it may be that the political situations in the two North American democracies are highly comparable. The issue of "why no socialism in America" remains with us, since social democracy in the advanced industrial societies of North America is still much weaker than leftist movements elsewhere in the developed world. The factors which have created the problem of American exceptionalism are still operative.

Stanley Rothman, professor of government at Smith College, author of European Society and Politics, *and coauthor of* Through Different Eyes, *has since 1970 turned his attention to the relatively new field of political psychology. Among the several articles he has published on this subject are "Sigmund Freud and the Politics of Marginality" and "Freud and Jewish Marginality." Professor Rothman's most recent study in this area,* The Radical Impulse in Europe and America, *will be published in 1977 by Oxford University Press.*

Anne H. Bedlington is an assistant professor in the Department of Government at Smith College.

Phillip Isenberg, M.D., is director of resident education at McLean Hospital in Belmont, Massachusetts, and is an assistant professor of psychiatry at Harvard University. Dr. Isenberg is also a practicing psychoanalyst.

Robert Schnitzer, Ph.D., is director of training in clinical psychology at McLean Hospital in Belmont, Massachusetts, and principal associate in psychology at Harvard University.

3

Ethnic Variations in Student
Radicalism: Some New Perspectives
Stanley Rothman et al.

On Student Radicalism in America

It seems only a very short time ago that a good many social scientists were arguing forcefully that a new liberated
generation had emerged in the United States.[1] At the time it
was predicted with some confidence that the student movement (the liberated generation) would most certainly produce profound changes in American life (even if it did not
usher in the "greening of America") and would continue to
grow. However, within two or three years the movement had
withered and died, leaving only small remnants behind.

To be sure, the events of the 1960s have had an important
impact on American life, for good or evil, depending on one's
views, and many of those who were active in the student
movement have continued their commitment, even where
they have come to accept middle class life styles.[2] It does
seem strange, however, that most of the factors which so
many authors saw as assuring that the movement would
continue to expand (for example, new "democratic and
warm" patterns of child rearing, and the "alienation" produced by American society), have not in fact had their

predicted effect.[3] College students today—including students at elite colleges—are less committed to traditional American values, and less supportive of the institutions of their society than they were in the 1950s, but they seem singularly unlike Lifton's "protean" type.[4] It does begin to look as if the factors which sparked the student revolt had more to do with the concrete issues of the period (civil rights and the war in Vietnam) than with any major personality changes in America's youth, although, obviously, changes in our social and cultural life also played a role.

If students in the movement, then, were not a new breed psychologically, what were these young people actually like? The picture which emerges from most of the studies completed in the 1960s is that these students represented to a considerable extent the best in America. They were "humanitarian"; "autonomous"; "nonauthoritarian"; "impulsively warm"; in contact with their "inner selves"; "intellectually alive and interested"; and "nondogmatic." Most of those who studied the students related these qualities to the warmth and intimacy which characterized their family life.[5] Kenneth Keniston and others also found them to be, for the most part, extremely "authentic" and "open"; unwilling to accept the "hypocrisies" of the society around them. They were, in Keniston's view and those of others, not rebels for the sake of rebellion, but individuals with a sincere concern for and identification with the weak and oppressed (blacks and Vietnamese), and a longing for a society that was more participatory and which would restore a sense of community.[6]

To be sure, these views were not shared by the mass of the citizenry who, by and large, tended to view student radicals as spoiled brats at best, or criminals or anarchists at worst. There were also those in the academic profession who were not persuaded by this analysis. Lewis Feuer saw many of the students as engaging in a self-destructive generational rebellion; Lawrence Kerpelman found little difference between radical and nonradical activists in major personality attributes; O. Glantz found radicals to be more punitive than nonradicals, and still other investigators have found them to be more paranoid and to have a lower concept of self than non-radicals.[7] The studies arguing that radical activists do not differ from other activists or that some of the attributes of radical students were less than totally exemplary have, however, been relatively few in number.[8]

If one carefully examines the studies which make these claims, one is impressed by a number of important weaknesses in their design and execution as well as by the questions left unanswered. For example, Keniston's *Young Radicals*, easily the most widely read study, relied on an extremely small sample, fourteen in all. More importantly, his interpretation is based on his own evaluations of interviews of a group with whose ends (and means) he clearly sympathized. There is no possibility of intersubjective checking or validation. Thus, Joseph Adelson, commenting on the work of Keniston and others, argues that many of those scholars have, because of their sympathies, idealized the young and ignored their "warts." His own perceptions of radical students, he noted, were far less favorable.[9]

Theoretically, studies containing larger, more randomly selected samples of students, and using objective measures, would be rather more free of the possibility of bias. In far too many cases, however, the instruments used are so designed that radical students, by definition, are characterized by personality traits or values which the authors of the studies, usually quite sympathetic to them, regard as good. Thus, in a study by Henry Finney, support for trade unions is included in a scale "measuring" support for civil liberties, insuring a relatively high score for radical students. Indeed, even when asking standard civil liberties type questions, Finney inquires primarily about attitudes toward left-wing groups.[10] Few, if any, questions attempt to determine whether respondents are as concerned with the rights of, say, racists as they are with those of communists or homosexuals. Finney is not alone in this. Most social scientists, even the most sophisticated, (for example, Samuel Stouffer) have tended to equate support for the civil liberties of leftist or deviant groups with support for civil liberties in general.[11]

Nor is such bias confined to purely political categories. All too many studies ask what are essentially questions of political ideology and then proceed to ascribe psychological characteristics to respondents on the basis of such questions. The famous "F" scale of authoritarianism is the most notable case, but despite the widespread criticism it has received from numerous scholars, variations of the type continue to be widely used.[12] Thus when relatively conservative respondents indicate that they would respond rather punitively to actions by Communist nations which are seen as hostile to the United States, they are described as "more aggressive" than liberal or radical respondents. Again such studies rarely raise the same questions with respect to racist or Fascist states or tap the willingness of the respondents to support revolutionary violence on the part of "oppressed" groups.[13] When they do, they often simply explain away some of their findings.[14]

Nor are the difficulties involved in obtaining unbiased measures of either certain political attitudes or personality attributes easily overcome. In the case of political attitudes even unbiased instruments may not tell us very much. Radical students checking off answers which indicate support for the civil liberties of "reactionary" groups may simply, as Lipset and Schaflander point out, be responding in terms of political response set which have little relation to their actual conduct.[15] Thus, at Harvard in 1971, those students who prevented a proadministration Vietnam policy teach-in from being conducted insisted that they believed in free speech, but argued that the whole thing was a "Nixon plot" and, thus, did not come under free speech guarantees (personal observation), or that free speech included the right to shout other people down.[16]

The same problem is faced by those who wish to measure personality variables, and thus a similar criticism can be leveled at the work of Block, Haan and Smith, and Troll and Neugarten, among others.[17] The instruments used by these authors often ask students to describe themselves along certain dimensions, or to describe the manner in which their parents raised them. If the students view themselves as

"tolerant of ambiguity," "creative," "open," and "percep-
tive," such qualities are regarded as representing, at least to
an extent, what the students are. When students (or their
parents) are asked to describe child rearing practices (usually
in full sentences), it is assumed that these are related in some
way to what actually happened. As Keniston points out,
however, most of these students and their parents are quite
"self-conscious" about their motives and life style.[18] They
know that they should be "tolerant of ambiguity," "warm
and open" with their children, and their responses may simply reflect this. Keniston believes that the "self-awareness" is
genuine, but, as most psychoanalysts who deal with intellectuals know, these self and parent descriptions are often merely rationalizations which serve a defensive function.

Aside from problems of questionnaire design, another issue
leads one to suspect that something was lacking in most of
the student studies completed during the 1960s. The evidence is fairly clear that, until 1966 or 1967 at least, students of Jewish background constituted anywhere from 50 to
70 percent of the New Left.[19] Initially, Jews at the key liberal
elite schools were, for all practical purposes, the New Left, as
Arthur Liebman[20] and Joseph Adelson (personal communication) point out. Indeed, the American Council of Education's
1966–1967 study revealed that the best single religio-ethnic
predictor of campus protest activity against the Vietnam war
or policies of the college administration in terms of input
characteristics was "present religion none, parents' religion
Jewish."[21] In our 1971 random sample of 344 Harvard students, 65 percent of the radical students were of Jewish
background in a student body which was about 29 percent
Jewish.

To be sure, many of these students of Jewish background
were "deracinated Jews" in that they no longer considered
themselves such. But, as we shall see, there is some reason to
believe that they have been influenced in fairly decisive ways
by their inheritance.

One may legitimately ask why this pattern of student involvement has so rarely been discussed. We suspect that many

scholars of Jewish background studying the students (and a very substantial portion of such scholars was Jewish) feared lest the reporting of such evidence be used by anti-Semites.[22] Still others undoubtedly thought and think of themselves as cosmopolitan intellectuals and thus refused to consider the ethnic component in its full implications.

Many of the Jewish radicals came from radical or at least liberal backgrounds. These were the students who, in studies by Flacks and Keniston, were carrying on the traditions of their parents, moving perhaps but one step further to the left.[23] On the other hand, as Sale and others have pointed out, and as we shall see later, most of the non-Jewish white students who became radicalized were often involved in a sharp battle with the *expressed* political values of their parents.[24] For many of these students, the move to radicalism involved breaking from their parents almost completely. Given this, one would expect that the motives which brought students of Jewish background into the movement would differ somewhat from those of non-Jews, as would their psychological makeup. The study we conducted deals largely with this question. To prepare the way for it, however, and for a better understanding of its purposes, a theoretical discussion is required.

A Theory of Jewish (and non-Jewish) Radicalism

Ever since their release from European ghettoes, Jewish intellectuals have served as a radical leaven in Europe and in countries settled by Europeans. Marx leveled a fundamental attack upon the basic values of European culture in the name of a universal ideology, as did Freud,[25] and Jews have played a very large role in radical socialist movements throughout Europe and Latin America. In the period before World War I, they had come to play a substantial enough role in the left of European socialist parties to lead Robert Michels to attempt an explanation of the phenomenon in his classic *Political Parties.*[26] They played key roles in the leadership cadres of the Russian Bolshevik party, although they did not join in really large numbers until after the Revolution.[27]

They also played central roles in the leadership of the communist parties of every East European country save Yugoslavia, Albania, and Bulgaria during the 1930s and in the immediate postwar period, where, as in the Soviet Union, they were heavily overrepresented in the secret police.[28] During the Weimar period they constituted a substantial proportion of the unattached left German intelligentsia, which so sharply attacked the Weimar Republic, and, in France, of those intellectuals who supported the French Communist Party. Further, they played key roles in the Austrian and Dutch left wing as well as in communist movements in Cuba and other Latin American countries.[29] In the United States, during the 1930s they constituted at least fifty percent of the membership of the Communist Party, as well as of the left-wing American Student Union.[30]

Since World War II, this participation has continued. In addition to their role in the student left in this country, Jewish students played a role far disproportionate to their size in the student movement in both France[31] and England. During the same period, Americans of Jewish background have been heavily represented among those in the intellectual community most sympathetic to what has been called the adversary culture. Lipset and Ladd have documented this for academics in general and Kadushin has for the general intellectual community. Halsey and Trow find the same pattern among academics in England.[32] A number of other writers have either hinted at the Jewish role or noted it explicitly.[33] Moynihan and Glazer, in fact, have gone so far as to call the emergence of the adversary culture a victory of the New York political and cultural style.[34] It should be stressed, of course, that radical Jews represent a relatively small proportion of the Jewish community, and that their role in radical movements tends to be salient only in the initial stages of such movements or while such movements remain relatively small in size. Further, the most radical tend to be, as indicated earlier, deracinated Jews who deny that their Jewishness plays any role in their political activities and even express a strong antipathy toward Jews and the Jewish religion.

The classic case, of course, is that of Marx, although one can find the same pattern in the life of Trotsky, Rosa Luxemburg, and other Jewish radicals including those most active in the so-called Frankfurt School of German Sociology.[35]

A number of attempts have been made to explain the prominent role of Jews in radical movements. Their extensive participation has been traced to the Jewish prophetic tradition and to humanistic, universalistic, and intellectual values in Judaism which lead to support for civil liberties.[36] It has also been ascribed to the marginality of Jews which gives them a clearer view of the evils of the society of which they are part, and enables them to perceive new universalistic alternatives to existing parochial attachments, and to the suffering of Jews which leads them to identify with the weak and the downtrodden.[37]

As Charles Liebman has pointed out, however, many of these explanations of Jewish radicalism are mythic.[38] Traditional Judaism was communal rather than universalistic and it was, at best, ambivalent regarding intellectuality. It contained important antiphilosophic elements and the pattern of Talmudic exigesis is not to be confused with the kind of rational system building of modern rationalistic radicals nor even of medieval Catholicism. Contemporary Jewish intellectuality is a postghetto phenomenon. Further, there is little evidence that the humane concerns of traditional Judaism were more pronounced than those of many other traditional religious creeds. Indeed, the more religiously conservative a Jew is today, the less likely he or she is to identify with universalistic ideologies or with the non-Jewish poor and downtrodden.

Jewish marginality within European society provides a much more plausible explanation of Jewish radicalism, though not necessarily for the reasons suggested above. After all, marginal status is as likely to narrow the vision of those in such a position as it is to broaden it. The oppressed see only the worst side of a culture or social system, and, indeed, it is rational for them to do so. Excessive suspicion as to the potential hostility of the dominant group and behavior based on that suspicion provide a greater margin of safety than an opposite perspective. Thus, marginal oppressed groups are as likely to exaggerate the negative features of a society as those who are comfortable with it are likely to exaggerate its good points.

Charles Liebman's treatment of the impact of marginality seems both more reasonable and less self-serving. He suggests that Jewish attachment to universalistic ideas of a radical or liberal nature which seek to undermine existing cultural norms is basically a mechanism for ending marginality by subverting the cultural categories which have defined Jews as marginal.[39]

Liebman's argument can be generalized. Groups can attempt to end their marginality (should they so desire) in one of three possible ways: they can assimilate to the culture which has defined them as marginal; they can attach themselves to a more universalistic ideology or movement which subverts the cultural categories which so define them; or they can, finally, develop an ideology or institutions which enable them to transform themselves into some kind of majority.[40]

For Jews the first path has involved conversion, or at least Reform Judaism. Radical secular rationalism, of which Marxism is the prime example, is a second path, although during the 1960s, the New Left's attack on rationality served a similar function. Finally, Zionism is prototypical of the third path. Of course many Zionists have attempted to combine elements of the second and third paths by uniting a universalistic creed (socialism) with their nationalism.

Given the peculiar relationship of Judaism to Christianity, one way of safely undermining the latter has been to attack the former. Thus, for deracinated Jews, attacks upon Judaism as a religion or upon bourgeois Jewish values may serve the double function of denying their own Jewishness and of undermining the religious categories of the dominant groups in the society.

Nor are Jews alone in facing these options. As Robert Haddad has pointed out, the role played by Syrian Christians in secular nationalistic movements in the Middle East can be explained in the same terms.[41] The replacement of Islamic consciousness by secular Arab states would, it was thought, eliminate the distinction between Muslim and Christian Arabs, and hence end the subordination of the latter, because all would become predominantly Syrians or Iraqis, etc.[42] Himmelstrand analyzes the reaction of the Ibo in Nigeria in much the same way.[43] In terms of their economic and social position, Nigerian nationalism had much more to offer the Ibos than tribalism, and they were its major proponents until a backlash forced them to an abortive attempt at an Ibo nationalist solution. And the analysis can also be applied to American blacks. In this case "passing" and conformity to middle-class white norms represent attempts at assimilation; radical Marxist movements, during the 1930s, and again today, the universalist solution; and various nationalist groups which emerged during the 1920s and the 1960s were, for blacks, the functional equivalent of Zionism. The key point is that for all of these groups, the basic attack of those choosing the universalist alternative (no matter how the attack is rationalized) is upon the institutions of the society which, in their eyes, define them as marginal.

The attitudes of the marginal man toward the dominant culture inevitably involve an admixture of love and hate. Often his supposed identification with the underdogs of the society is based less on identification with their suffering, than upon a desire to use these groups as a means for undermining the establishment. The difference between the liberal and the radical in this case is primarily one of degree. Philip Roth makes the point quite sharply in *Portnoy's Complaint*. Portnoy, of course, is only a quasi radical but, whatever he would like to think his real motives are, his tirade to the analyst makes it quite clear that his love for suffering humanity is far less important than his envy and hatred of WASPs and his desire to literally "screw" the "goyim," despite the fact that he despises his parents for their "anti-goyish" attitudes. The situation, however, is not quite so simple, for Portnoy also wants to become one of those strong, blond "goyim" who own America and whose brothers are "the engaging, good-natured, confident, clean, swift and powerful halfbacks for the college football teams." His unconscious hope is that he can somehow become a goy by sleeping with the "shikses." (In addition, he has hopes that some of his emotional problems will be solved if he goes to Israel, although he fails here too.)[44]

Portnoy is a caricature, and yet one can find the same aggressive themes discussed (with a similar interpretation) in Theodore Reik's analysis of *Jewish Wit,* and in the writing of a number of Jewish radicals. Thus, Jerry Rubin ascribes his own radicalism to being Jewish, and finds that Cohn-Bendit shares the same feelings. Roger Kahn writing about the Columbia conflict keeps remembering how badly Jews are treated by the WASP establishment.[45]

In short, the aim of the Jewish radical is to estrange the Christian from society as he feels estranged from it. The fact that the United States is no longer Christian in any real sense, or that Jews have moved to positions of considerable power and influence, is of little import, for its Christian base is still seen, unconsciously for the most part, as the decisive oppressive element by many radicals of Jewish background. Nor should this come as a surprise. We know that socio-political stances adopted in the wake of traumatic experiences tend to be self-perpetuating. In France, the radicalism of the Midi can be traced back to the Albigensian Crusades, and the radicalism of certain Northern regions to Jansenism. Areas which voted left in 1848 were still voting left in the 1960s.[46] Thus, many radical Jews, even when they do not identify themselves as Jews, retain a generalized hostility to Christian culture.

While the evidence for the following hypothesis is largely indirect or clinical, it seems reasonable to assume that Jewish marginality has had consequences for Jewish personality of a type first outlined by Nietzche, and supported from a psychoanalytic perspective by Rudolf Lowenstein and Theodore Reik.[47] Surrounded by an enemy who was too strong to fight, Jewish males could only survive by controlling the urge to strike back at their tormentors. The Jewish family, then, began to place tremendous emphasis upon inhibiting the *direct* physical expression of aggression by male children. The standard stereotype of the emasculating Jewish mother may have its roots here. Despite their refusal to admit these things publicly, most Jews will acknowledge privately, as does Portnoy, and some of the students interviewed by the senior author, that Jewish boys do not engage in street fights, and that Jewish males are more timid physically than Christian males. Good studies of Jewish personality traits are few in number for a variety of reasons, not the least of which is, as Victor Sanua points out, that scholars have tended to avoid the subject.[48] However, there is some evidence to support these notions. Zborowski and Tursky and Sternbach found that Jewish subjects seemed to have lower pain thresholds than Protestants.[49] Argyle, Lowenstein, and Goldberg as well as others have noted the low rate of crimes of violence (although not of embezzlement) among Jews in both Europe and the United States.[50] Bieri, Lobeck and Plotnick have associated high rates of social mobility among some Jews with avoidance of occupations which call for direct aggressive behavior. These Jews seek professions in which the expression of aggression is more indirect (verbal).[51] Usually such professions require higher levels of educational attainment.

The low rate of alcoholism among Jews has frequently been noted. Most commentators, however, have avoided dealing seriously with Kant's suggestion that Jews do not drink to excess for fear of acting in unseemly ways in the context of a Christian community.[52] However, McClelland, Kalin, Wanner and Davis have demonstrated convincingly that both cultures and individuals characterized by strong power drives and *strong needs to inhibit these* drives are also characterized by low to moderate drinking patterns.[53] On the other hand, cultures and individuals with high power drives and low need to inhibit these drives were found to drink more heavily. Indeed Lowenstein explains the Jewish propensity for intellectuality in just these terms, i.e., the need to inhibit aggressive (power) drives.[54]

It is our argument, then, that the European diaspora and the ghetto experience encouraged among Jews the emergence of a particular family pattern; a pattern characterized by mothers who were protective and controlling, especially with their male children. It was not enough to teach such children to curb the *direct* expression of aggression against the Christian enemy, for under such circumstances control might be lost in a crisis situation. Rather aggression must be driven underground by appropriate child rearing practices.

The institutionalization of this pattern was to have profound effects upon both Jewish males and Jewish females, effects which have been already alluded to in part and are spelled out in some detail by Bibring and Wolfenstein.[55] The Jewish family became, in Bibring's terms, a kind of matriarchy in which the husband was perceived by the children as more fearful, less capable and weaker than the wife who cared for and somewhat dominated him in crucial areas, whatever his professional and/or business achievements.

In its benign form this family pattern and the mode of socialization associated with it could be highly adaptive for both male and female children in advanced industrial societies. Certain of its positive qualities, i.e., the substitution of intellectual mastery and verbal capacity for the direct expression of aggression, have already been alluded to, and will be further discussed below. Nevertheless the pattern can also lead to a particular sequence of developmental problems which, if not adequately managed, can prove maladaptive.

Both Bibring and Wolfenstein suggest that the oedipal phase and its resolution in such families will be quite different from such developments in the predominantly patriarchal families of the society.[56] Since the father is considered inadequate, castration fears may be lower among Jewish males. We are not asserting, in the discussion which follows, that the particular pattern of socialization described is more likely to result in pathology than (for example) patriarchal types. Each childrearing pattern produces its own kind of developmental crises. However, with the mother continually perceived as a seductive, devouring preoedipal figure (and the

father as a fellow sufferer), males raised in this family setting
may doubt their masculine potency. They may alternate
between pseudohomosexual panics, seeking to identify with
males who are "really" potent, and attempting to deny the
reality of sexual differences.[57] Thus the identification of
some Jewish males with the Russian proletariat during the
Soviet Revolution, with Irish and Italian workers during the
1930s and with the black "underclass" today have other
motives than mere sympathy with the underdog.

Slavin found that while favorable attitudes toward female
equality tended to vary inversely with scores on a scale of
"threatening female imagery" derived from responses to
TAT pictures, one group of respondents deviated from the
norm.[58] This group, which was 60 percent Jewish (Jews constituted 20 percent of the sample) scored extremely high on
"threatening female imagery," and "female equality" both. It
also scored relatively low on measures of "castration anxiety." There is some evidence, too, that in the family pattern
for middle-class Jewish schizophrenics an overprotective
mother is more common.[59] Fred Strotbeck's evidence indicates that women do play a more dominant role in Jewish
than in non-Jewish families. The salience of the Jewish mother has also been documented by Joseph Giordano.[60]

The modal personality pattern of diaspora Jews outlined
above closely resembles Jules Nydes' "paranoid masochistic
type."[61] The high level of defensive projection[62] characterizing such types stems ultimately from an inability to cope
with their own feelings of aggression and a desire to be pun-
ished for such feelings.

Theodore Reik feels that the paranoid-masochistic character is modal among Jews and he is partially supported by
Lowenstein.[63] Evidence for high levels of defensive projection among Jews is to be found in Greeley who, analyzing a
national study by Kohn, found that Jews scored lowest on a
"trust in people scale" of any ethnic group.[64] Whiting and
Child offer empirical support for the theoretical proposition
from the analysis of a large number of primitive cultures.
They find that, in general, paranoid suspicion varies directly

with the emphasis a given community places upon the repression of aggressive drives.[65]

In general, then, the extensive participation of Jews in liberal and radical movements in Christian societies is seen as a function of several interrelated variables, including marginality and family structure. The adoption of universalistic ideologies has been both ego-syntonic and adaptive. (By the 1960s, of course, such participation was being passed on from parents to children via normal socialization.) The adoption of more revolutionary stances which involve high levels of identification with mass lower-class movements, and commitment to revolutionary action, is fostered by a family structure which tends to produce a certain modal personality type. Where persons of this type have, in fact, dealt successfully with problems of maturity, the results can be high levels of intellectual (or artistic) productivity, and a strong commitment to universalistic egalitarian values. The aggressive (power) needs of such individuals are directed to ends which, in many cases, serve both themselves and the larger society.

When for some reason (an unusually weak father and/or an unusually protective and seductive mother for example) the maturation process has gone awry, the neurosis of choice will be that described by Nydes. Adolescence, especially, will be characterized by a partial desublimation of (power) aggressive drives, and a high degree of defensive projection. Intensive and recurring efforts will be made to find external sources of strength in powerful male figures. At the same time such individuals will become compulsively competitive as they attempt to demonstrate their masculinity to themselves. This competitiveness will be justified by fears of attack which such persons will continually seek to provoke. Many of them, especially during adolescence, will be caught in a bind from which there is no easy escape. Longing to merge with their mothers (to return to the lost Garden of Eden in Keniston's formulation)[66] they will fear the loss of ego boundaries and will, thus, at the same time, engage in a desperate flight from her.

In times of relative social stability the neurotic pattern may be highly personal. Where moderate outlets for radical activism are present, at least a portion of those characterized by such a modal personality will tend to justify aggressive behavior on grounds that they are warding off attacks from an evil, threatening "establishment." They will find it increasingly easy to identify with a (powerful) militant working class movement or with militant blacks (in the 1960s) because they will be able to convince themselves that they view this group as weak and oppressed. It is well to emphasize here, once again, that the sociological and psychological dimensions are of equal importance. The same personality type, with a different ethnic background and historical experience, might very well adopt a quite different political stance.

The United States, as numerous writers have pointed out, has been faced with a series of crises during the past 15 years which have seriously weakened the structure of authority in the society. In such crisis situations the external props which a society creates to help adolescents and adults achieve or maintain strong ego boundaries and effective sublimation are weakened, and both regression and acting out are encouraged. Indeed, for adolescents especially, so is narcissism, for the destruction of external authority weakens those forces pushing the adolescent to adult commitments and encourages the fantasy that such commitments can be postponed indefinitely. Attempts at narcissistic fulfillment can thus be justified as attacks upon an evil system. As Fred Weinstein and Gerald Platt have cogently argued, societal crises always encourage the reactivation of childhood conflicts.[67] The key issue here is that various groups involved in revolutionary situations are acting out, in part, different kinds of problems. In the 1960s, for example, the same slogans probably meant quite different things, on a psychodynamic level, to radicals of Jewish and Italian background. In any event many Jewish adolescents and adults chose the adversary culture and/or radical political activism during the 1960s. They were able to call upon the sympathies of a much larger segment of liberal

Jews for the simple reason that many Jewish liberals are sublimated radicals even as many conservatives are sublimated reactionaries. Thus, as Dotson Rader notes, many liberal (Jewish) intellectuals were drawn to the movement at its height because of its vitality and strength.[68] Tom Wolfe initiated the term "radical chic" for the phenomenon.[69]

Some caveats must be offered here. First, the argument is not simply reductionist. The United States faces real problems. However, even if the analysis of these problems by radicals were entirely correct, their motives could be as described. One can, indeed, make a very good argument to the effect that the origins of psychoanalysis itself lay partially in Freud's unconscious desire to destroy the Christian culture which he found oppressive.[70] This would neither deny the validity of the observations of psychoanalysis, nor constitute an argument that one factor *alone* explains its emergence at a particular historical time.

Second, we are not suggesting that all Jewish radicals conform to the Nydes type. We are speaking of modal personality. Especially in the later stages of the student movement (as with any movement) many Jews and non-Jews undoubtedly became involved whose personalities in no way conform to the above. They were merely conforming to the pressures of their peers. For a time, however, the movement was able to activate latent elements in their personalities, which is why, in periods of social crisis, as Glantz notes, the more punitive individuals come to dominate and direct movements in which there are a substantial number of nonpunitive types.[71] And, of course, we would argue that at least some Jewish students in the movement were characterized by the personality type which we hypothesize as modal among non-Jewish movement participants, i.e., Nydes' sadistic type, i.e., the "authoritarian,"[72] just as some non-Jewish radicals may conform to the "paranoid-masochistic" type.

Third, we are not suggesting that the Nydes typology is characteristic in its pure form of all or even *most* Jews; only that it is more characteristic of Jews than it is of other groups in the United States. Nor are we suggesting that the type, even when combined with the other variables mentioned, inevitably leads to radicalism. Additional variables may be involved. For example, student political activity of the type which characterized the 1960s is peculiarly middle class. Poor Jews may be too busy surviving economically even to contemplate the issues. For many Jews, individual experiences may lead in other directions.

We do, however, believe that we will find a significant correlation between political attitudes and family and personality structure among Jews. Thus we expect to find that radicals of Jewish background are more likely than (politically) conservative Jews to come from family backgrounds characterized by overprotective controlling mothers and are more likely than conservative Jews to be characterized by a high level of power needs, and high levels of defensive projection (among other things). We would expect to find liberal Jews standing somewhere in between, sharing (but more effectively sublimating) power needs, but less characterized by defensive projection, and not impelled as strongly by the desire to identify with (physically) powerful male figures. We expect to find that liberals of Jewish background come from families in which the mother is perceived as rather less intrusive and the father as rather more salient than is the case with radical Jews, although the father will not be as salient as for conservative Jews.

In short, radicalism among young males of Jewish background is the result of four interacting variables: historical marginality; a matriarchal family structure which has resulted in a particular modal personality; a radical tradition; and social crisis.

Our hypotheses regarding the psychodynamics of white youth of Christian background who entered the radical movement are based on Nydes' model of the "sadistic" personality.[73] The sources of the type are, we suspect, described best by Erikson in his essay, "The Legend of Hitler's Childhood."[74] These young people have, by and large, grown up in family situations in which they perceive both parents as distant and punitive. The families are patriarchal, dominated by a controlling father who, however, is seen as flawed.

For the Christian radical of this type, the weakening of political authority provided an opportunity both to rebel against hated parents by rejecting their values and to take out his pent-up anger against a society he perceives as weak (in the image of both his father and himself) by a pseudoidentification with the underdog. Dynamically he somewhat resembles the classical American racist; both project their own violent tendencies onto blacks. For the racist, the partial legitimation of black assertiveness and violence by the elite culture is a threat to his own self-control, and his desire is directed to restoring that control and/or destroying or at least punishing those who by their example threaten it, i.e., blacks and their allies. For many radical Christians, on the other hand, the partial legitimation of black violence offered an opportunity to legitimize the expression of their own violent urges and to act out their adolescent fantasies. Thus they identified with the Black Panthers, not because they were perceived as weak and oppressed, but rather because they were perceived as strong and violent.[75]

As Kirkpatrick Sale notes in his very sympathetic study of the SDS (1973), these non-Jewish students were part of a new breed:

> For now SDS was starting to become the home for a new breed of activist, a younger, more alienated, more committed student. . . .
>
> These were people generally raised outside of the East, many from the Midwest and Southwest . . . more violent, more individualistic, more bare-knuckles. . . . They were non-Jewish, nonintellectual, nonurban, and often without any family tradition of political involvement, much less radicalism.[76]

Jewish youngsters, even when their parents were not particularly activist, could be almost sure that they would not be disowned. Aside from the closeness of family ties, the parents, deep down, regarded children's activism with some pride. For Christians like Jeff Shero, however, the situation was very different:

If you were from Texas . . . you couldn't go home for Christmas. Your mother didn't say, "Oh, I see you're socially concerned." In most of these places it meant, "You Goddamn Communist."[77]

Toward the end, in fact, these non-Jews entering the movement included an increasing number who moved from very tight control to free and almost casual violence. Indeed, for some of them, violence had become an obsession. Even Dotson Rader, himself fascinated by violence, was disturbed by the casual way in which these young people talked about blowing up representatives of the establishment.[78] The ultimate result was, in a few cases, murder barely masquerading as social purpose:

But . . . Charlie Simpson is never quite more than just one of those disturbed kids who latched onto the ideas of the Movement as expressions of their own inarticulate troubles and seized its occasions and excuses for cathartic violence.[79]

Our discussion of male Christian white radicals is far less complete than that of Jewish radicals, for we are far less certain of all the dimensions of their radicalism. Surely there were differences between those from "old stock" families and youth of Irish or Italian background. However, these remain to be explored. We have said little, too, about women in the movement. Our ideas in this area are not sufficiently formulated, and also await further analysis of our data. Finally, we have not touched on black students or youth of other minority groups (Chicanos, Indians). Our sample did not include a sufficient number of persons from these groups, and the analysis of personality patterns would require, we think, instruments other than the ones we have used. It would also require an understanding of group cultural patterns which is beyond our competence at this time.

Operationalizing and Testing the Theories

In an attempt to test the hypotheses just described, the senior author, during the academic years 1971-1972 and 1972-1973, developed a questionnaire which was administered to a sample of 1,195 students of whom 60.3 percent were male and 39.7 percent were female. Of the total sample 443 or 37.1 percent were Jewish and 749 or 62.7 percent were non-Jewish. The sample was drawn from Harvard University, Boston University, the University of Massachusetts at Amherst, and the University of Michigan. Thirty-six of the students (all volunteers who were paid twenty-five dollars) were interviewed by the senior author and Dr. Phillip Isenberg, M.D., for periods ranging from one to four hours. Rorschachs and clinical TATs were administered to this group. Those projective tests were interpreted by Dr. Robert Schnitzer, director of clinical training at McLean Hospital, Belmont, Massachusetts. Since Dr. Schnitzer was aware of the purposes of the study, six of the protocols scored by Dr. Schnitzer were chosen at random and "blind" clinical evaluations were obtained from Dr. Thea Goldstine of the Psychological Clinic at the University of Michigan. Her analysis closely paralleled that of Dr. Schnitzer.

It is legitimate to ask whether a study completed at the end of the student movement tapped the same kind of person who was active in the early or middle periods. We are confident that it did. Although our questionnaire contained an activity scale which we plan to use to compare activists with nonactivists, we relied upon the radicalism scale devised by Gold, Friedman and Christie for classifying students as radicals.[80]

Our interest at this point is in analyzing students who are radical, whether activist or not. The advantage of this procedure for present purposes is obvious. By 1971, the Progressive Labor Party had taken over SDS, and membership in SDS had declined for a variety of reasons, among which the tactics of the new leadership was but one. An attempt was made to continue an earlier SDS tradition at some schools by creating new radical organizations which adhered to the SDS ideology of the early and middle 1960s. However, these attempts failed to get off the ground. We feel that many of the students whom we have classified as radical were of a type who would have been active in the SDS in an earlier period, even if, for various reasons, they were now somewhat disillusioned. Our impression is confirmed by those students whom we interviewed. Most of them were very much like those with whom we were acquainted from an earlier period.[81]

To determine whether a student was a radical we used items with high loadings which had been suggested by Gold et al. on three of the five Gold scales, i.e., "Revolutionary Tactics, New Left Ideology and Traditional Moralism."[82] The scales contain items to be rated on a continuum from one to seven (agree or disagree). For purposes of preliminary analysis, we decided to examine only those respondents who scored at either end or the middle of the scales. Radicals were defined as those with combined scores on the three scales exceeding 4.95, liberals included those with combined scores between 3.75 and 4.25, and conservatives included all students scoring 3.25 or lower. The mean scores of the three groups are (approximately) 5.6, 4.0 and 2.8 respectively.[83] Our subsample N of these groups is 584 of whom 59.6 percent are male and 40.4 percent are female. To simplify the analysis, only white students who had grown up in the United States were included in our analysis. The original sample had included 67 nonwhite students. In an effort to insure that it contained a sufficiently large number of radicals, we also used contacts to obtain entrée to a number of radical, predominantly student, groups in the Boston area, and at the University of Michigan. We also took a random sample of 75 students from the reputedly radical Project 10 program at the University of Massachusetts to which we had access. Thus, the actual proportion of radical students in our samples comes to (by our definition) 17.6 percent of the total (N 210).[84] Our sample, however, does not contain a proportionate number of the most radical students. The attempts we made to administer questionnaires to such students usually met with rejection.

Our final sample compares favorably with many other attempts to study radical students, e.g., Block, Haan and Smith; and Troll, Neugarten, et al.[85] In any event, since we were concerned with studying types per se, rather than describing their general distribution, we felt that complete randomness was less important than it might otherwise have been.

Our choice of instruments was dictated by the desire to find measures which were not subject to response set and yet would enable us to test propositions derived from our theory. We decided quite early to rely heavily upon projective tests which would be scored in standard ways. Projectives, of course, have some drawbacks in terms of questions of reliability and interpretation. Given our goals, however, their advantages far outweighed their limitations. As Knutson and others have noted, projective tests reduce the likelihood of response set by enabling the investigator to explore motives of which the respondent is unaware or only barely aware, and which even an unbiased investigator is unlikely to intuit. And, especially, they provide an opportunity to examine motives which are considered by the respondent to be socially undesirable or which are ego alien.[86]

We decided to use the system for scoring thematic apperception type pictures developed by McClelland et al.[87] The traditional clinical Thematic Apperception Test (TAT) was developed by Henry A. Murray in the late 1930s. It consists of a series of cards containing ambiguous pictures about which respondents are asked to tell short stories. Theoretically the stories told under such circumstances reveal a good deal about the motives and wishes of respondents. The standard pictures have been used widely in clinical work and are regarded as extremely useful by clinicians with psychodynamic orientation.[88]

While we administered clinical TATs to a small sample of respondents, it would have been prohibitively expensive and time consuming to do so to the total sample. The development of standard TAT scoring of measures of motivation has been carried out in a fairly systematic and rigorous manner by McClelland, Atkinson, Winter and others over three decades. With perhaps the exception of the recent attempts by Stewart to develop a technique for scoring level of psychosexual development, the scoring systems have been derived within an experimental setting.[89]

The TATs we administered were scored for five motives, viz.: the need for power (*n* Power), personal and social power (*p* and *s* Power), hope of and fear of power (*h* and *f* Power), the need for affiliation (*n* Affiliation) and impulse control. The system of scoring TATs for *n* Power has been in use for some years.[90] Winter's revision was empirically derived by attempting to determine what themes are accentuated in TAT stories in situations in which it can be reasonably assumed that the desire to control, command, or to heighten one's sense of power would be increased.

McClelland originally developed the scoring system for *p* and *s* Power in an effort to measure whether *n* Power was directed toward personal or social goals, i.e., the extent to which power drives were sublimated or inhibited. Later research by McClelland, however, indicated that a *s* minus *p* Power score was not an adequate measure of sublimation or inhibition.[91] While the score did, in certain cases, comport with predictions about the inhibitions of power drives, it failed to predict satisfactorily in other key cases. McClelland is now persuaded that *s* minus *p* Power measures the manner in which the power drive is rationalized to the self.[92] To get a better measure of inhibition or sublimation of power motives, McClelland turned to the cross cultural analysis of folk tales. He and his colleagues discovered that the use of the word "not" in such stories was closely associated with inhibition (impulse control),[93] and that the use of a relatively large number of "nots" in stories did indeed predict inhibition, and the sublimation of power drives to larger social purposes.

Given our theory of the psychodynamic sources of radicalism, we were interested in obtaining a good measure of defensive projection. Paper and pencil tests of defensive projection are notoriously poor. Many of those used by political scientists question respondents about their attitudes toward political elites and institutions and are subject to bias induced by given political situations. Thus, to suggest that a member of the John Birch society is paranoid because he believes that conspiracies abound to destroy those things he holds dear, is no more reasonable than ascribing paranoia to the New Left on the same grounds. Paper and pencil tests which try to ask nonpolitical questions suffer from another difficulty.[94] Very suspicious respondents are *suspicious of the questions* and can usually succeed in figuring out the answer which is non-paranoid. This is probably even more true of student populations than of the general public. On the other hand TAT pictures (especially if they do not deal with political themes) tend to draw upon deeper, more permanent dispositions and, thus, are less subject to current experiences. Further, unless respondents know the scoring system, they are unlikely to be in a position to "con" them.

Some work by David Winter enabled us to rely on TAT pictures to determine levels of defensive projection. Winter had developed a scoring system for hope of and fear of power. Basically stories are classified as "fear of power" if the power goal is for the benefit of some other person or cause, or if the person or story writer reacts to power with doubts, conflict, irony, or feelings of deception.[95] Winter found that paranoid schizophrenics scored substantially higher on fear of power in relation to hope for power than nonparanoid schizophrenics or a normal control group. He also found that students relatively high in fear of power generally prefer being alone to being in groups, are characterized by deteriorating performance under stress, and exhibit other behaviors which suggest higher levels of defensive projection.[96]

The need for affiliation (*n* Affiliation), the final motive used in scoring, theoretically measures the desire to maintain or restore good interpersonal relations. (It may also measure fear of rejection, but the behavioral correlates are the same.)

McClelland et al. have directed major efforts toward discovering the behavioral correlates associated with clusters of such scored-for motives. He concludes that persons high in *n* Power and low in *n* Affiliation fit the model of the authoritarian personality in that they exhibit considerable willingness to achieve their goals without concern for the wishes or interests of those they so manipulate.

Actually, McClelland's most recent work develops a somewhat more complex typology, differentiating among three types of individuals who score relatively high on *n* Power. He labels these the "imperial," "conquistador," and "personal enclave" personality or character structure.[97]

Males exhibiting the imperial pattern score high in *n* Power, low in *n* Affiliation and high in activity inhibition, as determined by the relation of the number of times the word "not" is used in stories as compared to *n* Power scores. On the other hand, conquistador types, while scoring high in *n* Power and low in *n* Affiliation, also score relatively low in measures of activity inhibition. Finally, the personal enclave type scores high in *n* Power, relatively high in *n* Affiliation but low in activity inhibition.

In general imperial types are good managers. They are willing to subject their power drives to larger organizational goals, and to enforce universalistic codes of justice within such organizations. As compared to conquistador types, individuals exhibiting the imperial pattern are more likely to join organizations, to consult an expert for personal help (rather than parents), and less likely to list admired individuals as inspiring them. Such individuals also tend to enjoy their work, to control their anger, and to keep their feelings to themselves. They are more likely than either of McClelland's other two types to support charities, and to report that their parents taught them sociocentric values.

Conquistador types, on the other hand, tend to fight more, drink more, and boast more about their sex lives. They tend to reject institutional responsibility and to be insensitive to the needs of others and the harm which they might do them. In McClelland's terms they behave like classic tough guys or miniature war lords. On measures of psychosexual development they score heavily at the phallic stage. They are, in short, rebels against authority, but their rebellion (whatever its rationalization) is always for self-aggrandizement.

McClelland's personal enclave types are oriented around

prephallic (mostly oral) stages of psychosexual development. They are always seeking strength from external sources to make up for their feelings that they lack strength. Not surprisingly, in line with psychoanalytic theory, they score relatively low on Slavin's measure of castration anxiety.

While McClelland's types are not ours, it can perhaps be seen how they might enable us to check our hypotheses. We would predict on the bases of our theoretical assumptions that non-Jewish radicals would resemble most closely the conquistador pattern (scoring high on n Power, low on n Affiliation, and low on inhibition), while radicals of Jewish background would (as compared to other groups) combine elements of that pattern and the personal enclave pattern (high on n Power, low on n Affiliation, but higher than the Christian radicals, low on inhibition and low on castration anxiety).[98]

What about s and p Power and defensive projection? These scores should enable us to differentiate both non-Jewish and Jewish radicals from liberals and conservatives. If our theory is correct, both Christian radicals and radicals of Jewish background have a reduced capacity for sublimation or even self-rationalization. Thus, even to themselves, their power striving should appear as directed largely toward personal aggrandizement. Both groups should also score high on defensive projection as compared to the control groups. On the other hand, for reasons outlined earlier in this paper, we expected liberals of Jewish background to score relatively high in s Power minus p Power and relatively low on defensive projection.

Our theory suggests that radical males of Jewish background should score relatively low on castration anxiety as compared to radical males of non-Jewish background. It also suggests that while radical females of non-Jewish background would score low on castration anxiety, radical females of Jewish background would score relatively high. This follows from Freud's suggestion that, in our culture at least, most women satisfy their power needs by identifying, in part, with males, i.e., fathers and/or husbands. Coming from families with ineffective fathers and controlling mothers, Jewish females would feel strongly the need to develop their own power, i.e., to become males. On the other hand, given their family patterns, radical females of non-Jewish background would tend to conform to more traditional patterns.

We used one other projective technique in our work, i.e., the semantic differential, developed by Osgood, Suci and Tannenbaum.[99] The work of Osgood et al. is well known, and questions of reliability and validity have received extensive attention.[100] Osgood et al. divide semantic space into three major dimensions, viz., the power (potency), activity, and evaluative. Certain clusters of bipolar adjectives load on each of these dimensions and *not* on any of the others. Thus weak-strong and (less obviously) light-heavy, and smooth-rough load primarily on power. Respondents were asked to rate several pictures along the power dimensions (without being told this). Adjectives from other dimensions were included to confuse the issue. The set of pictures analyzed consists of: (1) a black militant (just the face) obviously angry; (2) a black professional man, with shirt and tie, in front of a microscope; (3) a white police officer; (4) a brawny truck driver (blue-collar worker); and (5) a militant student, in the midst of a crowd, his hand raised in a fist.

We had two purposes in mind in using the semantic differential. First, we wished to see how our groups compared the black militant with the middle-class black scientist in terms of power scores, and how they compared the white militant student with the middle-class black scientist along the same dimensions. Second, we wished to develop an index of power perceived of as physical power, i.e., the police officer, the militant student, the brawny truck driver, and the black militant, as against power perceived as (sublimated) intellectual power, i.e., the middle-class black scientist. Our procedure in this case was to add the *differences* between the ratings of the various physical power pictures and the sublimated power picture and label the total a physical power score. It should be remembered that the determination of what aspect of power is important to the respondent is made by the respondent. Thus a respondent might regard a black militant as physically strong but socially weak, in that he is oppressed. If, however, he rates him as powerful, it is plausible to assume that it was the power or strength of the black militant which is most salient.

If the self-description of radical students were correct, our radical respondents should have rated the black militant and the radical student as relatively weak. Further, the physical power score of our more radical respondents should have been relatively low. On the other hand, we predicted that, as compared to other groups, both Jewish and Christian radicals would rate the militant student and the black militant as relatively powerful as compared to other groups, and would score relatively high on our physical power index.

We faced a problem in dealing with Jewish liberals. In general their identification with power as physical power should, according to our theory, be relatively low, and that was our prediction. On the other hand they do "resonate" with Jewish radicals in a period of crises. What predictions should we make as regards their ratings of the militant student and the black militant? We assumed that, as of 1971–1972, they would still regard the black militant as relatively powerful, and so predicted. The rating of the student militant was more problematic. According to our theory such a rating should have risen with the growth of the student movement, so that, at its peak in 1968–1969, the ratings of the power of the student militant by liberal and radical respondents of Jewish background should have been comparable. As the student movement declined, however, the power rating of militant students by Jewish liberals should have dropped off more rapidly than the ratings given by radicals of Jewish background, which we predicted.

Thus far we have said nothing about family patterns. To obtain information of respondent's perceptions of their parents we relied on the Parent-Child Questionnaire devised by Jacobs, Spilken, Norman, Anderson and Rosenheim. The Questionnaire has been used by Jacobs et al.[101] to investigate which specific faulty relationships between parents and children were characteristic of some illness groups and not others.

The scales on the Jacobs et al. questionnaire ask respondents to characterize their parents in terms of certain short phrases which contain descriptions of behavior. Respondents are asked to rate first one parent then the other. The total questionnaire consists of six scales of ten items each, viz., parents seen as benevolent, overprotective, controlling, ineffective, punitive and abandoning.

We felt that such a questionnaire was far less likely to yield response set bias than scales which ask respondents to talk specifically about their relations with their parents in full sentences, especially since respondents were urged to work as rapidly as possible. We were encouraged by the fact that Jacobs had found little or no difference between the results of this questionnaire and a set of TATs which he had used.[102] We were also encouraged by the fact that he and his colleagues had been able to successfully distinguish among the family patterns of "normals," or ordinary "neurotics" (clinical judgments), respondents with asthma and hayfever, and respondents characterized by chronic upper respiratory infections. Nevertheless, the questionnaire cannot probe to the same depth as projectives, and also is open to a greater possibility of response set bias than are projectives. It should be emphasized, in any event, that the questionnaire does not measure actual parental behavior, but only the perceptions of parents by the respondents. This, of course, is true of all such questionnaires. It should also be noted that the scales are designed (except for the benevolence scale) to elicit perceived negative traits. Thus, the controlling scale consists of such items as "bossy," "interfering," "authoritarian," et cetera.[103]

Our predictions, following from our theory, differentiated sharply between radicals of Jewish and Christian background. We predicted that Jewish radicals would perceive their families as matriarchal. Radical females of Jewish background would perceive their mothers as nonbenevolent, controlling, cold (abandoning) and punitive and their fathers as relatively ineffective. Radical males of Jewish background would have the same perceptions of their mothers by and large, but would also see them as overprotective. (The perception of the mother as abandoning by radical males of Jewish background is, of course, defensive.) Again, the father would be seen as ineffective, and relatively low on control as compared to the mother and to the father of other respondents.

Radicals of Christian background, on the other hand, would perceive their families as fundamentally patriarchal. We predicted that both parents would be characterized as nonbenevolent, controlling, abandoning and punitive, with the fathers receiving higher scores on all of these dimensions. However, we also expected the fathers of Christian radicals to be perceived as relatively ineffective (flawed) in line with our hypotheses.

We expected liberals of Jewish background to resemble radicals, in that male respondents would perceive their mothers as overprotective. However, we also expected to find that fathers would be psychologically more salient than was the case with Jewish radicals, as indicated by higher controlling and punitive scores and lower ineffective scores as compared to the mother than was the case with radicals. Further we expected relatively higher ratings on benevolence and lower ratings on punitiveness and abandonment scales than was the case for radicals.

We expected the families of both Christian and Jewish conservatives to be patriarchal as compared to other groups, with relatively controlling fathers. The mothers of conservative Jews would, perhaps, be perceived as somewhat more overprotective with regard to male children than would the mothers of conservative non-Jews, but the fathers would be perceived as quite salient for both groups, even though not quite as controlling in Jewish families as in non-Jewish. In the case of both conservative Jews and non-Jews we expected both parents to be regarded as relatively benevolent, nonabandoning and nonpunitive.

Finally, we predicted that moderate (or liberal) students of non-Jewish background would fall in between radicals and conservatives with relatively egalitarian families (although somewhat patriarchal). We also predicted that such respondents would perceive both parents as relatively benevolent, warm and nonpunitive.[104]

Table 1

THEMATIC APPERCEPTION TESTS—TOTAL SCORE FOR SIX PICTURES,[a] MALE STUDENTS. GROUP STATISTICS AND RESULTS OF PLANNED COMPARISON TESTS.

Motive	Radicals		Liberals		Conservatives		t-value	Significance Level[b]
	Jewish	Non-Jewish	Jewish	Non-Jewish	Jewish	Non-Jewish		
n Power								
Mean	17.254	16.454	17.642	15.716	14.166	15.258		
Standard deviation	5.566	3.349	4.025	5.304	4.740	4.544		
Number of cases	19	34	9	33	10	41		
Comparison	.3	.3	.3	-.3	-.3	-.3	2.280	.024
n Affiliation								
Mean	4.065	3.742	4.454	4.766	6.502	5.281		
Standard deviation	2.469	2.520	2.876	2.332	2.413	2.922		
Number of cases	18	33	8	32	10	36		
Comparison	-.3	-.3	-.3	.3	.3	.3	2.713	.008
n Power - *n* Affiliation								
Mean	12.960	12.560	12.923	11.028	7.101	9.439		
Standard deviation	7.039	4.489	5.059	5.769	6.017	4.360		
Number of cases	18	33	8	32	9	35		
Comparison	.3	.3	.3	-.3	-.3	-.3	3.316	.001

Social-Personal Power								
Mean	1.878	1.199	3.277	1.707	.728	1.185		
Standard deviation	2.023	1.058	1.730	1.959	1.054	1.288		
Number of cases	20	34	9	33	9	41		
Comparison	-.2	-.2	1.0	-.2	-.2	-.2	3.593	<.001
Power-"nots"								
Mean	2.206	-.751	2.003	-2.169	-4.948	-1.675		
Standard deviation	6.345	4.754	6.516	6.869	5.231	6.768		
Number of cases	19	34	9	33	9	41		
Comparison	.3	.3	.3	-.3	-.3	-.3	3.289	.001
Hope - Fear of Power								
Mean	.987	2.034	4.018	3.036	4.447	3.386		
Standard deviation	7.154	4.689	4.841	4.167	4.999	4.339		
Number of cases	19	33	9	34	10	42		
Comparison	-.5	-.5	.25	.25	.25	.25	2.339	.021

NOTES: For the planned comparison tests (an extension of the difference of means test), a like weight indicates that groups were predicted to have the same mean. A positive weight means that the average was predicted to be high relative to the low mean of negatively weighted groups. See Hubert M. Blalock, Jr., *Social Statistics* (New York: McGraw-Hill, 1972), pp. 330-334.

aIn cases where a linear relationship exists between the number of words written about a story and the score a subject received for that story, the residuals from regression analysis were used as the scores for that picture, the residuals being that portion of the original scores unexplained by story length.

bThese computer-generated p-levels for the t-tests are exact.

Some Initial Findings

The results of our analysis of the projective and semiprojective tests we administered confirmed most of our predictions (see tables 1, 2, and 3). As compared to other groups radicals scored relatively high on *n* Power, low on *n* Affiliation (and especially *n* Power minus *n* Affiliation), and low on impulse control. They also exhibited high levels of defensive projection, and were *not* particularly high on *s* Power minus *p* Power as compared to other groups. Finally, they rated the black militant and the student militant as more powerful than the black middle-class scientist as compared to other groups and had a much higher physical power score than our control groups.

Table 2
CASTRATION ANXIETY SCORES,[a] MALE AND FEMALE
RADICAL STUDENTS. GROUP STATISTICS AND RESULTS
OF PLANNED COMPARISON TESTS.

Castration Anxiety Score	Jewish		Non-Jewish		t-value	Significance Level[b]
	Male	Female	Male	Female		
Mean	.786	4.938	2.929	-2.333		
Standard deviation	11.033	13.777	11.274	9.436		
Number of Cases	14	16	28	21		
Comparison	-.5	.5	.5	-.5	1.781	.079

NOTES: For the planned comparison tests (an extension of the difference of means test), a like weight indicates that groups were predicted to have the same mean. A positive weight means that the average was predicted to be high relative to the low mean of negatively weighted groups. (See Blalock, 1972, pp. 330-334.)

[a]The castration anxiety score is obtained by subtracting scores on four adjectives on the scale which do not identify death with castration imagery, from those four which do.

[b]This computer-generated p-level for the t-test is exact.

Jewish liberals resembled Jewish radicals in their relatively high power and low affiliation scores, their relatively high power and low impulse control scores, and on their rating of the black militant. On the other hand, defensive projection does not appear to be high, power needs are still perceived of in terms of social power, and sublimated intellectual power is rated more highly than physical power as compared to the radicals.

As a group radicals of Jewish background differed from non-Jewish radicals in their lower castration scores, pointing to some personal enclave features in their personalities. Affiliation scores were also higher, but the differences were not statistically significant. However, given the evidence of the clinical tests (see below) and the fact that the set of TAT pictures scored for did not particularly pull on affiliation motives, we do not regard this result as a major setback. In our future analyses we plan to score a larger number of respondents for n Power and n Affiliation and also to check our predictions by the use of the system developed by Stewart for scoring level of psychosexual development. We did not, incidentally, convert our scores to standard scores as McClelland often does, but such a procedure would not materially affect our results.

The results of our predictions on the parent-child scale were equally satisfactory. For female respondents all predictions were borne out at very good levels of significance, as were others not mentioned in the text. In most cases here significance levels were smaller than .001 (see table 4).

Of particular interest are the father-mother comparisons. In contrast to all other groups, radicals of Jewish background saw their mothers as relatively less benevolent, more controlling, more abandoning and more punitive than their fathers. The scores on these comparisons for radicals of non-Jewish background indicated as much patriarchy in family structure as for conservatives.

In attempting to validate our predictions about male radicals of Jewish and non-Jewish background we found ourselves faced with a serious difficulty. On some of the more important subscales, i.e., "protective mother," "ineffective father," as many as 18 percent of our male Jewish radical respondents had not completed the items. Other subscales

Table 3
SEMANTIC DIFFERENTIAL PICTURE SCORES, MALE STUDENTS. GROUP
STATISTICS AND RESULTS OF PLANNED COMPARISON.

Power Score[a]	Group						t-value	Significance Level[b]
	Radicals		Liberals		Conservatives			
	Jewish	Non-Jewish	Jewish	Non-Jewish	Jewish	Non-Jewish		
Black Militant—Middle-class Black								
Mean	5.652	11.182	6.526	.837	3.875	3.677	3.507	.001
Standard deviation	6.450	10.916	8.859	5.740	3.284	10.196		
Number of cases	23	11	19	43	16	31		
Comparison	.3	.3	.3	-.3	-.3	-.3		
Militant Student—Middle-class Black								
Mean	1.905	8.364	1.500	.578	-2.118	.515	3.363	.001
Standard deviation	6.180	7.298	7.137	6.415	4.675	8.800		
Number of cases	21	11	16	45	17	33		
Comparison	.5	.5	-.25	-.25	-.25	-.25		

Physical Power Score[c]

Mean	30.789	47.000	21.000	16.229	15.467	25.286	
Standard deviation	22.548	31.366	30.002	19.293	14.659	29.327	
Number of cases	19	11	15	35	15	28	
Comparison	.5	.5	-.25	-.25	-.25	-.25	
						3.599	<.001

NOTES: For the planned comparison tests (an extension of the difference of means test), a like weight indicates that groups were predicted to have the same mean. A positive weight means that the average was predicted to be high relative to the low mean of negatively weighted groups. (See Blalock, 1972, pp. 330-334.)

[a] The power score is the sum of the scores on five bipolar adjectives which load on the potency dimension of semantic space, and do not load on other dimensions.

[b] These computer-generated p-levels for the t-tests are exact.

[c] This score was constructed by subtracting the potency score for the middle-class black picture from the potency score of each of the other pictures (police officer, militant white student, truck driver, and black militant) and summing the results.

Table 4
JACOBS PERCEPTIONS OF PARENTS SCALE SCORES, FEMALE STUDENTS. GROUP STATISTICS AND RESULTS OF PLANNED COMPARISON TESTS.

	Group							
	Radicals		Liberals		Conservatives		t-value	Significance Level[a]
Scale	Jewish	Non-Jewish	Jewish	Non-Jewish	Jewish	Non-Jewish		
MOTHER								
Benevolent								
Mean	58.407	58.435	67.763	64.848	74.615	67.357	5.311	<.001
Standard deviation	14.368	17.509	10.921	10.581	7.456	14.296		
Number of cases	54	46	38	46	13	28		
Comparison	-.5	-.5	.25	.25	.25	.25		
Controlling								
Mean	47.808	42.341	37.842	39.864	31.143	39.667	4.040	<.001
Standard deviation	15.513	17.547	12.765	14.905	7.284	12.496		
Number of cases	52	44	38	44	14	27		
Comparison	1.0	-.2	-.2	-.2	-.2	-.2		
Abandoning								
Mean	33.450	34.800	22.781	27.944	18.100	23.444	5.203	<.001
Standard deviation	14.590	16.539	10.740	12.090	5.820	13.435		
Number of cases	40	40	32	36	10	27		
Comparison	.5	.5	-.25	-.25	-.25	-.25		

Punitive								
Mean	42.128	42.108	30.938	32.429	22.000	28.600	5.420	<.001
Standard deviation	16.515	18.667	12.662	14.061	12.619	14.637		
Number of cases	39	37	32	35	9	25		
Comparison	.5	.5	-.25	-.25	-.25	-.25		

FATHER

Benevolent								
Mean	57.288	50.721	62.368	56.822	70.462	60.483	3.774	<.001
Standard deviation	14.278	18.342	15.088	15.426	6.132	18.073		
Number of cases	52	43	38	45	13	29		
Comparison	-.5	-.5	.25	.25	.25	.25		
Controlling								
Mean	42.863	49.073	37.676	42.409	41.513	45.852	1.801	.073
Standard deviation	16.338	19.712	15.129	15.240	12.317	14.158		
Number of cases	51	41	37	44	12	27		
Comparison	-.3	.3	-.3	-.3	.3	.3		
Ineffective								
Mean	34.700	32.282	29.256	31.727	23.846	25.552	2.677	.008
Standard deviation	14.389	13.889	11.991	11.451	7.777	10.315		
Number of cases	50	39	39	44	13	29		
Comparison	.3	.3	.3	-.3	-.3	-.3		

Table 4—*continued*

Scale	Group						t-value	Significance Level[a]
	Radicals		Liberals		Conservatives			
	Jewish	Non-Jewish	Jewish	Non-Jewish	Jewish	Non-Jewish		
FATHER, continued								
Abandoning								
Mean	32.132	42.289	26.500	33.229	23.444	32.464		
Standard deviation	10.545	19.098	11.648	14.136	6.521	17.422		
Number of cases	38	38	32	35	9	28		
Comparison	-.2	1.0	-.2	-.2	-.2	-.2	4.980	<.001
Punitive								
Mean	36.081	47.889	30.063	33.588	30.444	33.962		
Standard deviation	16.137	21.638	14.115	15.443	11.304	23.073		
Number of cases	37	36	32	34	9	26		
Comparison	-.2	1.0	-.2	-.2	-.2	-.2	4.346	<.001
FATHER-MOTHER								
Benevolent								
Mean	-.840	-6.977	-5.730	-8.548	-4.154	-5.714		
Standard deviation	17.894	18.964	16.791	17.012	8.999	18.899		
Number of cases	50	43	37	42	13	28		
Comparison	1.0	-.2	-.2	-.2	-.2	-.2	1.856	.065

Controlling								
Mean	-5.347	6.098	.297	3.171	10.833	5.308		
Standard deviation	20.701	23.776	16.066	18.066	13.259	15.136		
Number of cases	49	41	37	41	12	26		
Comparison	-.10	.2	.2	.2	.2	.2	3.258	.001
Ineffective								
Mean	-2.388	-4.923	-4.641	-7.146	-11.769	-9.393		
Standard deviation	20.136	16.133	17.983	14.498	12.431	12.965		
Number of cases	49	39	39	41	13	28		
Comparison	1.0	-.2	-.2	-.2	-.2	-.2	1.861	.064
Abandoning								
Mean	-2.297	7.703	3.719	7.303	4.889	7.741		
Standard deviation	17.867	19.240	15.683	15.797	8.964	16.762		
Number of cases	37	37	32	33	9	27		
Comparison	-1.0	.3	0	.3	0	.3	2.860	.005
Punitive								
Mean	-7.314	6.057	-.875	1.645	8.444	3.600		
Standard deviation	22.320	24.527	17.601	18.890	19.609	20.817		
Number of cases	35	35	32	31	9	25		
Comparison	-1.0	.3	0	0	.3	.3	2.865	.005

NOTES: For the planned comparison tests (an extension of the difference of means test), a like weight indicates that groups were predicted to have the same mean. A positive weight means that the average was predicted to be high relative to the low mean of negatively weighted groups. A group with a weight of zero was omitted from the particular planned comparison. (See Blalock, 1972, pp. 330-334.)

[a]These computer-generated p-levels for the t-tests are exact.

Table 5
JACOBS PERCEPTIONS OF PARENTS SCALES, MALE AND FEMALE STUDENTS. RESPONSE RATE PERCENTAGE.

	Group					
	Radicals		Liberals		Conservatives	
Scale	Jewish	Non-Jewish	Jewish	Non-Jewish	Jewish	Non-Jewish
MALES						
Protective						
Mother	82.1	94.0	88.2	87.5	90.0	85.6
Father	80.4	86.0	91.2	87.5	86.7	81.1
Father-Mother	75.0	84.0	88.2	83.0	83.3	78.9
Benevolent						
Mother	98.2	100.0	100.0	94.3	100.0	94.4
Father	91.1	92.0	97.1	95.5	96.7	95.6
Father-Mother	91.1	92.0	97.1	93.2	96.7	92.2
Controlling						
Mother	96.4	100.0	94.1	92.0	96.7	90.0
Father	87.5	92.0	91.2	93.2	93.3	85.6
Father-Mother	87.5	92.0	91.2	90.9	93.3	84.4
Ineffective						
Mother	89.3	98.0	94.1	93.2	93.3	93.3
Father	82.1	90.0	91.2	92.0	93.3	90.0
Father-Mother	80.4	88.0	91.2	90.9	90.0	88.9

Abandoning						
Mother	89.4	100.0	96.4	93.0	100.0	91.5
Father	85.1	89.1	92.9	93.0	90.5	91.5
Father-Mother	80.9	89.1	92.9	93.0	90.5	87.3
Punitive						
Mother	85.1	97.8	85.7	91.5	100.0	88.7
Father	78.7	91.3	75.0	93.0	90.5	81.7
Father-Mother	78.7	89.1	75.0	90.1	90.5	80.3
FEMALES						
Protective						
Mother	84.2	93.6	92.3	87.8	85.7	89.7
Father	82.5	85.1	94.9	81.6	85.7	86.2
Father-Mother	77.2	85.1	92.3	77.6	85.7	86.2
Benevolent						
Mother	94.7	97.9	97.4	93.9	92.9	96.6
Father	91.2	91.5	97.4	91.8	92.9	100.0
Father-Mother	87.7	91.5	94.9	85.7	92.9	96.6
Controlling						
Mother	92.1	93.6	97.4	89.8	100.0	93.1
Father	89.5	87.2	94.9	89.8	85.7	93.1
Father-Mother	86.0	87.2	94.9	83.7	85.7	89.7

Table 5—*continued*

	Group					
	Radicals		Liberals		Conservatives	
Scale	Jewish	Non-Jewish	Jewish	Non-Jewish	Jewish	Non-Jewish
FEMALES—continued						
Ineffective						
Mother	93.0	97.9	100.0	93.9	92.9	96.6
Father	87.7	83.0	100.0	89.9	92.9	100.0
Father-Mother	86.0	83.0	100.0	83.7	92.9	96.6
Abandoning						
Mother	88.9	95.2	100.0	94.7	90.0	96.4
Father	84.4	90.5	100.0	92.1	81.8	100.0
Father-Mother	82.2	88.1	100.0	86.8	81.8	96.4
Punitive						
Mother	86.7	88.1	100.0	92.1	90.9	89.3
Father	82.2	85.7	100.0	89.5	81.8	92.9
Father-Mother	77.8	83.3	100.0	81.6	81.8	89.3

also received lower response rates than either the female or other male groups, although the response rate of non-Jewish conservative males was also rather low on some of the more sensitive items.

As table 5 indicates, the general pattern is as follows: both males and females (Jews and non-Jews) completed the benevolence subscale in large numbers. Women tend to complete the more sensitive subscales in higher percentages than men. Radicals of Jewish background fail to complete the more sensitive subscales in larger proportion than other groups, and male radicals of Jewish background are rather less likely than are radical women of Jewish background to complete the scales which contain "negative" items. The male-female differences are in line with a good deal of the literature on the subject. In general, women in our culture seem more willing to reveal themselves than men on psychological tests.[105] The differences between radicals of Jewish background and other groups support our contention that the psychological mindedness of many radicals of Jewish background reduces the level of usefulness of nonprojective tests for understanding them.

Despite the relatively low response rate, many of our predictions as to family structure were supported by our results, although the expected differences were less pronounced than was the case for female respondents (see table 6).

In general, Jewish males perceived their mothers as more protective than did non-Jewish males. However, using the controlling scale as an index and subtracting the score of the mother from that of the father, the latter appears to be perceived as more salient in the case of both liberals and conservatives of Jewish background than is the case for radicals of Jewish background.

Once again the non-Jewish radicals resembled both Jewish and non-Jewish conservatives in the perceived patriarchal character of family relations, with relatively controlling fathers. And again the major difference seemed to lie in the quality of family relations. Non-Jewish radicals saw both parents as punitive and cold, while conservative (and liberal)

Table 6

JACOBS PERCEPTIONS OF PARENTS SCALE SCORES, MALE STUDENTS. GROUP STATISTICS AND RESULTS OF PLANNED COMPARISON TESTS.

| | Group | | | | | | | |
| | Radicals | | Liberals | | Conservatives | | | |
Scale	Jewish	Non-Jewish	Jewish	Non-Jewish	Jewish	Non-Jewish	t-value	Significance Level[a]
MOTHER								
Protective								
Mean	53.804	50.106	53.267	48.130	52.815	50.610		
Standard deviation	10.323	11.243	8.673	9.673	8.871	9.330		
Number of cases	46	47	30	77	27	77		
Comparison	.3	-.3	.3	-.3	.3	-.3	3.021	.003
Benevolent								
Mean	63.291	59.780	67.735	62.253	65.700	65.529		
Standard deviation	13.195	12.228	9.577	10.481	10.784	12.862		
Number of cases	55	50	34	83	30	85		
Comparison	-.5	-.5	.25	.25	.25	.25	2.613	.009
Abandoning								
Mean	33.452	33.326	29.741	29.833	28.095	28.077		
Standard deviation	12.461	14.668	9.737	9.905	10.606	11.851		
Number of cases	42	46	27	66	21	65		
Comparison	.5	.5	-.25	-.25	-.25	-.25	2.776	.006

								F	p
Punitive									
Mean	36.375	38.044	31.542	34.138	31.524	33.016		2.321	.021
Standard deviation	15.266	15.767	14.142	13.088	12.671	14.823			
Number of cases	40	45	24	65	21	63			
Comparison	.5	.5	-.25	-.25	-.25	-.25			
FATHER									
Benevolent									
Mean	58.000	55.957	61.848	60.119	61.379	61.093		2.235	.026
Standard deviation	13.337	18.313	12.935	11.782	16.192	15.859			
Number of cases	51	46	33	84	29	86			
Comparison	-.5	-.5	.25	.25	.25	.25			
Controlling									
Mean	41.122	46.565	42.226	42.159	50.964	44.870		3.291	.001
Standard deviation	14.956	15.703	12.683	13.520	13.993	13.097			
Number of cases	49	46	31	82	28	77			
Comparison	-.3	.3	-.3	-.3	.3	.3			
Abandoning									
Mean	34.525	37.805	34.423	33.106	33.681	32.200		1.780	.076
Standard deviation	12.828	16.778	13.014	10.919	15.442	15.387			
Number of cases	40	41	26	66	19	65			
Comparison	0	1.0	.25	-.25	-.25	-.25			
Punitive									
Mean	39.730	39.524	35.524	32.985	36.368	35.000		1.574	.117
Standard deviation	16.940	17.454	16.648	13.086	16.833	17.328			
Number of cases	37	42	21	65	19	58			
Comparison	0	1.0	-.25	-.25	-.25	-.25			

Table 6—*continued*

Scale	Group						t-value	Significance Level[a]
	Radicals		Liberals		Conservatives			
	Jewish	Non-Jewish	Jewish	Non-Jewish	Jewish	Non-Jewish		
FATHER-MOTHER								
Protective								
Mean	-7.738	-4.024	-5.500	-4.178	-4.160	-5.577	1.800	.073
Standard deviation	10.673	11.031	9.160	9.099	9.745	10.198		
Number of cases	42	42	30	73	25	71		
Comparison	-1.0	.2	.2	.2	.2	.2		
Controlling								
Mean	-.755	.261	1.677	-.575	7.357	2.026	1.614	.108
Standard deviation	18.313	19.918	15.278	16.146	18.896	14.393		
Number of cases	49	46	31	80	28	76		
Comparison	-1.0	0	.5	0	.5	0		

NOTES: For the planned comparison tests (an extension of the difference of means test), a like weight indicates that groups were predicted to have the same mean. A positive weight means that the average was predicted to be high relative to the low mean of negatively weighted groups. A group with a weight of zero was omitted from the particular planned comparison. (See Blalock, 1972, pp. 330-334.)

[a] These computer-generated p-levels for the t-tests are exact.

respondents tended to perceive their parents as benevolent, nonpunitive and relatively warm. This negative view of parents was also shared by radicals of Jewish background. However, while direct statistical comparisons were not made for this paper, the fathers of Jewish radicals seem to be perceived rather less negatively by their male children, than do the fathers of non-Jewish radicals, as would be expected from our theoretical model. Both Jewish and non-Jewish liberals fall between the radicals and conservatives. Liberals of Jewish background share some perceptions of parents with radical Jews but differ on other dimensions.

A number of our predictions were not borne out by the data, namely those dealing with mother perceived as controlling and father perceived as ineffective. However, a varimax rotated factor matrix with a Kaiser normalization revealed some other possibilities. Our analysis indicated that while the original Jacobs scales hold up, some of them are not completely homogeneous.[106] The "ineffective" scale, for example, contains two subscales, one of which (weak, passive, often fearful, et cetera) loads primarily on a weakness factor, and another which seems to be identified primarily with indulgence (always gives in, too easy going). The latter, however, does not contain enough items with high enough loadings to be very useful.

Similarly the controlling scale consists of two subscales. One of these (a discipline scale) loads upon such items as strict, authoritarian, et cetera. For perceptions of mothers, another (an intrusive) subscale emerges which loads on such items as intrusive, bossy, interfering, et cetera. While some of these items also load on an intrusive scale for perception of father, this subscale does not contain enough items with a large enough loading to be useful.

Following our theoretical model, we predicted that, while the mothers of non-Jewish radicals would be perceived as both intrusive and disciplinarian, the mothers of radicals of Jewish background (given tendencies to overindulgence) would only be perceived of as intrusive. Similarly we predicted that while the fathers of both non-Jewish and Jewish

Table 7
JACOBS PERCEPTIONS OF PARENTS ITEMS, AVERAGE SCOREa ON ITEMS WITH HIGH FACTOR LOADINGS, MALE STUDENTS. GROUP STATISTICS AND RESULTS OF PLANNED COMPARISON TESTS.

Factor	Group						t-value	Significance Levelc
	Radicals		Liberals		Conservatives			
	Jewish	Non-Jewish	Jewish	Non-Jewish	Jewish	Non-Jewish		
MOTHER								
Intrusivenessb								
Mean	4.386	4.426	3.859	4.173	4.273	4.006	1.731	.084
Standard deviation	1.560	1.727	1.464	1.350	1.574	1.669		
Number of cases	56	50	34	86	30	89		
Comparison	.5	.5	-.25	-.25	-.25	-.25		
Disciplined								
Mean	3.631	4.267	3.505	4.060	3.806	4.266	2.797	.005
Standard deviation	1.659	1.933	1.501	1.345	1.540	1.577		
Number of cases	56	50	34	86	30	89		
Comparison	-.25	.5	-.25	-.25	-.25	.5		

FATHER

Weakness[e]							
Mean	3.95	4.05	3.88	3.44	3.83	3.642	
Standard deviation	1.74	1.45	1.56	1.27	1.72	1.316	
Number of cases	56	50	34	86	30	89	
Comparison	.5	.5	-.25	-.25	-.25	-.25	1.696 .091
Discipline[f]							
Mean	4.006	4.804	4.162	4.401	4.994	4.808	
Standard deviation	1.984	2.271	1.639	1.943	1.819	1.709	
Number of cases	52	46	33	86	29	86	
Comparison	-.3	.3	-.3	-.3	.3	.3	2.980 .003

NOTES: For the planned comparison tests (an extension of the difference of means test), a like weight indicates that groups were predicted to have the same mean. A positive weight means that the average was predicted to be high relative to the low mean of negatively weighted groups. (See Blalock, 1972, pp. 330-334.)

[a] A factor analysis of the 56 Jacobs items with varimax rotation was formed. For those items with a high factor loading (≥.491) on a factor, the mean item score was computed.

[b] The items with high factor loadings (≥.543) on this factor are bossy, interfering, intrusive, controlling, and pushy.

[c] These computer-generated p-levels for the t-tests are exact.

[d] The items with high factor loadings (≥.570) on this factor are strict, authoritarian, and disciplinarian.

[e] The items with high factor loadings (≥.491) on this factor are passive, wants to be led, weak, and often fearful.

[f] The items with high factor loadings (≥.641) on this factor are strict, authoritarian, and disciplinarian.

radicals would be perceived of as weak, only the fathers of non-Jewish radicals would be perceived of as disciplinarians (see table 7). All our predictions were borne out for both male and female respondents. (Because the results of our female respondents did not change, they are not reported here.)

Given the relatively small number of items in each of these subscales (from three to five), one can raise questions about the reliability of the scales. However, given our data the findings are highly suggestive. In all they would seem to bring seriously into question the image of the New Left projected by the New Left itself and many of those scholars who studied it in the 1960s.

Much remains to be done, including, as already indicated, the examination of other variables in relation to our scores, a comparison between non-Jewish radicals of Protestant and Catholic background, and a comparison of radicals of various ethnic backgrounds (e.g., Irish, Italian, et cetera). Further, aside from these matters and others already mentioned, we have not yet measured the strength of the association of variables, nor have we engaged in the kinds of analyses which would enable us to determine what portion of the variance in political ideology is explained by personality factors.

There are other considerations as well. We are dealing with average scores for certain groups. S. Robert Lichter has found important differences between revolutionary radicals, philosophic radicals, and the merely alienated (as measured by the Christie scores).[107] In later analysis we also plan to compare radicals with relatively low power scores to those with high power scores along a number of dimensions.

The Clinical Evidence

The clinical evidence (Rorschachs, TATs and interviews)[108] supports and enriches the findings of the questionnaires. Our groups were all diverse; the Jewish radicals were the most homogenous, but even here individuals were far more complicated than any simple categorization can capture.

As indicated earlier, thirty-six white male students were

interviewed from two to four hours, in one-hour sessions. Clinical Rorschachs and TATs were also administered. These respondents were volunteers who had indicated their willingness to be interviewed on their questionnaire at the time that it was administered. The group was divided equally among radicals and moderates of Jewish and non-Jewish backgrounds.

The radical group fairly closely resembled the larger set of radicals from which it was chosen, at least in terms of political ideology. (The mean radicalism score for the radicals of Jewish background was 5.7; that of non-Jewish radicals 5.9.) The moderates, on the other hand, were chosen both from relatively conservative and relatively liberal students, and thus were politically more heterogenous. (The mean radicalism score for Jews equalled 3.4; for non-Jews 3.5.)

The following discussion is preliminary. It must be noted that, especially in the case of adolescents, Rorschach and TAT interpretations tend to overemphasize pathological elements in those studied.

The key variables on the projectives which differentiated Jewish radicals from non-Jewish radicals were: (1) the presence of wandering and exile fantasies, which we interpret along with Keniston[109] as associated with the desire to merge with a strong mother and fear of this desire; (2) the theme of flight from the mother; (3) the salience of the mother; and (4) the emphasis on "machismo," i.e., the need to demonstrate masculine processes.

Jewish and Christian radicals shared the desire to establish a negative identity. However, given the salience of a flawed father in the projectives of the Christian radicals, it seems clear that the parent against whom rebellion was directed was different for these two groups. Both Jewish and non-Jewish radicals also shared a tendency to treat people as concepts, as against moderate respondents.

We did not discover any significant personality variables which differentiated Jewish moderates from Christian moderates in the clinical projectives. However, we did have the impression that Jewish subjects (of whatever political persuasion) tended to be more caught up in their minds and lives with their families than did Christian respondents.

Many clinicians of a psychodynamic persuasion will rely on scoring systems for the Rorschach only as an aid in determining pathology; there are no clinical scoring systems for the TAT which are widely used. Clinicians tend to respond to these projectives as a whole and hesitate to isolate particular responses. Yet, one can, for both groups of radicals, pick out responses which illustrate characteristic themes. For example, the combination of negative identity, flight from the mother, and exile are brought up again and again by radicals of Jewish background on the TAT.

On Card 6BM of the TAT one respondent (No. 343) tells the following story which illustrates all these themes and the concern with "machismo":

> "Well, Ma. I had to do it (laughs)." Jeff is trying to console his aging mother for his ne'er do well life which has recently culminated in a senseless attack on a young couple . . . which resulted in the death of the young woman and injuring the young man. Thus, after having served in the armed forces . . . he's been tried for car theft, but he had a good defense. His mother's been aware of his somewhat illicit activities, partly involved in the drug rackets in New York City. He has now come back to their home in Long Island to almost lean on her shoulder, cause he's scared for the beatings, murders he's committed. The old lady has tried her best to raise a good son but has never been able to understand her son.
>
> And at this point what he really needs is a slap in the face. At a time when he'd better get out of the state, she is simply going to stand there watching Long Island Sound from the window. He'll wander the Eastern seaboard several years before finally being picked up on an assault and battery charge in Georgia where he slugged a gas station attendent. . . . And he will get two to six for that.

The "machismo" theme comes out even more strongly for many subjects on Card 17BM of the TAT, a picture of a rather muscular male climbing a rope. The radical Jewish students tended again and again to emphasize the muscles, as, for example, the story told by respondent No. 700:

> This guy looked—This looks like a really macho guy. And very kind of muscular and exercising all his masculinity by climbing these ropes and he's looking on to the audience, to the arena saying . . . "Dig it! I'm a man. And look at my muscles. Look at how I'm climbing up, climbing up this rope. It's a look at me. Hot shit!"

Several Jewish radicals interpreted the inkblot on Card 1 of the Rorschach as an eagle. This perception tends, clinically, to be associated with paranoid grandiosity. Attitudes toward the father also come out clearly on Card 4 of the Rorschach, a card which is generally interpreted as representing masculine authority. One respondent saw the card as an ugly frightening troll, but really very weak and ludicrous. Still others saw in the picture a kind of fusion of two forces unable to separate themselves, indicative of a kind of masochistic surrender. For example subject No. 701 described the card as follows:

Free Association

> I see some kind of collision and I have the feeling of two people sort of very tightly holding on to each other . . . sort of enmeshed in each other.

Inquiry

> Subject: I guess I just saw a variation in color and things coming together and colliding as two people sort of just wrapping on to each other. Not easy to separate them from each other. There's not a lot of exactness. Like I didn't see this as their legs or that as their legs but I saw more just everything coming together.

Case reports on two respondents who are reasonably representative can perhaps add some depth to the examples just given. Respondent No. 640, a radical of Jewish background, had just graduated from Boston University and had joined a revolutionary organization, which he did not identify. He was the son of two fairly high level Washington bureaucrats, who, from his description of them, were very liberal politically and no longer identified themselves as Jews.

The respondent gave the impression both in the interviews and on the TATs of essentially drifting, without life plans. It was fairly clear, too, that he was using his political activism as a grandiose scheme to bring him security.

He saw his father as a distant figure who did not interfere with him too much and his mother as a rather more formidable and aggressive person. The projective test confirmed the patient's own perceptions, with additions. It was quite clear from them that the major pressures in his life were seen as deriving from his mother, and that he felt discouraged at being unable to live up to her expectations. His TAT stories indicate also intense anxiety with respect to the possible attractiveness of his mother and the adoption of a negative identity to avoid possible intimacy. On the other hand it was also clear that his father had disappointed him in some way.

Masochistic fantasies were very apparent in his responses to the projectives, including a strong desire for a kind of masochistic surrender to something larger than himself. The extensive use of projection defensively also came through quite clearly, especially on the Rorschach.

Respondent No. 1006 was a graduate student at the University of Michigan who was very active both in University and Ann Arbor radical politics. He came from a lower-middle (upper-working) class background. His father was a plumber. He was born a Catholic, and, at the time of the interview, considered himself an atheist, although he reported a recurrent dream which suggested that he still yearned for something which was once provided by the Church.

The respondent had been active in political affairs for a long time. He felt that his interest in politics went back to when he was eight or nine when he became "totally independent from his parents." He had come to feel at that point that he could not trust his parents, especially his father. He saw his father as a disciplinarian and he felt very badly for his mother, given the manner in which he perceived his father as having treated her. On the other hand he resented the fact that, in the fairly affluent suburb in which he lived, his father was a nobody.

On the projectives the respondent came through as essentially borderline with a great deal of underlying depression and dependency needs which he dealt with by denial, hypomanic activity and projection. Indeed he projected all responsibility outward, seeing his parents as responsible for all the bad things that had happened to him in his lifetime. In some of his responses to the projectives he appeared to caricature his father's authority and all authority. Yet he thought of all relationships in terms of domination and submission. The TAT responses give the sense of a flawed—in some of the stories a criminal—father, indicating rejection. And yet, he apparently identified with this father as well, seemingly hoping to use the power which he fantasied father as having against father and controlling father with his own weapons.

He was probably among the most sadistic of all the respondents we interviewed. The degree of control he had over himself was minimal at times, and he very much enjoyed fantasies of aggression and sadism.

One last case study is of some value, because the respondent, No. 701, had attained some level of partial insight into himself, and his past. The subject had left school at the University of Wisconsin without having finished work toward an advanced degree. He had been a member of both the SDS and the Weathermen, and had now rejected traditional radical politics for Jewish gay liberation, having finally decided to openly accept his own homosexuality. At the same time, he had somewhat reestablished relations with his parents, especially his mother, and his attachment to Judaism, which he had so long renounced, although, as he put it, he always knew that the renunciation was not complete. The projectives reveal a subject with considerable pathology, and still show a sense of exile.

He noted that he originally went to Columbia University as an undergraduate to escape from the neighborhood in which he was born, even though it was financially difficult for his parents. Although he did not quite say so, it is clear that he meant to escape from being a Jew:

> I suppose there was a thing in my head about not wanting to be with the same kind of people I went to high school with, and there would be some new kind of people there who were not, I suppose, petty bourgeois and who would be cultured.

> Well I think . . . I was trying to get away from the Jewishness of . . . and into a cultured world. I probably saw that as not Jewish.

Columbia, however, was a disappointment. Most of his friends turned out to be Jewish. He was intimidated by the Christians there and hated them at the same time.

It seemed to him that all the Jewish girls were looking for WASP males. He compensated by being an aggressive intellectual and then a radical intellectual. He admitted that it was his hatred of the WASPs at Columbia that led to his fantasies about a possible mass revolutionary movement at Columbia and then led him to participate in it. He admitted, too, that the "energy coming from the black community" contributed to radicalization. Finally, he recognized that his actions (and those of others like him) had something to do with his Jewishness, but he still does not quite understand the mechanisms involved.

> Of course you know I compensated for it in a typically Jewish way, I think, by being super brilliant and intellectually aggressive. I was miserably unhappy and a lot of the way moved to pour out the tremendous hatred of society by becoming a revolutionary.

> Let me put it this way—its clear that Columbia couldn't have happened if Columbia men were traditional WASPs. It only happened because it became 80 percent Jewish and the Jews were susceptible to energy coming from the black community and the war in Vietnam. (Of course) we did not move self-consciously as Jews— did not say we were Jews—because we didn't know that, we weren't able to do that. We were still having to rebel against a lot of repressed aspects of being Jews.

His discussion of Weatherman leadership indicates quite clearly *some* of *his* reasons for becoming involved:

> A lot of the Weatherman leadership was Jewish and had never been tough street kids, and I really believe that a tremendous amount of what they were doing was overcoming their own fears about their masculinity, by taking on . . . male standards. Most of them . . . had been intellectually aggressive, but all of a sudden they were trying to be tough street kids. . . . I think there was a lot of self-hatred going on.

The respondent eventually decided "to give up trying to prove himself," and became openly homosexual, at which point he felt he could acknowledge his Jewishness and even reestablish some kind of relationship with his parents. At the time of the interview he was still a revolutionary against "straight" society but he distrusted Christian revolutionaries, for he felt that they would not protect Jews.

Some Very Preliminary Conclusions

It seems to us that the evidence of the questionnaire, the clinical tests, and the interviews hold together very nicely and even reinforce one another to support the theory which we developed at the beginning of this essay.

The radicals of the 1960s were not a new type of "protean" person characterized by warmth, openness and desire for community. They were not part of a liberated generation in a postindustrial society. Rather the evidence indicates that radicals of Jewish background were both acting out an historical role which involved the desire to estrange Christians from their society, and to which was added a personality pattern which drove them to identify with the power of the black underclass. Liberal students of Jewish background resonated with the ideas of the radicals because they resembled them sociologically and, to a certain extent, in personality. They differed from the radicals primarily in their greater capacity for sublimation and their relative lack of paranoia. The difference seems to be related to a family pattern in which the father was somewhat more salient psychologically.

Radicals of Christian background were drawn to the movement because it gave them an excuse to act out sadistic impulses and engage in a rebellion against their own perceived weakness of their fathers, at the same time identifying with them. They only barely concealed their desire for personal aggrandizement behind a facade of social purpose. (This probably states the case too strongly, but we wish to make the point clear.)

In a preliminary analysis, S. Robert Lichter has found a similar pattern among German students. Using essentially the same questionnaire developed for this study, he found that radical German students perceived their parents as cold and punitive. The father was perceived as controlling, but with a flaw (ineffective). On the semantic differential the radicals rated the picture of a soldier firing a field piece as more powerful than obviously middle-class types, as compared to nonradicals.

The ideology of the student movement, then, was linked to underlying motivations in a manner which raises some serious questions not only about the self-awareness of the radicals themselves, but about much of the response of American and European social scientists. We ourselves are not clear why the particular themes were chosen. Nor are we saying that the radicals have necessarily been wrong in their programs for change. Probably most of the great revolutions which have occurred in human history have been led by individuals whose underlying motives were other than they thought they were. The analysis of motives is no substitute for the analysis of issues.

More precisely put, it seems to us that: (1) we have raised some very serious questions as regards the conclusions reached by Keniston, Flacks and others; (2) we have seriously undermined interpretations of Jewish radicalism which relate it to humanitarian impulses sparked by marginality; and, (3) we have established the initial *plausibility* of an argument which sees the personality variables and family structure we outlined as a causal factor in Jewish radicalism, and by doing so, also established the initial plausibility of our theory of the effects of marginality upon the political behavior of some students of Jewish background. The establishment of a stronger case must await our completing a more sophisticated statistical analysis of our data.

It should be added that, whatever the motives involved, new ideologies, once articulated, can have an independent influence. It seems clear that America and Europe are being changed in key ways by the experience of the 1960s and that these changes will have a lasting impact.

Sidney Tarrow is professor in the Department of Government at Cornell University. Coauthor of Communism in Italy and France *and author of* Peasant Communism in Southern Italy, *Professor Tarrow's most recent study,* Between Center and Periphery: Grassroots Politicians in Italy and France, *will be published by Yale University Press in 1977. A specialist in political development and modernization of Western Europe, Professor Tarrow has held fellowships from the Guggenheim Foundation and Ford Foundation. He is currently working on problems of economic planning in Western societies.*

4

From Cold War to Historic Compromise: Approaches to French and Italian Radicalism
Sidney Tarrow

Radicalism in France and Italy: for some the archaic residue of the total oppositionism of the interwar period, for others the best hope of revolution in a Europe approaching postindustrial consensus. Radicalism in France: for Marx the most concrete expression of Europe's revolutionary class vanguard, yet the fountainhead of the most abstract schemes that radical intellectuals could cook up.[1] Radicalism in Italy: for Bakunin a potential spark of revolution for oppressed classes and regions, yet for others the source of a maximalist rhetoric that had "squandered the capital of revolution in an orgy of words."[2] Why have Italy and France preserved this radical potential into the 1970s?

For their comments on an earlier version of this paper, I am grateful to Luigi Graziano, Stanley Hoffmann, Peter Katzenstein, Marc Kesselman, Peter Lange, and the participants in the Workshop on the Sources of Radicalism and the Revolutionary Process, Research Institute on International Change, Columbia University, February 5, 1975.

Neither political sociologists, with their images of the gradual Americanization of Europe, nor the Marxists, with their
prediction of increasing social polarization, foresaw the combination of affluence and protest that have coexisted in both
of these systems since 1968. Three dimensions have dominated major views of French and Italian radicalism that will
be analyzed in this chapter:[3] first, its cultural and historical
determinants; second, the static characteristics of each society which have preserved radical parties and protest movements within and against each system; and third, the relationship between social change in each society and the modernization of its radical movements.

Although most students have stressed all three themes—
origins, systemic characteristics and change—I shall argue
that in the sociology of knowledge of French and Italian
radicalism, both national and temporal factors have been
unusually powerful in determining which elements have been
stressed. I will show that, with the regeneration of the left
after World War II, there developed an emphasis on the origins of radical movements; that from the long static period
of left-right confrontation in the 1950s and 1960s, there
followed an emphasis on static systemic characteristics; and
that following the radical renewal of the late 1960s, a greater
emphasis on the dynamics of change began to appear. National factors have also been important in the themes, the
logic, and the outcomes predicted for radical movements in
each country. In the case of France, the state has been at
the center of attention, while in Italy it is the party system
that has gained much more notice. Recent developments in
each political system have shaped the themes, the emphases,
and the interpretations that have been given to the study of
radicalism.

In discussing the work of four students of radicalism chosen from the first two postwar periods, I shall argue that our
lack of understanding of French and Italian radicalism is due
to two factors in particular: to inadequate attention to the
relationship between state and society and to the failure to
analyze the strength and composition of the ruling groups

that have conditioned the development of radical movements. I shall then interpret the recent period of radical revival in each country in terms of the crises in their ruling social coalitions and of the changing role of the state in capitalist society.

The Birth of the Postwar System
and the Origins of Protest

What do Italy and France, so frequently linked in history and popular culture, have in common that justifies linking their radical traditions?[4] Observers have often stressed a number of similar features in the historical traditions of the two countries, features which quite early influenced the paths of radical movements. First, with an uneven record of the extension of rights to the lower classes, deep social cleavages, and strong conservative traditions, neither country was likely to develop either a consensual politics or a stable liberal democracy. In addition, each suffered a church-state conflict well into the twentieth century. Exacerbated in Italy by the presence of the Vatican, in France it was perhaps more intense owing to a more deeply rooted and virulently anticlerical revolutionary tradition.

Second, in both countries the political elite was deeply divided. In nineteenth century Italy, the unresolved issue of unification was so pressing that the *questione politica* was tackled while the *questione sociale* was largely ignored. In France, with a longer national tradition, political leaders were able to confront the crises of industrialization with less concern for problems of national unity. On the other hand, a structure of deep conflicts within the political class intensified France's political cleavages and led to massive ministerial instability. In Italy, so bereft was the prefascist liberal state of political organization that the dominant political problem was the *trasformismo* that rendered cabinets incapable of coherent policies.

Third, in both countries industrialization was both partial and unbalanced, with enormous regional differences and many small paternalistic firms surviving well into the twentieth century. In this context the large-scale economic sector that emerged had enormous economic and political power. In the rural sector, a traditional peasantry survived in most of the country, with pockets of rural radicalism that even predated the industrial revolution. The penetration of commerce worsened the plight of the peasantry, guaranteeing rural support for powerful radical movements until well after World War II.

But by the end of the First World War, some differences were clearly obvious in each country's social and political traditions. France's democratic heritage was more solid, and could survive the crises of the 1920s, whereas Italy's tenuous liberal institutions did not withstand the strains of the 1918-1921 period. By World War I, the French socialists were predominantly republican while the Italian socialists were heavily influenced by their maximalist tradition. In addition, the French right was both ideologically and organizationally fragmented, compared to the potentially great unifying force of the Vatican and the bloc of conservative forces that began forming around it even before fascism. Finally, the French state was more coherent in its impact on society and less vulnerable to petty political influences, especially after 1945.

These differences would eventually shape the configuration of both left and right. The future character of Italian communism—born during the death-throes of the "liberal" state—was fundamentally shaped by its twenty-year struggle against fascism, while the French Communist Party (PCF), which grew up in the liberal atmosphere of the Third Republic,[5] remained much longer under Stalinist influence. French socialism's convergence with republicanism left it a moral heritage separate from the communists' that would strengthen its independence in the Fourth Republic and prepare the way for its revival in the Fifth, while the Italian socialists, with little distinct ideological tradition, emerged from the war deeply dependent on the Communist Party of Italy (PCI).[6] The French center and right, finally, which had closed ranks in 1940 after allowing the left an opening in the mid-1930s, began to fragment again after 1945, just as Italian conservatism was becoming dominated by the great populist force of Christian Democracy. The result was the early necessity for the Italian left to seek terms with the church while the French left—founded on anticlericalism and encouraged by the division to its right—never moved theoretically beyond the idea of a *Front Populaire*.

As if to deny these differences, however, France and Italy emerged from World War II with some remarkable similarities. Each had undergone experiences of fascism and occupation, of bitter armed resistance and liberation. Each had strong communist and socialist parties and popular Catholic movements, and developed a high degree of ministerial instability that contrasted with the staying power of its bureaucracy. Finally, internal cleavages became deeply interwoven with the international conflicts that were developing between East and West. Although Russians and Americans justified their meddling in the name of democracy, their combined intervention helped to rigidify the cleavages between left and right and threw up new obstacles to the development of a pragmatic politics of change. The historical differences between the two systems faded into the background before their common fate as battlegrounds in the cold war between East and West.

Historical Subcultures and the Absence of Political Exchange

Oddly, however, the international context was absent from the content of the first attempts to systematically explain the regeneration of postwar radicalism in France and Italy. In the foreground of these explanations were the inhibitions to political bargaining that resulted from the historical cleavages within each country. As Almond and Powell, working in a tradition pioneered by Almond in the early 1950s, would later write: "The parties aggregate interests only within subsections of . . . major cultural fragments. . . . The fragmented multiparty system in Italy transmits conflicting and ideologically rigid demands into a fragmented legislature and a coalition Cabinet."[7] And as they observed of France, its "political culture, although manifesting a strong national identity in some respects, appears to be so fragmented as to make effective political performance almost impossible except in crisis, or under an authoritarian regime."[8]

From these characteristics, Almond in 1956 developed the concept of "continental European systems," in which France and Italy would figure prominently. Essential in barring political exchange from such systems was the embedding of social identifications within party subcultures.[9] Almond wrote: "The political actors do not come to politics with specific bargainable differences but rather with conflicting and mutually exclusive designs for the political culture and the political system." This means, he concluded, "that political affiliation is more an act of faith than of agency."[10]

The most typical case of such principled, nonpragmatic political activism was found on the left: "The normatively consistent, morally confident actor . . . is the militant who remains within the confines of his political subculture, continually reaffirms his special norms and scolds his parliamentarians."[11] But, while espousing radical ideologies, these were highly *conservative* activists, for their commitment to principle prevented them from adapting to change by modernizing their parties' appeals. Thus the party system, which in pragmatic, Anglo-American systems helps social changes to percolate into politics, becomes a bar to political change in continental European systems.

Almond's image of the party militant owed much to his pathbreaking study of communist defectors in *The Appeals of Communism.*[12] But although the modal communist defector in that study (not to be confused with the modal activist) had had a deeply principled, psychologically intense commitment to his subculture, this was more typical in Britain or America than in France or Italy.[13] Where principled commitment is the modal form of involvement for all parties, radical parties can draw on a larger and more "normal" spectrum of the population than in "pragmatic" political cultures. Thus ideology and "political market behavior," for Almond contradictory, grow to coexist in the same political system, and even in the same political activist. This is the situation in

Italy and France today, after thirty years of institution-alized opposition to the system.[14]

In fact, the division of French and Italian society into mutually exclusive ideological subcultures was never total. First, there was the residual solidarity of the Resistance, from which many postwar leaders had entered public life. Second, there was a small "third force" which could transmit messages and from time to time find accommodations between left and right. Third, subcultural models of politics assume a degree of organizational structuring that was lacking in these two societies with their weak associational traditions, their cultural and regional splits that cross-cut social and economic cleavages, and their increasingly high geographic mobility.[15] Even the left never developed the level of organizational penetration and encadrement found in classical models of class-mass parties derived from Northern and Central European examples.[16]

Missing from Almond's formulation, as from those of other students of political subcultures, was the role of the state, so essential to the strategy of both government and opposition in countries of Roman Law tradition. The state could force left-wing parties into a pattern of negative opposition, as had occurred in Imperial Germany; split the left through the cooptation of its more moderate segments, as in France in the Fourth Republic and in Italy in the 1960s; or it could accept the legitimacy of the left but relegate it to permanent opposition, as was attempted in Italy in the 1950s and in France in the Fifth Republic. The pivotal role of the state became crucial with the expansion of its economic and social activities after World War II.

Behind these various state strategies lay the dominant social coalition in each society. By the mid-1950s, the French bourgeoisie had regained its traditional hegemony and was attempting to restrict the social gains that had been made by the working class before and after World War II. Intermediate groups like shopkeepers and small farmers were also being squeezed, and populist forces like the M.R.P. (*Mouvement Républicain Populaire*), which cushioned the struggle between

left and right in the early postwar years, were in disarray. All
that the French bourgeoisie lacked was an ideology to legitimate its hegemony and a political elite to represent it. These
it found in the Gaullist-led coalition of the Fifth Republic
and in the higher civil service whose planning ideology dove-
tailed so well with modern bourgeois values. The position of
the French left was deeply compromised, first by the successful resurgence of the bourgeoisie in the 1950s, and, second,
by the ideology and institutions of the Gaullist regime which
constructed a "productive" social coalition around it in the
1960s.[17]

In Italy, where the bourgeoisie had emerged from fascism
too compromised, too divided, and too traditionalistic to exercise power, it fell to the one legitimate part of the establishment—the Catholic Church—to organize political power on
behalf of a populist social coalition. Peasants, Catholic workers, the industrial bourgeoisie of the north, and the parasitic
petty bourgeoisie of the south became the reservoir of forces
on which the Christian Democrats (DCs) depended to organize power. The prospects and strategy of the left were deeply affected by the weakness of the Italian bourgeoisie and by
the breadth of the "coalition for patronage" organized by the
DC.[18] Although effective in buying the votes of many middle-
class and lower-class Italians, the DC coalition, through the
misuse it made of the state, posed the danger over the long
run of eroding its legitimacy and policy-making capacity.

These various elite coalition strategies and the use they
made of the state could not be integrated into models of
radical behavior that were based upon the presence or absence in society of political subcultures. Where the state
became an important political actor—as it did in both countries—"political market behavior" was understandably resisted by the opposition, for in such a market the state held
all the cards. But if the prospects of the left were hurt in each
country by the new capitalist planning state, there were important differences. The weakness of the Italian bourgeoisie
and the domination of the state apparatus by a populist
coalition left open to the PCI the possibility of penetration

through social presence and political skill, a possibility that was far less obvious vis-à-vis the French state, with its coherence and its direct links to the upper bourgeoisie. Among other factors, too numerous to elaborate on in this context,[19] this led to a more rapid adaptation of the Italian communists to life in an advanced capitalist political system, while the French communists preserved their apartness until quite recently. The strength of the French state was thus an important factor in preserving the subcultural character of French communism, while the dispersion of the Italian state encouraged the more rapid evolution of its Italian counterpart.

The Stalemate Society and the Archaism of Protest

More country-specific, and for that reason more conscious of the role of the state, was a second model that focused on the origins of revolt: that of the "stalemate society" of Stanley Hoffmann.[20] Beginning with the France of the Third Republic, Hoffmann started from four interrelated observations:

1. Economic bases: France under the Third Republic developed as a relatively static economy with a low rate of growth, a preindustrial value system and an equilibrium between the bourgeoisie, the lower middle class and the peasants, excluding the working class from social ascent.[21]

2. The political system reflected this emphasis on low growth, social balance, and exclusion of the working class by a low governmental profile which essentially benefitted the bourgeoisie, a paternalism toward the peasantry, and a tendency to policy immobilism that led to frequent paralysis.[22]

3. The party system: partly as a reflection of the society, but also as a result of institutional arrangements, France developed a weak and fragmentary party system, divided both along the lines of historical splits in French political thought, and along organizational lines within many of the major tendencies.[23]

4. Authority relations: A style of authority, neither liberal nor authoritarian, but "noninterventionalist," developed within and between these elements to protect the individual's autonomy and, not incidentally, to prevent the state from imposing its will on society.[24] This style of authority could be traced to the school, the family, and the peergroup.[25]

What were the characteristics of radical movements in such a context? Because they were excluded from the coalition of bourgeoisie, lower middle class and peasants, French workers in the Third Republic retreated into a negative, totalistic and defeatist ghetto of protest. "Workers," in Hoffmann's words, "could not but adopt an attitude of protest against the established order and dream of revolution or revenge. But the very numerical inferiority of the workers made their dream a rather hopeless one: here we find the roots of negativism, 'totalism,' and defeatisim in working-class movements."[26] No less archaic than the society it grew up in, for Hoffmann, French working-class protest was a cry of rage against a paternalistic management that treated workers "according to the degree of loyalty shown by them towards their employers."[27]

The negativism, totalism and defeatism of working-class protest extended to other radical movements. Because the republican synthesis required a noninterventionist state, neither a strong executive, a clearcut set of economic policies, nor an effective party system could emerge. "Parliament was supreme but immobile," wrote Hoffmann. "Its role was deliberative rather than representative; law was the product of a compromise between opinions rather than the result of a weighing of forces."[28] As a result, syndicalists, Catholics, nationalists, monarchists and numerous others took up antiparliamentary positions of protest. "The parliamentary game . . . was bound to antagonize people who celebrated values of activism and violence and who rejected an atmosphere of verbalism and stagnation."[29]

Strangled by a culturally patterned associational incapacity, the party system did not provide adequate ventilation for the expression and redress of grievances either. Conflicts were dealt with, not by cooperation and compromise, but by referral to a higher level of authority. An urge to preserve the individual's right to protest survived alongside and reinforced a remote and hierarchical authority system. Hoffmann wrote: "The citizen is not a militant; he wants to be left alone; he abandons decisions to elites he distrusts and leaves the task of supervising those elites to representatives whom he also distrusts." The result was periodic crises of authority interspersed with periods of social peace in which the protestors would slink away into churlish *ressentiment*.[30]

Like all good historical theories, Hoffmann's interpretation of French society in the Third Republic is solidly grounded and has been frequently vindicated. France, even into the Fourth Republic, had a small-unit, low growth economy, one that was restrained by a low infusion of capital, a limited labor supply and a lack of entrepreneurial dynamism.[31] The parliamentary history of both the Third and the Fourth Republics combined interparty and intraparty strife with cabinet instability and policy immobility.[32] Moreover, the party system reflected both associational weakness and an uneasy balance between political radicalism and social conservatism.[33] Finally, that France combines a tendency to centralized authority with a flair for individualism has long been evident.[34] Thus as a synthetic description of the *conditions* under which French radicalism developed, Hoffmann's model is unsurpassed.

But his analysis of radical movements is less persuasive. First, on the working class: its position was indeed marginal, because of a successful coalition between the French bourgeoisie, the lower middle class and much of the peasantry, as Hoffmann argues. But why did this result in defeatist and totalistic protest waged "in archaic ways on behalf of an archaic archetype?" The advanced social legislation of the Popular Front was scarcely archaic; today's social welfare system still rests on its foundation. The main sources of working class protest were not archaic; they came, not from the small towns, the paternalistic firms, and the inefficient

industries of the stalemate society, but from the best organized and most modern industries in the country.[35] The demands of the French working class were far from archaic
either; in a country which failed to even tax property gains
until quite recently, workers might justly claim that undue
burdens were borne by the producers of wealth.

When we see this stalemate society for what it was—the
system of apparently easygoing, but actually rigid, hegemony
exercised by the French bourgeoisie in the Third Republic—
the explosive aspects of French working class revolt become
quite understandable. The stalemate society was a deftly
exploitative system, and the strategy of the left—extreme
forms of action and "total" demands—was a response by the
left to its exclusion from a number of key social and economic rights. As for the defeatism of French radical protest,
this was no more than defeat repeated over and over at the
hands of a strong and compact industrial bourgeoisie and its
system of cultural and political hegemony.

The survival of the original characteristic of French protest
into the 1970s has been seen by Hoffmann and others as the
sign of its archaism. But radicalism responds to the strength
and strategy of the ruling social coalition, and these, following an uncertain period in the Fourth, became more powerful
with the coming of the Fifth Republic. If the same traits of
French protest were found in the Events of May 1968—when
the stalemate society was long dead—as had been observed in
the 1930s, this suggests not that protest is archaic, but that
it takes its form from the continuing elements of class struggle in France, which in turn depends on the strength and
implantation in the state of the French bourgeoisie.

The linkage that Hoffmann tries to draw between older
and more modern forms of French protest depends on a parallelism between the individualistic, paternalistic authority
relations of the past and the organized, semipublic management system of contemporary France. Thus, for Hoffmann,
the student movement of 1968 was a wild *chahut* against
"the intolerable weight of the structure of authority";[36] the
peasant uprisings of the 1960s parallel the Dorgères revolt

of the 1930s; trade unions and civil rights groups protest today for the "preservation of established forms and lines of
authority";[37] as for the cadres and white collar workers who
lent support to the Events of May, they protest because of
"the effect of postindustrial society on France's preexisting
social order."[38]

What links these modern elements of protest to the past,
for Hoffmann, is the French "style of authority," which not
only persists, but has in some ways hardened. But how useful
is a concept, the French "style of authority," which collapses
into the same category individualistic protest against the
limited state of the Third Republic and collective opposition
to the Fifth Republic, by Hoffmann's account "an authoritarian bureau-technocracy that takes little or no account of
grievances and that experiments in the dark?"[39] Is not the
real link the power of the French bourgeoisie in both periods
and the use it has been able to make of the state to buttress
its hegemony? In the Third Republic the key was a noninterventionist state which acted in the name of a dominant bourgeoisie and a subaltern lower middle class and peasantry.
With the rapid decline of the peasantry and the urbanization
of French society, a new coalition had to be established. This
was the function of Gaullism as a political movement: integrating a large part of the petite bourgeoisie of the provinces
that used to be on the left into a political coalition with the
managerial bourgeoisie and the remainder of the peasantry
and the lower middle class.

The result has been a *productive* coalition led by an elite
of technocratic reformers and animated by an ideology of
national renewal and productive investment. Such a coalition
fosters different policies than the ones that Hoffmann identified for the Third Republic: policies to complement that
concentration of wealth by a technocratic rationalization
of the economy which claims to make up in economic pro-
pulsion for its defects in distribution. Radicalism still thrives,
not because the protest movements are "negative, totalistic
and defeatist," but because the ruling power is divisive,
authoritarian and technocratic. In its very modernity at the

head of a neocapitalist system, combined with the authoritarianism of the administration it controls, the state gives ample reason for opposition movements to continue to preserve their radical élan.

The Static Equilibrium of the Cold War Period

Images of radicalism thus often take on the properties of the period they are born in. If, in the early postwar period, it was the origins of radicalism that impressed observers, as the postwar bloom of parties and movements ground down into a standoff between left and right, attention shifted from the sociocultural roots of radical politics to the static equilibrium of the political system or of the state in relation to society. It was logical that a period of static equilibrium, like that of the Cold War, should give rise to theories larded with static imagery, such as the "vicious circle" of bureaucratic inertia of Michel Crozier or the "centrifugal democracy" of Giovanni Sartori.

The Stalled Society and the Vicious Circle of Protest

Although perfected only in 1970 in *The Stalled Society*, Crozier's model of "blocked" society was a product of his work on bureaucracy carried on before 1960, and first gaining notice in *The Bureaucratic Phenomenon* in 1963.[40] Central to the theory is the notion of a system in equilibrium, expressed through the metaphor of the "vicious circle" of bureaucratic dysfunction. And as in many theories of French society from Tocqueville on, Crozier's begins with an internal analysis of the state and proceeds from there to the character of radical movements and of French society as a whole. In both the internal life of the bureaucracy and in the broader problems of French society, Crozier saw cyclical patterns of stagnation, protest and bureaucratic response which between them worked to prevent any positive change from occurring. Bureaucracy thus becomes a metaphor for society as a whole, and antibureaucratic sentiment a shorthand for social protest.

Bureaucracy, though it first emerged to rationalize society's functioning, creates vicious circles of inefficiency through:

1. the well-known characteristic of large organizations to become highly stratified internally;
2. the lack of communication between strata and the resulting recourse to impersonal rules that gives greater and greater discretion to those at the highest levels of the organization;
3. the lack of fit between the abstract rules and the variety of concrete tasks that those at the base of the organization must perform;
4. all of which leads to a malaise among the personnel at the base, tension between strata in the organization, a set of informal internal understandings to keep the wheels turning, and periodic crises when the informal understandings are insufficient.

The vicious circles come in the last phase, when the rules of the organization become more impersonal while its operation is more and more erratic. Crisis occurs when the gap between rules and operation leads to paralysis, when the personnel at the top are cut off from their subordinates, and when those at the bottom finally revolt.[41]

Originally developed to understand the dysfunctions within organizations, Crozier's model was extended to comprehend the whole of French society in *The Stalled Society*. The impersonal rules at the top become the arbitrary enactments of government; the gaps between strata are expanded to class conflicts, the "informal arrangements" of bureaucracy become feudalities and privileges in the state that the citizens find unacceptable; and the concept of bureaucratic cycles of dysfunction and change is extended to the cycles of revolt and complacency in modern French history. Crozier writes, "French society as a whole suffers from the same problems as its government bodies."[42]

Crozier's view of radical protest in France follows from these extensions of his bureaucratic model to society as a whole. The extension is both general and specific. Since bureaucracy is now universal in modern society, the character of reaction against it becomes equally universal. Where bureaucracy is modern and enlightened, "the impulses which before could be expressed only in contradictions and paralysis of bureaucracies or hierarchies . . . can now be resolved more rapidly and efficiently."[43] But where, as in France, the bureaucracy is laden with dysfunction, where communication between summit and base is lacking, and where change can occur only through periodic crisis, then demands for change take on a "radical totalitarian character."[44] As Crozier concludes of the crisis of the French university system, "The totally integrated system provoked total contestation. Resurgence of a chiliastic and totalitarian ideology was a natural consequence of the crisis rather than its cause."[45]

Crozier is quick to admit his debt to Tocqueville, whose "vigorous tirade against that 'regulating and constricting administration' [the Ancien regime]," seems to him "just as fresh and relevant today as when he wrote it."[46] But Tocqueville was not writing about today's French bureaucracy which, among other things, has presided over an astonishing record of postwar economic growth, much of it state-led. He was writing about the venal and parasitic, hierarchical and refeudalized administration that led to the French Revolution. The paradox is that, while Crozier describes French administration in negative Tocquevillian terms, he has idealized the potentialities of large-scale organization in general. He writes:

> The evolution of large modern organizations, indeed, does not seem to be tending toward the image of oppression and bureaucratization which is popularized in superficial analyses. Constant improvement in forecasting methods permits greater flexibility in the application of rules. Not as much conformity is needed in order to function.[47]

Thus he concludes that France's problems can be solved through organizational reform based on improved information flow and greater participation in decisions, more open recruitment into the elite, and increased bargaining between organizations.[48]

As an example of peaceful organizational reform, Crozier cites the cases of the French rural world and of French Catholicism, which have overcome their irresponsible protest of the past through a process of "institutional investment" whereby "responsible leaders and activists . . . are establishing constructive goals: technical and economic training, technical and commercial research and experiment, discussion of the structure of the milieu."[49] Although there have been "echoes of the *jacqueries* of the past in road barricades and assaults on local government officials," the overall strategy has been one of the formation of new attitudes among the young, the spread of information, and the acceptance of the power of other organizations that characterize modern society at its best.[50] This, he argues, is the right path to positive change in French society, in contrast to the path of revolt.

But collectivities like "the rural world," or "the Catholic world," although they have strong organizational traditions, are not really equivalent to organizations, neither in the rules governing their behavior nor in the actions which bring about change. Crozier's extension of the bureaucratic model to society as a whole has led him to the error of supposing that "institutional investment" *within* a social group can bring about change in the society as a whole, as if the group were, in itself, an authoritative source of values and commands.

This is dubious on both empirical and theoretical grounds. The French peasantry did not achieve its current survival by following the rules of more open organization, expanded information and participation, and the acceptance of the power of others; it did so through *protest* against the state and against the market forces which constricted its profits while raising prices for the consumer. This protest brought about a fundamentally *political* response from the state during the 1960s.[51] As for the Church, it was bought off through a financial solution to the old religious school question and its assurance that the Gaullist regime posed it no threat.

But there is a larger problem involved in assimilating social protest to antibureaucratic resentment. In dismissing protest as a residue of an older tradition of destructive rebellion, Crozier ignores the fact that neither bureaucratic systems nor market economies—and France is both—budge very easily without pressure for change from outside. Moreover, in

supporting his view, Crozier has chosen sectors of society—
the rural world and French Catholicism—that are extraordinarily *well*-organized. What can the *dis*organized do in react-
ing to bureaucratic power except to protest? "The risks of
blockages," writes Francois Bourricaud, "do not derive at all
from the style of a society's organizations, but from the relations between organized and unorganized sectors within the
larger society."[52]

Crozier's antibureaucratic view of radical protest is thus
profoundly conservative. Take the French student rebellion.
Crozier sees it as "the true revolt against France's bureaucratic mode of organization and against the authoritarian
aspects of the French style."[53] He complains of the "retro-
gressive aspects of the revolutionary movement of 1968"
which ultimately led to "accommodations with tradition,"
to "an obsessional retreat of large numbers of young people
and intellectuals back to millenarian ideologies favoring
total change," and to "a very strong force for blockage, in
that much of the potential for change is thus spent in conservative action." Any real change in the University, Crozier
maintains, must come from intrabureaucratic and interbureaucratic reform: of the *grandes écoles* from which higher
civil servants are recruited; of communication and participation between and within organizations; and of acceptance by
all the players of the real pluralism of power in the system.[54]

But far from being the archaic protest of one stratum of a
bureaucracy against another, the student revolt was a particularly articulate expression of a broader phenomenon: the cry
of rage of unorganized sectors of the population against the
"large modern organizations" whose behavior Crozier would
see rationalized. By demanding that such expression of revolt
give way to reasoned interbureaucratic and intrabureaucratic
bargaining, Crozier would deprive the unorganized of their
only weapon against the power of the center.

Where is the party system in Crozier's analysis of radicalism? And where are the class conflicts that bubbled to the
surface after the first confrontation between the Paris students and the police in 1968? The absence of both from

Crozier's scheme is not only the result of the tendency to see society as a bureaucracy writ large; it is a reflection of the period prior to 1968, when an authoritarian government kept the traditional parties on the run and the economy moving ahead through a combination of inflated nationalist rhetoric and deflationary economic policies. Although May 1968 took antibureaucratic forms, this was not because society has been bureaucratized but because the state has linked its fate with management in an economic system in which public and private power can no longer be disentangled.[55]

May 1968 was a revolt against the economic policies of the Gaullist regime, their socially regressive effects, and the tendency to substitute the state for the managerial class as the ultimate arbiter of the market. In fact, it was not the student revolt which made France an exception in 1968. There was more violence in Tokyo, a greater number of deaths at Kent State, a greater number of class-days lost at Berkeley, and more buildings occupied in Rome. What made the French student revolt exceptional was its fusion with a *working-class* uprising which paralyzed the society, brought a revival of the French party system and led to the current strength of the left. There is a far deeper connection between the student revolt and the working-class movement of May–June 1968 than antibureaucratic rebellion. In its volatility and power, its sense of outraged justice, and its immediate identification of the state as the common enemy of both workers and students, the movement of May 1968 drew on a tradition of anticapitalist revolt that could comprehend both the corporate demands of the workers and the more abstract goals of the students. In this sense, the Events of May were not a wild and isolated revival or protest against the Napoleonic state, but an archetype of anticapitalist revolt that would feed into the more organized and institutionalized growth of the left we see today throughout Europe.

Polarized Pluralism and the Growth of the Italian Left

If it was the relations between the bureaucracy and the individual that was the basis of theorizing about radicalism in France in the 1960s, it was the static equilibrium in the party system that struck observers' attention in Italy. This led, among other things, to attempts to apply economic models of voting choice to the Italian electorate. The vote, students like Anthony Downs had argued, could be used much as economists used the currency: as a universal measure of political purchasing power. The voter, in this model, was a consumer, and political parties were little more than competitive marketing organizations, offering their products in the form of alternative policy sets and changing their policy proposals in response to changes in electoral opinion. Since the bulk of unattached voters, at least in bipolar political systems, were found in the center, it followed that these competing appeals were made to attract moderate opinion.[56] With more elegant language and less appeal to science, this was exactly the premise that underlay the "catch-all party" thesis of Otto Kirchheimer and others in the 1960s.[57]

If it is surprising that such an approach should have been applied to the Italian party system, this paradox could be understood in terms of an electorate that was so stable and so spatially-oriented that it could more plausibly be placed on a left-right continuum than almost any other.[58] It was when students turned to Italian parties that the economic model would pose some problems. How could the "fragmented multiparty system" with the conflicting and mutually exclusive designs for the political system described by Almond be adjusted to an approach which viewed parties as "maximizing" actors? Moreover, how could the group voting and collective action widespread in Italian politics since the war be dealt with by the individualistic voting choice studied by the economic model of politics? And what of the left, with its principled appeal to class and sectoral interests: how could its continued success in Italy be reconciled with a model of political parties as almost identical marketing organizations?

In a well-known article,[59] Giovanni Sartori tried to deal with this problem by exempting the extreme left (along with the extreme right) from the appeal to moderate opinion. Sartori tried to preserve the underlying model of voting choice from the economic approach (parties are "maximizing" actors), but argued that in some political systems, which he chose to call systems of "polarized pluralism," the appeal was to extreme, rather than moderate, opinion. In these "centrifugal" systems, he argued, the government is based on a centrist coalition; it is attacked by opponents on both poles who seek support from the extremes; coalitions are fragile and inefficient and no effective opposition is possible.[60]

Both left and right were defined in terms of this overall dynamic. Instead of their appeals to the voters converging in the center, they diverged towards the extremes. Extremist party leaders appealed to the electorate with platforms which attempted to outbid the government. Two conditions were responsible: first, the "central position is physically occupied in a way that removes moderate electoral opinion from competition"; second, for parties on the extreme poles, "it is in their interest to split the system apart by diverging."[61] The extremes therefore grow at the expense of the center, and the latter responds by seeking the vote of adjacent moderate parties, thereby forcing them as well towards the extremes in search of new supporters.

Before turning to the Italian party system, it is worth noting how Sartori defines the concept of an "extreme pole," which is the term he uses indifferently for radical parties of the right and left. The image is fundamentally physical, and assimilates left and right into the same relationship to the center. For example, Sartori wrote,

> "polarity" and "polarized" are the terms used as indicators of strong distance; and "polarization" and "depolarization" are defined dynamically to mean a centrifugal process towards disruption of basic consensus and, vice versa, a centripetal process towards reunification of basic consensus.[62]

Left and right are thus conceived purely physically—neither in terms of the intensity of cleavage nor of the character of their strategies, but in terms of a situation "in which the distribution of opinion covers the *maximum conceivable distance*."[63] They also gain support jointly, both of them at the expense of the center.

But do the left and right represent "poles" of the political system in the same sense? In Italy the extreme right is not a pole but a fringe of shifting protest voters, while the left has a solid subculture of mainly constant support.[64] The Italian extreme right has never represented much more than 10 percent of the electorate, even at its peak in 1972, and has always had a strong regional concentration in the south.[65] The left-wing pole, the Communist Party, has more than one-third of the electorate and has continued to grow steadily, while the growth of the right was erratic and has been reversed several times. If one pole of the system grows so much larger than the other, then the natural outcome is not a centrifugal trend—with both extremes growing at the expense of the center—but bipolarity, which is exactly what has occurred in Italy since 1968.

Another problem in Sartori's interpretation concerns the relationship between the growth of the left and the nature of its appeals. Since he defines the key term "polarization" in terms of the amount of political space in the system, it follows that the left must grow through an appeal to an electorate susceptible to extremism. First, on the electorate: it is incorrect that centrist voters are unavailable to the PCI because the center is physically occupied. Because of the nature of the DC's ruling coalition and its foundation on patronage, the loyalty of its electorate has been both instrumental and contingent. Once the Italian model of economic development began to collapse in the late 1960s, these centrist voters became eminently available to other parties.[66] Who captured them would depend on which of the opposition parties was able to make the broadest *national* appeal, and not on outbidding the DC.

Second, Sartori calls the strategy of the communists "outbidding," and postulates that it must be "divergent" by virtue of the PCI's position "outside the system." But this is a purely nominal, and not an empirical, designation. It is well known how heterogenous, both regionally and sociologically, the PCI's support base is. Many studies have shown how the party's electoral appeals, far from "outbidding," tend to converge with those of the DC in its electoral and policy targets.

With respect to the communists' attitude to the traditional sector of the middle class, for example, Suzanne Berger writes, "Their objective seems to be that of reducing the hostility of this sector to socialism."[67] And as Giacomo Sani writes of the party's strategy in the south, "a fundamental trait of the position of the PCI is . . . to render it acceptable to an ever-wider circle of voters belonging to diverse social classes."[68]

Thus while Sartori's model did predict an expansion of the left, it did so for exactly the opposite reason for the PCI's current success. This has been rooted in its ability to construct a broad coalition of workers, peasants, regional interest groups, intellectuals and white collar workers, in opposition to the populist coalition organized by the Christian Democrats. There is no evidence that the Italian communists "outbid" more than any other opposition, and their behavior in Parliament, in local government, in the trade unions and in the area of civic reform has been so moderate as to make many party sympathizers uneasy.[69]

In fact, if we compare the impressive successes of Italian communism in the past two decades with the volatile and frequently disappointing showing of the French communists, the difference seems to lie in the PCI's capacity to construct a broad coalition to reflect more sensitively the demands of new or recently transformed social groups, and to be present wherever social change is occurring. These successes emerge from what Alessandro Pizzorno has called the PCI's strategy of participation and presence,[70] which has been the party's response to the nightmare memory of fascism, to the strength of Catholicism as a political force and to the weak hegemony of the bourgeoisie. In a society like Italy's, the PCI's strategy of presence was not only tactically advantageous (in fact, it had some political disadvantages, as in the south for instance);[71] it held out the long-range hope of laying the groundwork for a rival hegemony of the left and for the development of a different model of social development than the one offered by the bourgeoisie.

The changes in Italian society in the 1960s and 1970s gave

the PCI encouragement in expanding its strategy of presence into one of entente with progressive Catholicism. In the 1960s, the postwar governing coalition was steadily eroded, and was only temporarily shored up by the addition of the socialists to the government in 1964. Three trends coalesced to produce this result. First, as southern peasants moved north they broke their clientele ties with the DC and became available as potential voters for the left; second, the older middle class—artisans, shopkeepers, clerks—divided into a parasitic state bureaucracy, inherently loyal to the government, and a new productive middle class only instrumentally so; third, the Italian model of growth, which had been based on cheap labor from the south and on exports, was challenged as this pool of labor began to dry up and the unions brought about increases in factory wages which lessened Italy's export advantage.

As the subaltern social partners in the dominant political coalition began to drop away, the DC responded neither by shifting solidly to the right (though there were attempts to do this) nor by turning back to its populist roots, but by an expansion in the techniques of "individualistic mobilization"—e.g., patronage—that it had perfected over two decades of power. While this could temporarily stem the erosion of its support, it ultimately led to an absence of policy control and of political cohesion which left the government unable to face its growing economic problems. The communists could thus expand their appeal by the promise of constructing a coalition that could manage the existing system according to more universal and efficient policy criteria. For an alternative to the coalition for patronage designed by the DC to hold power, the PCI promises a coalition for universalism through its formula of a great historic compromise between Marxists and Catholics. Thus, far from gaining votes by diverging, the PCI has increased its support and gained a share of power by anticipating and shaping the dominant currents of dissatisfaction with the existing system. This is far from a revisionist sellout, but it is not the strategy of an antisystem party either, since its programs include the civic reforms, the call for efficiency, and the universalism ideally, but not inevitably, brought about by bourgeois democratic revolutions.

Political Change and the Search for New Models

From Cold War to historic compromise, interpretations of French and Italian radicalism have been shaped by the periods in which they were coined. These can be briefly summarized. The resurgence of the left after World War II led analysts to stress the subcultural and historical origins of radical movements. This could take general forms, as in Gabriel Almond's work, or national ones, as in Stanley Hoffmann's. The static period of left-right stalemate of the late 1950s and 1960s led to an emphasis on the systemic constraints surrounding radical movements: either through the hand of a bureaucratic tradition, as in Crozier's work, or in the logic of electoral equilibrium, as in Sartori's. Both periods of theorizing were marked by an absence of attention to international factors, to the relations between state and society, and to the character of the dominant social coalition in each country.

National differences have also been important in the sociology of knowledge of radical movements in these two periods. If the two theorists of France, Crozier and Hoffmann, began from the strength of public authority, this only reflected the greater historical strength of the state in France. Conversely, if Sartori and others concentrated on the party system in Italy, this related to the growing politicization of Italian public life and to the division of the country into two imperfectly-organized subcultures, the Marxist and the Catholic one. With respect to neither country has there been systematic attention to the relationship between political and social change and the increased power of the left. On the contrary: through all the interpretations of radicalism that we have surveyed there runs at least the implication that radicalism is the result of the *backwardness* of the social structure, or that of the left itself, of its tactics and its psychology.

Enough has been said above to make unnecessary an extended discussion of what is wrong with such an approach. Although both countries preserve substantial pockets of backwardness in their social structure, the left has not been notably successful in these areas and, even within them, its success is greatest where change is more advanced. Even the growing antistate sentiment of the late 1960s and the 1970s is due, not to the traditional authority of the bureaucracy, but to its growing economic and social impact on the citizens. This cannot be assimilated to the simple image of the welfare state in the two countries, but is shaped by the divergent character of the links between the state and the industrial bourgeoisie in each country. In the Italian case, there has been a growing emphasis on "assistance capitalism," which has produced a parasitic public service class and an individualistic mobilization of the middle strata at the cost of the most productive groups in the population;[72] in France the state's economic impact has been felt more through its control over investment, in the passion that its planners feel for concentration, and in the ultimate reshaping of the public services to facilitate economic rationalization.[73]

These contrasting emphases in the state's economic role, which emerge from, and reinforce, the differences in the dominant social coalition, ought to be central to any attempt to understand the future of radicalism in each country. In recent years, the French and Italian left have been bracketed together, just as they were after World War II, under the generic term "Eurocommunism." Although there are strong similarities now, as there were then, the differences may prove equally important. These can be summarized under three general headings: international, internal, and systemic.

First, the two countries' international position is different; France is at the center of the Western alliance, and its political future is far more important to both the Soviet Union and the United States than Italy's. It is true that Italy is more susceptible to international pressures than France, but the left in France (witness the polemic over Portugal in 1975) is more likely to be divided by external events. The most likely such event in the new few years would be an increase of tension in Central Europe, or the accession of a left-wing government in Italy or on the Iberian peninsula. Either occurrence could easily add to the appeal of the current governing coalition in France and cause strains in the opposition alliance between the PCF and the Socialist Party (PS). In contrast, there is growing unanimity on foreign policy in many sectors of Italian opinion.

Second, the forces on the left are weighted towards the communists in Italy and towards the socialists in France. It was the PS of François Mitterrand that gained the large influx of former members of the student movement in France, while, in Italy, the PCI made the greatest gains from this source in recent years. The French communists are attempting to move in a very few years over a territory of change that the PCI took thirty years to cover. Despite changes in a few key doctrinal tenets and a recent increase in new members, these changes have yet to filter down into the French party's internal life, and its voters may still feel them to be superficial. In the PCI, in contrast, so many changes have been made in the party's doctrines, in its leadership and in its internal life that the remaining signs of orthodoxy—membership in the "Third International" and democratic centralism—appear increasingly out of place by comparison. After the electoral successes of June 1975 and 1976, even the internal balance of power between the party organization and its elected officials appears to be changing in favor of the latter, who share responsibility for pulling the country out of its profound economic crisis.

Third, this leads to the nature of Italian capitalism, which is, as it always has been, far weaker than its French counterpart. The Italian bourgeoisie is not, nor has it ever been, a true ruling class in the full economic, social, cultural, and political sense of the term. The weakness of Italian capitalism, alongside the strategy of presence favored by the PCI for so many years, gives the left in Italy a real chance to establish a new hegemony over Italian society, and it is towards this goal that the communists' incremental strategy is aimed.

In France, despite the current bickering in the majority, a strong, modern, and fairly coherent bourgeoisie lies behind its political power, and this creates far more problems for the left than in Italy. It is for this reason that the strategy of the

French left—both communist and socialist—is predominantly electoral, while that of the Italian left is electoral, social, and economic. The French left has not yet gone beyond the idea of an electoral Popular Front, either conceptually or politically, while the Italian left has gone so far towards establishing bridgeheads in the fabric of Italian civic society that its electoral success is no more than a symbol of its social and cultural presence.

Related to this difference of strategic perspectives is the contrasting role of the state in social transformation. While the increased economic role of the state would afford the left a promising, if flawed, instrument for socialist transformation in both countries, the power and efficiency of the French state are immeasurably greater. The Italian bureaucracy is inflated, with power centralized in Rome, but each ministry is a feudal entity, and many of the state's important economic activities escape their control. In contrast, short of an actual electoral breakthrough, the French state is relatively impermeable to left-wing penetration, even assuming that the Gaullists—as seems increasingly likely—begin to lose their grip.

This raises the problem for the PCI, should it achieve its goal of a historic compromise with the Christian Democrats, of reforming the Italian state apparatus. It is easy to campaign against parasitism and inefficiency from the opposition, as the communists have effectively done since 1972. It is quite another matter to reform the bureaucracy without carrying out wholesale purges of inefficient, corrupt, and frequently reactionary bureaucrats. The failure to reform the state would mean the failure of any serious program of social and civic reforms; while the purge of the bureaucracy (unlikely in coalition with the DC) would raise the spectre of a PCI return to Stalinist methods. The regional reform of 1970, reinforced by left-wing gains in the regional elections of 1975, was a step towards a reform of the state at its lower levels. But the real problem, which remains at the center, demands a far more basic housecleaning of the bureaucracy.

This takes us to recent attempts to understand the evolution of the Italian political system since 1968, for the social and political changes since that time have stimulated a new debate on the future of the left and on the appropriate models to understand the current changes in each party system. How, students have begun to ask, can political pluralism survive with the communists accepted as legitimate players in the political game, and even as participants in a government coalition? And what shape will the new governing coalition take should this occur?

To find an answer, some have looked to those European systems, like Holland, Belgium, Austria, and Switzerland, in which multipartyism and low political consensus have been able to coexist with political stability for a long period.[74] In trying to understand what these other societies rested on, Arend Lijphart proposed a solution based neither on the number of parties in the system, nor on the extent of polarization, but on the character of elite interaction.[75] Lijphart showed how, in the Dutch case, systems of communication and political exchange had grown up between leaders of various partisan subcultures at the top to bridge the cleavages between the groups they represented. He then described an entire system of rules of the game developed by the leaders of the Dutch parties to overcome cleavages; otherwise, without such rules there might have been a less stable political system. Consociational democracies, Lijphart writes, are characterized by an ability to forge solutions for the divergent demands of their subcultures, the ability to recognize the dangers inherent in a fragmented system, a commitment to system maintenance, and an ability to transcend subcultural cleavages which persist at the base by bargaining at the elite level.

But to reconcile subcultural fragmentation and elite consensus, such systems needed a number of complementary properties: first, the common perception of a common external threat, at least historically; second, a subcultural balance so diversified that it reduced the fear of any one player destroying the others; third, sufficiently increasing prosperity to financially afford the policy duplications and waste inevitable in a proportional process of policy allocation; fourth, a political class with the skills to create and utilize conciliar decision-making structures; and fifth, the bases of support in the political subcultures to permit leaders to bargain with opposing parties over their heads.

Along none of these dimensions does Italy appear to be a promising candidate for consociational decision-making. First, the perception of an external threat is there, but it is divided between the Soviet Union and the United States. Second, the subcultures are far from diversified and the fear that one player, the PCI, may overcome the others is both great and legitimate. Third, there is not the prosperity necessary to afford policy *proporz*; on the contrary, this has been one of the causes of the current crisis. Fourth, the political class has not shown the talent or the restraint in the past to create conciliar decision-making structures. Finally, except for the communists, the support of the base is insufficiently disciplined to provide party leaders the security that they will be followed in compromises that affect their followers' interests, and not even the communists may have the necessary control over their trade union affiliate to prevent a recurrence of high wage claims in a program of economic austerity.

In the absence of any real possibility of consociational democracy, then, the PCI's historic compromise strategy may add up to little more than the expansion of the network of mutual dependence that has been observed between it and its opponents in Parliament, in local governments, and in the regions. But convergence at the center without a change in the current distributive policy bias of the government will only further erode the legitimacy and solvency of the system. The communists can only break through these problems by building a majority for universalism—the proposal of collective solutions to collective problems—and by choosing their allies on the basis of their fitness to conceive and carry out such solutions. The left, in other words, must have the courage to seek broad-based changes in order to make incremental ones; which is exactly the opposite of the logic of consociational democracies, with their penchant for making policy through mutual adjustment between coalition partners.

If the combination of the international situation, a permeable state and the incremental strategy of the Communist Party threatens to lead to convergence at the center in Italy, does the stronger French state and a more narrowly-based Communist Party suggest a bipolar outcome for France? If so, then there should be revived interest in France in theories of elite circulation like Schumpeter's or Mosca's, just as Italians have been turning to consociational models as a theoretical reference point for their system's future. It seems logical that, in a system that has grown increasingly bipolar, in which the left has achieved its highest degree of unity since 1936, and in which presidentialism reinforces bipolar choice, students of politics would look to such theories for guidance.

No such development is currently evident in France, for what seem to be two reasons. First, because the state is so strong, the assumption is common that left-wing electoral success would naturally lead to either a struggle between a left-wing government and a conservative civil service, or to a total subjugation of society through the bureaucracy, by the communists, in which case one-party government might well ensue. In neither case would alternation in power lead to a continuous circulation of elites: in the former one, a standoff between government and bureaucracy would develop and, in the latter, political alternation would only happen once.

Second, the growing strength of the communist-socialist alliance has threatened the government, but it is not clear that it has transformed the political system to one with a truly bipolar logic. In contrast to Italy, where much of the electorate is still moored in a set of relatively stable partisan attachments, the French electorate retains a good deal of the fluidity that gave support to "flash parties" in the Fourth Republic, led to the surge and decline of Gaullist support in the Fifth, and has always made the future of the left difficult to read. Much of General de Gaulle's success was based on his appeal to a persistent strain of antipartisan ideology in the French electorate. Part of his failure was that he left his party without firm control over the mass of unaffiliated voters who would return to the Gaullist fold in moments of danger, but

were liable to stray into casual alliances, as in May 1974. And
the strategy of the Giscard regime is to capitalize on this
marais (swamp) of unaffiliated voters to construct a new
populist coalition based on reformist programs.

That this is not an easy enterprise was illustrated by the
tortuous legislative history of the real estate tax reform of
1976. This episode not only illustrates the political weakness
of a majority based on three parties, of which the largest does
not control the presidency; it also demonstrates the continued strength of French capitalism, which has always been
based as much on property as on production. The fluidity of
the French electorate gives the government the chance to
gain mass support in the center through such programs as tax
reform; but the strength of French capitalism poses the
threat of simultaneously losing elite support on the right. The
only plausible outcome would be a solid shift to the right on
the basis of a traditional anticommunist electoral appeal or
an expansion of the government's majority to the left by appealing to the socialists for a semicoalition after the 1978
legislative elections. The first strategy raises the threat of
throwing the PS into a firmer communist embrace and of
losing power altogether; while the second one might well
throw the Gaullists, with their capacity for eroding the government's support among business, into the opposition.

The problem for the French left is that it too suffers the
threat of uncertain electoral support and, as a result, has not
come to grips with the real policy options it would favor if
it came to power. The alliance has survived in part because
neither party has been willing to claim supremacy over the
other, and this inhibits its ability to establish clear policy
goals for a left-wing alternative. Many of the programs that
were hammered out in the *Programme commun*, for example,
were taken over from the unions, which to some extent compete with the parties of the left for working-class loyalty.
Others were dredged out of the past and still others represented a joint grasping at issues that could unite the two parties at the risk of possible irrelevance to the voters. The striking aspect of the common program is its failure to come to

grips with the radically new relationship between French capitalism and the state, and its politically inspired lack of attention to the issue of workers' control.

The changes in French society since 1968, unlike those in Italy, have left the social and political power of the bourgeoisie virtually unscathed. The current disaccord in the majority—as much a result of personality differences as of disagreements on programs—leaves open the possibility of continued left-wing gains in future years. But the French state remains a bulwark of policies which advance the collective interest of the bourgeoisie, and the changes in French communism are too recent, too hurried and too elitist to inspire confidence that the PCF is following its Italian counterpart in the slow and patient construction of a system of left-wing hegemony. It is for these reasons that France seems to be headed, not towards a new political polarity, but towards a reinforcement of the social polarity that has always existed: between capital and labor.

But in these two political systems, marked by policy immobilism, political instability, and the incubus of the Cold War until quite recently, something has begun to change. Models of radicalism will also need to change to cope analytically with the new reality, and in so doing must take account of shifting social coalitions, of the left's strategy in attempting to form its own coalition, and of the role of the state in responding to demands from old supporters and from new opponents.

Henry A. Landsberger is professor of sociology at the University of North Carolina at Chapel Hill. He is author or editor of numerous articles and books on peasant movements and peasant organizations, including Latin American Peasant Movements *and* Rural Protest: Peasant Movements and Social Change. *An expert on Latin American politics, Professor Landsberger has served as vice-president and president of the Latin American Studies Association of the United States.*

5

The Sources of Rural Radicalism
Henry A. Landsberger

Peasant Radicalism or Peasant Militancy[1]

In urban settings—and in dictionaries—the term "radicalism" refers to an extreme point of view. It is used to describe a position at the level of ideology rather than of behavior. A crude definition of radicalism might be that it is "an ideological position which includes a desire for a very substantial, extreme change in the structure and/or in the basic values of a broad spectrum of societal institutions—economic, political and social."

The term "radicalism" has, however, been used only rarely in connection with rural movements. A rich variety of peasant parties established themselves in the East European countries between the two world wars.[2] They were to some extent guided by elaborate ideologies, at least in comparison with peasant movements elsewhere. Nevertheless, the word "radical," while on the tip of one's tongue because it was "almost" appropriate, was ultimately not often applied to these parties. Similarly, the many farmers' movements in the south and midwest of the United States in the decades before and after the Civil War have not been called radical but were referred to by specific names: the Farmers' Alliances, the

Greenback Movement, the Nonpartisan League, the Populist Movement.[3] At least by United States standards, these movements were among the most class conscious in its history and demanded more institutional change than most movements in America supported by other classes. Their demands exceeded all but those of small sectors of the American labor movement. Yet it is a rare writer—Seymour Martin Lipset is one—who feels justified in bracketing these rural movements under the term "Agrarian Radicalism."[4]

In most of the literature on American farmer movements the term "radicalism" is not extensively used. Moreover, when these movements are examined in detail, it turns out that they demanded, at most, that specific links on which the farmer depended—banks, railroads, processors, suppliers, and buyers—be prevented (occasionally by nationalization, but more frequently by demands for regulation) from exploiting the farmer's weakness. No major change was advocated in the agrarian structure itself; no rural communes, no nationalizing of land, no cooperative farms (as distinct from marketing and purchasing co-ops). Nor was radical change consistently sought in institutions which did not directly affect the farmer's economic well-being.

Implicit in the infrequent application of the label "radicalism" to rural events seems to be a recognition that peasant[5] movements and peasant protests usually do not quite meet the requirements for its accurate use. No detailed, precise, and generally accepted definition of the term "radicalism" exists. But a close examination of peasant unrest can clarify our ideas about it, as well as certain ambiguities in the conceptualization of "radicalism."

"Negative" vs. "Positive" Radicalism

The first ambiguity is that the concept "radicalism" includes (in part simply by not spelling out the difference between the two) both *negative radicalism* and *positive radicalism:* both the desire to see the disappearance of the institutions which exist, *and* the desire for a very different society to replace what exists. Failure to distinguish between the two makes it easy to slide unwittingly into the assumption that those who are vehemently against an important aspect of the present social structure must also have a clear vision of what they want in its stead. Whether this is the case ought to be a matter for empirical investigation rather than for unrecognized assumption. Once this assumption is brought out into the open, it does not seem very plausible. Few people engage in speculating about, and drawing up comprehensive and detailed plans for, a future ideal society. Rejection of this or that existing institution, on the other hand, might be expected to be quite frequent among the groups which suffer from the defects of these institutions. In any case, confusing the two types of radicalisms and radicals makes it difficult to analyze coherently their different origins, the groups to which each kind of radicalism (and the enormous varieties under each) appeals, and so forth.

More or Less Radicalism

Second—although Marxists might object—there is a quantitative characteristic in radicalism, however difficult it may be in practice to quantify and measure. Surely, the issue arises *how many,* and *which,* institutions a certain ideology or group wants to see changed, and by *how much?* Marx—unlike, for example, Gandhi, who wanted to go back to the hand loom—was eager to retain not only modern technology, but also such administrative structures and social relations as high technology necessarily entailed. Engels spelled this out quite specifically for the rural sector, and Castro has partly applied this idea, expecting that the traditional small-holding peasant would see that the technologically determined, large factory-in-the-field could satisfy his needs better than the bourgeois possession of a relatively small, uneconomic plot of land.

In any case, peasants (and workers, I believe) are apt to focus their demands for change on a relatively limited range of institutions. We indicated this in the case of the American farmer, but it is equally true of the Peruvian peasant of the 1960s. He wanted, first and foremost, to abolish unpaid labor services as a method for paying rent, to increase the wages he received, and to recover land of which his community had been deprived by fraud. It was far from his mind to question the existence of large estates *per se,* that is, to demand the systematic division of all *haciendas* (and far from the mind of the Mexican peasantry in the early years of the Mexican Revolution), let alone to challenge the principle of private ownership of land as such, and even less the institution of "private ownership of the means of production."

There is, then, the possibility that even in their negative aspects, in their rejection of the present structure, different groups and ideologies single out different aspects of that structure, and a broader or narrower range of institutions. The *problematica* of radical movements, and especially the *problematica* of relations between peasants and urban radicals, cannot be understood without first clearly understanding the different critiques and the different degrees of criticism of the present which each group proposes.

Radicalism vs. Militancy

Certain groups—again, most likely to be found among the urban intelligentsia—which are intensely against almost all aspects of a certain society, may exaggerate the extent to which broad segments of the population are equally comprehensively against the entire system on ideological grounds. This exaggeration is due partly to wishful thinking. But it is also due to fusing and confusing two phenomena which, again, need to be kept very much apart so that their complex relationship can be better clarified: the relationship between radical ideology on the one hand and militant behavior on the other. The temptation is to think that extreme militancy in behavior, e.g., violence, is bound to spring from a comprehensively radical critique of society. There may be a positive correlation, but it is unlikely to be perfect, any more than is its reverse: radical ideology need not lead to militant behavior. These are two very different phenomena, and should not be linked by definition.

It was conceptually confusing (and politically disastrous) to apply the label "radicalization" to the peasantry of, for example, Chile in the latter part of the 1960s and the early 1970s merely because Chilean *campesinos,* or at least some groups among them, were increasingly militant, that is, prepared to seize farms, organize unions, demonstrate, and strike. The extent to which this represented a total rejection of the then-existing system, let alone the extent to which it represented potential positive allegiance to some specific alternative system, was quite, quite doubtful. Yet in the literature on the Latin American peasantry, the term "radicalization" is often used to summarize a situation where we know for certain only that peasant activism has increased but where little is known about underlying ideologies, if any.[6]

While it may be wrongly labeled, it is in fact militant behavior, regardless of whether or not it reflected radical ideology, which has historically mattered not only in the countryside but also in helping to determine major historical events in society at large. In France in 1789; in Mexico in the second and third decade of this century; in Russia in 1917 and 1918; in Bolivia in 1952; in China from the latter part of the 1930s to 1949; and in Vietnam from the early 1950s onwards—in all these countries it was militant peasant action which helped to destroy the existing societal structure. The destruction was far greater than all but a handful of urban intellectuals (or the peasantry) had advocated, and because it was so thorough, it also helped to create a new society the exact nature of which, in most countries, no one had advocated, neither peasant nor intellectual! Even rural banditry can have such unintended disintegrating effects.[7] Differences in society at large, rather than differences in peasants' discontent, determine the differential impact on society of peasant unrest.

The role of the peasantry in China and Vietnam was very

different from its role in the other four countries to which we have referred: it was much more integral to the revolutionary process. But this, as we shall see, was due far less to any difference in its own ideology, than to the context in which peasant activism evolved. And the same is true when all six of the above countries are contrasted as a group with other countries *without* revolutions in which peasants played a part. What differentiates them as a group, we believe, is not so much peasant militancy as such nor any difference in the degree of underlying peasant discontent on which it is based, but rather the kinds of adventitious allies which the peasantry had available, the tactics of these allies, and the lack of strength of the opposition.

The following theses, admittedly exaggerated somewhat to bring out their unorthodox nature, are the essence of this paper:

1. Peasant discontent has been widespread, intense, and more constant than not, throughout history.

2. The discontent of peasants is directed at important but nevertheless relatively limited, concrete aspects of their life situation. It is misleading to use the word "radicalism" to denote this discontent, or to use any other word denoting a desire for comprehensive and profound change in overall social structure. There are well known exceptions to this, but they are indeed exceptions and they have generally not occurred where peasants have been involved in radical change.

3. Peasant unrest (militancy) which expresses this discontent has also been much more widespread than it would seem from just looking at the "peasant revolutions" (a very misleading term) of the twentieth century. Admittedly peasant unrest has been less widespread than discontent (for several reasons, of which repression is one). But it has been widespread nonetheless.

4. Despite the relative constancy both of peasant discontent and of peasant militancy, only recently have peasants begun to play crucial roles in bringing about actual radical social change. This implies that it is not

necessary to be an ideological radical in order to bring about radical change.

5. Given the peasantry's unchanged lack of radicalism and its chronic readiness to express discontent in unrest, the new historical role of the peasantry—at its extreme in China and Vietnam—implies that not the peasant, but the context in which peasant unrest now occurs, has changed.

These points will be elaborated in the main body of this paper.

Peasant Radicalism vs. the Culture of the Peasantry

Methodological Problems

Any discussion of peasant ideology, its existence and possible content, has to begin by drawing attention to what is really self-evident: systematic evidence about peasant ideology is likely to be scarce. Peasants, unlike intellectuals, do not write down their thoughts and are not even given to extensive speculation orally. Even if they were, there would still be the problem (true also for intellectuals) whether to take verbal expressions of belief—written or oral—at their face value. How does one ultimately know that someone is committed to an ideology, especially when commitments can take so many forms? Indirect evidence—such as voting for parties with radical ideologies—cannot be used, because to clarify the relationship between belief and behavioral support for radical causes is precisely the issue. Hence, to assume a direct relationship sweeps the issue under the rug. There is in any case the danger of committing the "ecological fallacy" of attempting to infer from overall voting percentages, based on electoral districts, the behavior of groups of individuals within these districts.

Methodological problems aside, there are substantive problems of interpretation. Electoral support by some sectors of the French peasantry for the French Communist Party, for example, is generally interpreted not as showing great peasant affection for communism, but merely as a ploy to frighten the government into not taking the peasantry for granted.[8] This kind of subtle ploy may be peculiar to the sophisticated French peasant. However, research in the relatively few other areas of the world in which peasant voting patterns, including voting for Marxist parties, could be analyzed, e.g., in Chile or in India, similarly lends itself only to inconclusive interpretations. It may well be the case, as Donald Zagoria has shown, that the worse the land tenure situation, the greater the vote for the communist party.[9] While it is fair to assume that voting communist represents some kind of protest (which is, in fact, all that Zagoria was interested in showing), we have no precise idea what it meant in ideological terms to the peasants concerned. The same is true of studies of rural voting in Chile, where the danger that the ecological fallacy was committed is actually substantial, and where the translation of voting patterns into "radicalism" was quite dubious.[10]

Hofheinz, in his ecological analysis of the strength of the Chinese Communist Party in rural areas, has been most sensitive to the problem of which kind of behavior to use as an index of commitment to an ideological position: what intensity of commitment each indicator might represent, and precisely to what.[11] Most of his indicators measure the impact of the Communist Party on a certain area, e.g., its control of it. As Hofheinz points out, inferring peasant attitudes from this is quite hazardous. Hofheinz finds only two other direct measures of peasant mobilization: party membership and military participation. For most countries, these are either not available or would again be quite ambiguous in significance.

Therefore, the precise relation between the great varieties of peasant protest behavior on the one hand and the attitudes and ideologies possibly underlying it on the other will always remain a matter of uncertain speculation rather than definitive proof.

Studies of peasant mentality. There is, however, one available source for the study of peasant mentality: the writings of anthropologists. With the exception of European peasants,

peasants have until recently been studied by anthropologists.[12] The anthropological literature confirms indirectly but very strongly our assertion that neither positive radicalism nor even comprehensive negative radicalism are realms on which the peasant spontaneously dwells. The peasant attitudes around which the anthropological literature revolves are (supposed) peasant apathy and fatalism, peasant reluctance to accept new ideas, to risk and to innovate (in all realms, including the political) and, above all, the air of mistrust and uncooperativeness which supposedly pervades peasant life.

This literature is associated especially with the names of George Foster and peasants' "image of limited good," and Edward C. Banfield and the concept of "amoral familism."[13] Their thesis—and the controversy surrounding it—is very similar to that revolving about "the culture of poverty." Interestingly enough, it was Oscar Lewis, an anthropologist well versed in tensions in peasant communities, who coined the phrase "culture of poverty" in describing the urban poor.[14]

Foster and Banfield, as well as others, have maintained that peasants are submissive, fatalistic and apathetic; mistrustful of others and therefore unwilling to cooperate with their peers; concerned only with their own and their family's fortune, and not that of their community; suspicious that if one person has more, another is bound to have less, etc. This kind of point, especially if somewhat misunderstood, quickly raises academic temperatures, and positions become exaggerated out of all proportion. The opposition usually asserts that there is good situational cause for these characteristics. The riposte to that, in turn, is that the proponent of the original thesis had himself said this quite plainly. If there is a genuine difference, it really only revolves about how deeply ingrained these traits are. Would the adult change almost immediately if put into a different opportunity structure? Or are these traits relatively permanent by then, but could be changed if, for example, the adolescent had different experiences? Finally, is the culture transmitted from generation to generation in early childhood so that it is difficult to break the chain? Although the answers in this overheated argument tend at times to be influenced by the writer's own ideological position, there is also disagreement among scholars of similar political sympathies. For example, a left-oriented writer such as Gerrit Huizer believes in the almost instant reversibility of these traits among peasants, while James Petras and Hugo Zemelman have accepted their persistence and a high degree of materialistic individualism.[15] Interestingly, Marx himself sketched a character portrait of the small-holding peasant in the *Eighteenth Brumaire* not unlike that drawn by today's supposedly conservative writers and left the impression that this character, reflecting the mode of production, was fairly deeply ingrained.[16]

To the extent that the characterization is even temporarily true, it would account in some measure for certain widely noted peasant attitudes and behavior patterns: the great reluctance, due not only to fear, with which most peasants break with their *patron* to join peasant movements; the intense rivalries and divisions which have often beset peasant movements, with one village fighting another; the reluctance of peasants to move far from their own homes; and the great difficulty in getting them to conceptualize their own problem as a systemic one, or at least, to act upon such a conceptualization. It is my impression that those closest to the peasantry and those activists most sympathetic to the plight of the peasantry have been most explicit in complaining of its passivity and have accepted pretty much the existence of a character syndrome as portrayed by Foster. Those furthest removed have read ideological "radicalization" into events with which they had only indirect contact. Thus there appears to be considerable validity to the proposition that one difficulty in arousing the peasantry, both ideologically and for militant action, lies in a particular peasant psychology which, at least in the short run, is not changeable. Few authors now join Fanon in declaring that "the peasants alone are revolutionary," and most would agree with James Scott that

> the central goals envisioned by peasants are often limited. . . .
> They take up arms less often to destroy elites than to compel them

to meet their moral obligation. Where a shred of the paternal normative structure remains, peasants often invoke it; where such a restoration is inconceivable, peasants often attempt to drive out the collector of taxes and rents (or move beyond their reach) and to reestablish an autonomous community. In those cases where the threat to subsistence routines seems cataclysmic and irresistible the response appears more often to take on millennial overtones.[17]

The reference to "millennial overtones" is relevant not only to Southeast Asia—e.g., the Cao Dai in South Vietnam; the *Iglesia Ni Cristo* in Luzon—but also on occasion to Latin America, at least in earlier times.[18] Moreover, religious ideology may stiffen peasant support *for* the established system, and *against* a revolution supposedly helping their cause, as the *Cristero* unrests in Mexico in the mid-1920s showed. This was a church-fomented, landlord-supported movement against the still shaky new postrevolutionary government, and against land reform specifically. Both its footsoldiers and its targets were peasants. It is not only the Spanish Civil War that can be described as a civil war among the peasantry.[19]

In the writings of anthropologists, therefore, there is no reference to peasant radicalism. A number of them (and we would strongly agree) insist that peasant fatalism and apathy are not only superficial and reactive, but in part not even genuine: they form a protective mask which serves as a way to get back at the *patron,* as well as to hide intense hatred for him and fear of the consequences of that hatred.[20] In other words, these authors see constant, intense discontent, on the existence of which we would also insist. Of radicalism, however, there is no mention.

Recently, political scientists and historians have joined anthropologists in their study of peasantry. We have already referred to Scott, who posits at most a backward-looking radicalism—restoring the past—and indicates that, for the most part, this covers only those institutional segments which are necessary for the peasants' immediate survival. Other political scientists, however, who by disciplinary inclination are more intrigued than anthropologists to establish whether peasants are or are not radical, have indeed begun to concern themselves with the issue. Migdal (whose work covers different parts of the world, though his main interest is in Asia) and Petras and Zemelman (who are most concerned with Latin America) have designed "scales" of ideology and class consciousness which are quite similar to each other. Midgal's scale has steps beginning with "seeking individual gains," going on to "seeking gains for a community or sector," up to "raising the peasantry as a whole." Petras and Zemelman define "political consciousness" (to these authors, the highest form) as no more than becoming an "antagonist group" which seeks the elimination of the *patron* as both necessary and possible.[21] Significantly, even the most extreme points on these scales do not postulate that the peasant formulates his problem except as it affects him. No society-wide vision is posited, or is allowed for only in negative terms (that is, in terms of what needs to be removed; there is no vision of a "new society").

The requirement that institutional change be seen as both possible and—very significantly—as necessary *before* the peasantry can acquire revolutionary or radical consciousness was first introduced by Wolpe[22] and has since been much utilized by other writers.[23] But little empirical evidence has been adduced for this claim, nor for any other empirical assertion about consciousness: e.g., its content, prevalence, differential incidence in various strata of the peasantry, and so forth.

Concerning the prevalence of radical ideologies among peasants as discussed by political scientists, we may cite Migdal as one of the few authors who not only state that behavior support for radical movement exists (this is undeniable, of course) but also speak about consciousness and ideology. At the very end of his excellent book, Migdal asserts that peasants originally join revolutionary movements to redress personal grievances (the lowest level of consciousness in his scheme, after "accommodation"). Later, however, they recognize communal ills which need to be alleviated, and they ultimately become conscious that society as a whole must be changed. But interestingly enough, Midgal points to no evidence for this claim in an otherwise meticulously documented work.[24]

Perhaps the most telling example of nonradical consciousness is provided in Petras' and Zemelman's Chilean case study. They found that what really motivated the leader of the peasants, who was also the most loyal to Chile's (very left) Socialist Party, was his desire to free himself from the old *fundo* system in order—so help us!—to become a private owner and entrepreneur selling in the market! Thus, the most active and ideological of their *campesinos* saw class conflict as leading ultimately to their replacement by themselves of the *patron*.[25] No wonder that this led to the development of "attitudes of social differentiation toward other peasants," to the heightening of internal stratification among the peasantry.[26] Six years after the takeover of the estate by the peasants and after much political agitation, these authors could still discern no more than the dimmest outlines of a new consciousness which consisted of no more than a negative awareness that the new system did not work as well as expected. The authors place their hope for a totally changed peasant mentality in the establishment (by those in charge of a society) of a "broad context of a completely new system of relations and information."[27] In other words, peasant mentality is so "sticky" that it could be changed only *after* a revolution, by living within new, postrevolutionary institutions. No claim is made by these relatively radical writers that peasant radicalism would precede, and be effective in bringing about, a changed institutional structure.

Peasant Discontent, Peasant Unrest, and Its Containment

The Ubiquity of Peasant Discontent

To focus too narrowly on the dramatic "peasant revolutions" of the twentieth century may convey the false impression that both discontent and the unrest which under certain circumstances results from it are recent and exceptional.

Our position is that as long as there has been stratification in the countryside, there has been discontent with it. *Norms* and *exchanges* may have assuaged it to some extent, and *coercion* will have further limited its expression in unrest. But all three have resulted in no more than very delicate and unstable balances, easily upset by any change in the forces on which the balance has been poised.

The rural "premobilization" situation (a misleading term, because it implies a previously quiescent state of affairs) is no longer portrayed by most analysts as necessarily and invariably a harmonious one. Few now regard as prototypical the *Gemeinschaft* type of community in which there either were no class distinctions based on wealth, power and the *de facto* repression and exploitation that go with these; or in which such differences were legitimated by tradition and therefore accepted painlessly. Most analysts now recognize that while patterns of superordination-subordination may have been traditional, and of long standing, they were often not wholly accepted and certainly not without some internalized resistance. Redfield's presentation of the integrated folk society as typical of agrarian life outside Europe until the early twentieth century is no longer regarded as valid.[28]

In the case of Mexico and its Aztec empire, for example, political, economic and cultural subordination existed before the arrival of the Spaniards, that is, it antedated European colonialism and neocolonialism. Indeed, the unrest and resistance it engendered were crucial to the success of Cortes and the very small group of Spaniards he led. The same is true of the Inca empire in Bolivia-Peru and its collapse before Pizarro's equally outnumbered band. India experienced peasant unrest before the appearance of the British, and so did Japan. China had a history of peasant discontent well antedating the late nineteenth century, when European trade began to exert a major influence on that country's entire internal development. And Popkin is at pains to stress that intravillage tensions antedated the economic and political impact of French rule in Vietnam. European peasant unrest goes back to the eighth century at least.[29]

Peasant unrest outside Europe, therefore, has not been contingent on the most recent phase of total and intensive world economic integration (the imperialist stage of capitalism, according to Marxists), just as inside Europe, too, peasant unrest, while indeed related to the interplay between commercialization, urbanization, and technological changes in agricultural production, often occurred well before the beginning of capitalism, precisely because changes in commercialization, urbanization, and agricultural technology themselves also far antedated the rise of capitalism. Marx and Engels saw class conflict as beginning with the movement of society beyond "savages and semi-savages." Since this was well before the advent of capitalism and industrialism, the exploited classes were necessarily peasants and it was they, therefore, who were involved in conflict.

The Paradigmatic Situation

With the recent growth of comparative studies of peasantry, attempts have been made to describe and understand the peasant's plight in terms which can be generalized beyond the specifics of a certain situation. One part of this literature focuses on differences among the peasantry, that is, "types" of peasantry which recur (landless workers, tenants, sharecroppers, workers on modern plantations, etc.). These differences are ultimately based on differences in the relationship to land, to markets, and to each other, of dominant and subordinate (peasant) classes, as well as on differences in crops and technology. A classic article by Stinchcombe opened this discussion in the early 1960s.[30]

Another part of the literature has addressed itself to a portrayal of what is common to all peasants regardless of type. Its most graphic formulation is that of Peruvian sociologist Julio Cotler, who coined the phrase "the triangle without a base" to describe the relationship among peasants, between peasants and those who control the essential means of production, and between peasants and the sociopolitical environment.[31] The structural basis of all these relationships is, as Wolf puts it, "a social order in which some men,

through their power, can demand payment from others . . .
'peasant' denotes an asymmetrical structural relationship
between producers of surplus and controllers."[32] Barrington
Moore calls the same phenomenon "exploitation" and
refers to the fact that the peasant has to strike a bargain
in which he receives less—protection, land, and money—
than he gives.[33] Most people (this author very much among
them) would agree that the phenomenon, whatever its particular label—expropriation of a surplus, exploitation, asymmetrical relationship, unbalanced bargain—is a very real
one. Yet like Marx's original concept of "exploitation," it
is not objectively provable except through a series of taut-
ologies and definitional assumptions which nullify its usefulness.

In essence—and this is what the "triangle without a base"
described—a combination of circumstances and institutions
keep the peasant either objectively on the margin of existence, or at least subjectively severely deprived in comparison with others. The legal structure and the ultimate and
often immediate backing by physical force enable a relatively
small group which dominates the economic, religious, or
political institutional structure to keep control of the essential scarce resources: land and water above all, but also credit
and access to markets and supplies. Demographic pressure on
the peasant often reinforces his weakness because he lacks
control of these scarce resources.

Whether living on the *hacienda* or in his own community,
the individual peasant is economically much more dependent on the controller of key resources than vice versa, and
political power assures that this remains the case. When the
Black Death made labor scarce in England in the middle of
the fourteenth century, wages did not rise, they were fixed
by Parliament, and peasants were prohibited from leaving
their employment. The controlling classes isolate the peasant
as much as possible from political elements (e.g., towns)
which might ally with him against the landlord; from economic resources which might increase his bargaining power
(direct access to markets, migration to produce labor scarcity,

etc.); and, above all, by preventing peasants from communicating and combining forces with each other. All institutions are so designed that the peasant is dependent only upwards, on the landlord, not horizontally, on other peasants. Hence the metaphor of the "triangle without a base." It was, of course, this same isolation of French peasants from each other which Marx diagnosed more than a century ago as the source of their weakness and lack of class consciousness.

There is widespread agreement on this description of the peasant's position, although a recent dissertation by Gitlitz warns seriously that the picture of helpless oppression, total isolation, and extreme one-way dependence can be severely overdrawn.[34] There is less agreement on the degree to which the peasantry reacts to this situation with either unalloyed hostility or partial acceptance.

Those who emphasize the large role which coercion does and has to play in order to keep peasants subjugated, obviously postulate severe discontent and an ever-present readiness to revolt. Ernest Feder has written in great detail about the vast arsenal of coercive methods—economic, ideological (the threat of damnation), political, and physical—which are available to landlords.[35] Our own view is that a substantial degree of coercion is almost invariably present. Others, however, emphasize that some kind of a bargain, an exchange of utilities (land or wages, or payment in kind for labor or product) does after all go on. Discontent is then expected to be severe only if the terms of the bargain suddenly worsen.

Finally, there are those who emphasize the existence of normative elements which lessen discontent. Two kinds of normative elements have been discussed, applicable to two very different kinds of situation. One, on which Scott focuses, assumes an already existing peasant-lord dependency relationship, but asserts that it is governed by a "norm of reciprocity": the elite owes it to the peasant to guarantee his "right to subsistence" even if, in a disastrous year, this means foregoing the rent which would otherwise be due. Both sides accept this moral obligation. To the peasant living on the margin of existence, the right to subsistence has the highest value, and inequality and exploitation are accepted provided that this right is guaranteed.[36] The other type of normative constraint on discontent is found in what Migdal calls "free-holding" villages,[37] similar to Wolf's "closed" communities.[38] In these, there was no landlord who provided any kind of service, only an external state which extracted taxes. Here, norms controlled the behavior not of landlords, but of members within the community, especially of its wealthier members. Norms limited their exchanges with the outside (in order to reduce insecurity and the possibility of divisive stratification) and obliged them to help those in need (thus preventing internal stratification and assuring subsistence for all). Our own view is that such normative elements, which imply that there is genuine acceptance of the situation by peasants, should be viewed as a surface layer which permits both sides to rationalize a situation essentially based on coercion.

Hence, the coercive, utilitarian, and normative elements keep in check the expression in overt unrest of the perpetual peasant dissatisfaction. The precariousness of this balance between discontent and its containing forces is indicated by the frequency with which peasant unrest erupts. Although the nonspecialist is apt to think of peasant protest as relatively rare, all detailed agrarian histories show an almost continuous series of protests, but mostly on a scale insufficient to be included in "great" history or to be more than noted in passing by major figures and documents.[39]

Tipping the Balance of Discontent: Structural Changes

All writers agree that a *change* of some magnitude, detrimental to the peasantry, is the key causal link between what may have been, at best, a situation of uneasy tension with sporadic unrest on the one hand, and on the other, a wide range of acts of more massive militant protest. Theoretically, such change could be exclusively subjective—for example, a rise in aspirations leading to increased frustration. No author defends that position, however, even though in the last few decades rising aspirations stimulated by mass media may well have had *some* independent effect. And certainly social psychological theories of "relative deprivation" have been in vogue to explain more general societal unrest. But to our knowledge, all authors concerned with the peasantry accept that an objective, institutional change of some kind occurs and is of primary importance.

If the theses of various authors are juxtaposed, there is an appearance of disagreement regarding the kind of change involved. Yet, there is no particular reason for insisting that economic changes are always primary over political ones. In the case of Russia in the eighteenth and nineteenth centuries, the political phenomenon of growth and rationalization of the state resulted in pressure on landowners and, ultimately, on peasants. In other cases—Mexico, for example—the economic integration of the State of Morelos into the world sugar market at the end of the nineteenth century was primary; while in Vietnam, both economic and political changes (French taxes and a new administrative system) played a role. Given a Marxist orientation, political changes such as we have mentioned are considered to be ultimately rooted in the economy. But while this may well be correct, it is one stage further back in the analysis. The recent work by the Tillys, dealing with collective violence in France, Italy, and Germany, also questions an exclusive and direct link between economic changes and unrest. *The Rebellious Century* places heavy emphasis on political factors.[40] In any case, the two institutions—political and economic—are generally so intertwined that they should not be thought of as providing alternative explanations.

Hence, in this critical area of analysis, we find varied but compatible emphasis, with differences depending not so much on the author as on the reality of the case under consideration. In some cases it is political, in others economic change which aggravates discontent. The effect on the peasantry is sometimes mediated via the landlord who seeks to exploit opportunities in a new market, or pass along new taxes and obligations. In other cases—a collapsing rice market—the change has a direct impact on the peasant. The change can be positive for the landlord—an opportunity to adopt machinery, to change from labor intensive crops to pasture—or it can be a negative squeeze. It can be steady downward pressure on the peasantry or the greater uncertainty of being subject to an unpredictable trade cycle. There may even be some situations in which it is the uneven degree of improvement that intensifies peasant dissatisfaction to an explosive degree.This occurred in the century preceding the English Peasant Uprising of 1381 and the French Revolution of 1789. In the case of France, however, it has been seriously questioned whether the lot of the average peasant really had improved. In the twentieth century at least, the phenomenon of uneven improvement does not seem to be an important one in explaining rising discontent.

In line with earlier arguments, the kinds of objective negative consequences of change—in addition to plain immiserization—which are likely to intensify peasant discontent are: increased uncertainty; the greater probability of falling below the level needed for survival; the changing balance of utilitarian bargains; and changing fulfillment of moral commitments which bind both landlords and better-off community members to help those in need and generally restrain individually-oriented behavior. Because integration into more distant markets brings uncertainty with it, such integration is often accompanied by peasant discontent. And, similarly, the increased discontent associated with the monetization of exchanges is related to the fact that money rents, or wages, or taxes—especially those imposed by alien governments—are likely to be less flexible in case of emergency than exchanges in kind and thus increase the possibility that the poorer peasants have left to them less than is needed for survival.

Detrimental changes in the demand and supply for land and labor—the *utilitarian* aspect of the exchange relationship—will be seen by peasants as breaches also of the *normative* aspect of the previously existing precarious balance. The literature on peasant unrest frequently refers to the experience of injustice (not only of hardship) and the delegitimation of the landlord, or of the agents of the state, as higher and more rigid rents and taxes are imposed, and personal and communal emergencies are no longer taken into account.[41]

Changes of such magnitude may occur that the elite (the landlord or the state) renders no recognizable services to the peasant at all, political or economic, so that the "exchange" is completely one-sided. Such extreme elite parasitism is, of course, most likely to lead to delegitimation. The belief that the state was not necessary is one of the explanations for rural anarchism in Spain, and for peasant revolts at the time of the French Revolution.

Many authors stress that a frequent effect of structural changes is increased inequality in the countryside. In other words, not only are the poorer being pushed downward, but the originally better-off, or some of them, are maintaining or even improving their position. This accelerates the delegitimation of the system. Reference here is not so much to the already rich landlords as to better-off sectors within the peasant community.[42]

Changes in economic relationships with landlords, and their consequences for utility and legitimacy, blend into changes in other relationships. Thus Migdal emphasizes the weakening of the constraints and social control exercised by the village as a whole on those peasants within the community who were better off, and who previously limited their accumulative tendencies. This occurs precisely at a time when the less well endowed are unable to cope with what Migdal calls "incomplete market structures," namely, lack of credit and of other inputs, and of access to markets. In other words, there is a general breakdown of consensus on norms, as new opportunities or pressures upset utilitarian and normative balances which in any case had been precarious.[43]

In addition to giving precedence to structural over subjective changes, most authors agree substantially on one further aspect of change. The *scope* of changes which push peasants toward large-scale unrest is not local nor even confined to the agrarian sector. However "parochial" the response of each peasant group may be, the cause of what ultimately impinges on him is, as Wolf terms it, "overwhelming societal change" and "great social dislocation."[44]

Linking major peasant unrest with major social change might seem to imply that peasant unrest should be periodic, which we previously asserted was not the case. Is not great structural change episodic? Not necessarily so. Great changes, even in the past, let alone since the beginning of this century, have often been prolonged and continuous. The "Industrial Revolution" did not begin suddenly in 1760, nor was it preceded by several centuries of general stability. The West did not force its way into an India, China, or Latin America which were even remotely stable. This is in accord with the facts concerning unrest which we described above. The intensification of peasant unrest, the dependent variable of large scale change, has been much more frequent in most countries and eras than is known by all but students who have specialized in the agrarian histories of their respective countries, because change too has been much more continuous than is generally assumed.

Tipping the Balance of Discontent: Accelerating Factors

While the specific changes in the economy and the political system which we have just discussed are the most important in intensifying the ever-high level of peasant discontent, demographic change may have the same effect. There are, further, certain exogenous-accidental events which may affect the peasant-elite relationship, and the peasantry itself, in such a way as to heighten the preexisting level of tension, so that any changes will more readily lead to unrest.

Demographic Pressure

There is widespread agreement in the literature on the association between an absolutely high level of demographic pressure—and especially of *increased* demographic pressure—and peasant discontent.[45] Whether population pressure leads to the subdivision of the small owner's and the tenant's plot until subsistence becomes impossible; whether it leads to higher rents and shares because the demand for land to rent intensifies; or whether the consequence is an increase in the mass of landless laborers, an increase in rural population is likely to lead to immiserization and to an increasing threat to survival. "Self-exploitation" and "agricultural involution" can be carried only so far (and in any case imply a deterioration in living standards).[46]

An interesting characteristic of demographic pressure as a cause of heightened discontent is that in the past it has generally not been recognized as such by the various actors in the rural drama, even at the national level. There have generally been more visible demons to blame for peasant misery, such as landlords and hostile governments. It is only after friendly governments have divided up at least a fair proportion of large landholdings and the peasant's condition is still not a great deal better that the importance of demographic pressure becomes apparent, at least to some observers. There is a man/land ratio which—with existing technology and existing systems of production and organization—puts a low ceiling on the number of peasants who can be satisfied, and the degree to which they can be satisfied. This was the situation in several Eastern European countries between the wars,[47] and it is the case in several Latin American countries today, notably Peru, where the division of large estates and the more effective utilization of their land would still leave hundreds of thousands of peasants without land.

"Exogenous factors" in the peasant-elite relationship. There are a number of fortuitous factors which may either add to the tension intrinsic to the peasant-elite relationship, or—if they cut across the relationship—may defuse that tension. Among the two most important are national-ethnic differences on the one hand, and religious differences on the other. If landlords are divided from the peasantry by these, then economic tensions are thereby compounded. This was the situation of Indian creditor landlords in Burma in the 'thirties and 'forties; of Spaniards vs. Latin American Indians over several centuries; French colon and administrator vs. North African or Indochinese; Normans vs. Saxons in the thirteenth and

even still in the fourteenth century. The same factors can, of course, also undermine class unity (in exactly the same way as in urban-industrial settings) if, instead of reinforcing class cleavages, they cut across them. The peasantry of interwar Poland was divided within itself by the fact that some were Poles, others White Russians, and still other Ukrainians; in Yugoslavia the Croat Peasant Party—originally one of the most promising—in time became essentially an anti-Serb and antiorthodox nationalist party allied with the Croation middle class, so that no united action with Serb and Slovene peasants materialized. Similarly in Czechoslovakia, Slovak separatism (and Roman Catholicism) triumphed as orienting ideologies over peasant class interests. In the United States South, the unity of poor farmers was typically broken by black-white ethnic differences, often accentuated by elites for that very purpose.

Factors "Radicalizing" the Peasantry

Scholars agree that a number of influences increase the likelihood of peasant militancy or, at least, the likelihood that those individual peasants affected by them will become militant. Experience outside the village is one of these influences. And because service in armies during wartime affects so many peasants (Russia, 1914-1917; Bolivia, 1929-1932), the level of discontent and militancy among the entire peasantry may be raised by it. Especially powerful is the effect of a lost war, in which the peasant often sees the previously all-powerful elite in a position of incompetent helplessness. However, military service is only one kind of extra-village experience which gives peasants the self-confidence and the comparative perspective on their situation to make them more militant. Migration in search of employment, with a subsequent return to the village after a seasonal or a longer absence, is likely to have a similar effect. Other major influences on the individual are reputed to be the influence of the mass media and education. We enter here the realm of speculation, or of passing on conventional wisdom. For there are no sophisticated studies showing the effect on individual (or group-aggregate) militancy of these two factors when other correlated factors are held constant.[48] However, they are generally accepted as effective causes of militancy, and this seems plausible even though exact empirical verification is presently unavailable.

Structuring the Goals of Rural Discontent: Tenure and Labor Systems

We have so far explained only the intensification of discontent and unrest. We now need to explain the specific directions which the unrest takes, that is, its goals, as well as the subgroups of the peasantry most likely to become militant. It is useful to remember that industrial labor movements, at least until the 1920s, differed greatly in whether they sought (1) the restoration of the traditional master-journeyman systems of the past; (2) a worker-controlled (syndicalist) industrial system; (3) improvements in the new employer-worker relationship; or (4) the transfer of the ownership of industry from private to social ownership. Preoccupation with the concept of "radicalism"—in this case, deciding to which of these four goals the term "radical" should be applied—seems less useful even in the urban context than exploring the conditions under which labor movements set themselves one or the other goal.

The goals of rural movements have varied in ways quite comparable to those of industrial labor. There are trade unions looking for "no more" than better wages and working conditions. There have been movements seeking to restore the past. There have been cooperative movements and peasant parties, especially in Europe, which can be equated to some extent with syndicalism in their emphasis on sectoral autonomy, and even on peasant dominance and a belief in the peasant's capacity for self-direction, as well as suspicion of the state as it exists. Finally, nationalization has been advocated by some—though the proportion of "outsiders" to "peasants" has been far greater than in the case of industry, where workers themselves have been massively behind this aim. There are, of course, many other differences between the goals of urban and rural movements, but some degree of parallelism undoubtedly exists. In any case, our main point in raising here the issue of qualitatively different goals, and the need to investigate the conditions which determine the selection of one and the rejection of the other, is to question the fruitfulness of any undifferentiated concept of "radicalism" as applied to rural movements.

In the case of industrial movements, the two chief determinants of their goals have been seen as stemming from (1) the specific historical evolution of the class system in each society; and (2) the nature of the ownership structure and of the productive process of the industry regardless of the specific society. Similarly in agriculture, (1) the historical specifics of the relationship of peasants to society at large, and (2) the nature of the landowner's and peasant's income, and their relationship to the means of production, regardless of societal specifics, are crucial in determining the orientation of peasant movements. We shall concentrate here on the effects of income sources and tenancy, and on the relative militancy of different sectors of the peasantry.

Who Is Most Militant?

This line of investigation goes back to Marx and Engels.[49] The answer to the question: "which subclass among the peasantry is the most militant?" varies. Some authors cast the middle-level, landowning peasantry into the most militant role, while others think it the most conservative and the landless laborers the most militant. But the disagreement is substantially resolved if there is (1) more precise specification of the conditions under which each is supposed to be true; (2) knowledge of the stage which the movement has reached; and (3) the distinction kept between intense discontent and short-term uprising based on it, as against longer term commitment to militant action.

Eric R. Wolf has asserted that it is the landowning middle peasantry which is the most likely to be "instrumental in dynamiting the peasant social order."[50] Yet Malefakis found that the case of Spain did not substantiate this thesis of the revolutionary "landowning middle peasantry." He shows convincingly that the landless proletariat of Andalusia and Estremadura was the most militant (a possibility Wolf seems specifically to deny), while the property-owning peasants of Spain were as conservative as Marx, a century ago, had said they were and would always be in France.[51] Zagoria's writings also stress the role of the landless, most impoverished peasantry, whether hired laborers, sharecroppers, or tenants.[52] Hofheinz, too, is well known for his scepticism about encountering stable correlations between *any* peasant or contextual characteristic and the spatial distribution of radical, i.e., communist, influence in pre-1949 China—especially since that distribution itself varied so much from one period to another.[53] Yet something can probably be salvaged from the attempt to link class of peasants with militancy.

According to Malefakis, the Andalusian rural proletariat and that of Estremadura was and had been highly discontented and to some extent genuinely radical in ideology, rare though that is. However, once it attempted to move from belief to militant action it was quickly suppressed. This was the case because—as Wolf would have put it—the rural proletariat was not sufficiently marginal in relation to control from the outside. In other words, this group of laborers was located close to urban centers of power—a second condition posited by Wolf.[54] Second, as Malefakis dramatically recounts, the Andalusian peasantry was quickly crushed because it was physically and psychologically too weak to resist, which is what Wolf and I had asserted.[55]

Although the distinction may not have been made with sufficient clarity, Wolf and I were predicting neither the degree of discontent nor the readiness to act and engage in spontaneous uprisings of the middle peasantry, but rather its capacity for sustaining a prolonged revolt with some chance of success and, in Wolf's case, for sustained revolutionary warfare. Landless laborers clearly will engage in (relatively hopeless) uprisings when sufficiently threatened and when they perceive a chance of success, whether realistic or not. But it is only the middle peasantry which, if and when it does decide to rise—and it may hold back a long time—has the capacity for sustained action.

This, too, is the kind of situation portrayed in Hobsbawm and Rudé's *Captain Swing*.[56] Agricultural laborers can rise up, but they are too weak in resources to stay the course. The poor peasantry also plays a considerable part in the thinking of those influenced by Maoism. But let it be noted that its role in eliminating first the rich, and then even the middle peasants, develops *after* revolutionary forces have won complete control over the power of coercion at the level of the state. The poor peasantry is, then, "revolutionary" in the very different (but of course very important) sense of changing the structure of property for the second time (the first being the elimination of the nonworking landlords which occurs much earlier in the revolutionary process).[57]

It seems appropriate to elaborate these points in order to substantiate one theme of this paper: there is a good deal of agreement in the literature, but much of it is latent and dependent on reconciling supposed disagreements by more careful formulation of proposed generalizations. In particular, we need to be precise about (1) the *exact phenomena* to which the generalizations are expected to apply ("radicalism" in what sense?); (2) the *conditions* under which the assertion is expected to hold; and (3) the *stage of the development* of a movement to which it applies. Of course, no generalization can ever be perfect. In statistical terms, no correlation is ever at the level of 1.0. Hence the existence of negative cases should not necessarily lead to abandoning a hypothesis. That a strong state is capable of suppressing even groups highly susceptible to rebellion does not invalidate the idea that some groups are indeed more susceptible, other things being equal.

The different goals of different sectors of the peasantry. We regard this question as more tractable than the one concerning "who is more militant?" which really depends as much on the situation as on the group in question. By far the most elegant work on differential goals, both conceptually and statistically, is that of Jeffrey Paige.[58] His starting points are three key pieces of work by Stinchcombe, Steward, and Wolf, all of which break down "the peasantry" into three to five different groups according to the kind of agricultural enterprise in which they work (old-style manor or *hacienda*, family tenancy, plantations, etc.), and then link these groups to the kind of goals they have. These, in turn, are related in complex ways to degrees of class consciousness, radicalism, conservatism, etc.[59] According to Paige, however, the evidence adduced by these three authors is not systematic, nor are the theoretical linkages tight. Furthermore, there are substantial contradictions between authors. As we have already noted, Wolf thought small-holders to be "revolutionary" while Steward though them conservative and plantation workers class conscious, a view shared by neither Stinchcombe nor Wolf.

Paige himself converts these "empirical" typologies into what he believes to be their theoretically more relevant underpinnings: whether the income of each side is based on *land* or on *money* (wages in the case of peasants, capital in the case of the landowning and controlling class). From this he obtains a two-by-two table: (1) the *hacienda*, in which the *owner* depends on *land* (he has little capital) and his "serfs" are paid in *land* for their labor; (2) sharecropping and tenancy in which the *owner* again has only *land* and relatively little capital, but the *sharecropper* or tenant is paid in the *money* left over from the sale of his share of the crop; (3) the plantation, in which the *owners* have to have a good deal of *capital*, and workers get paid in *cash*; and finally (4) *small holders*, who themselves have *land*, but the *upper class* obtains its "cut" via *capital* (in the form of control of bank credit, marketing, etc.).

From the source of their income Paige then deduces whether the peasants' organization will be weak or strong. They will be weak where income is based on land, because peasants will be in competition for it, more likely to be isolated, heterogeneous, etc. If the upper class, too, is based on land (*hacienda*) there will be ineffective revolt. Where it is based on capital (in the case of the opponents of smallholders) there will be commodity reform movements (U.S. farmers' movements) which, again, will be highly sporadic, having the control of credit, railroads, tariffs, money supply, etc., as their goal.

Where peasants receive their income in the form of money, however, they are likely to be more homogeneous, less in competition and therefore able to mount stronger organizations. In the case of plantations, this should lead to strong unions, bargaining with capitalists over wages in a reform-style fashion. In the case of sharecroppers and tenants, however, who face an upper class based on land, the situation is explosive. If they lose much land, they lose everything—their capital, not just part of the income from it. Their inflexibility leads the peasants to adopt socialist or nationalist revolutionary goals. It results in movements whose goal is the ousting of the present owners and the establishment of owner-managed farms.

In addition to theoretical elegance, Paige has attempted to test this theory very painstakingly and with great statistical sophistication, including "path" and "factor" analyses coding agrarian events in seventy countries. His analysis takes into account the possibly "explosive effect" of the simultaneous presence of key variables, i.e., the interaction of key variables with each other, achieving at one point correlations of .90.[60] In this specific example, an intensive study of the distribution of unrest in Peru, it is the simultaneous existence in a zone of very unequal land distribution (large *haciendas* control a high percentage of land) *and* of many traditional communities *and* of export orientation which predicts land invasions ("revolts") with a high degree of certainty. There are some severe methodological problems inevitably built into this kind of research, such as the uneven distribution of events between countries. Paige is fully aware of this, and attempts to take it into account, but it is unclear whether this is ultimately possible. But one feels reluctant to cavil at this magnificent effort, in which specific types of agrarian structures are linked to specific types of goals, and these in turn to specific types of militant actions: strikes are linked to commercial plantations, in which unionized workers have higher wages as their objectives; concern over marketing, credit, etc. are associated with small-holders; sporadic "peasant revolts" including land invasions are associated with *haciendas* in which workers are "paid" with subsistence plots; and a total change in the property system seems to be sought by tenant farmers and sharecroppers.

There are additional phenomena which Paige's scheme does not attempt to cover. Thus, it is a recurrent theme in rural history that peasants who are differentially placed with respect to the means of production may not only have different goals, but may be in conflict with each other. (This is quite separate from the fact of disunity *within* a certain type of peasantry.) Typically, communities trying to recover lost lands from large *haciendas* may meet resistance from "serfs" resident on the *hacienda*. This occurred in Peru in the early 1960s[61] and in Russia in 1905.[62] In Chile, too, conflict became a serious problem during the Allende years, between landless laborers on the one hand, and small-holders as well as farm laborers who were attached to farms and were benefiting from agrarian reforms, on the other. Indeed, small-owners in Chile allied themselves at times with right-wing large land-owners, as they did in Northern Germany in the 1920s and early 1930s, in Spain during the Civil War, and in Northern Italy before Mussolini's rise to power. Yet these same small-holders may be oriented toward the radical left if the threat comes from surrounding large landholders.[63] In short: the goals of a group will depend on who is, at a given point, the opponent—and this may not be the "upper class" but another group of peasants structurally differently located. Whatever the specifics, the severity of conflicts within the peasantry can hardly be overestimated.

The difference—indeed, conflict—noted above between unattached farm laborers and farm laborers regularly attached to a farm also draws our attention to the fact that the rural stratification system is more complex than a mere three or four classes. Even at the lower end there may be six or seven classes, and peasants may simultaneously belong to several of them; they may be both small owners and laborers. No wonder that the exact prediction of choice of goal is difficult if the status on which it is based is itself ambiguous. Finally, as we already pointed out in the previous section, the choice of goal may be affected by other cleavages. A clash which is at bottom economic may take on an ethnic or nationalist tinge if the upper class happens to be of another ethnic group.

The interwar peasant parties of Eastern Europe are an interesting example of selecting a goal which, in part, at least, goes beyond the rather limited patterns we generally expect. These parties obtained their main support, though not their leadership, from small owners. Demographic pressure was a considerable though unrecognized problem, so that, despite substantial land-reform, a high percentage of owners disposed of too little land. To the extent that the parties desired the further break-up of large estates and the distribution of land, and to the extent that they had "commodity" goals (e.g., support of cooperatives, better credit facilities), they do fall within the above scheme.

But in addition, they seem to have been pervaded by a broader, genuine "peasantist" ideology: an exaltation of the quality of rural life, an idealization of peasant personality (including conservatism), hostility to the cities and to industry and, particularly, depreciation of urban professionals and intellectuals (and Jews).[64] With this went a certain amount of antiparliamentarism, an antipolitics, antiparty outlook, shading into a desire to restore an organic, conflict-free society in which "the people's will" would prevail.

How can we account for these rather unusual goals? There may well have been something unusual about the East European peasantry and its relation to this unusual "opponent," the city. There was enough direct contact so that these peasants (unlike those of Latin America) were very much aware of the immense cultural gap separating them from the towns. The towns were heavily influenced by Western Europe, so that the gap was indeed substantial. It could also have been due to a relatively homogeneous and, at the same time, relatively well educated peasantry (again, as compared with those of Latin America and Southeast Asia). In certain countries, no other parties—e.g., religious ones—were forthcoming or suitable, and the relative effectiveness of the political (that is, parliamentary) structure of the nation made it highly desirable for each group to have a party represent it.

Our point here is to emphasize that over and above the general tendencies which may be highlighted by studies such as those of Paige, there will be local or regional facts of history and social structure which may modify the general rule. There is really no reason why the search for general tendencies should in any way preclude the simultaneous acceptance of certain *ad hoc* explanations.[65]

Nevertheless, the main determinant of the type of goal (or better, types of conflicting goals) which peasants seek in order to alleviate their discontent would seem to be their relationship to the means of production, and to the landowners, as well as the position in which the landowners find themselves vis-à-vis market and state, and the repercussions this has for the peasantry. The position of the landowners is certainly as crucial as the position of the peasant in shaping the goals of a peasant protest.

The Forms of Unrest: From Individual Protest to Revolution?

Stages of Protest

Rural protest has certainly taken many forms. The totally individual unorganized protest has existed in the countryside from time immemorial. Theft, sabotage, the murder of a landowner or his bailiff by a peasant, as well as turnover (moving from one landlord to another)—all these are familiar stories in the countryside. They parallel the early stage of industrial protest—"the strike in detail"—conceptualized by Kerr et al.[66] Apathy and passivity, too, can be a form of protest, as we have already stated. Migration, whether to the towns or to the frontier, whether by individuals or by groups, was a protest mechanism in Russia throughout the nineteenth century and before, not to mention the United States.[67]

Hobsbawm has described in several books yet another form which repressed hostility may take: systematic support for "Robin Hood" type bandits who ostentatiously rob the rich and powerful (and *may* give part of the loot to the poor). The support of dissident religious movements, including messianic and revitalization movements, is generally interpreted as an indication of tension and distress, if not yet of focused hostility.[68] The final chapter of Scott's work gives an excellent description of the great variety of forms which the expression of discontent may take, including, of course, simply living with it, or escaping to cities.[69]

There is also no doubt that spontaneous group action—more or less localized demonstrations, riots, land invasions—has been widespread. It is the form of peasant unrest we believe to be the most frequent. At times of exceptional unrest, local revolts stretching over several villages have had a good deal of organization and have even had communication—though not coordination—with other areas.[70]

What is in doubt is whether higher levels of class consciousness, or even—in the absence of ideology—levels of organization above the local are ever reached by peasants, comparable to the tight national unions and union confederations of industrial workers. We take a firmly skeptical line, both at the level of ideology and at the level of organization, thus differing, for example, from such Latin American sociologists as Quijano, who some ten years ago saw a continuous upward trend in both levels.[71]

The First Watershed

The French Revolution seemed to be a watershed at least in the scope of the societal *effect* peasant unrest might have and in the kind of role the peasantry might play in bringing about major social change. In contrast to the almost equally massive but unsuccessful revolts of late medieval times, this was the first uprising which was substantially successful from the point of view of the peasantry itself. Precisely because the peasantry abolished the privileges which the French church and the aristocracy possessed to exploit it, the power of these two elites was undercut in society at large, since that power rested substantially on the peasantry. This pattern was very similar in other countries in the twentieth century. In

Mexico in 1911, in Russia in 1918, as well as in Bolivia some thirty years later, very widespread peasant revolts (each one of them, however, local) again helped to change drastically the pre-existing socioeconomic system.

The question is whether there was anything fundamentally different between these peasants and those of the past, either in spirit (ideology) or at least in behavior, i.e., in organization and tactics. Certainly, in each of these countries, structural changes as well as the additional, exogeneous changes had occurred which we stipulated previously as heightening peasant discontent and militancy. Was this an example of a Marxian dialectic: a change in the quantity of discontent and unrest finally turning into a qualitative change? We do not think that, in the last analysis, there was a sufficiently substantial difference between the more modern peasantries and those of England in 1381 or Germany in 1525 to account for the success of the modern peasantries.

The real differences were external to the peasantry. First, these more recent peasant uprisings coincided with a parallel revolt of a sizable bourgeoisie which simply did not exist before, and which certainly had been unwilling to challenge the established system. These urban groups were initially often relatively uninterested in the problems of the peasantry, or else they were wooing the peasantry only to enlist its temporary help for their own benefit. They had no ultimate goals of bringing about the kind of rural structure the peasantry itself wanted. Lenin is typical of this, and Che Guevara was also explicit about it.[72] The peasantry in its turn had little interest in, or even awareness of, the goals of its urban allies, whether these goals were the explicit ones of political liberty, or the more debated ones of economic power. The rural-urban coalition of which so many authors speak[73] as being essential for a successful revolution must be visualized, therefore, as existing only in the realm of mutually supportive behavior. There was not any deliberate pact at top organizational levels, at least not on the part of the peasantry, which has had neither the organization nor the consciousness for it. Hence, it is not surprising that in most

of the cases, while the peasantry may have made some positive gains—one cannot altogether write off the agrarian reform sector of Mexico, Venezuela and Bolivia—ultimately,
the peasant loses out.[74] Peter Lord some time ago summarized the situation for Mexico, Bolivia, and Venezuela by
stating:

> In all three countries . . . a political role for the peasantry has de-
> veloped because political leaders needed its vote, its militia, or its
> general support. . . . Thus, political leaders have organized the
> peasantry and brought it into the political system to serve their
> own purposes.[75]

Thus the peasant may help to bring about more revolution
for others than for himself, or he may help others to reach
their aspirations more than he does his own. However the
matter of postrevolutionary betrayal may stand, the existence of an independent, revolution-minded urban bourgeosie
was the first difference between, say, the Mexico of 1911 or
the France of 1789 and the medieval peasant revolts in Europe or even in Peru before 1950.

The second difference is that the established systems
which were being assaulted were much more fragile than
those the peasants had attacked previously. When the chips
were down, the earlier regimes could count, with some defec-
tions, on support from all kinds of groups—the lower aristocracy, the still weak urban bourgeoisie soon frightened by
peasant violence, whatever kinds of armed forces existed at
the time, and the big nobles. The later regimes, however,
were generally deserted by all groups and sectors of society:
Profirio Diaz in Mexico in 1911; the Czar in 1917; Louis
XVI in 1789.

But these are not really the peasant revolutions which have
been the most startling, since they were in fact *not* peasant
revolutions. They were peasant revolts not too different from
previous ones, except that they took place in societies whose
established system was already succumbing to urban, middle-
class attackers who were acting quite independently of
the peasantry, and usually ahead of the latter. The role of

peasant militancy was crucial nonetheless. The urban middle class or the urban revolutionary parties might well have been unable to hold on to their newly seized power had not the peasantry undermined the remaining strength of the various *anciens régimes*. While this is speculative, it is notable that where the peasantry failed to support an urban revolution— in France and Germany in 1848, in France in 1871, in Spain in 1936—the established regime, or at least the classes supporting it, essentially held their own.[76]

The Second Watershed: Real Peasant Revolution?

The most obvious, extreme, and historically the most novel form of peasant unrest is a peasant movement which gives prolonged integral support to a revolutionary movement and constitutes its main base. The peasantry constitute the soldiers even though others may be the officers. This frequently used simile is also literally true. China and Vietnam are the best known examples because they were dramatically successful. Yet the Huk rebellion in the Philippines and various movements in postwar Burma, Laos, Korea, and above all Indonesia and India,[77] represented a close enough fusion between radical leaders and at least some sections of the peasantry to be regarded at least as partially peasant revolutionary movements, albeit unsuccessful ones.[78]

It will be noted that the two successful ones—China and Vietnam—had national liberation as their aim, as well as social revolution. All of them, the unsuccessful as well as the successful ones, were originally nurtured under foreign occupation, whether Western or Japanese. Indeed, a great deal of attention has been paid to the relative importance of the two aims (nationalist liberation vs. social revolution), and especially to their relative significance in eliciting that extra peasant support which might have made the difference between success and failure. Writers like Chalmers Johnson assign a decisive role to the existence of a foreign enemy,[79] while others rightly draw attention to the lack of a Japanese threat in some of the areas in which peasant support of radical movements was strong, e.g., in parts of China. This is certainly an unclarified area, but let us give endogenous forces the benefit of the doubt.

How is it that the peasantry could be mobilized so intensively? Those who have written about the Chinese and Vietnamese revolutions seem to be quite agreed on the scenario. No more than ever before were these nation-level, tightly-organized movements truly peasant revolutions. As White says, referring to Vietnam: "We are far from simply a 'peasant revolution.'" The leaders were "long familiar with modern organization, technology and ideas, namely revolutionary intellectuals and workers—they led revolutionary movements as early as 1930."[80] The same, of course, was true of China. Peasant revolts from the Middle Ages onwards had usually benefited from substantial infusions of nonpeasant leadership. These nonpeasant elements helped to formulate such broader ideological goals as sometimes appeared in fourteenth century peasant revolts and to broaden peasant goals in modern times, for example, during the Mexican Revolution. The radicalization of their goals was a reflection of the increasing leadership of urban intellectual populists.

Nor should this need for outside aid come as a surprise. If even the industrial workers, according to Lenin, needed the ideological guidance and organizational leadership of dissident bourgeois intellectuals, how much more likely is this to be true for the peasantry? The problems which urban revolutionaries face are the same with respect to both classes: the tendency to limit the fight and to remain content with immediate economic gains. Indeed, up to the Chinese and Vietnamese revolutions, nonpeasant elements had been no more than counsel and tacticians to local groups, though they tried to be more. They had never succeeded in welding them into a single organized force at the national level.

Why have urban revolutionaries been able to change so completely the form of peasant militancy since the early part of the twentieth century? Obviously, one reason could be the increased receptivity of the peasants due to rising discontent. The central thesis of this section is, however, that we see here the first successful implementation of the social concept put forward by Marx and elaborated by Lenin: of a revolutionary elite whose task is not to make a revolution by itself (Blanquism), but to mobilize "the masses." One may or may not "like" the idea; one may or may not regard Lenin's emphasis on discipline as a break with Marx's supposedly more libertarian, egalitarian spirit. But one must regard the idea of a mass-mobilizing revolutionary elite as a major social invention. Unsuccessful attempts to implement this had been made before (outside Marxian theory, in the case of the Russian *narodnikii* of the late nineteenth century). But now enough has been learned from past errors for successful implementation.

The Chinese Communists, symbolized by Mao Tse-tung, are generally credited with recognizing that in those cases where the peasantry is the "mass" to be mobilized, the task could only be accomplished if the urban revolutionaries were willing to get very close to the peasantry and to employ a complex variety of tactics which would be in accord with the different stages of the revolution.[81]

In order to adapt tactics realistically to the different stages of the revolution, the threat to middle and even rich peasants (as distinct from landlords) was kept to a minimum in the early stage, as for example in the Chinese land redistribution and rent reduction policies after 1930, and in the compromise agrarian program of the early 1940s in Vietnam.[82] Yet the very fact that land could be taken away from the powerful and rent reduced, fostered and was intended to foster self-confidence among the weaker peasants (and their confidence in the urban cadres) as well as to dissipate the fear which usually paralyzes the lower strata of the peasantry. Self-confidence, especially among the poor peasants, was further strengthened by having committees of all peasants decide which lands to confiscate and how to distribute them,[83] and by organizing separate "poor peasants' corps" and farm labor unions. Thus, the readiness of Wolf's "independent" middle peasant to be activist in the early stages of a revolution was utilized, even while preparations were made to continue the revolution beyond the point to which these middle peasants would wish to go.

To make sure that the revolution would continue, the mobilization of the lower strata of the peasantry was combined with proper leadership. In China, the "To the Village" movement of 1942 (*hsia-hsiang*) apparently epitomized the careful attempt to bridge the seemingly inevitable gap between urban intellecuals and lower peasants. Although most administrative positions seemed to be held by outsiders,[84] for the first time members of the community were called upon to make important decisions. Over time, these decisions became more frequent and extensive so that outside cadres merely aided in local self-government rather than administered decisions made bureaucratically far away. These were important factors in integrating the peasantry into the initially small revolutionary cadre. The continual struggle against the bureaucratization of the party, the perpetual emphasis on community organization and on asking peasants for ideas were novel tactics, very different from the ideological preaching generally associated with urban-rural contacts.

Above all, however, peasants were won over because the urban outsiders addressed themselves to the concrete problems which peasants deemed important. The NLF, and the Chinese Communists before it, recognized fully that "the main interest of the farmer . . . is in land" and Seldon cites an NLF document as stating that "the Party knew well how to make use of the farmer's interest in land" in its "political and armed struggle, in its administration of the rural area, and in other revolutionary tasks."[85] Land was, however, not the peasant's only known interest; education was another and urban revolutionaries frequently provided it, thereby highlighting the failure of the existing governments to fulfill this desire.

Finally, the peasant's alienation from the established government was nurtured by confronting him with the hostility of that government. This ranged from demonstrating the futility of operating within the existing legal structure to exposing the peasants to government military countermeasures. An example of the latter was the bombing of Nghe An in 1930,[86] which had a dramatic radicalizing effect, to say nothing of later activities of the U.S. and South Vietnamese governments. Chile, according to Petras and Zemelman, provided an example of radicalization through frustrating experiences with the government in the course of employing legal methods. Obviously, exposing peasants to frustration and retaliation is very much a double-edged sword, and can push peasants away from a revolutionary movement as well as towards it, a well known example being Guevara's unsuccessful attempt to establish a guerrilla movement in Bolivia in 1967. His failure is an example that all the above tactics, well known to Guevara, by no means work automatically. Unless a strong groundswell of peasant discontent is already present, or unless an existing Red Army can move into and control an area to protect peasants from retaliation, none of these tactics will be successful.

Yet even in these two revolutions no simple homogenous role must be imputed to the peasantry. Essential reading for anyone interested in the enormous difficulty in evaluating even the factual role of the peasantry in any revolution, let alone the motivation underlying it, is Gil Carl AlRoy's analysis of the peasantry in the Cuban Revolution.[87] It is undisputed that Castro's army consisted mostly of peasants. Yet, had Castro operated in the cities, he could have found an equal number of recruits there. How many peasants were *reluctant* to join? Why did some peasants join?

> We should remember that traditional, negative orientations toward government, so typical of backward peasants, may well produce the same behavior ("support") that would also result from an appreciation of any traits peculiar to an insurgent movement. It would be easy, and often tempting, to confuse the two.[88]

AlRoy wonders whether the type of peasant who joined was not, perhaps, running away from the land altogether rather than seeking any improvement in his condition on it.

It is certainly legitimate to query whether the Cuban peasants supporting Castro did so because they sought title to the land. AlRoy stresses also that a semipoliticized outlaw type of "guerrillaism" had a long tradition in Cuba.[89] This affinity for guerrillaism, reinforced by Castro's deliberate policy of sharing lifestyle hardships with peasants, may explain much of the peasant support, rather than agreement at policy levels. The sharing of lifestyles and of urban revolutionaries getting down to the concrete concerns of the peasant are much emphasized in the literature on Vietnam and China.

In any case, the main point here is not about a set of universally successful tactics *per se,* but about the fact that systematic and very pragmatic thought on how a revolutionary elite can best mobilize a rural mass constitutes in itself a new social invention. This has contributed to bringing about successfully the phenomenon to which it is directed: revolutions led by urban intellectuals, but based on substantial peasant support.

Whether or not such revolutionary efforts are successful depends not only on those efforts but at least as much if not more on the strength of the opposing elite and its supporters. Governments may be flexible enough to initiate or, at least, to promise convincingly a sufficient range of reforms to undercut support for the revolution, as was the case in the Philippines in the mid-1950s.[90] Or the elite may dispose of sufficient force, in relation to the organizational strength of the revolutionaries, to crush the attempted revolution, as happened all over Latin America in the early and mid-1960s. This is true not only of revolutions, but also of more localized revolts and of any encounter between peasant and landlord. A number of independent conditions have to be present for discontent to turn into action, and for action to be successful.

Nor is the future likely to be any more uniform than the past. Some writers, such as Scott, appear to predict that, on balance, peasants are henceforth more likely to resolve their problems in forms other than revolts and support for revolutions.[91] Governments are becoming adept at introducing a modernized clientelist system which prevents unity of action. Alternatively, migration to cities to participate in the "scavenging possibilities of the extra-village economy"[92] is now so available an option, especially for young adults most likely to be rebellious, that the recruits for organized unrest could diminish.

Just as Engels in his last writings revised downwards the possibilities of armed revolt by industrial workers because of the increased efficiency of the weapons of the armed forces opposing them, so, too, the efficiency of rural counterinsurgency may be thought to be increasing.[93] While these may seem to be mere speculations, they are certainly congruent with the easy suppression of attempted rural revolutions in Latin America in the 1960s. The effectiveness of counterinsurgency is a partial explanation of the failure of guerrilla movements in Guatemala, Peru and Venezuela,[94] but it is very clearly belied by later events in Vietnam, where the United States, with all the sophistication of its weaponry and reconnaissance techniques, could not contain the NLF. Similarly, migration and cooperation through reform and clientelism may avert revolts and revolutions in some places, but may be insufficient in others. And some elites will be strong and cohesive enough to withstand organized challenges successfully, while others will not.

One analytical point is clear. As contrasted with the period 1789-1952, when peasant revolts were parallel to urban revolutions, urban radicals today, at least in the Third World, are very likely to regard the potential for revolt in the countryside as an integral, if not the key element, in their strategy. The point made by Lenin, and reinforced by Mao, is now an ineradicable part of revolutionary thinking, even if in practice the situation simply may not be ripe for a revolution.

Conclusion

The following have been the main theses of this paper:
1. Radicalism is perhaps not an appropriate concept to use in connection with the various forms of *rural unrest.*

The term "radicalism" is, rightly, intimately connected with explicit *ideologies* which revolve around a total critique of the principles underlying an existing social order, with a view to either establishing a new order or resurrecting an old one. Even though peasants have at times supported actions which have in fact changed institutions, generally they have not been moved by explicit radical ideologies. East European peasant parties between the two world wars may be the most notable exception, but even this is debatable. Certainly voting for parties with radical ideologies is not a reliable indication of commitment to that ideology.

2. Rural discontent has been endemic to agrarian societies, and has been prevented from crystallizing into *outbreaks of rural unrest* only by a set of counterforces (coercion, minimal service, some normative support). Because the balance has been precarious, it has frequently been upset. This is indicated by the large absolute number of peasant revolts, local or regional, over the centuries, even though relatively speaking such outbreaks have not been frequent.

3. The *susceptibility to actual outbreaks of unrest,* and the particular goals to which such unrest addresses itself, are linked to the specific relationship of both landlord and peasant to the means of production. The perennial question remains, who is most likely to revolt: the rural proletariat, the tenant, or the small landowning peasant?

4. The *commercialization of the world* and its integration into a single complex market system in the twentieth century may have tipped the balance in various parts of the world, and produced certain qualitative changes in the form of peasant unrest, but it did not create the underlying tension.

5. The relatively new phenomenon of *societal revolution,* or *attempted revolution based on peasant support* is therefore due not so much to a change in the position of the peasantry, but to changes in the urban elites who lead these, and other, revolutions. These elites, beginning

with the *narodnikii* of Russia have: (a) included the peasants in their ideology or, at least, in their *tactical* conceptions of how to make a revolution; and (b) they have "learned," at least in some instances, how to *make themselves acceptable* to the peasantry, which initially they were not. This is the lesson of China and Vietnam.

6. Closer *communication* of all kinds between town and country has played an important role in the ability of urban elites to mobilize rural masses, and in the receptivity of the latter to the message of the former—although rural skepticism has not really changed quite so much.

7. *Success*, present, past, and in the future, as in the case of all revolutions, depends at least as much on the strength of the elites and of their backers as it does on the strength of the attackers.

William H. Overholt, a political sociologist specializing in political development, Asian politics, and foreign policy, has served on the research staff of the Hudson Institute since 1971. Principal author of several book-length studies for Hudson, Dr. Overholt has also published many articles on land reform, organization of political movements, and revolutions. His study, Political Revolution, *is to be published by Westview Press in 1977.*

6

Sources of Radicalism and Revolution: A Survey of the Literature
William H. Overholt

"Sources of Radicalism and Revolution" could well serve as title for a history of social science thought over two millennia, for there is very little in the social sciences which does not directly address the sources and varieties of discontent among individuals and the reasons for stability or fundamental changes in social or political or economic systems. Any survey is therefore necessarily idiosyncratic, and this one is no exception.[1]

Some Definitions

The word "radical" is used in both absolute and relative senses, and sometimes denotes one end of the political spectrum, other times both ends. In its absolute sense, radicalism refers to a congeries of views that advocate more fundamental restructuring of society than liberalism; in this sense Harry Truman was a liberal, but C. Wright Mills was a radical.

But what is called radical tends to vary over time, so even the absolute concept of radicalism varies over time. A more thoroughgoing relativism makes the concept completely relative to its political context; thus for many purposes

Liu Shao-chi was viewed as relatively conservative whereas Chiang Ching, Mao Tse-tung's widow, is called a radical. Likewise, in Ethiopia during the 1960s any advocate of the most minimal democratization of the regime was called a radical.

Sometimes radicalism refers solely to left-wing ideas, sometimes to both left and right. In the first sense, radicalism is the opposite of reaction or of whatever is labeled right-wing; in this sense the John Birch Society and the German Nazi party are not radical. On the other hand, radicalism frequently refers to any views dramatically different from whatever is regarded as centrist or normal. Thus a famous collection of articles on the recent right wing in American politics is titled *The Radical Right.*[2] This latter concept of radicalism is consistent with the evidence that members of the extreme right and the extreme left often share certain psychological characteristics and that extreme right and extreme left polities frequently share structural characteristics.

When radicalism refers exclusively to the political left, it is often broadened to include any view vaguely associated with Marxism, with social classes, with economic determinism, or even with the view that social, political, and religious institutions tend to support the interests of an economic elite. Thus military-industrial-complex explanations of government decisions are often termed radical. Among economists there are three theories of unemployment: the orthodox, which views the labor market as atomized; the dual market theory, which views the market as stratified; and the radical theory, which emphasizes the importance of competitions among strata and groups.[3] The substance of the radical economic theory is often presented along with a penumbra of dialectical materialism and devil-theory perspectives on the capitalist class, but what is most striking to the noneconomist is not this penumbra, but rather the automatic association of the most elementary sociological considerations (viz., group cohesion and conflict) with radicalism.

If one views radicalism as extreme deviation from a society's median political views, then one faces further ambiguities. Is a man radical if he is alienated from his society and as a result opts for quietism and depoliticization? Or does radicalism require active demands for restructuring society? If radicalism requires active demands for restructuring society, then what do we do with the man who desires restructuring but does not actively seek it because of fear?

A more abstract concept of radicalism defines the latter as a single-minded attempt to explain or prescribe social action by reference to some single ultimate principle. Egon Bittner, following Max Weber, employs such a definition, specifying in addition that radicalism implies unreasonableness and disregard of contrary evidence.[4] Stripped of the latter (nonessential and possibly biased) specifications, this definition ties radicalism to the tradition of Western rationalism and to zealous carving of reality with that ultimate principle of modern science, Occam's Razor. Using such a definition one can comprehend key linkages between modern science and modern radicalism, such as the congeniality many groups of scientists have felt for Marxism. (The linkage with modern science is more direct than one might imagine. It has been argued that the concept of the critical experiment can only arise in cultures based on fanatical—i.e., radical—religions. In cultures with tolerant religions, the concept of "many mountains up to God, many roads up each mountain" tends to preclude rigid distinctions between truth and falsehood.[5])

This linkage with modern science creates difficulties for this definition. Identification of, for instance, Einstein's urge for simplicity of explanation as a form of radicalism would be anomalous. A scientist seeking simplicity is behaving conservatively even if his conclusions prove novel. If, to avoid this difficulty, one insists upon Bittner's specification of unreasonableness and disregard of evidence, then the concept of radicalism becomes restricted within boundaries far narrower than is customary in scholarly usage and tainted with invidious judgments whose implications would make even conservative American politicians squirm.

I shall avoid final choice among these definitions, but will discuss various forms and sources of discontent which might create, or prove useful to, advocates of fundamental restructuring of society.

"Revolution" is an equally slippery concept. In popular literature virtually any substantial change is labeled revolution: the Green Revolution, the revolution of rising expectations, the sexual revolution, and the communications revolution. Any writer who fails to perceive a revolution in his subject is surely a scribbler at loose ends. Students of revolutions have usually employed restrictive concepts of revolution, however, frequently distinguishing social revolutions, which are major structural changes in society, from political revolutions, which are major changes of government and politics.

Because so many phenomena can lead to fundamental social change, social revolution is too broad to study under a single rubric. Therefore most writers have focused upon political revolution. Huntington has chosen the most restrictive concept of political revolution, namely a "rapid, fundamental and violent domestic change in the dominant values and myths of a society, in its political institutions, social structure, leadership, and government activity and policies."[6] Moreover, Huntington views revolution as a phenomenon occurring narrowly in time, as a sometime concomitant of the modernization process of the last few centuries. In contrast, Tilly advocates broadening the concept to include all forms of "multiple sovereignty," that is, of struggles by more than one group for political hegemony. There are indeed solid justifications for examining Huntingtonian revolutions, coups d'etat, and internal wars together, but clearly there are also important distinctions: if Tilly expands the word "revolution" to cover all situations of multiple sovereignty, then eventually some new words will be required for the very special phenomenon of political changes which go much deeper than coups and civil wars. Why not retain "multiple sovereignty" as the overreaching category? For this reason, and because there is an exciting, cohesive, and distinctive subject matter and literature on "revolution" narrowly conceived, and also because the narrower concept dovetails best with a discussion of radicalism, I shall employ a definition just a little broader than Huntington's.

A revolution occurs when a domestic insurgent group or groups displace the government of a society by means which are illegitimate according to the values of the existing regime and when fundamental political institutions are destroyed or transformed and fundamental values of the system are dramatically changed. An abortive revolution occurs when a domestic group attempts to carry out a revolution without success. Fundamental political institutions are those without which a regime would be illegitimate in terms of its own values. For instance, competitive elections are fundamental political institutions in the United States because they implement the value of political equality. Fundamental values are those which serve as basic legitimating principles for the political system.[7] The reference to illegitimacy of means in the eyes of the old regime eliminates the logical possibility that the changes in groups, values, and institutions would result from the normal and legitimate processes of the system, such as from elections in a democracy; such a situation does not conform to most intuitive conceptions of revolution.[8]

This definition includes as revolutions the French, Russian, Nazi, Meiji, Chinese (1911-49), Cuban, and Mexican revolutions, as well as successful revitalization movements,[9] and the transformation which occurred in China from the disintegration of the later Han dynasty to the stabilization of the T'ang dynasty.[10] It excludes simple coups, imperial conquest, wars of independence, civil wars which are mere struggles for power, transformations of the international system, political changes which do not overthrow the central government, and nonpolitical changes (though the transformations of institutions and values during a revolution virtually always coincide with major socioeconomic transformations).

Revolution is not mere change.[11] The *speed* at which the transformations occur[12] is not mentioned because there is no way to construct an index which would in all cases differentiate revolutionary rates of change from nonrevolutionary ones. The definition includes no reference to war[13] or violence,[14] although war and violence frequently accompany revolution; such references would add little additional precision and would eliminate a useful empirical question of the possibility of nonviolent transformations of this kind. The identity and political attitudes of the revolutionaries[15] are not part of the definition, because such a specification would drastically restrict the inquiry, as would specification of the type of society in which the revolution occurs.[16] Moreover, we reject a criterion of progressiveness[17] or sense of novelty or freedom[18] or modernity,[19] because such criteria are ambiguous and can impose arbitrary restrictions on the scope of inquiry, and because events which are universally accepted as being revolutions (e.g., the French revolution) fail to meet these standards in important ways. If revolutions invariably advance freedom and progress, by whose standards shall we judge Russia in 1917? The concept of revolution originally referred to an attempt at restoration.[20] Revolution can be in large part a revolt against freedom.[21] The aims of the groups which initiate revolution frequently consist of the restoration of *old* rights.

Several concepts frequently employed to characterize revolution prove misleading or unfruitful. Revolution is not the antithesis of evolution. Revolutions may be the punctuation marks of evolution (Marx), or the selection mechanism of evolution, or short-term setbacks of evolution, but never its opposite. "Discontinuity," a term often used erroneously to describe accelerated, nonmonotonic, or nondifferentiable change,[22] does not adequately describe guerrilla warfare situations where authority, territorial control, and so forth, change continuously. Discontinuity, disintegration, strain, incongruence, and disequilibrium,[23] when they accurately describe a revolutionary event, do not facilitate analysis of the internal processes, struggles, and sequences of revolution. Instead, they reduce revolution to the disruption of a system, and leave revolution itself as an unanalyzable black box.[24]

The Psychological Bases of Radicalism and Revolution

Studies of the psychology of radicalism and revolution range along a continuum from an exclusive emphasis on individual psychology to an empathetic concern for the existential dilemmas faced by members of key social groups. That is, they range from those which emphasize what goes on inside the head of a radical to those which emphasize the social situation confronted by his peers. With some crucial exceptions, studies of revolutionary leaders emphasize individual psychology, whereas studies of the followers emphasize social psychology. In accordance with Michelet's dictum that in revolutions "the people were usually more important than the leaders"[25] the sociological studies of mass groups have generally proved more fruitful.

The discontents in which modern social psychology has located the roots of radicalism and revolution have generally derived from the existential dilemmas of those social groups uprooted by the disintegration of the medieval synthesis and those created by the industrial revolution. The basic themes of these analyses are that people, or specific groups, have been torn from their secure relationships to God and society, deprived of the full development of their individual personalities, isolated from their fellow men, and deprived of guidance regarding the proper means and ends of their lives. Marx's analysis of the proletariat picked up all the major themes of alienation and radicalism: frustration at absolutely or relatively declining living standards, powerlessness as a cog in an incomprehensible industrial machine, personality mutilation, and intolerable identity as a man with his diverse potentialities subjugated to the performance of a single menial task. Weber perceived the oppression and alienation of the bureaucrat who must subordinate his whole personality to professional tasks. Erich Fromm, David Riesman, and C. Wright Mills provide similar analyses of the alienation of commercial man, the sales personality, and white collar man. Durkheim paints a broader picture of modern man isolated from his fellows and condemned to infinite striving in a normless world. Robert Merton has picked up these themes of Durkheim, formalized them, and employed them in a sketch of the dilemmas faced by men whose lives are structured by social demands for monetary success. Paul Goodman has portrayed students as an oppressed minority which is charged tuition for the privilege of having their personalities remolded to fit social roles. A host of writers analyzing peasant society has developed the themes of insecurity and anxiety in a subsistence world invaded by the aspirations and demands of a monetary economy and deprived of the security provided by traditional ties to landlords.[26]

These studies of social dilemmas and their psychological consequences have yielded a set of labels for specific psychological conditions, namely *frustration, anomie, search for identity, isolation, powerlessness,* and *anxiety.* Having derived such a list from studies of particular groups, social scientists have tended to reverse their perspective: they assume that the psychological states are the basis of radicalism, and then seek generalized descriptions of social situations which would produce such psychological states. Thus we find Ted Robert Gurr, the Feierabends, and many others arguing that economic improvement, or decline or fluctuation, can stimulate frustration and thereby induce radicalism, violence, and possibly revolution.[27]

As a psychology of membership in radical movements, the above list probably needs broadening. *Boredom* may well be a central source of radicalism for certain social groups, particularly in previous centuries when boredom constituted a principal psychological problem of the elites from which part of the revolutionary leadership was drawn. *Compulsive conformity* probably provided a principal source of participation in radical movements in Nazi Germany and in revolutionary China—and, in a very different way, in some contemporary university upheavals as well. Moreover, in all revolutions it is clear that for many the motivation for joining revolutionary movements has been *opportunism,* in the sense of choosing the politics that will best facilitate pecuniary or status advancement. Such opportunism is particularly marked among peasant revolutionaries, since peasant youth often see the revolutionary organization as their sole opportunity for escaping from the tedium of village life. Similarly, scholars since Burke have noted that ideological movements attract intellectuals, since all great ideologies require more scholarly exegesis than do the myths of routinized and instrumentalized old regimes.[28]

Analyses of revolution must explain why nonradicals and nonmembers of the revolutionary organization lend their support to revolutionary movements. Such support may be the product of terrorization as well as opportunism, and may take the form of passive nonsupport of the government as well as active insurgency. Neither responses to terror nor the reasons for passivity rather than activity are well understood. But a revolutionary movement may derive much of its information, taxes, and obedience from the uncommitted, and thus studies of the psychology of revolution are imperfect without explanations of the behavior of the uncommitted. In a country where the government does not penetrate far into the countryside, radical groups may tap virtually unlimited resources simply because they have no competitors. Similarly, bureaucrats who perceive their role as entirely instrumental may make a government an object to be captured rather than an active force defending itself.[29] Although there is a large collection of studies which focuses upon one special kind of bureaucracy, namely the military, in conflictful situations, even the most insightful studies of professionalization, ideology, organizational structure, and organizational and personal interests, do not satisfactorily explain why some militaries intervene frivolously in politics, why others react relatively passively to vast political changes, and why still others intervene only when the most basic structures of the polity are threatened.

The excessive narrowness of psychological studies of radicalism becomes extreme in single-variable explanations which emphasize frustration as the exclusive source of violence, radicalism, or revolution, and relative economic deprivation as the exclusive source of frustration. If such simplification could adequately explain violence, radicalism, or revolution, it would be highly desirable. But the numerous psychological bases for radicalism described above all have considerable empirical support, and most of them cannot be subsumed as subcategories of frustration caused by relative deprivation.

Supposing that one possesses an adequate typology of discontents which stimulate radical attitudes or behavior, several tasks remain: first, to identify the logical and psychological connecting links between the particular discontents and radical or revolutionary behavior; second, to identify the social and political conditions under which these links will activate concerted political action or political change; and, third, to identify anew the precise groups likely to experience such discontent and to organize politically.

The psychological and logical links between discontent and radicalism identified in the literature take two distinct but not mutually exclusive forms: radical or violent or revolutionary behavior is explained first of all as a result of psychological phenomena and alternatively as a result of rational, problem-solving choices. The psychological links are not difficult to establish. Frustration leads to anger and anger leads to violence, radicalism, or revolution. Anomie produces an anxious and conflict-ridden individual seeking order and discipline. Lack of an adequate identity or possession of an intolerable identity can stimulate a desire for metaphorical death and rebirth, for cleansing through violence as advocated by Frantz Fanon,[30] and for identification with a cause which will lead one's group or society or all mankind into a better order of things. Escape from isolation and powerlessness can be achieved through sadomasochism, authoritarianism, destructiveness, or automaton conformity.[31]

These psychological analyses explain the characteristic features of radical ideologies. For the frustrated and powerless there is absolute assurance that success is inevitable, that God or history is on the side of the insurgent.[32] For the anomic there is a fully integrated set of values and norms, an ideology which provides "a unified and internally consistent interpretation of the meaning of the world" allowing its holder to reason from a rigidly supreme principle to all occasions of actual conduct.[33] The need of the anomic for such an ideology explains the overwhelming emphasis on doctrinal purity found in many radical movements. For people with inadequate or intolerable identities, revolutionary ideologies invariably offer extravagant praise for the worker or other downtrodden individual and assure him of a historically important role.[34] For isolated personalities there is the fraternity of the radical movement.

Rational choice explanations of radicalism and revolutionary ideology sometimes complement these purely psychological explanations and sometimes contradict them. Chalmers Johnson argues—without evidence—that revolutionary paths are chosen only when all alternatives have been exhausted.[35] Certainly most revolutions do display a gradual groping around among the nonrevolutionary alternatives, and, if such alternatives fail, a gradual expansion of support for groups which pursue revolutionary goals. But history provides numerous examples of groups and group leaders who have adopted revolutionary goals long before nonrevolutionary alternatives have been exhausted. Barrington Moore emphasizes that societies turn revolutionary when the ineffectiveness of key institutions has been demonstrated, a view strongly supported by the so-called Western revolutions, where the disintegration of government has long preceded the rise of powerful revolutionary movements.[36] Likewise, groups naturally turn radical or revolutionary when they perceive the government as being, or as allied to, a dangerous, hostile enemy. Thus when the Czar orders his troops to fire on peaceful protesters, or when the Ngo Dinh Diem government in Vietnam invades Buddhist temples, they naturally stimulate revolutionary attitudes and behavior. Finally, manifest inconsistencies between institutions and the prevailing values or the prevailing social myths naturally stimulate radicalism. For instance, the great military dictator who loses a war, the landlord class which abrogates paternal responsibilities to the peasants, and the "democratic" party which rigs an election, all risk the rise of radical movements.

However, to establish these links of psychology and logic between discontent and radicalism is not to explain the rise of radical movements, much less their success. The linkages are weak; they bind in some cases and not in others. Frustrated people can abandon their goals, or divorce their wives, or work compulsively, rather than join radical movements. Powerlessness, isolation, and anomie can be overcome through Calvinist religion, through Marine Corps fraternity, through feverish accumulation of Mitsubishi profits, through dedication to one's family, through Nazi party violence, or through peaceful Vietnam War protest. Herman Kahn has remarked, correctly, that one of the American strata suffering most from relative deprivation, defined as a gap between inculcated expectations and value received, is the group of ugly, upper-middle-class girls. But these frustrations vent themselves peacefully at the boutiques rather than violently at the barricades. Citation of this case may seem frivolous, but there is little in the theory to tell us why this kind of frustration would be less significant than another. Relative deprivation theorists dominate much of the literature on revolution, violence, and radicalism, despite having unconsciously ignored all the forms of relative deprivation which fail to support their case, and despite having failed to distinguish among different kinds of deprivation, some of which clearly differ in their consequences. Likewise these theorists make much of correlations between social class and radicalism, while ignoring stronger correlations with such variables as youthfulness and unmarried status.

Under what conditions, then, does psychological discontent lead to a radical consciousness in a psychological sense, and in what cases does such purely psychological consciousness lead to consciousness in the Marxist sense, namely a radical political organization? Practical revolutionaries universally acknowledge that usually neither form of consciousness arises spontaneously. Lenin maintained that the labor movement could never work out an independent ideology for itself and cited Kautsky's argument that socialism arises from bourgeois science rather than from class struggle.[37] Mao complained that:

> Wherever the Red Army goes, it finds the masses cold and reserved; only after propaganda and agitation do they slowly rouse themselves.[38]

The accessibility of an appropriate ideology is certainly a key factor. Chilean peasants adjacent to radical mining towns tend to vote radical regardless of class differences, whereas peasants not adjacent to such towns divide their votes along class lines.[39] American farm laborers choose radical ideologies because, helpless without outside organizational leadership, they find that the only leadership available to them has radical political orientations.[40] As Barrington Moore puts it:

> The partial failure of a set of institutions to live up to what is expected of them provides an atmosphere receptive to demands for a more or less extensive overhaul of the status quo. At this juncture the future course of events depends heavily upon the models of a better world that become available to various strategic groups in the population.[41]

Degree of discontent is another key factor. Since radicalism is in some sense an extreme response to discontent, it probably results from particularly extreme forms of discontent. Thus, whereas moderate frustration might lead to reformist activities, extreme frustration might lead to revolutionary acts. But the hypothesis is neither self-evident nor empirically established beyond question. Absolute repression seems to work, even though it must maximize frustration at least temporarily.

A third criterion for adoption of a revolutionary ideology clearly must be that the ideology provide a plausible explanation for the individual's or group's problems and, explicitly or implicitly, offer some solutions. What is plausible depends, of course, upon the individual's or group's experience and patterns of thought; for instance chiliastic religion may no longer be plausible for many highly secularized modern groups.

By far the most promising explanation of group acceptance of a revolutionary or radical perspective has been that such acceptance occurs in response to blatant infringement by the government or by another group of those *older* values which the group or that society holds most sacred. Prerevolutionary French peasants saw themselves as *counterattacking* against nobles who were threatening existing rights; the nobles in turn thought that they were *regaining* old rights which had been gradually nibbled away. American revolutionaries demanded the *old* rights of Englishmen. The Chinese dynasties, whose legitimacy was based in large part on the personal virtue of the emperor, often ended with revolt against a corrupt emperor. This brings to mind Hannah Arendt's observation that the term "revolution" originally referred to restoration.

If the specific values of a society constitute the means by which discontent becomes politically or socially radical, then the conditions under which radical ideologies are adopted will vary among societies. Rigging an election would stimulate radicalism in the United States but not elsewhere. Since individuals and groups respond to infringement of those *distinctive* values which they hold sacred, Lupsha has suggested a distinction between "relative deprivation" on the one hand and "righteous indignation" on the other—where righteous indignation is the response to infringement of ultimate values.[42] Lupsha's concept is not really a substitute for "relative deprivation" but rather a subcategory of frustration/anger, namely frustration/anger that has been channeled in a particular direction because of the uniquely important values that have been infringed. Understood in this way, it may be useful.

One virtually universal source of such righteous indignation is the failure of a government or a society to provide some minimal degree of law and order. This responsibility of government is almost universally acknowledged and is a key feature of all political philosophies, except anarchism and other utopian theories which claim to solve the problem of order without recourse to government. Emphasis on law and order as a key responsibility is particularly noteworthy among traditional peasants, who frequently receive little else in return for their taxes and obedience. For such peasants, governments which do not maintain law and order are inherently evil. Such is the justification for revolution in Mencius's Mandate of Heaven, and such are the less-articulated feelings of peasants in all other societies with which this writer is familiar. Middle-class Americans frequently express similar views.

Having identified the varieties of radical discontent, and the groups experiencing such discontents, one must then explain why particular members or sections of such groups adopt radical ideologies or join revolutionary movements whereas others do not. Only about two percent of American students joined radical protest movements at the height of the Vietnam era in the United States. Only a tiny proportion of Chinese peasants ever participated in the Communist Party or the Red Army or active local level organizations. Only a small proportion of the German lower middle class ever joined the Nazi organization. Given that a group is somehow oppressed or discontented, who from that group joins and who does not? Are the differences explained by different experience or by different character or by something else? Research on the subject provides a variety of insights but no satisfying answers.

Contemporary research on ideology initially assumed that each ideology attracted a single kind of personality, such as an "authoritarian personality" identified with fascism.[43] But subsequent evidence has shown that certain personality types are susceptible to ideologies of either the far left or the far right—or even to oscillation between them. Attempts to distinguish these personality types from more middle-of-the-road personality types have included distinctions between the "open" and "closed" mind,[44] and more recently between personalities which display little ability to tolerate cognitive dissonance and those able to tolerate greater dissonance.[45] More detailed psychoanalytic studies may yet restore some distinction between those personalities attracted to the extreme left and the extreme right. Other studies have begun to explain susceptibility to radicalism as a consequence of the interaction of different forms of discontent (e.g., when low self-esteem is accompanied by powerlessness or frustration).[46]

More detailed than these studies of mass radicalism are biographical studies of great revolutionary leaders. Some of these have confined themselves to what might be called micropsychological hypotheses about the individuals involved. For instance Wolfenstein's study of Lenin, Trotsky, and Gandhi discovered unresolved difficulties in relationships with the leaders' fathers;[47] these were later projected onto a political scene that happened to provide an arena for working out their personal problems. Mao of course experienced similar difficulties with his father.[48] Wolfenstein also employs studies of Gandhi, Nasser, and Lenin to argue that an individual leader's propensity for violent means to achieve social change is inversely proportional to his sense of active guilt, proportional to masculine identification, and proportional to the perceived dangerousness and animosity of the enemy.[49] One can find various peculiarities in the backgrounds of many revolutionary leaders. For instance, Edmund Wilson tells us that Bakunin "was in love with one of his sisters" and "apparently remained impotent all his life." LaSalle had terrible conflicts with his sister and his classmates. Lenin's attitude toward liberals was affected throughout his life by his friends' desertion of him at the time of his brother's arrest; and so forth.[50] But how does one make more out of these observations that mere cocktail gossip? Tumultuous, unusual upbringings and lives may well be characteristic of most great men, conservative, reactionary, and revolutionary alike. Energy, imagination and intelligence are far more predictable qualities among such leaders than any particular psychological quirks, except perhaps for the unsurprising finding that future revolutionaries so frequently conflict with authority figures such as their teachers and fathers.

At a much higher level of generality, Erikson's studies of the quasi-revolutionary personalities of Luther and Gandhi discern correspondences between personal crises and broad social crises.[51] These men experienced personal crises directly related to the broadest social problems of their day and managed to encompass and to articulate those crises so clearly that they as individuals became symbols of the crises and of their resolutions. At a similar level of generality, Fromm asserts that the character structure of the individual who creates a new doctrine and the character structure of the followers of that doctrine are likely to be similar. "If the same ideals appeal to them their character structure must be similar in important respects."[52] At first blush these two great hypotheses of Fromm and Erikson appear to be complementary, but they could hardly be further apart. If one combines the insights of the various micropsychological hypotheses with Erikson's conclusions about the ability of these great men to somehow encompass within their own experience the broadest crises of a society or civilization, few things are more obvious than the distinctive characters and personalities of the great men. These great creative figures in fact are as different from their followers as the charismatic politician from the obscure bureaucrat. And indeed most revolutionary organizations display an extraordinary contrast between the creative, volatile, charismatic top leader and the highly disciplined bureaucratic followers.

Indeed one of the central insights that should have been gained from studies of the psychology of revolution, but generally has not, is that people become radicals and join revolutionary organizations for a broad variety of reasons. Charismatic leaders may join because only the role of revolutionary leader will permit them to act out and resolve their great personal crises. Intellectuals may join because of the attractiveness of being in the avant-garde, because of admiration for the systematic logic of revolutionary theory, and also because revolutionary ideology requires so much systematic exegesis that intellectuals have great opportunities for high-ranking positions. Bureaucrats may join for reasons of pure efficiency or opportunism. Poor peasants and oppressed workers may join because of intolerable economic frustrations. Middle peasants and rich peasants whose motivations are not particularly radical may eventually join successful radical peasant movements in order to play the same organizing roles in the new society that they played in the old. Crucially, the revolutionary organization needs all of these different motivations and skills, and uses them at different levels of the organization.

Ultimately it is to be hoped that studies of the psychology of radicalism and revolution will provide means for distinguishing cranks from charismatic leaders, for identifying which members of a society with the specified sources of stress will join a movement, and for predicting which types will tend to rise to the top. It is further to be hoped that such psychological studies will establish links to the sociology of revolutionary organization and of social change. Does the revolutionary society produce more revolutionary leaders or does it simply give the existing reservoir of leaders an opportunity to exercise their personalities? For instance, do periods of socially disruptive change produce more sons who cannot work out satisfactory relationships with their fathers or with other social authority figures? Or do they merely provide more opportunities for such discontents to focus upon politics? Or both?

Economic/Psychological Theories

There is an entire genre of theories whose principal content is psychological—although sometimes embroidered with a few hypotheses about the balance of coercive capabilities—and whose methods and data are almost exclusively economic. These theories not only interpret violence or radicalism or revolution as a response to relative deprivation, but they also assume that the principal sources of this relative deprivation are economic and that the sole forces channeling the expression of the frustration and anger are a few cultural and coercion variables. If one reads the substantive theory and then imagines the appropriate methods, one summons up an image of Freud interviewing a peasant on a couch. If one looks exclusively at the supportive evidence, one sees graphs which seem to demonstrate that revolutions or violence occur when economies rise, that likewise they occur when economies fall, that they also occur when economies rise and then fall or when they simply fluctuate; finally, if for some reason expectations rise, then revolutions or radicalism or violence will occur even if the economies remain constant.

Such relationships prove absolutely nothing about the basic frustration/aggression hypothesis, since the links between the sociological variables and the psychological hypotheses are never really established. In fact, the findings are consistent with any of the pure sociological models, to be discussed later, which completely ignore psychological variables.

For example, one such study considers the effects of regime coerciveness on political violence. It finds that moderate levels of coerciveness and inconsistent levels of coerciveness are associated with political instability and violence. From this it concludes that "coerciveness at first stimulates violence until a certain point is reached. Then coerciveness, in the form of tyranny, seems just as apt to bring internal peace as more violence." It concludes that "regimes that resort to force, especially if they use force inconsistently, must expect political instability and violence."[53] The data do not support this interpretation over an opposite interpretation, namely that regimes troubled by violence and instability are forced by the situation to be at least moderately coercive but are often too weak to employ adequate force to suppress the violence. Inconsistent use of force would seem to indicate the same kind of organizational weakness that made it impossible for the regime to employ great force.

A rich variety of similar studies now exists. All implicitly or explicitly focus their analysis on the psychological frustration/aggression hypothesis, and all test that hypothesis with primarily economic data. Most use correlations or linear regressions as their primary statistical tool. They vary in several ways. Some, like James C. Davies' famous paper on the

J-curve, rely on a vague concept of "need satisfaction,"
which, because it is not constructed in any objective empirical fashion, is impossible for any other investigator to repli-
cate or test;[54] but most recent studies emphasize easily measurable variables, such as poverty or social inequality. Eco-
nomic/psychological studies also vary in whether they use
aggregate data for an entire nation, or whether they focus on
specific social groups within nations.[55] Finally, they differ
in the other variables that they happen to include in the analysis; other variables which have been used include regime
coerciveness, alien ideological influence, strategic terrain
(Mitchell), and various broad social process variables such as
Hofheinz's modernization. Perhaps the most complete data
of this kind are those on land inequality and peasant societies. Here the resulting statistics typically show very weak
and sometimes even negative relationships between violence
or radicalism and land inequality within countries, thus
seeming to conflict with Russett's finding of a positive global
relationship between some discontent variables and violence.[56] Finally, Hofheinz's study of rural influence patterns
in China demonstrates that neither modernization nor inequality nor any of the other variables relied on by the simple empirical theories can adequately explain peasant support for the Chinese communists.

When one examines what kind of theory of revolution
these statistical analyses actually test, it becomes obvious
that they are in effect testing pure mass uprising theories—
i.e., theories where mass discontent leads directly to support
for revolution. Comparative historians have persuasively
discredited such theories. (Spontaneous mass uprisings
frequently do occur, but gain historic importance only on
those rare occasions when they are accompanied by organizational phenomena which these theories cannot explain.)
Until some way is developed to include the relative organizational capacities and achievements of the insurgents and the
government, these statistical analyses will lack explanatory
power. Some of the authors of these empirical studies have
come to this conclusion themselves. Thus Hofheinz proposes

a theory of "organizational dynamism," and Averch, Denton, and Koehler speak of a "self-perpetuating organization" rather than discontent as the reason for insurgency. That organizational phenomena are the key to analysis is correct, but organization is not an *alternative* explanation. Discontent is just one of several prerequisites of revolutionary organization.

The economic/psychological studies of revolution, violence, and radicalism are the epiphenomena of a curious convergence among the methodological fetishes of behaviorism, the simplicity of economic variables, and the substance of vulgar Marxism. To be sure, no major author of such studies is a Marxist, much less a vulgar Marxist. But the present generation of behavioralists allows method and data to dominate substance, and economic data are the easiest to obtain and manipulate. Thus simple economic variables tend to dominate analysis as in vulgar Marxist discussions. Ultimately these studies tell us that economic change is somehow related to discontent, which sometimes, somehow, is channeled into violence or radicalism or revolution. Organization, politics, strategy, and any but the most primitive military considerations are ignored, and with them the essence of the process under consideration.

Sociological Theories of Radical Movements and Revolution

The psychological theories just discussed provide contemporary versions of the old Mass Uprising theory and the Great Man theory of revolution. Most sociological theories are modern versions of disharmony theory or of conspiracy theories. There are also a few modern versions of the Idealist theory, namely modern studies of the influence of political ideas and ideology on society and politics.[57] Marx provides the paradigm of contemporary disharmony theories, and interpretations of Leninist writing and experience provide the paradigm of contemporary conspiracy theories.

Disharmony theories hold that political or social stability depends upon proper dovetailing of various components of society or of the universe and that disruption in one component will cause disruption in the other components. Modern disharmony theories tell us that revolution and radical movements are consequences of social strain, dysfunction, disequilibrium, incongruence, stress, discord, contradictions, distress, leads and lags, and the like.[58] The literature of modern disharmony theories testifies to the capacity of modern social science to promulgate literary metaphors. The adequacy of these metaphors as scientific theory is less clear.

Modern disharmony theories have distinguished predecessors. Sung neo-Confucianism described society and the universe as a hierarchy of interrelated parts, with the emperor mediating between heaven and earth and maintaining general harmony through his personal virtue. The Great Chain of Being provided later Western society with a parallel theory of considerable sophistication and broad acceptance.[59] Contemporary disharmony theories are descendants of the Great Chain of Being, even though students of Shakespeare's *King Lear* are more likely to recognize the lineage than students of society and politics. These older disharmony theories, like some contemporary theories of revolution as a concomitant of the modernization process, are limited in their applicability to certain kinds of societies. But particularly in the case of Sung neo-Confucianism, there is a useful concreteness and specificity behind the grand metaphors. One knew what the emperor had to do to retain the Mandate of Heaven and what the consequences of disharmony or lack of virtue would be: namely, famines, border wars, breakdown of the irrigation system, and so forth. Modern variants of the disharmony theory have tended to lack this redeeming precision. The most recent disharmony theory to which such criticism does not apply is that of Karl Marx.

For Marx, revolution was a consequence of social contradictions arising out of the division of labor.[60] At this aery level of generality Marx's theory resembles contemporary versions of the disharmony theory. But Marx vivified his metaphor of contradictions with detailed analysis of all other key aspects of bourgeois revolutions. The resulting theory is scientifically testable, despite its high level of generality and broad applicability to a class of events roughly equivalent to Huntington's concept of revolution. Marx argues that the proletariat would find its life experiences so contrary to prevailing bourgeois ideology that the old social myths would become unacceptable; their *susceptibility to a new ideology* and their increasing numbers made probable transformation of the basic social myth of the society if they could gain power. At the same time, their concentration in factories, their increasing homogeneity, and their training in industrial skills provided the resources necessary for *political organization*. Economic competition ensured absolute or relative deterioration in their standards of living,[61] while economic growth ensured rising aspiration,[62] and the meaninglessness of the work which provided the workers with their identities degraded them;[63] all of these ensured revolutionary *discontent* among individual workers, in Marx's view. Simultaneously, wealth became more concentrated, and therefore the *possessors of wealth became fewer and more vulnerable.* Business cycle crises would further weaken the capitalists' position and would *precipitate* the revolution.

Most of Marx's specific predictions about revolution have failed. Crucially, the semiskilled workers eventually became more differentiated, less numerous as a proportion of the population, better paid, and—through unions—more politically influential. But Marx's theory, although wrong, provides a model of scholarly craftsmanship, just as Isaac Newton's theory of motion, although wrong, provides such a model. Consistent with the evidence available to him, Marx's theory accounted for individual discontent, political organization, value transformation, the precipitants of revolutionary struggle, and the triumph of new institutions. Contemporary disharmony theories have never even aspired to comparable standards of craftsmanship.

Functionalist theories of revolution assert correctly that specification of the conditions of stability constitutes specification of the conditions of instability. But Chalmers Johnson goes further and argues that

a knowledge of morbid conditions in animals depends upon a
knowledge of healthy conditions in the same species. . . . the sociology of functional societies comes logically before the sociology
of revolution.[64]

The problems with the analogy between society and the ani-
mal body are familiar. But even if the analogy were accurate,
a complete theory of health is *not* logically antecedent to a
theory of the causes, sequences, and consequences of some
particular disease; indeed, medicine has fully analyzed most
diseases in the absence of an overarching theory of health.

Johnson's *Revolution and the Social System* maintains
that revolution results from multiple dysfunction plus elite
intransigence plus an accelerator.[65] The alleged need for elite
intransigence is not supported and, more important, merely
constitutes a type of dysfunction. Separate mention of it
confuses levels of analysis and serves merely to introduce into
the theory Johnson's unsupported belief that all revolutions
are avoidable. Moreover, all societies suffer from multiple
dysfunction, but not all societies are revolutionary, yet Johnson provides no criteria for the importance of dysfunction or
for situations in which multiple dysfunctions will reinforce
one another. Contemporary American society suffers from
serious dysfunctions in its police and criminal justice system,
its economic and welfare system, its educational system, its
family system, and to a lesser extent, in its political and military systems, yet it is clearly not on the verge of revolution.

In *Revolutionary Change* Johnson maintains that revolution
results from disequilibrium (i.e., lack of congruence between
values and environment), power deflation (increasing need
for the government to employ force to obtain obedience),
loss of authority (decreasing governmental legitimacy), and
an accelerator.[66] He links individual discontent to system disequilibrium by saying that noncongruence between values
and environment leads to personal tension and by arguing:

Utilizing the concept of the social system, we can distinguish
between those instances of violence within the system that are

revolutionary and those that constitute criminal or other forms of behavior.[67]

But this is precisely what he cannot do; he fails in his attempt to provide independent measures of personal tension and system disequilibrium, and does not even attempt to provide empirical distinctions between revolutionary and nonrevolutionary violence.

Another flaw in this disequilibrium theory is its treatment of accelerators. Johnson maintains that accelerators trigger the revolution, make it appear that the elite is unable to maintain its monopoly of force, and determine the success or failure of the revolution.[68] Most writers have preferred a more limited concept of precipitant, which is merely a trigger of the revolution.[69] There is no logically necessary connection between an event that triggers a revolution and the conditions which determine success or failure. Edwards saw the Boston Tea Party as a precipitant of the American Revolution,[70] and Marx saw the expulsion of unmarried workers from the *ateliers* as a precipitant in France,[71] but neither of these events determined the success or failure of the revolution. Johnson's class of possible accelerators is rather small: weakening of the elite's armed forces, ideological belief in insurgent success, and the launching of special operations like guerrilla warfare against the elite's forces.[72] But the latter is the thing triggered, not the trigger itself. Johnson's theory also omits the possibility that a government's capabilities and its opponents' discontent remain the same, but that social change provides the opponents with new resources which make them stronger than the government. Even if these difficulties were solved, Johnson's theory still could predict only the breakdown of the system and never the internal processes, sequences, and outcomes of the revolution.

Arnold Feldman argues that societies should be conceptualized as tension-management mechanisms, a view which can explain both stability and change and therefore avoids the characteristic difficulties of functional and conflict theories of society. In his view a revolution occurs when tensions become greater than the capacity for tension management. In this theory, tensions result when society is fragmented into subsystems (e.g., classes and functional divisions), and when individuals are placed in inconsistent status positions. The capabilities to manage these tensions result when change is slow and predictable, and when all social groups assign a high priority to tension management.[73] But other writers have identified the fragmentation of society as a source of stability—indeed fragmentation ruined Marx's theory of revolution. And Feldman does not really identify tension-management mechanisms, only conditions (slow change, high priority for management) which would allow such mechanisms to operate if they did exist. Once again, we have a metaphor without content. Feldman and Johnson and others agree that revolution occurs when something gets out of whack, but as Bienen says, "What is out of whack is never clear."[74]

Organization Theories of Revolution and Radical Movements

The second major division of sociological theories of revolution and radical movements includes the descendants of the conspiracy theory, namely the studies of the rise and fall of political organizations. Because conspiracy theories have been so abused in the past, both as intellectual tools and as excuses for victimizing particular groups, they have rightly been neglected. But this writer takes the position that studies of political organization constitute the only theoretical tools making it possible for a single theory to explain all of the following phenomena:

1. The goals of revolution
2. The participants in revolution
3. The role of ideology
4. The structure of revolutionary organization
5. The causes of revolutions
6. The sequences of revolution
7. The precipitants of revolution
8. Strategies of revolution and counterrevolution
9. Consequences of revolution

In short, organizational theories of revolution and radical movements are capable of an intellectual imperialism which absorbs the other kinds of theory, whereas the other theories are inadequate bases for such a synthesis.

Within organizational studies of revolution there is a fundamental division between those which emphasize the forest and those which emphasize particular trees. The favorite trees coming under scrutiny are the intricacies of insurgent organization building and the processes of political decay of old regimes. Lenin's essays on the organization of a revolutionary party, the importance of professionalism, and the uses of a newspaper, have collectively become a classic. Philip Selznick's book, *The Organizational Weapon*, provides parallel analyses.[75] Franz Schurmann's classic study of the Chinese Communist Party[76] is particularly insightful regarding the role of ideology in organizing a revolutionary party, a revolutionary state, and a revolutionary society. For instance, Schurmann tells us that pure ideology, which states values, can be used to mobilize mass support; practical ideology, which states norms of behavior, can be used to mobilize support from "the line component of the middle tier organization"; and nonideological ideas can be used to mobilize professional staff.[77] Studies of social movements provide similar insights although these are generally neither so detailed nor so fruitful as the studies of revolutionary organizational building. Parallel to the studies of revolutionary organization *building* are the studies of *decay* of old regimes. Samuel P. Huntington is largely responsible for focusing contemporary political scientists' attention on political decay, but his contribution has been not so much to analysis of this particular tree as to providing one sketch of the forest as a whole.[78] The primary students of the process of political decay are the comparative historians, particularly those who study the sequences of revolution.

Analysts of sequences of revolution have received roughly the same acclaim from contemporary social scientists that numerologists receive from professional mathematicians. Since it has proved difficult to incorporate the sequences into other kinds of theories, such sequences have generally been treated as prescientific folklore imbued with the same quaintness as the Greek division of the universe into earth, air, fire, and water. But in fact most of our concrete, generalizable knowledge of revolutions is indebted to these discoverers of sequences. Moreover, neglect of these studies is a principal reason why "theorists by and large are trying to explain why men rebel rather than why revolutions occur and why governments collapse."[79]

Lyford Edwards, the original and principal student of descriptive sequences,[80] believed that alienation of the public from a regime typically increased over four generations. Individualized discontent becomes general, oppressed people acquire new capabilities, intellectuals' loyalties shift toward the oppressed, the rulers lose faith in themselves, discontent focuses on a single institution, and diversionary wars or circuses fail. A new social myth provides a novel set of values, a justification of alternative modes of property ownership, and assurance of success to insurgents. The revolution is then precipitated by some trivial event. Moderates initially gain control of the government and persecute the conservatives. Public opinion becomes radicalized, conservatives undermine the moderates from within and without, and the moderates demonstrate incompetence at using force. Thus the radicals take over. The radicals face internal insurrection, foreign invasion, and their own inexperience at governing. But the new social myth becomes entwined with defense against invasion, and effective military command becomes supplemented by political control of the military. Bureaucratic revolt is quelled by purges and threats of pension loss. Popular revolts are ended by a few highly visible acts of terror and by war weariness. A period of factionalism and corruption is followed by the formulation and institutionalization of a new constitution. Crane Brinton elaborated this sequence,[81] and Anthony Wallace discerned a very similar sequence for revolutionary phenomena ("revitalization movements") among primitive tribes.[82]

Not all revolutions have followed the western sequence,

however, so the search for sequences must either be abandoned, or supplemented by one or more new sequences, or continued at a higher level of generality. Huntington adds a new sequence,[83] which he identifies as the eastern revolution, which begins at the periphery of society and has the government fall at the end of the revolution rather than at the beginning. Moderates are eliminated early and the primary struggle is between government and radicals. Such sequences are useful insights, but do not constitute theories. Huntington's explanation of why one sequence occurs in one place and the other sequence in another depends in part upon an unsatisfying distinction between elites which have lost their will to rule and those which have not. Moreover, new sequences are neither ruled out nor predicted.

Other writers, primarily theorists of social movements, have described sequences at a much higher level of generality, sequences which we may term *analytic* as opposed to the *descriptive* sequences described above. Rex Hopper condensed the Edwards-Brinton sequence into four primary sequences which can be labeled (somewhat differently from Hopper's labels) individual excitement, organization, struggle, and institutionalization.[84] Hans Toch says that social "problem situations" create "problems" for individuals, who in turn become "susceptible" to certain beliefs and to mobilization by movements which advocate them. Toch fails to provide empirical criteria for discriminating social problem situations from individual problems, and he has the social movement enter the theory as a *deus ex machina*.[85] Ted R. Gurr provides a sequence, basically similar to Toch's, in which discontent is generated, becomes politicized, and then becomes actualized in violence. Gurr's more detailed hypotheses can be strung together to form alternative sequences based on such criteria as the relative strength of government and insurgents, but crucial phases, such as organization, are omitted from his sequence.[86]

Smelser provides the most convincing analytic sequence, a sequence applicable to all forms of collective behavior.[87] A revolutionary movement occurs when (1) the revolutionary movement is structurally possible, (2) the society is subject to strain, (3) a generalized belief grows "which identifies the source of strain, attributes certain characteristics to its source, and specifies certain responses to the strain as possible or appropriate," (4) precipitating factors focus attention on a concrete problem, (5) participants are mobilized for action, and (6) social controls succeed or are overwhelmed. Smelser's discussion of revolution argues the necessity for charismatic leadership, for institutionalization of various organizational features, and for appropriate tactics; these emphases are welcome in a literature which otherwise neglects organizational problems and ignores human purpose. But Smelser's analysis is not tied to measurable variables and his discussion of each element in the sequence is inadequate. For instance, in discussing the structural possibility ("conduciveness") of a value-oriented movement, he mentions differentiation of the value system from other components of action, availability of means to express grievances, insulation and isolation of value-oriented movements, and communications. Supposing these preconditions satisfied, and the first five elements of the sequence fulfilled, how does one know whether the revolutionary movement will carry the day? What kind of mobilization is required in the fifth element of the sequence? Such questions remain unanswered.

Examining these various sequences carefully, one discerns that there are really two distinct sequences being discussed. One is the rise of an insurgent organization: individual discontent becomes group discontent and then an organized political actor that eventually clashes with the government and sometimes gains control of society. The analytic sequences and the literature on social movements focus on this rise of a protesting group. In the special case when the group is revolutionary, it evolves into a full-fledged revolutionary organization like that described in the work of Lenin and Selznick. The second sequence, detailed in the descriptive sequences but generally ignored in the analytic sequences, is the organizational decay of the government and the concomitant decadence of the governing elite. The western sequence of revolution predominates when the decay of the government almost entirely precedes the rise of a revolutionary party. Huntington's eastern sequence occurs when the decay and collapse of the government is so slow and prolonged that the sequential development of the insurgent movement occurs while the government remains a powerful political actor.

The literature on the development of radical movements, including revolutionary ones, and the parallel literature on the decay and collapse of governments, are complementary in every respect except for the differing jargons employed. Together they focus on the essence of revolution, namely the triumphant rise of a radical regime and the collapse of a government. Psychological studies of revolution are easily absorbed as part of the discontent phase of the sequences of organizational rise and decay. Disharmony theories are transformed from metaphors into theories by examining social stresses in terms of their effects on the organization of an insurgency and the disorganization of a government. Studies of the psychology of particular groups involved in a revolutionary insurgency divide neatly into studies of which groups would be motivated to join particular parts of a revolutionary organization. Following Franz Schurmann's previously noted insights we can then trace the motivations of the leadership, of the staff, of the mass base, and of other differentiated parts of the organization, and we can assess the extent to which the groups have the capacity to perform as an integrated organization facing a hostile environment.

What remains is to incorporate into such an overall organizational perspective on revolution the insights of studies of ideology, of revolutionary strategy, and of precipitants of revolution.

Samuel P. Huntington has sketched the framework within which most current organizational theories proceed.[88] His key concepts are "political mobilization and participation," by which he means the emergence and activity of political organizations in a modernizing society, and "political institutionalization," by which he means organizational stability. Revolution in these terms is an explosion of participation and a concomitant failure of institutionalization. Since "participation" covers everything from voting to interest group activity to revolutionary insurgency, it in effect encompasses all of politics under a single word. Likewise "institutionalization" encompasses everything known about the stability and instability of organizations. Not surprisingly, then, the concepts require a great deal of intricate differentiation and analysis before they are applicable to any particular situation. Nevertheless, during the modernization process, and in revolutionary situations generally, there is a general expansion of political participation of all kinds, and there are systematic, multiple failures of institutionalization. And it is more fruitful to start from such broad, insightful characterizations of the situation and work down to greater details than it is to try to piece together a broad picture from numerous studies of seemingly unrelated details.

Even more ambitious, and just as successful, is Barrington Moore's neglected general analysis of the processes by which groups (revolutionary and nonrevolutionary) acquire power.[89] According to Moore, active search for power begins (1) when a society undertakes activities requiring high coordination, (2) when "external shock or internal decay produces a movement for the forced reintegration of society around new or partially new patterns of behavior,"[90] or (3) when "rulers of one segment of a loosely ordered system gradually expand their control over the whole system or a substantial part of it."[91] In the first case, coordination is typically required to allocate large resources in frequently changing ways, to persuade or compel a large number of people to act contrary to their inclinations, and to realize a competitive advantage accruing "to that social unit which can mobilize or control the larger quantity of resources."[92] In the second case, the center may be strengthened or other extensive changes may occur, depending on available concepts of a better world. The third case occurs because of personal ambition.

In Moore's theory, desire for change results from discontent, which in turn results either from the desire of the outs to be in or from dissatisfaction with the performance of institutions. The latter leads to formation of a charter myth, which chooses between nativism and xenophilia, and between hierarchy-discipline and equality-freedom. The myth allocates authority, designates interpreters of the myth, and delineates membership. At this point, conditioned by the situation, the movement chooses an internal structure (segmental, feudal, bureaucratic, or totalitarian) and defines its relations with external groups. In a stable society with diffused levers of power, broad coalitions are necessary to maintain power and such coalitions are necessarily loose. In a stable despotism, minimal alliances are necessary and power can be acquired by appeasing a few groups. In both of these situations little change occurs. Transformation of society requires a movement to seek a mass base and then to "atomize those segments of society that have maintained some degree of corporate identity."[93]

Out of these sequences of choices come four basic patterns: *totalitarianism* results from external shock or internal decay and a charter myth emphasizing hierarchy. *Monarchical absolutism* results from the piecing together of societal fragments by an ambitious ruler. *Feudalism* emerges from decay of a centralized regime or from tying together of fragments; here loyalty is to a person and this limits the system. A *highly centralized nontotalitarian system* (unnamed by Moore) results from the rise of activities requiring high coordination contrary to popular desires, whereas *egalitarianism* may result from the need to coordinate activities consistent with popular desires (e.g., in the English industrial revolution). Moore's historical patterns do not constitute highly integrated theory, but his approach is far more consistent with evidence, far more testable, and much more convincing in the way it relates individual movement and ideology, than its functionalist or tension-management or internal war counterparts.

Leites and Wolf have attempted a general theory of *Rebellion and Authority*[94] organized around a simple systems analysis in which both the rebellion and the authority receive endogenous and exogenous *inputs* which a conversion mechanism transforms into *outputs* for conflict with the opponent and for generation of new inputs. Leites and Wolf emphasize that organization is central to the strength of rebellion and to its analysis,[95] but in fact they emphasize inputs and outputs and deemphasize the conversion mechanism. They rely heavily on analogies with market theory (indifference curves to explain individual behavior, supply and demand for revolution as an explanation of conflict), which take the structure of the organization as given. Their failure to separate the inputs necessary for construction and maintenance of the conversion mechanism from the inputs necessary for strategic resources, and their failure to analyze strategies and structures of organization, make their book primarily a useful contribution to strategic literature of Sun Tzu, Mao Tse-tung, and Vo Nguyen Giap, rather than to the organizational literature of Lenin, Barrington Moore, Philip Selznick, and Frank Schurmann, despite the authors' frequent contrary assertions.

My own work has also focused on a broad synthesis of theories of revolution based upon studies of organizational development and conflict.[96] In this organizational perspective, a revolution is fundamentally a conflict between two political organizations in which the insurgency shatters the government and restructures the society. The first question such a theory asks is: under what conditions does a government in effect spontaneously disintegrate or weaken? Second, what social groups or coalitions of social groups are capable of forming a potent political organization? It turns out that virtually the whole literature of political sociology bears upon and revolves around an answer to this question. Theories of interest groups, of social stability, of organization, and of social stratification concur that groups can organize politically only if they possess certain key attributes, including goals that are visible and salient, communications, leadership, time, and autonomy. Third, the structures of revolutionary organizations are explained by examining the structural requirements of an organization threatened with destruction if it does not achieve secrecy, discipline, rapid decision-making, and so forth. Fourth, ideology turns out to be a prerequisite of successful revolution because of its key role in enhancing the organizational resources of the group, legitimizing the organizational structure of the insurgency, and providing tools and strategies for revolutionary conflict. Fifth, sequences of revolution are explained by the interacting sequences of rise and fall of insurgency and government. Sixth, the causes of revolution are those social phenomena which facilitate the rise of a revolutionary organization and enhance the decline of a government. Seventh, the precipitants of revolution turn out to be, not inexplicable chance phenomena, but rather classes of events which precipitate *decisions* by either the government or the insurgency; the precipitants are subject to analysis because the decision processes of the two conflicting parties are susceptible to analysis. Finally, strategies of revolution and counterrevolution are susceptible to systematic analysis in terms of the organizational and strategic weaknesses of the two conflicting organizations.

Some Concluding Perspectives

The role of psychology in studies of revolution remains controversial. The behavioralist movement promulgates reductionist theories, which must be dismissed as methodological fetishism; psychological and economic variables have been allowed to dominate political, organizational, and military questions simply because polls and economic data happen to fit the kind of statistics which political scientists are being taught these days.

Tilly[97] suggests dismissing psychological analyses altogether, leaving a pure political/social theory of revolutions. Certainly the possibility of such a theory can never be ruled out. But revolution seems to require distinctive kinds of political organization whose existence and effectiveness depend in turn upon acceptance of distinctive ideologies. These ideologies tend to be accepted only by individuals experiencing certain kinds of psychological pressure. If such psychological pressures were fully understood, and if they followed fairly automatically from certain gross features of social structure, then the prospects for a purely socio-political theory would be auspicious. However, all our experience so far suggests that the psychological pressures, the acceptability of ideologies, and the abilities of groups to organize depend upon some fairly fine features of social structure. To be more concrete, if social inequality, tenancy, and absentee landlordism automatically stimulated peasant radicalism and peasant political organization, then reference to psychological and other variables would be unnecessary. But it turns out, for instance, that the Philippines, with far greater tenancy rates than China, does not generate powerful peasant organizations like those of China—for reasons connected in part with the psychological conse-quences of religion, family structure, village social organi-zation, and politics. Hopefully it will turn out that all these complexities simply result from an erroneous perspective or a failure to grasp some fundamental point, but for now we seem doomed to trade with the psychologists.

Tilly's view of multiple sovereignty as a competition among abstract groups for political power, and Huntington's concept of a general expansion or explosion of political participation also raise other, purely socio-political, issues. So long as one imbues such models with an historian's wealth of differentiation and detail, they provide useful images, but unless one is terribly careful it can be fatal to think in terms of abstract groups instead of particular groups. Some groups can organize and carry through political action; others cannot. Because Marx showed *French* peasants incapable of political action *at a certain date,* generations of Marxists mistakenly believed peasants in all places and at all times incapable of such organization. Following the successes of Mao Tse-tung and Ho Chi Minh, men like Robert McNamara came to believe that all peasants in all places were organizable. Marx himself foundered on a similar point, and Edmund Wilson's analysis of his error is worth quoting at length:

Karl Marx had arrived at his vision of the working class expelling the capitalists by way of two false analogies. One of these was a probably unconscious tendency to argue from the position of the Jew to the position of the proletarian. The German Jews in Karl Marx's time were just escaping from the restrictions of the ghetto, which meant also the system of the Judaic world; and in this case the former victims of a social and economic discrimination, with their ancient religious discipline and their intellectual training, were quite easily able to take over the techniques and the responsibilities of the outside modern world. The proletariat, however, unlike the Jews, had no tradition of authority; they were, by their very position, kept ignorant and physically bred down. The country—industrial England—in which Marx prophesied that the widening gulf between the owning and the working classes would first bring about a communist revolution, had turned out to be the country where the progressive degradation of the underprivileged classes had simply had the effect of stunting them and slowly extinguishing their spirit. The other false analogy of Marx was his argument from the behavior of the bourgeoisie in the seventeenth and eighteenth centuries to the behavior to be expected of the working class, in their turn, in relation to the bourgeoisie. The European middle classes who finally dispossessed the feudal landlords were, after all, educated people, accustomed to administering property and experienced in public affairs. The proletariat, the true ground-down industrial workers on whom Marx was basing his hopes, were almost entirely devoid of any such experience or education; and what we now know invariably happens when the poor and illiterate people of a modern industrial society first master advanced techniques and improve their standard of living, is that they tend to exhibit ambitions and tastes which Karl Marx would have regarded as bourgeois.[98]

Since identification of specific groups and their capacities is crucial, some obvious but frequently neglected theoretical and methodological points follow: First, studies which examine the relationships between gross economic indices of a whole society, such as GNP trends, Gini indices of inequality, and so forth on the one hand, and political variables like violence, radicalism, and revolution on the other are very crude; they have made a limited contribution, but they have little additional to add to our understanding of revolution. Second, crude distinctions between elite and mass also have little value in such studies, since revolutionary organizations display a far more complex stratification. Third, it is crucial that the inventory of groups which are scrutinized for potential radical or revolutionary behavior be complete. The literature on the lumpenproletariat, blue collar workers, white collar workers, and the subcategory of white collar workers with menial tasks and little hope of advancement, is thorough and impressive. On peasants there is great volume of writing, but crucial errors recur.

Whole categories of groups are systematically excluded from analysis. In many revolutions youth and women have played crucial roles, and those roles have typically been ignored. For instance, in the Chinese Revolution, Mao made a central point of organizing women's groups and youth groups as well as peasant groups. These organizations tapped central sources of discontent in Chinese society and played central roles in reorganizing that society. In his writings, in his revolutionary organizing, and in his recent political struggles, Mao has emphasized the role of women and youth. Anthropological observers in Chinese villages were invariably impressed by the potency of such organizations, and the Chinese media continue to highlight their roles. Despite the increasing attention devoted to youth and women after the Western experiences of the 1960s, and despite the political development literature on these groups, it remains true that social scientists have systematically neglected the roles of women and youth. The literature also tends to systematically neglect ethnic bases for radicalism and revolution in favor of class bases. Studies of peasant revolts in the Philippines have invariably uncovered ethnicity as the strongest predictive variable. Rwanda experienced a revolt in which ethnic bases clearly predominated over class considerations. Fortunately the work of Moynihan and Glaser[99] and others may be initiating a process of legitimization of discussion of the ethnic basis of American politics, and Jewish students of Jewish radicalism may be legitimizing the study of that subject.

Finally, intellectuals studying radicalism and revolution need to be particularly self-conscious about their own role. Intellectuals are the group most vulnerable to the Durkheim and Weber varieties of alienation: infinite aspiration, normlessness, isolation, and even abandonment of personality to role requirements. Scholars tend to project their own discontents onto other groups, for instance in overrating the alienating effects of the meaninglessness of assembly-line work. Scholars also tend to reach, by one route or another, the conclusion that the solution to societies' problems is rule by the intellectuals and that such rule is imminent; on this point there is a noteworthy convergence in the views of Plato, Lenin, Galbraith, C. Wright Mills, David Apter, and Daniel Bell.

Although the lower-middle class has received considerable scrutiny as a potential radical or revolutionary or authoritarian force, there is a conspicuous neglect of the upper-middle class as a group defending its class interests, perhaps because the unmaskers of class interests tend to be drawn from this class. Throughout modern history the upper-middle class has occupied a peculiarly precarious position. Lacking the security that comes with being truly wealthy, this group finds itself constantly threatened by the rising wealth of the rest of society. Maids become unavailable, commuting to work from the suburbs becomes burdensome, the increasingly well-to-do lower-middle-class groups have the temerity to clutter the landscape with "ticky-tacky" housing developments, and the quiet rural lake previously containing one upper-middle-class house on its shore and one large upper-middle-class boat on its surface becomes cluttered and noisy because of lower-middle-class cottages and boats. Not surprisingly, "quality of life," which means having only one cottage on the lake, comes to replace "standard of living" as a principal theme of upper-middle-class magazines.[100]

A substantial proportion of this class raises its interests to an ideology that the world is being made worse and threatening its own destruction by continued economic growth. A somewhat smaller proportion of this class begins to view high consumption of resources as a crime. Use of resources by industrialized nations comes to be viewed in terms of the now-famous life raft analogy, in which a dozen men on a life raft possess a single barrel of water and one of the men insists on taking a bath in the barrel on the flimsy excuse that he owns the water. If this set of views proves not to be a passing fad, it could prove to be one of the great sources of radicalism and revolutionary fervor of the future. Built into the (dubious) intellectual arguments about resources are justifications for linkages between upper-middle-class minorities in some rich countries and deprived majorities in poor countries; for terrorism directed against power plants and other conspicuous symbols of economic development; for a new ideology of steady-state economies; and for political domination by a mandarinate of scholar-bureaucrats rationing resources. Henceforth discussions of radical and revolutionary groups cannot afford to ignore the revolutionary potential of this group with this issue.

Once an adequate inventory of groups is in hand, the next concern must be adequate analysis of the motivations and capacities of each group. With few exceptions, students of radicalism and revolution have emphasized motivation to the exclusion of questions of organization and strategy, and they have stressed economic sources of motivation to the exclusion of noneconomic. For instance, almost universally the literature assumes that peasants are exclusively economic animals. If peasants revolt it must be because the economy in which they reside is going up, or because it is going down, or because it is fluctuating, or because subsistence is being threatened, or because the balance of exchange with landlords is changing. Now all of these factors are terribly important. But politics counts too. Nationalism has been a central factor in most recent peasant revolutionary movements. In China and Yugoslavia the governments were destroyed by the Japanese and the Germans, and the revolutionaries merely administered a final blow. In the Philippines a democratic political system short-circuited most of the potential for peasant rebellion. The failure of the Philippine Congress to seat two peasant movement representatives precipitated the rebellion in the early 1950s, and the lines of communication established by the democratic political system turned out to be the key to destruction of the guerrilla movement.[101] A more recent uprising of Muslims has been primarily an ethnic conflict triggered by the ending of the democratic system and by government attempts to confiscate weapons which served as symbols of masculinity and status in Muslim households. At no time in the postwar period were Muslim or communist areas threatened with loss of subsistence or with severe degradation of traditional exchange balances. Regression studies of political behavior throughout the Philippines have invariably turned up ethnic and linguistic factors as the best predictors of political behavior. Thus, by ignoring crucial ethnic and political factors, traditional economic-focused studies have consistently fallen wide of the mark.

Neglect of political *variables* is complemented by neglect of broad political *perspectives,* especially neglect of strategies and strategic situations. Sociologists and political scientists have almost completely abandoned analysis of political strategy and strategic situations to historians, and of military strategy and strategic situations to ex-colonels. When social scientists do confront issues of strategy, they tend either (1) to jump out of their own discipline and lose themselves in military thought; or (2) to focus on the *tactics* of a specific situation like Vietnam; or (3) to focus on the politics and social psychology of a situation and to dismiss military and international considerations as trivial. As a result there is *no* social science study which integrates serious military considerations into a broad sociopolitical analysis. Sheldon Wolin is right in criticizing the "militarization" of studies of revolution and counterrevolution, and in denouncing excessive concern with "technique," because of the proliferation of guerrilla warfare books.[102] But it is simultaneously true that, whereas colonels have become aware of political and social considerations, social scientists have utterly failed to integrate political strategy and military variables into their work. Had Mao been a better sociologist and a worse military strategist he probably would have lived a short life. Had Aidit of Indonesia built upon less peasant discontent but created a competent army, he would have ruled Indonesia. But nothing in contemporary social theory would tell us so.

In China and Yugoslavia, the Japanese and German invasions, respectively, created political/strategic situations in which mobile, rural, radical groups could organize and fight, and in which geographically fixed groups were subject to blackmail. Analyses of discontent, strain, and military strategy are simply incapable of incorporating such political/strategic considerations. What is wrong with our theories is fragmentation, trivialization, methodological fetishes, academic contempt for military issues, and neglect of the essence of politics, namely choices and strategy.

It may be well to close with another comment by Sheldon Wolin, one which questions the worth of the entire enterprise just surveyed. He asserts that social science demeans revolution "by using categories which trivialize or devitalize revolutionary thought and action,"[103] and that revolutionaries enamored of technique do the same thing. His comment is correct, but pointless. Any scientific study trivializes and devitalizes its subject. The great crime of Copernicus was to trivialize man and to demean God's universe. Studies of the physiology of human mating trivialize and demean sex. Psychobiography trivializes and demeans the processes of creative genius. Such trivialization and demeaning are the price we pay for analysis, for the acquisition of systematic, scientifically valid information. So Wolin's criticism is invalid, considered as a comment on the achievements of social science in light of the standards of social science. Nonetheless, in two larger senses Wolin is correct. First, by a kind of Gresham's Law the behavioral revolution has come to mean that methods drive out substance. As a corollary, because our elementary statistics can test only trivial or fragmented ideas, our knowledge becomes increasingly fragmented and trivial. Second, empirical social science has become an imperialistic ideology driving philosophy into those corners of the library reserved for the quaint. The genes of Taine pervade social science. Poor men's Lenins spring up wherever the dragon's teeth of consulting fees are sown. But the descendants of Burke and Jefferson and Babeuf have been banished to the computer center. We are poorer for this.

Notes

Notes to Chapter 1

1. Questions relating to the psychological dimensions of the sources of radicalism are not discussed in this introduction. The study of these questions is of enormous importance, however, as is evidenced by the best writings from the radical perspective. For instance, David Kettler remarks: "Historians and social scientists cannot disregard the evidence, for example, which links revolutionary doctrine and practice with the social and psychological type of 'the saints' even though such evidence is commonly presented in the context of genteel disdain for radical social change or of venomous defense against critical challenge to prevailing privileges" ("The Vocation of Radical Intellectuals," *Politics and Society* I, no. 1 [November 1970] : 42-43). After mentioning the work of Walzer, Cohn, Talmon, Popper, Van Hayek, and Oakeshott, Kettler concludes: "A conception of radicalism which cannot come to grips with the materials in such studies simply blinds itself to realities" (ibid., p. 43, fn. 28).

2. Dr. Overholt's essay obviates the need for extensive bibliographical references in these introductory remarks.

3. The papers given at the workshop were substantially revised following the discussion. Professor Lipset gave an oral presentation at the

Sources of Contemporary Radicalism

workshop and wrote his paper later. Regrettably, an important paper by Professor Linz, "The Sources of Radicalism in the Iberian Peninsula," is not included, since other commitments made it impossible for him to prepare it in time for publication.

4. Stanislaw Ossowski, *Class Structure in the Social Consciousness* (New York: The Free Press, 1963), pp. 165-166.

5. Reinhard Bendix, "The Age of Ideology: Persistent and Changing," in *Ideology and Discontent,* ed. David B. Apter (New York: The Free Press, 1964), p. 294.

6. See, for example, *The Shorter Oxford English Dictionary,* vol. 2, 3rd ed. (Oxford: Clarendon Press, 1975), p. 1738. The first use of the term "radical" in a political sense is generally associated with Charles J. Fox, who at the end of the eighteenth century proposed a "radical reform" in England—a drastic expansion of the franchise. Throughout most of the nineteenth century the term "radical" in European politics continued to be closely associated with the struggle for universal suffrage for the male population.

7. On the functions, purpose, and variety of types of definition in the social sciences see Hans L. Zetterberg, *On Theory and Verification in Sociology* (Totowa, New Jersey: The Bedminster Press, 1965), chapter 3.

8. This distinction of course follows the well-known Weberian classification of types of action, e.g., "political and politically oriented" vis-à-vis "politically relevant" actions. See Max Weber, *The Theory of Social and Economic Organization,* edited with introduction by Talcott Parsons (New York: The Free Press, 1964), esp. pp. 145-157.

9. B. N. Ponomarev, ed., *Politicheskii Slovar* (Moscow: Gosudarstvennoe Izdatelstvo Politicheskoi Literatury, 1958), p. 469.

10. On the nature and meaning of direct action and other forms of protest behavior see April Carter, *Direct Action and Liberal Democracy* (New York: Harper Torchbooks, 1974).

11. For an excellent critical review of the relation of violence to political order and especially to social change see Henry Bienen, *Violence and Social Change* (Chicago: University of Chicago Press, 1968). Especially pertinent is the quote from William Kornhauser's *The Politics of Mass Society* with which Bienen concludes his review of current literature on the subject: "The readiness to assimilate all politics to either order or violence implies a very narrow notion of order and a very broad notion of violence" (p. 106).

12. The persons whose contributions to the workshop discussion appear in either the text or notes of this chapter are not identified, since, unlike the authors of papers, they had no opportunity to revise, reconsider, or clarify their remarks.

13. The adherents of Maoist radicalism, varieties of New Left Marxian dissidents in Eastern Europe, and Western socialists express no less stridently than the Soviets and their followers outside the USSR conviction in the authenticity of their own forms of radicalism, criticizing vigorously not only Soviet radicalism but each other as well. For Soviet criticism see especially E. Batalov, *The Philosophy of Revolt: Criticism of Left Radical Ideology* (Moscow: Progress Publishers, 1975). For a traditional Western communist view see Jack Woods, *New Theories of Revolution* (New York: International Publishers, 1972). For a Trotskyist view see Jack Barnes et al., *Towards an American Socialist Revolution—A Strategy for the 1970's* (New York: Pathfinder Press, 1971). For one variety of New Left views see Daniel and Gabriel Cohn-Bendit, *Obsolete Communism: The Left Wing Alternative* (New York: McGraw-Hill, 1968) or the collection edited by Carl Oglesby, *The New Left Reader* (New York: Grove Press, 1969).

14. Barrington Moore, Jr., *Reflections on the Causes of Human Misery and Upon Certain Proposals to Eliminate Them* (Boston: Beacon Press, 1973), p. 192.

15. The difficulties which the question of means and especially of violence entails in the analysis of radicalism (some of which are stressed in Professor Landsberger's paper) include the entire question of the relation between radical rhetoric and action. Their detailed discussion belongs more properly in the introduction to the third volume of this study, where they will be considered together with the question of "de-radicalization."

16. These differences and the various typologies that can be built around them are not limited to the obvious distinctions between single issues versus totalistic orientations (which are so much stressed in all discussions and in comparisons between the successive and relatively short-lived radical movements in the United States and the stable and long-entrenched European radical parties). Typologies of radicalism can be based on the different degrees to which specific aspects of particular belief systems (e.g., socialism, nationalism, populism) and their combination are central to the goals of radical movements. That populism is more than an elusive and contradictory concept and that it does have an intellectual unity of underlying tendencies is argued with some

success in the first organized attempt to clarify its meanings. See Ghita Ionescu and Ernest Gellner, *Populism, Its Meaning and National Characteristics* (New York: Macmillan Co., 1969), especially the chapters by Donald MacRae, Peter Wiles, and Peter Worsley. Another kind of commonsense typology which combines the differences regarding the scope of radical goals with differences in judgment about how they can be attained is suggested by Steve Kelman in "The Feud Among the Radicals" in *The End of Ideology Debate*, ed. Chaim I. Waxman (New York: Simon Schuster, 1969), pp. 352-372.

17. Robert C. Tucker, *The Marxian Revolutionary Idea* (New York: W. W. Norton, 1969), p. 182. The second volume of our study is devoted entirely to this subject, the diverse visions of the future to which radicals aspire.

18. Reinhard Bendix, "The Age of Ideology: Persistent and Changing," pp. 295-296. The use of the term "ideology" here does not imply a perfectly integrated, dogmatic world view but rather the interpretation, well argued by Joseph La Palombara, that the term includes symbol systems which vary widely in such properties as dogmatism, probability of realization, rationality, integration, and rhetorical passion. See Joseph La Palombara, "Decline of Ideology: A Dissent and an Interpretation," *The American Political Science Review* LX, no. 1 (1966). And, as William Delaney adds, "ideologies are also more deliberately created by specialized intellectuals than political cultures." See his article, "The Role of Ideology: A Summation," in *End of Ideology Debate*, ed. Waxman, p. 297.

19. Jacques Ellul, *Autopsy of Revolution* (New York: Alfred A. Knopf, 1971), pp. 299-300.

20. This point of view was articulated in the most explicit and far-reaching way by one participant in the workshop as follows:

> I want to address myself to what strikes me as an extraordinary amount of epistemological confusion that has been circulating in this room and which has culminated in a number of points brought up by a number of people, in what to me is the rather remarkable notion that one can infer or determine from the immediate target of a revolt the root causes of that revolt. Some have suggested that because certain kinds of revolts or protests in advanced capitalist societies have not addressed themselves directly to capitalism or to the capitalist mode of production but have addressed themselves to bureaucracy and certain cultural issues, that we can conclude from this that capitalism is not the

root cause of these protests. Some of the others have suggested that because the immediate target of these revolts has been one involving ethnic grievances or racial grievances, we can therefore conclude from this that capitalism is not the root cause of these protests.

Now, it would logically follow that one could conclude that protests against bureaucracy, ethnic and racial deprivation, even science, did not have their roots in capitalism if bureaucracy, ethnicity, racism, and even science in a capitalist society had nothing to do with capitalism and the capitalist mode of production. In order to make somewhat clearer what I am trying to say, I think it helps to draw on Marx's distinction between the concept of a mode of production and the concept of a concrete social formation and in particular the concept of a capitalist mode of production and a capitalist social formation. By the capitalist mode of production Marx means, of course, a mode of production through which surplus value is produced by means of commodity production produced by workers who sell their labor power in return for a wage. Capitalist social formation, however, implies the notion that along with the dominant capitalist mode of production there can coexist other modes of production, including precapitalist modes of production; it also implies the hypothesis that the capitalist mode of production in a capitalist social formation, or, if you will, the commodity form, is determinative in the sense that it is that kind of "ether," in Marx's words, which colors all the rest of the parts of that society and which determines in some fundamental sense all the other parts of that society whether they be the state and its bureaucracy, whether they be ethnicity, whether they be race, whether they be cultural issues. All the parts of that society take on a certain form in relationship to a dominant whole, which is the commodity form.

Or to put it in another way, the state or bureaucracy in a capitalist social formation is a radically different phenomenon from the state and bureaucracy in a noncapitalist social formation. Similarly, ethnicity is a radically different entity in a capitalist social formation than ethnicity in a noncapitalist formation. Similarly, even science, one could argue, is a radically different phenomenon in a capitalist social formation than in a noncapitalist social formation.

Once we realize that the task is to come to understand how the capitalist whole and particularly the commodity form is present within all the various parts of the society, then it becomes rather simplistic to conclude that because a revolt has as its immediate target one particular level or one particular part of that whole, capitalism is not the root cause of that revolt. Rather the task becomes to understand the very complex mediations between the capitalist mode of production, the whole and all the various parts of that society which are colored and in some sense determined by that whole. So to suggest that a revolt in a capitalist society which has as its immediate target the state does not have capitalism as its cause is to propose the ridiculous, to me, argument that the state in a capitalist society is not a capitalist state. Or to propose that a revolt which has as its immediate target science in a capitalist society is not a revolt against capitalism, is to suggest what to me is a ridiculous proposition that the way in which scientific enterprise is conducted in a capitalist society is not in some sense colored in a very important, if not determinative, way by the dominant capitalist mode of production.

So I would suggest that in order to avoid the simplicity of jumping to the conclusion that because the target of a revolt is not explicitly capitalism, therefore capitalism is not the cause, you have to proceed from an epistemology which makes the distinction between the mode of production and the social formation, and to realize that the beginning of social understanding is to grasp the way in which the whole of a particular society is interiorized in each of its parts and begin to establish those mediations.

21. Paul M. Sweezy, Reply to Charles Bettelheim, "On the Transition from Socialism to Capitalism," *Monthly Review* 20, no. 10 (March 1969):15.

22. See Charles Bettelheim, *Les Luttes de Classes en URSS 1917-1923* (Paris: Maspéro/Seuil, 1974).

23. Rossana Rossanda, "Die sozialistischen Länder: Ein Dilemma der westeuropäischen Linken," *Kursbuch* no. 30 (Berlin: Kursbuch Verlag/ Wagenbach, December 1970):30.

24. This position is associated with views which interpret the meaning of ideology in the narrowest possible way as incarnate irrationality and unreason and therefore see radicalism as ideological daydreams at best and nightmares at worst. For an excellent review of the positions concerning the inevitability of inequality, ranging from explicit statement

to circumlocution, see Steven Lukes, "Socialism and Equality," *Dissent* 22, no. 2 (Spring 1975):154-168.

25. J. H. Plumb, *The Death of the Past* (Boston: Houghton Mifflin Co, 1971). He states his thesis as follows:

> The use of the past in this way, that is, the confirmatory annals that justify not only the structure of society but its rulers, may not be dead, but it is mortally sick—at least in the West. There is little sense in any Western nation that their past is impelling them towards a certain future. For them . . . the concept of Manifest Destiny is stricken, a threadbare refuge for politicians, for ageing rulers of society, but from which all strong social emotion is rapidly draining away.

26. Alexis de Tocqueville, *Democracy in America*, vol. 2 (New York: Alfred A. Knopf, 1945), p. 331.

27. One of the most recent and comprehensive attempts to synthesize the elements of this crisis from the political point of view may be found in Michel J. Crozier, Samuel P. Huntington, and Joji Watanuki, *The Crisis of Democracy* (New York: New York University Press, 1975). The most recent and impressive diagnosis from a different vantage point, where the crisis is considered primarily as the disjunction of the social structure, the polity, and the culture, with principal stress on the latter, is found in Daniel Bell's *The Cultural Contradictions of Capitalism* (New York: Basic Books, 1975).

28. Alvin W. Gouldner, *The Dialectic of Ideology and Technology: The Origins, Grammar and Future of Ideology* (New York: The Seabury Press, 1976), p. 250.

29. This failure in the deepest sense, then, is the absence of the key alternatives as they were conceived and understood in the past and which, while of increasingly limited relevance by themselves, did not disappear from intellectual consciousness. Daniel Bell writes:

> It is too easy to say, as many radicals do, that this is all a consequence of *capitalism*. And even more deceptive is the implied answer that there is a normative alternative called *socialism* which is economically viable and philosophically justifiable. All that the radicals have done is to beg the question. Whether socialism is economically viable in an advanced industrial society and a democratic polity that is responsive to the diverse needs and desires of diverse groups, without coercion and the loss of liberty, is quite debatable. And other than the promise of an *abundance* that

would dissolve all social conflicts, we have not had any political or philosophical schema in the name of socialism that justifies the new distributive rules of such a society.

See Bell, *Cultural Contradictions of Capitalism*, p. 249 (emphases in original).

30. The vision of such replacement underlies to a large extent the theses of the new knowledge-dominated society that pervade the futurologist literature. This replacement is presented either as largely accomplished or as the dominant tendency toward which society is moving. See, among others, John K. Galbraith, *Economics and the Public Interest* (Boston: Houghton Mifflin, 1973); Daniel Bell, *The Coming of the Post-Industrial Society* (New York: Basic Books, 1973); Alain Touraine, *The Post-Industrial Society* (New York: Random House, 1971); Zbigniew Brzezinski, *Between Two Ages, America's Role in the Technetronic Era* (New York: Viking Press, 1970); but especially Peter S. Drucker, *The Age of Discontinuity* (New York: Harper Row, 1969), part 4. The most recent criticism of these visions from positions of democratic socialism is provided by Michael Harrington in *The Twilight of Capitalsm* (New York: Simon Schuster, 1976), chapters 9 and 10, especially pp. 220-224.

31. For various interpretations of the French revolt of 1968 see Stanley Hoffman, Jacques Ellul, and Maurice Duverger in *Struggles in the State*, eds. George A. Kelly and Clifford W. Brown, Jr. (New York: John Wiley Sons, 1970), pp. 482-551.

32. Perry Anderson, *Lineages of the Absolutist State* (London: NLB, 1974), p. 359 (emphasis in original).

33. Michael Walzer, "Radical Politics in the Welfare State," *Dissent* 15, no. 1 (January-February 1968):36-37.

34. To a large extent these propositions have their intellectual grounding, if not their contemporary empirical base, in the arguments advanced by Joseph Schumpeter about the inherent tendency of capitalism to bring about its own delegitimization. See Joseph A. Schumpeter, *Capitalism, Socialism and Democracy*, 3rd ed. (New York: Harper Torchbooks, 1950). "Unlike any other type of society," he concludes, "capitalism inevitably and by virtue of the very logic of its civilization creates, educates and subsidizes a vested interest in social unrest" (p. 145).

35. An excellent survey of the question of the Russian intelligentsia may be found in Richard Pipes, *Russia under the Old Regime* (New

York: Charles Scribner's Sons, 1974), part 3. Martin Malia provides the most concise and telling analysis of the Russian experience in his article, "What is the Intelligentsia?" in *The Russian Intelligentsia*, ed. Richard Pipes (New York: Columbia University Press, 1961). A recent interpretative essay on the subject offers some very suggestive reconsiderations of the phenomenon of the Russian intelligentsia and lays particular stress on the chronological limitations of this phenomenon even in the Russian nineteenth century. See Michael Confino, "On Intellectuals and Intellectual Traditions in Eighteenth- and Nineteenth-Century Russia," *Daedalus* 101, no. 2 (Spring 1972).

36. Crane Brinton, *The Anatomy of Revolution* (New York: Vintage Books, 1960), pp. 41-52.

37. It is interesting to note Brinton's remark that "one can make a case for the statement that from about 1900 on there has been desertion of the intellectuals in the United States. Yet the United States does not seem in this century ripe for revolution, does not seem to be a society in marked disequilibrium" (ibid. p. 48).

38. Samuel P. Huntington, "Social and Institutional Dynamics of One-Party Systems," in *Authoritarian Politics in Modern Society*, eds. Samuel P. Huntington and Clement H. Moore (New York: Basic Books, 1970), pp. 36-37.

39. Claus Mueller discusses these themes in *The Politics of Communication, A Study in the Political Sociology of Language, Socialization, and Legitimation* (New York: Oxford University Press, 1975). He concludes: "The socialization strategies, values, and language code of the upper-middle class make it the class least vulnerable to the constraints on communication imposed by the political-economic system. Its communicative patterns permit the articulation of needs and demands that go beyond those sanctioned by dominant interests" (p. 170). In addition to the changing attitudes toward legitimating rationales which underlie the estrangement displayed within this stratum, however, he stresses very strongly another factor—the changing context of professional work which intensifies the erosion of the stratum's support for the system (see pp. 173-177). Of major relevance to our subject is the very systematic and imaginative analysis of the role of communications in the creation of order, disorder, and counterorder by Hugh Dalziel Duncan in *Symbols in Society* (New York: Oxford University Press, 1972).

40. Moore, *Causes of Human Misery*, p. 174.

Notes to Chapter 2

1. Werner Sombart, *Warum gibt es in den Vereinigten Staaten keinen Sozialismus?* (Why is there no socialism in the United States?) (Tubingen: J.O.B. Mohr, 1906). Selections of this work have been translated as "Study of the Historical Development and Evolution of the American Proletariat," *International Socialist Review* 6 (1905-1906):129-136, 293-301, 358-367; and as "American Capitalism's Economic Rewards," in *Failure of a Dream? Essays in the History of American Socialism*, ed. John H. M. Laslett and Seymour M. Lipset (Garden City, New York: Doubleday-Anchor Books, 1974), pp. 593-608. A summary of the book may be found in Jane T. Stoddart, *New Socialism: An Impartial Inquiry* (London: Hodder and Stoughton, 1909), pp. 233-242.

2. Karl Marx, *Capital*, vol. 1 (Moscow: Foreign Languages Publishing House, 1958), pp. 8-9.

3. On Marx's views see Lewis S. Feuer, *Marx and the Intellectuals* (Garden City, New York: Doubleday-Anchor Books, 1969), pp. 198-209. On the Workingmen's parties see Nathan Fine, *Labor and Farmer Parties in the United States, 1828-1928* (New York: Rand School of Social Science, 1928), pp. 13-14; Edward Pessen, *Most Uncommon Jacksonians* (Albany: State University of New York Press, 1967), pp. 183-189; Walter Hugins, *Jacksonian Democracy and the Working Class* (Stanford: Stanford University Press, 1960), pp. 13, 18-20, 132-134.

4. Thomas Hamilton, *Men and Manners in America* (Edinburgh and London: William Blackwood and T. Cadell, 1833). See also Feuer, *Marx and the Intellectuals*, and Maximilien Rubel, "Notes on Marx's Conception of Democracy," *New Politics* 1 (1962):84-85.

5. Feuer, *Marx and the Intellectuals*, p. 206.

6. Rubel, "Notes," pp. 84-85. The selections from Hamilton are from pp. 160-161 and 166 in the English language edition.

7. Karl Marx and Friedrich Engels, *The German Ideology* (New York: International Publishers, 1960), p. 123.

8. Michael Harrington, *Socialism* (New York: Saturday Review Press, 1972), p. 114.

9. Saul K. Padover, ed. and trans., *The Karl Marx Library*, vol. 2, *On America and the Civil War* (New York: McGraw-Hill, 1972), p. 7.

10. Karl Marx and Friedrich Engels, *Selected Works*, vol. 2 (Moscow: Cooperative Publishing Society of Foreign Workers in the U.S.S.R.,

1936), pp. 458-459. This passage appears in Engels's introduction to Marx's essay "The Civil War in France."

11. Friedrich Engels, "The Conditions of the Working Class in England," in *Marx and Engels: Basic Writings on Politics and Philosophy*, ed. Lewis S. Feuer (Garden City, New York: Doubleday-Anchor Books, 1959), p. 491. This passage appeared in the introduction to the 1887 American edition of Engels's "Conditions."

Engels reiterated this formulation in other discussions as well. In a letter to F. A. Sorge, August 8, 1887, Engels noted that America "is a land without tradition (except for the religious), which has begun with the democratic republic." See Engels to Sorge, August 8, 1887, in "Unpublished Letters of Karl Marx and Friedrich Engels to Americans," *Science and Society* 2 (1938):361 (hereafter cited as "Unpublished Letters").

On another occasion Engels noted that America's "purely bourgeois foundation with no prebourgeois swindle back of it, the corresponding colossal energy of development . . . will one day bring about a change that will astound the whole world." See Engels to Schlüter, March 30, 1892 in *Letters to Americans*, Marx and Engels (New York: International Publishers Co., 1953), p. 243.

12. Engels to Sorge, December 7, 1889, *Letters to Americans*, p. 221.

13. Engels to Sorge, February 8, 1890, in *Karl Marx and Frederick Engels: Selected Correspondence, 1846-1895*, trans. Dona Torr (New York: International Publishers, 1942), p. 467 (hereafter cited as *Selected Correspondence*).

14. Engels to Sorge, December 31, 1892, *Selected Correspondence*, p. 501.

15. Engels to Sorge, June 29, 1883, "Unpublished Letters," p. 231.

16. Quoted in Sidney Hook, *Marx and the Marxists* (New York: D. Van Nostrand Co., 1955), p. 64.

17. Engels to Sorge, November 29, 1886, *Selected Correspondence*, pp. 449-450.

18. Engels to Sorge, May 12, 1894, *Letters To Americans*, p. 263.

19. Engels to Sorge, September 16, 1886, "Unpublished Letters," p. 358.

20. Karl Marx, "On the Jewish Question," in *Collected Works*, vol. 3, Marx and Engels (London: Lawrence and Wishart, 1975), p. 151.

21. Ibid., p. 155 (emphases in original).

22. Engels to Sorge, June 29, 1883, "Unpublished Letters," p. 231.

23. Engels to Sorge, March 10, 1887, *Letters to Americans*, p. 177.

24. Engels to Sorge, December 31, 1892, *Selected Correspondence*, p. 502. See also Engels to Sorge, February 8, 1890, *Selected Correspondence*, p. 467.

25. Engels to Sorge, January 6, 1892, "Unpublished Letters," p. 368; and Engels to Sorge, March 18, 1893, "Unpublished Letters," p. 371.

26. Engels to Sorge, November 29, 1886, *Selected Correspondence*, p. 451.

27. Engels to Sorge, April 29, 1886, and Engels to Sorge, September 16, 1886, "Unpublished Letters," pp. 354 and 358.

28. Engels to Sorge, December 31, 1892, "Unpublished Letters," p. 502.

29. Engels to Florence Kelley Wischnewetsky, December 28, 1886, *Selected Correspondence*, pp. 453-454.

30. Engels to Weydemeyer, August 7, 1851, *Letters to Americans*, p. 26.

31. Marx, *Capital*, vol. 1, pp. 769-770.

32. Ibid., p. 777.

33. Harvey Klehr, "Marxist Theory in Search of America," *The Journal of Politics* 35 (1973):319.

34. Engels to Sorge, October 24, 1891, *Letters to Americans*, p. 237.

35. Engels to Sorge, December 2, 1893, "Unpublished Letters," p. 375.

36. Karl Marx, "The Eighteenth Brumaire of Louis Bonaparte," in *Selected Works*, vol. 2 (Moscow: Cooperative Publishing Society of Foreign Workers in the U.S.S.R., 1936), p. 324.

37. Engels to Florence Kelley Wischnewetsky, June 3, 1886, *Selected Correspondence*, p. 449.

38. Engels to Sorge, January 6, 1892, "Unpublished Letters," p. 368.

39. Marx quoted in Harrington, *Socialism*, p. 115. Lenin also emphasized Marx's recognition of this American "petty-bourgeois movement as a peculiar initial form of the proletarian communist movement." See V. I. Lenin, "Marx on the American 'General' Redistribution," in *Collected Works*, vol. 8 (Moscow: Progress Publishers, 1965), p. 328.

40. Saul K. Padover, ed. and trans., *The Karl Marx Library*, vol. 3, *On*

the First International (New York: McGraw-Hill, 1973), pp. 499-500 (emphases in original). Marx expressed these sentiments in a letter to Sigfrid Meyer and August Vogt on April 9, 1870.

41. Engels to Schlüter, March 30, 1892, *Selected Correspondence*, pp. 496-497.

42. Engels to Sorge, December 2, 1893, "Unpublished Letters," p. 375.

43. Engels to Sorge, December 2, 1893, "Unpublished Letters," p. 374 (emphasis in original).

44. Engels to Sorge, January 6, 1892, *Letter to Americans*, p. 239 (emphasis in original).

45. Friedrich Engels, "The Condition of England," in *Collected Works*, vol. 3, p. 446.

46. Engels to Sorge, December 2, 1893, "Unpublished Letters," p. 375.

47. Padover, *On America*, p. 7.

48. Marx to Engels, August 19, 1852, ibid., p. 38.

49. Engels to Florence Kelley Wischnewetsky, February 3, 1886, *Letters to Americans*, pp. 149-150.

50. Engels to Florence Kelley Wischnewetsky, August 13, 1886, *Letters to Americans*, p. 160.

51. Engels to Sorge, December 31, 1892, *Letters to Americans*, p. 244 (emphasis in original.).

52. Sam Dolgoff, ed., *Bakunin on Anarchy* (New York: Alfred A. Knopf, 1972), pp. 110-111.

53. David Hecht, *Russian Radicals Look To America* (Cambridge: Harvard University Press, 1947), pp. 62, 64-65.

54. Dolgoff, *Bakunin on Anarchy*, p. 112.

55. Cited in R. Laurence Moore, *European Socialists and the American Promised Land* (New York: Oxford University Press, 1970), p. 77.

56. Ibid., pp. 58, 102.

57. Ibid., p. 70.

58. Ibid., pp. 78-79.

59. Ibid., p. 91.

60. Max Beer, *Fifty Years of International Socialism* (London: George Allen and Unwin, 1935), pp. 109-110.

61. Ibid., pp. 112-115.

62. Cited in Gerald Friedberg, "Comment," in Laslett and Lipset, *Failure of a Dream?*, p. 351.

63. Morris Hillquit, *History of Socialism in the United States* (New York: Funk and Wagnalls, 1910), p. 361.

64. H. G. Wells, *The Future in America* (New York: Harper and Brothers, 1906), pp. 72-76.

65. Ibid.

66. Max M. Laserson, *The American Impact on Russia 1784-1917* (New York: Collier Books, 1962), pp. 396-397.

67. Sombart, "Economic Rewards," pp. 596, 600, 601, 605, 607.

68. Ibid., p. 602.

69. Sombart cited in Moore, *European Socialists*, p. 114.

70. Sombart, "American Proletariat," p. 135.

71. Editor's note in a review of Sombart's "Why Is There No Socialism in the United States?," *International Socialist Review* 7 (1906-1907):425.

72. Cited in Moore, *European Socialists*, pp. 119-120.

73. Ibid., p. 122.

74. Ibid., pp. 124-125. See also Rosa Luxemburg, *The Accumulation of Capital* (New Haven, Conn.: Yale University Press, 1951), pp. 395-410.

75. Moore, *European Socialists*, p. 126.

76. David Hecht, "Plekhanov and American Socialism," *The Russian Review* 9 (April 1950):114, 118-121.

77. Moore, *European Socialists*, pp. 148-150.

78. Wells, *Future in America*, pp. 105-106.

79. Leon Trotsky, *My Life* (New York: Pathfinder Press, 1970), p. 271.

80. Hillquit, *History of Socialism*, p. 140.

81. Robert W. Smuts, *European Impressions of the American Worker* (New York: King's Crown Press, 1953), pp. 26-27.

82. Cited in Moore, *European Socialists*, p. 110.

83. C. Leiteizen, comp., and T. Dexter, ed. and trans., *V. I. Lenin: On Britain* (Moscow: Foreign Languages Publishing House, n.d.), p. 51. This observation appeared in Lenin's essay "Preface to the Russian Translation of 'Letters by J. Ph. Becker, J. Dietzgen, F. Engels, K. Marx and Others to F. A. Sorge and Others.'"

84. Ibid.

85. Ibid., p. 61.

86. Ibid., p. 51.

87. Hillquit, *History of Socialism*, pp. 358, 139-140.

88. Beer, *Fifty Years*, p. 113.

89. Sombart, "American Proletariat," p. 363.

90. Hillquit, *History of Socialism*, p. 349.

91. Moore, *European Socialists*, p. 129.

92. Yehoshua Arieli, *Individualism and Nationalism in American Ideology* (Cambridge: Harvard University Press, 1964), pp. 238-239.

93. Hillquit, *History of Socialism*, pp. 359-360.

94. Sombart, "American Proletariat," p. 133.

95. Ibid., p. 300.

96. Moore, *European Socialists*, p. 162.

97. C. Leiteizen and T. Dexter, *On Britain*, p. 49.

98. Moore, *European Socialists*, pp. 205-206.

99. H. G. Wells, *Social Forces in England and America* (New York: Harper and Brothers, 1914), pp. 345-346.

100. V. I. Lenin, *Collected Works*, vol. 36 (Moscow: Progress Publishers, 1966), p. 215.

101. Summarized briefly, the Commons-Perlman School identified as the five most important causes for the failure of socialism in America the purely middle-class character of American society; universal manhood suffrage; the presidential system of government; the antistatist nature of the American political tradition; and the unique sociological conditions which made it difficult for workers to view themselves in class-conscious terms. Not unlike Marxist analysts at the turn of the century, the Commons-Perlman School identified the highly individualistic nature of the American worker as a primary cause for the failure of socialism in the United States. As Commons noted in 1926, "the wide expanse of free land," to which the "poor and industrious" could escape—gained only after a political struggle which culminated in the homestead law—gave the American workers' movement not only its first expression of labor consciousness but also a character of "individualism rather than socialism." Universal manhood suffrage, granted

"with scarcely a struggle" to American workers two to three generations earlier than in Europe, "completed the endowment of the mech-
anic and laborer in the North with his equal share in sovereignty," and
eliminated to a large extent the sharp class distinctions which had become increasingly evident to European workers during their bitter
struggles to gain the right to vote. The decentralized nature of the
American system (which served to limit national power and maximize
state and local power, at least in the early years of the American republic) combined with the antistatist ideological tradition to produce a
labor movement which looked to industry rather than government to
enhance the position of the American worker. The special stress on
equal opportunity and equal rights in the Constitution of the United
States also reinforced the highly individualistic nature of the working-
man in America. For an in depth treatment see John R. Commons,
"American Labor History," in *History and Labour in the United States,*
vol. 1., ed. Commons et al. (New York: Macmillan Co., 1926) and Selig
Perlman, *A Theory of the Labor Movement* (New York: Macmillan Co.,
1928). The quotes in the above passage can be found in Commons,
"American Labour History," pp. 4-5.

102. On the Communist Party, see Theodore Draper, *The Roots of
American Communism* (New York: Viking Press, 1957), and *American
Communism and Soviet Russia: The Formative Period* (New York:
Viking Press, 1960); and Irving Howe and Lewis Coser, *The American
Communist Party: A Critical History,* 1919-1957 (Boston: Beacon
Press, 1957.

103. Draper, *Roots,* pp. 247-248. See also Emma Goldman, *Living My
Life,* vol. 2 (New York: Alfred A. Knopf, 1931), pp. 764-765.

104. Draper, *Roots,* p. 256.

105. Ibid., p. 266.

106. Draper, *American Communism and Soviet Russia,* pp. 269-272.

107. Ibid., pp. 277-278. For an elaboration of Lovestone's position, see
Harvey Klehr, "Leninism and Lovestoneism," *Studies in Comparative
Communism* 7 (Spring/Summer 1974): 7-12.

108. Draper, *American Communism and Soviet Russia,* p. 284.

109. Ibid., pp. 409-410.

110. Joseph Stalin, speech to the American Commission of the Communist International, May 6, 1929, in Special Committee on Un-American
Activities, House of Representatives, Seventy-Sixth Congress, *Investi-*

gation of Un-American Propaganda Activities in the United States (Washington, D.C.: United States Government Printing Office, 1940), Appendix—Part 1, pp. 883-884.

111. Ibid, p. 884.

112. See speeches by Stalin, Kuusinen, and Molotov, and "An Address by the Executive Committee of the Communist International to All Members of the Communist Party of the United States," ibid., pp. 876-903.

113. Leon Trotsky, "Extrait d'un Rapport à la Fraction Communiste du 10e Congrès des Soviets," in Trotsky, *Europe et Amérique* (Paris: Librairie de l'Humanité, 1926). pp. 111-112.

114. Ibid., p. 59.

115. Ibid., p. 89.

116. Ibid., pp. 90-91.

117. Ibid., pp. 93-94.

118. Leon Trotsky, *The Living Thoughts of Karl Marx* (New York: Longmans, Green & Co, 1939), pp. 25-26, 35, 40.

119. Ibid., p. 36.

120. Antonio Gramsci, *Selections from the Prison Notebooks* (New York: International Publishers, 1971), pp. 21-22.

121. Ibid., pp. 272 and 318.

122. Ibid., pp. 281, 285, 305.

123. Ibid., pp. 286-287.

124. Trotsky, *Living Thoughts of Karl Marx*, pp. 38-39.

125. Hermann Keyserling, *America Set Free* (New York: Harper and Brothers, 1929), pp. 237-239.

126. Ibid., pp. 239-240.

127. Ibid., pp. 244-252.

128. Leon Samson, *Toward a United Front* (New York: Farrar and Rinehart, 1935), pp. 16-17. For my earlier discussion of Samson, see Seymour M. Lipset, *The First New Nation* (Garden City, New York: Doubleday-Anchor Books, 1967), pp. 393-394, and *Revolution and Counterrevolution* (Garden City, New York: Doubleday-Anchor Books, 1970), pp. 151-152.

129. Samson, *United Front*, pp. 16-21, et seq.

130. Ibid., p. 40.

131. Ibid., p. 41.

132. Ibid., pp. 45, 49.

133. Ibid., pp. 47-48. It is important to note that Warren L. Susman advances a thesis of "surrogate socialism" that stands in contradistinction to Samson's analysis. Even though one may view Americanism as surrogate socialism, suggests Susman, "it is possible to see as well those values and beliefs associated with industrialism easily acceptable in Americanism: a belief in order, rationality and science; a respect for production, efficiency, power, discipline and above all work." Susman, "Comment," in Laslett and Lipset, *Failure of a Dream?*, pp. 450-451.

134. Samson, *Toward a United Front*, pp. 84, 27-28.

135. Harrington, *Socialism*, p. 118.

136. R. L. Bruckberger, *Image of America* (London: Longmans, 1960), pp. 203-207. Historians Allan Nevins and Frank E. Hill point out that Ford could have won the lawsuit or gained a compromise settlement had he emphasized that his policy for lowering prices was a condition for expansion which was for "the ultimate good of the stock holders" and "immensely profitable for the company." Ford, refusing to compromise his position, stressed instead that the new policy "enables a large number of people to buy and enjoy the use of a car" and "gives a large number of men employment at good wages." Stated Ford, "we aim to give employment and send out the car where people can use it . . . and incidentally to make money. . . . If you give all that, the money will fall into your hands; you can't get out of it." Although he lost the legal battle, Ford then bought out the Dodge Brothers' stock for $25,000,000. See Allan Nevins and Frank E. Hill, *Ford, Expansion and Challenge 1915-1933* (New York: Charles Scribner's Sons, 1957), p. 105.

137. Gramsci, *Selections*, p. 302.

138. Louis Hartz, *The Liberal Tradition in America* (New York: Harcourt, Brace and World, 1955), p. 4. See also Louis Hartz, *The Founding of New Societies* (New York: Harcourt, Brace and World, 1964), pp. 69-122.

139. Hartz, *Liberal Tradition*, pp. 6, 234.

140. Ibid., p. 235.

141. Ibid., pp. 252, 291-292.

142. Ibid., p. 10, 264.

143. Hartz, *New Societies*, pp. 111-112.

144. Marc Karson, *American Labor Unions and Politics 1900-1918* (Carbondale, Ill.: Southern Illinois University Press, 1958), pp. 290-292.

145. William M. Dick, *Labor and Socialism in America: The Gompers Era* (Port Washington, New York: Kennikat Press, 1972), pp. 183-184, 116.

146. Norman Ware, *Labor in Modern Industrial Society* (Boston: D. C. Heath & Co., 1935), pp. 49, 496.

147. Melvyn Dubofsky, *We Shall Be All: A History of the Industrial Workers of the World* (Chicago: Quadrangle Books, 1955), pp. 483-484.

148. Robert L. Tyler, "Comment," in Laslett and Lipset, *Failure of a Dream?*, pp. 291-292. See also Robert L. Tyler, *Rebels in the Woods: The IWW in the Pacific Northwest* (Eugene: University of Oregon Press, 1967), especially chapter 1.

149. Gus Tyler, "Comment," in Laslett and Lipset, *Failure of a Dream?*, pp. 574-575.

150. Seymour M. Lipset, *The First New Nation: The United States in Historical and Comparative Perspective* (New York: Basic Books, 1963), p. 341.

151. Ibid., p. 203.

152. Ibid., pp. 341-342.

153. See especially Lipset, *First New Nation*, pp. 318-348 and Lipset, "Equality and Inequality," in *Contemporary Social Problems*, 4th ed., ed. Robert K. Merton and Robert Nisbet (New York: Harcourt Brace Jovanovich, 1976), pp. 308-353. See also Seymour Lipset and Reinhard Bendix, *Social Mobility in Industrial Society* (Berkeley: University of California Press, 1959), pp. 76-113.

154. It is essential to note that Kolko's criticism of "consensual" theorists involves considerably more than a mere refutation of the theory of the classless nature of American society. In his view, not only is American society characterized by a static class structure, in which the interests and values of a ruling class serve as the "functionally dominant" concept, but even American radicals have accepted the mythology. Thus, argues Kolko, the failure of the Socialist Party "reflected the consensual and voluntarily accepted total domination of American

political ideology, an ideology that was conveniently described as class-less." The result, he concludes, is that "American radicals . . . tried to play the game according to rules that were quite irrelevant to social and political reality," and hence the socialist movement in the United States was rendered an unwitting tool of the "constituted order." See Gabriel Kolko, "The Decline of American Radicalism in the Twentieth Century," in *For a New America*, ed. James Weinstein and David W. Eakins (New York: Random House, 1970), pp. 209-210.

155. John H. M. Laslett, *A Short Comparative History of American Socialism* (New York: Harper & Row, forthcoming), chap. 1, pp. 15-16 of manuscript copy. Laslett is quoting Gramsci from his *Prison Notebooks*.

156. Ibid., chapter 1, p. 17.

157. Ibid., chapter 1, p. 20.

158. Ibid., chapter 1, pp. 21-22.

159. Ibid., chapter 1, pp. 23-24 (emphasis in original).

160. Ibid., chapters 2, pp. 2, 11; 3, p. 21; 4, p. 32; 5, p. 11; 6, pp. 21, 40; 7, p. 52.

161. Ibid., chapter 1, pp. 31, 29.

162. William Appleman Williams, *The Great Evasion* (Chicago: Quadrangle Books, 1964), p. 155.

163. Weinstein and Eakins, *For A New America*, p. 162. In his article "The Hoover Myth" in the book, Rothbard himself takes a very different point of view than Williams.

164. This impression of an egalitarian Jacksonian America has been conclusively refuted by a number of detailed quantitative studies. Thus before the American Revolution, the upper 10 percent in Boston and Philadelphia owned over half the property. By 1833, 4 percent owned almost 60 percent in Boston. "In the year of Andrew Jackson's election to the Presidency the wealthiest four percent of the population of New York City . . . owned almost half the wealth. . . . By 1845 the disparities had sharply increased." For a comprehensive survey of the evidence demonstrating the patterns of intense social and economic inequality from before the Revolution to the Civil War, see Edward Pessen, "The Egalitarian Myth and the American Social Reality: Wealth, Mobility and Equality in the 'Era of the Common Man,'" *American Historical Review* 76 (October 1971):989-1034.

165. C. Wright Mills, *White Collar* (New York: Oxford University Press, 1951), p. 10.

166. See "What's This?," *Dissent* 18 (August 1971): 395.

167. David Deitch, "Libertarians Unite in Drive to Reduce Tax Burden," *Boston Globe,* 10 April 1971, p. 7.

168. Clark Kissinger, "Who Supports George and Gene?," *Guardian,* 21 September 1968, p. 7.

169. Charles E. Fager, "Left, Right and Center with Lester Maddox," *Boston After Dark,* 2 March 1971, p. 1.

170. Fine, *Labor and Farmers Parties,* pp. 13-14; Pessen, *Uncommon Jacksonians,* pp. 183-189; and Hugins, *Jacksonian Democracy,* pp. 13, 18-20, 132-134.

171. Pessen, *Uncommon Jacksonians,* p. 185.

172. Hugins, *Jacksonian Democracy,* p. 143.

173. Daniel Bell, "The Background and Development of Marxian Socialism in the United States," in *Socialism and American Life,* vol. 1, ed. Donald D. Egbert and Stow Persons (Princeton: Princeton University Press, 1952), pp. 298-299.

174. Horowitz argues against the Samson/Lipset thesis that the "self-regulatory capacity" and the "omnipotent cooptation features" of the American social system are inherently successful. Dramatic changes in the system since World War I and the fact that blacks and other minorities have been excluded from participation in this system have, suggests Horowitz, considerably diminished the promise of surrogate socialism in America. See Irving L. Horowitz, "Americanism as Substitute Socialism," in Laslett and Lipset, *Failure of a Dream?,* p. 461.

Laslett, on the other hand, criticizes not so much the substance but the form of past analyses. The "broad, value-oriented, absence-of-feudalism type of analysis," suggests Laslett, "involves one in essentially a historical, determinist and oversimplistic kind of history," which ignores the impact of change and the extent to which outcomes might have been different, had socialists or others adopted different tactics at various decisive points in history. In his study of the significant role of socialism in six American unions between 1881 and 1924, Laslett supports this thesis by pointing out that during the period of industrialization, technological developments and economic crises "all helped to create discontents which were manifested, by a minority of workers at least, in demands for revolutionary change. These were no different from the causes which led to the growth of socialism in Europe." Laslett stresses, however, that once the strains of industrialization had eased, American socialists and other radicals, unlike their counterparts in Europe, lost their hold on the unions in which they had played a major role. See John Laslett, "Social Scientists View the Problem," in Laslett and Lipset, *Failure of a Dream?*, p. 69.

175. See Kenneth McNaught, "Comment," in Laslett and Lipset, *Failure of a Dream?*, pp. 405-420.

176. Kenneth McNaught, "American Progressives and the Great Society," *Journal of American History* 53 (December 1966):508, 511-512.

177. Kolko, "Decline," pp. 206-207.

178. Laslett, "Social Scientists View the Problem," in Laslett and Lipset, *Failure of a Dream?*, pp. 48-49, 52-54.

179. A detailed, highly sophisticated methodological critique with references to much of the methodological literature is Karl Ulrich Mayer and Walter Müller, "Progress in Social Mobility Research?," *Quality and Quantity* 5 (June 1971):141-147. For discussions of various methodological and theoretical issues in mobility research see the articles in Neil Smelser and Seymour M. Lipset, eds., *Social Structure and Mobility in Economic Development* (Chicago: Aldine, 1966), especially those by O. D. Duncan, H. L. Wilensky, W. E. Moore, and N. R. Ramsay, as well as the introductory chapter by the editors.

180. P. A. Sorokin, *Social and Cultural Mobility* (New York: The Free Press, 1959). This book was first published in 1927. David V. Glass, ed., *Social Mobility in Britain* (London: Routledge, 1954); Lipset and Bendix, *Social Mobility*; S. M. Miller, "Comparative Social Mobility: A Trend Report and Bibliography," *Current Sociology* 9, no. 1 (1960): 1-89; Thomas G. Fox and S. M. Miller, "Economic, Political and Social Determinants of Mobility," *Acta Sociologica* 9 (1965):76-93; Thomas G. Fox and S. M. Miller, "Intra-Country Variations: Occupational Stratification and Mobility," in *Class, Status, and Power: Social Stratification in Comparative Perspective*, ed. Seymour Lipset and Reinhard Bendix (New York: The Free Press, 1966), pp. 574-81; and Philips Cutright, "Occupational Inheritance: A Cross-National Analysis," *American Journal of Sociology* 73 (1968):400-416.

181. Peter M. Blau and Otis Dudley Duncan, *The American Occupational Structure* (New York: John Wiley, 1967), p. 433.

182. Cutright, "Occupational Inheritance." A similar conclusion was reached by K. Svalastoga, *Social Differentiation* (New York: David McKay, 1965), pp. 123-126. Pointing to the "pervasiveness of mobility," Svalastoga concludes that "even crude measurements produce the

finding that in any industrial society the majority is mobile." Ibid., p. 141.

183. Joseph Schumpeter, "The Problem of Classes," in Bendix and Lipset, *Class, Status, and Power,* p. 45.

184. See Wilbert E. Moore, "Sociological Aspects of American Socialist Theory and Practice," in Egbert and Persons, *Socialism and American Life,* p. 544; Edward A. Shils, "Socialism in America," *University Observer* (Spring-Summer 1947):98-99.

185. Stephan Thernstrom, "Socialism and Social Mobility," in Laslett and Lipset, *Failure of a Dream?,* p. 511.

186. Tom Rishøj, "Metropolitan Social Mobility 1850-1950: The Case of Copenhagen," *Quality and Quantity* 5 (June 1971): 131-140.

187. Bendix and Lipset, *Class, Status, and Power,* pp. 77-79.

188. *The Big Business Executive/1964: A Study of His Social and Educational Background* (a study sponsored by the *Scientific American,* conducted by Market Statistics, Inc., of New York City, in collaboration with Dr. Mabel Newcomer). The study was designed to update Mabel Newcomer, *The Big Business Executive—The Factors that Made Him: 1900-1950* (New York: Columbia University Press, 1950). All comparisons in it are with materials in Dr. Newcomer's published work.

189. Robert M. Hauser et al., "Temporal Change in Occupational Mobility: Evidence for Men in the United States," *American Sociological Review* 40 (June 1975):280. The authors cite a number of studies to this effect.

190. Stephan Thernstrom, *The Other Bostonians: Poverty and Progress in the American Metropolis, 1880-1970* (Cambridge: Harvard University Press, 1973).

191. Blau and Duncan, *American Occupational Structure,* p. 111.

192. Hauser et al., "Temporal Change," p. 280.

193. Christopher Jencks et al., *Inequality* (New York: Basic Books, 1972), pp. 7-8.

194. Ibid., pp. 179, 220.

195. Christopher Jencks, "The Effects of Grandparents on Their Grandchildren" (paper prepared for the Department of Sociology, Harvard University, Cambridge, 1975), pp. 15, 17.

196. E. P. Hutchinson, *Immigrants and Their Children* (New York:

John Wiley, 1965), pp. 114, 138-139, 171.

197. Harrington, *Socialism,* p. 132.

198. Karson, *American Labor Unions,* pp. 212-284.

199. Philip Foner, *The Policies and Practices of the American Federation of Labor, 1900-1909* (New York: International Publishers, 1964).

200. For a summary of the relevant data, see Lipset, "Equality and Inequality."

201. Jencks et al., *Inequality,* p. 220.

202. Paul W. McCracken, "The New Equality," *Michigan Business Review* 26, no. 2 (March 1974):6.

203. Edward Pessen, "Egalitarian Myth," pp. 989-1034, and *Riches, Class and Power before the Civil War* (Lexington, Mass.: Heath & Co., 1973). Pessen cites many relevant recent historical works bearing on the intense forms of inequality in this period.

204. Merle Curti et al., *The Making of an American Community: A Case Study of Democracy in a Frontier County* (Stanford, Calif.: Stanford University Press, 1959).

205. Simon Kuznets, "Income Distribution and Changes in Consumption," in *The Changing American Population,* ed. H. S. Simpson (New York: Institute for Life Insurance, 1962), p. 30. See also Selma F. Goldsmith et al., "Size Distribution of Income Since the Mid-Thirties," *Review of Economics and Statistics* 36 (February 1954):20. For a contradictory interpretation which concludes there has been little change in income distribution since 1910, see Gabriel Kolko, *Wealth and Power in America* (New York: Praeger, 1962), p. 13. Kolko's analysis, however, is based on data prepared by a private research group which has been rejected as too unreliable to be included in the *Historical Statistics of the United States* by a panel of the leading authorities on the subject in economics.

206. OECD Secretariat, "Inequality in the Distribution of Personal Income" (paper prepared for Seminar on Education, Inequality and Life Chances, Paris, January 1975), pp. 18, 20; and Herman P. Miller, *Income Distribution in the United States* (Washington, D.C.: U.S. Department of Commerce, 1966).

207. Kuznets, "Income Distribution," pp. 36-37.

208. Simon Kuznets, "Demographic Aspects of the Distribution of Income among Families: Recent Trends in the United States," in

Essays in Honour of Jan Tinbergen, vol. 3, *Econometrics and Economic Theory,* ed. Willy Selle Kzerts (London: Macmillan, 1974), pp. 223-246.

209. See Morton Paglin, "The Measurement and Trend of Inequality: A Basic Revision," *American Economic Review* 65 (September 1975): 598-609.

210. David Potter, *People of Plenty* (Chicago: University of Chicago Press, 1954), p. 102.

211. "Where the Grass is Greener," *Economist,* 25 December 1971, p. 15.

212. Gideon Sjoberg, "Are Social Classes in America Becoming More Rigid?" *American Sociological Review* 16 (December 1951):775-783.

213. Thernstrom, "Socialism and Social Mobility," pp. 512-517.

214. For a review of some of the literature on the subject see James Alden Barber, Jr., *Social Mobility and Voting Behavior* (Chicago: Rand McNally, 1950), pp. 9-12, 264-266. See also Sombart, "Economic Rewards."

215. Barrington Moore, Jr., *Political Power and Social Theory* (Cambridge: Harvard University Press, 1958), p. 183.

216. Herbert Marcuse, *One Dimensional Man* (Boston: Beacon Press, 1964), pp. xii-xiii.

217. Harrington, *Socialism,* p. 119.

218. Perlman, *Theory of Labor Movement,* p. 131.

219. Dubofsky, *We Shall Be All,* p. 163.

220. Edmund Burke, "Speech on Conciliation with the Colonies," in *Selected Writings of Edmund Burke,* ed. W. J. Bate (New York: The Modern Library, 1960), p. 125.

221. R. L. Bruckberger, "The American Catholic as a Minority," in *Roman Catholicism and the American Way of Life,* ed. Thomas T. McAvoy (Notre Dame, Ind.: University of Notre Dame Press, 1960), pp. 45-47.

222. Lipset, *First New Nation,* pp. 286-287.

223. James MacGregor Burns, *The Deadlock of Democracy* (London: Calder and Boyar, 1965), pp. 40-41.

224. Norman Thomas, *Socialism Re-Examined* (New York: W. W. Norton, 1963), pp. 117-120, and *A Socialist's Faith* (New York: W. W.

Norton, 1951), pp. 90-95.

225. Harrington, *Socialism*, p. 262; Thomas, *Socialism Re-Examined*, pp. 127-128, and *A Socialist's Faith*, pp. 252-255.

226. See Bell, "Development of Marxian Socialism"; Martin Diamond, "The Problems of the Socialist Party: After World War One," in Laslett and Lipset, *Failure of a Dream?*, pp. 362-379; Bernard Johnpoll, *Pacifist's Progress* (Chicago: Quadrangle Books, 1970); R. L. Moore, *European Socialists;* David A. Shannon, *The Socialist Party of America* (Chicago: Quadrangle Books, 1967); Foner, *Policies and Practices;* and Ira Kipnis, *The American Socialist Movement 1897-1912* (New York: Columbia University Press, 1952).

227. Bell, "Development of Marxian Socialism," pp. 221-222.

228. Shannon, *Socialist Party of America*, p. 260.

229. D. H. Leon, "Whatever Happened to the Socialist Party? A Critical Survey of Interpretations," *American Quarterly* 23 (May 1971): 250-251.

230. Henry Pelling, *American Labor* (Chicago: University of Chicago Press, 1960), pp. 88-89; see also Stuart B. Kaufman, *Samuel Gompers and the Origins of the American Federation of Labor 1848-1895* (Westport, Conn.: Greenwood Press, 1973), pp. 190-213.

231. Debs quoted in Karson, *American Labor Unions*, p. 190.

232. See, for example, Kipnis, *American Socialist Movement*, pp. 123-125.

233. Quoted in Shannon, *Socialist Party of America*, p. 248.

234. Will Herberg, "American Marxist Political Theory," in Egbert and Persons, *Socialism and American Life*, p. 504.

235. Earl Browder, "The American Communist Party in the Thirties," in *As We Saw in the Thirties*, ed. Rita James Simon (Urbana, Ill.: University of Illinois Press, 1967), pp. 238, 237.

236. Bell, "Development of Marxian Socialism," p. 292.

237. Shannon, *Socialist Party of America*, pp. 259.

238. Henry Pelling, *America and the British Left* (New York: New York University Press, 1957), p. 90.

239. Ibid., pp. 91-92.

240. R. L. Moore, *European Socialists*, p. 205.

241. James Weinstein, *The Decline of Socialism in America 1912-1925*

(New York: Vintage Books, 1969), p. 21.

242. Bell, "Development of Marxian Socialism," p. 301.

243. Ibid., p. 401; see also Johnpoll, *Pacifist's Progress,* pp. 292-293.

244. Kipnis, *American Socialist Movement,* pp. 403-406.

245. Ibid., p. 417.

246. Ibid., p. 418.

247. R. L. Moore, *European Socialists,* p. 207.

248. Weinstein, *Decline of Socialism,* p. 329.

249. Diamond, "Problems of the Socialist Party," pp. 375-376.

250. Georgy E. Mowry, "Social Democracy, 1900-1918," in *The Comparative Approach to American History,* ed. C. Vann Woodward (New York: Basic Books, 1968), pp. 271-272.

251. Ibid., pp. 278-279.

252. David A. Shannon, "Socialism and Labor," in Woodward, *Comparative Approach,* p. 241.

253. J. David Greenstone, *Labor in American Politics* (New York: Alfred A. Knopf, 1969), p. 7.

254. Harrington, *Socialism,* p. 251.

255. Ibid., p. 255.

256. Richard Hofstadter, *The Age of Reform* (New York: Vintage Books, 1967), p. 308.

257. Harrington, *Socialism,* p. 268.

258. Seymour M. Lipset, "Social Scientists View the Problem," in Laslett and Lipset, *Failure of a Dream?,* p. 40.

259. Ibid.

260. Marcuse, *One Dimensional Man,* pp. xii-xiii.

261. See Seymour M. Lipset, *Revolution and Counterrevolution,* pp. 37-75.

262. Ibid.

Notes to Chapter 3

1. Richard Flacks, "The Liberated Generation: An Exploration of the Roots of Student Unrest," *Journal of Social Issues* 23, no. 3 (July 1967):52-75; Kenneth Keniston, *Young Radicals* (New York: Harcourt Brace Jovanovich, 1968).

2. Paul Starr, "Who Are They Now? Rebels after the Cause: Living with Contradictions," *New York Times Magazine,* 13 October 1974.

3. For example, Keniston, *Young Radicals;* C. Bay, "Political and Apolitical Students: Facts in Search of a Theory," *Journal of Social Issues* 23, no. 3 (July 1967):76-91.

4. Robert Jay Lifton, "Protean Man," *Partisan Review* 35 (Winter 1968):13-27.

5. Keniston, *Young Radicals;* Flacks, "Liberated Generation"; Lillian E. Troll, Bernice L. Neugarten, and Ruth J. Kraines, "Similarities in Values and Other Personality Characteristics in College Students and Their Parents," *Merrill-Palmer Quarterly of Behavior and Development* (Autumn 1969):323-336; Jeanne H. Block, Norma Haan and M. Brewster Smith, "Socialization Correlates of Student Activism," *Journal of Social Issues* 25, no. 4 (Autumn 1969): 143-177.

For summaries see Seymour M. Lipset and Gerald M. Schaflander, *Passion and Politics* (Boston: Little, Brown & Co., 1971); Kenneth Keniston, *Radicals and Militants* (Lexington, Mass.: D. C. Heath & Co., 1973); and Charles Hampden-Turner, *Radical Man* (New York: Anchor Books, 1971).

6. Keniston, *Young Radicals.*

7. Lewis S. Feuer, *The Conflict of Generations* (New York: Basic Books, 1969); Lawrence Kerpelman, *Activists versus Non-Activists: A Psychological Study of American College Students* (New York: Behavioral Publications, 1972); Oscar Glantz, "New Left Radicalism and Punitive Moralism," *Polity* 7 (Spring 1975):281-304; Henry A. Alker, "A Quasi-Paranoid Feature of Students' Extreme Attitudes against Colonialism," *Behavioral Science* 16 (1971):218-227; Lipset and Schaflander, *Passion and Politics.*

8. The Keniston, Flacks, Troll et al., Block et al. view remains the dominant one in the field. See the bibliographies of various studies collected by Kenneth Keniston, *Radicals and Militants;* and Philip G. Altbach and David H. Kelly, *American Students* (Lexington, Mass.: D. C. Heath & Co., 1973).

9. Joseph Adelson, "Inventing the Young," *Commentary* (May 1971): 43-48.

10. Henry C. Finney, "Political Libertarianism at Berkeley: An Application of Perspectives from the New Left," *Journal of Social Issues* 27, no. 1 (1971):35-61.

11. Samuel A. Stouffer, *Communism, Conformity and Civil Liberties* (New York: Doubleday, 1955). See also John P. Robinson, Jerrold G. Rusk, and Kendra B. Head, *Measures of Political Attitudes*, Institute for Social Research (Ann Arbor: University of Michigan Press, 1968), pp. 161-186.

12. Richard Christie and Marie Jahoda, eds., *Studies in the Scope and Method of the Authoritarian Personality* (Glencoe, Ill.: The Free Press, 1954); John P. Kirscht and Ronald C. Dillehay, *Dimensions of Authoritarianism* (Lexington: D. C. Heath & Co.).

13. See for example Ira Rohter et al., "Attitudes About the Vietnam War: A Causal Theory and an Empirical Model" (mimeographed paper presented at the Annual Meeting of the American Political Science Association, Washington, 5 September 1968).

14. Monica D. Bumenthal et al., *Justifying Violence* (Ann Arbor:University of Michigan Press, 1972).

15. Lipset and Schaflander, *Passion and Politics*, p. 110.

16. Arnold Beichman, *Nine Lies about America* (New York: Simon & Schuster, Pocket Books Division, 1972), p. 87.

17. M. Brewster Smith, Norma Haan, and Jeanne Block, "Social Psychological Aspects of Student Activism," *Youth and Society* 1 (March 1970):261-288; Jeanne H. Block, "Generational Continuity and Discontinuity in the Understanding of Societal Rejection," *Journal of Personality and Social Psychology* 22 (June 1972):333-345; Block, Haan, and Smith, "Socialization Correlates"; and Troll, Neugarten, and Kraines, "Similarities in Values."

18. Keniston, *Young Radicals*, pp. 12-22.

19. As revealed by secondary analyses of Richard G. Braungart, "Status Politics and Student Politics," *Youth and Society*, vol. 3, no. 2 (December 1971):195-208; Troll, Neugarten, and Kraines, "Similarities in Values"; Flacks, "The Liberated Generation"; David R. Schweitzer and James M. Elden, "New Left as Right: Convergent Themes of Political Discontent," *Journal of Social Issues* 27, no. 1 (1971); Philip Meyer and Michael Maidenberg, "The Berkeley Rebels Five Years Later: Has Age

Mellowed the Pioneer Radicals?," mimeographed (February 1970); Robert S. Berns, Daphne Bugental, and Geraldine Berns, "Research on Student Activism," *American Journal of Psychiatry* 128 (1972):1499-1504. A fuller discussion is contined in our original paper of which this essay is a summary. The paper is available from the senior author, Smith College, Northampton, Mass., at a cost of $2.50 for printing and mailing.

20. Arthur Liebman, "The Jews and the Left," typewritten, 1974.

21. Alexander W. Astin, "Personal and Environmental Determinants of Student Activism," *Measurement and Evaluation in Guidance* 1 (Fall 1968):149-162 (N = 35,000).

Also, a small pilot study of student activists in 1966, supervised by Professor Joseph Adelson of the Department of Psychology at the University of Michigan, found that most of the SDS members in the sample listed their religion as "none," even though 12 of the respondents had recognizably Jewish names.

22. We have certainly worried about this issue, as have a number of our colleagues, and, indeed, it was raised by the National Science Foundation as a problem when funding for our proposal was being considered.

23. Kirkpatrick Sale, *SDS* (New York: Random House, 1973); Mrs. Erwin Angres, "Values and Socialization Practices of Jewish and Non-Jewish Parents of College Students," typewritten, n.d.

24. Sale, *SDS*.

25. Stanley Rothman and Phillip Isenberg, M.D., "Sigmund Freud and the Politics of Marginality," *Central European History* 7 (March 1974): 58-78; and Rothman and Isenberg, "Freud and Jewish Marginality," *Encounter* (December 1974): 54.

26. Robert Michels, *Political Parties* (New York: Collier Books, 1962), pp. 238-253.

27. Zvi Gitelman, *Jewish Nationality and Soviet Politics* (Princeton: Princeton University Press, 1972).

28. Leonard Shapiro, "The Role of the Jews in the Russian Revolutionary Movement," *The Slavonic and East European Review* (December 1961):148-167; R. V. Burks, *The Dynamics of Communism in Eastern Europe* (Princeton: Princeton University Press, 1961), pp. 150-170; Paul Lendvai, *Anti-Semitism without Jews* (New York: Doubleday, 1971).

29. See for example Francois Fejto, *The French Communist Party and the Crisis of International Communism* (Cambridge: MIT Press,

1967); P. Kruijt, *De Onkerheilkheid in Nederland* (Groningen: P. Noordhoff, 1933), pp. 265-267; Walter B. Simon, "The Political Parties of Austria" (Ph.D. dissertation, Columbia University, 1967), p. 263; Hugh Thomas, *Cuba, the Pursuit of Freedom* (New York: Harper & Row, 1971); Philip Williams, *Crisis and Compromise: Politics in the Fourth Republic* (New York: Doubleday, 1966); Walter Laqueur, "The Tucholsky Complaint," *Encounter* (December 1969):76-80; Martin Jay, "Anti-Semitism and the Weimar Left," *Midstream: A Monthly Jewish Review* (January 1974):42-50; Werner Cohn, "Sources of American Jewish Liberalism—A Study of the Political Alignments of American Jews" (Ph.D. dissertation, New School for Social Research, 1956).

It is extremely difficult to obtain accurate data as to the extent of Jewish participation. Before World War II, fascists stressed the issue and exaggerated the number and power of those of Jewish background involved in radical movements, while those on the left downplayed the issue. Until quite recently most respectable scholars both here and in Europe have chosen to ignore the question.

30. See for example Nathan Glazer, *The Social Basis of American Communism* (New York: Harcourt, Brace, and World, 1961); A. Liebman, "The Jews and the Left"; Lawrence H. Fuchs, *The Political Behavior of American Jews* (Glencoe, Ill.: The Free Press, 1956); Cohn, "Sources"; and Joseph DeMartini, letter to Professor Seymour M. Lipset, 8 February 1971.

31. For France, see Institute of Jewish Affairs, "Arab Propaganda throughout the World: A Survey," *Background Paper*, no. 17 (December 1969).

32. Seymour Martin Lipset and Everett Carl Ladd, Jr., " . . . And What Professors Think about Student Protest and Manners, Morals, Politics, and Chaos on the Campus," *Psychology Today* (November 1970): 49-51, 106; Charles Kadushin, *The American Intellectual Elite* (Boston: Little, Brown & Co., 1974); and A. H. Alsey and Martin A. Trow, *The British Academics* (Cambridge: Harvard University Press, 1971), pp. 413-419.

33. Nathan Glazer, "Revolutionism and the Jews: 3: The Role of the Intellectuals," *Commentary*, vol. 52 (February 1971):55-66; Eric F. Goldman, *The Tragedy of Lyndon Johnson* (New York: Alfred A. Knopf, 1969); Daniel P. Moynihan, *Maximum Feasible Misunderstanding* (New York: The Free Press, 1969); Victor Navasky, "Notes on a Cult, or How to Join the Intellecutal Establishment," *New York Times*

Magazine, 27 March 1966, p. 29; Tom Wolfe, "Radical Chic: That Party at Lenny's," *New York* (8 June 1970):26-54; and Peter Hamill, "Jews and American Politics," *New York Times Book Review,* 10 November 1974.

34. Nathan Glazer and Daniel P. Moynihan, *Beyond the Melting Pot,* 2d ed. (Cambridge: MIT Press, 1970).

35. Isaiah Berlin, "Benjamin Disraeli, Karl Marx and the Search for Identity," *Midstream: A Monthly Jewish Review* (August/September 1970):29-49; Joel Carmichael, "Trotsky's Agony," *Encounter,* vol. 38, no. 5 (May 1972):31-41, and vol. 38, no. 6 (June 1972):28-34; J. P. Nettl, *Rosa Luxemburg* (London: Oxford University Press, 1969); and Martin Jay, *The Dialectical Imagination* (Boston: Little, Brown & Co., 1973).

36. Michaels, *Political Parties;* Fuchs, *Political Behavior.*

37. Jerry Rubin, *We Are Everywhere* (New York: Harper & Row, 1971), p. 74; I. Deutscher, *The Non-Jewish Jew and Other Essays* (New York: Hill & Wang, 1970), pp. 27-39; and Fuchs, *Political Behavior,* p. 175.

38. Charles Liebman, *The Ambivalent American Jew* (Philadelphia: Jewish Publication Society of America, 1972); Charles Liebman, "Toward a Theory of Jewish Liberalism" in *Religious Situation,* ed. Donald R. R. Cuttler (Boston: Beacon Press, 1969), pp. 1034-1062.

39. Liebman, *Ambivalent American Jew.*

40. It must be stressed that even in societies dominated by Christian cultural values many or even a majority of Jews may not feel marginal in any sense. Thus Orthodox Jews might not feel marginal even in a society which defines them as subordinate. In the United States, because it is an immigrant nation, and because Judaism has become one accepted version of the American civil religion, many Jews feel that they can identify with the culture and still remain Jews. (Will Herberg, *Protestant, Catholic, Jew* [New York: Doubleday & Co., 1955], p. 10.) Incidentally, even Jews who feel marginal can accept this fact without desiring to change their situation or the culture of which they are part.

41. Robert Haddad, *Syrian Christians in Muslim Society* (Princeton: Princeton University Press, 1970), pp. 5-6 and passim.

42. Obviously adopting a secularist nationalist stance is not a universalist solution in the same sense that Marxism is. The point is that it

redefines the social universe so as to minimize the differences between the marginal and dominant groups by establishing an indentification which includes both. At the same time it serves to weaken the dominant values of the superordinate group. Islam, for example, is less likely to be as potent a force in a secular national state than in a traditional society.

43. Ulf Himmelstrand, "Tribalism, Nationalism, Rank Equilibrium and Social Structure," *Journal of Peace Research*, no. 2 (1967):81-103.

44. Philip Roth, *Portnoy's Complaint* (New York: Random House, 1969). Indeed some black radicals, most notably Stokely Carmichael and Harold Cruse, have suggested as much with respect to Jews. See Stokely Carmichael, "What We Want," in *Americans from Africa*, ed. Peter Rose (New York: Atherton Press, 1970), pp. 237-249; and Harold Cruse, *The Crisis of the Negro Intellectual* (New York: William Morrow & Co., 1967).

45. Rubin, *We Are Everywhere*, p. 75; Roger Kahn, *The Battle for Morningside Heights* (New York: William Morrow, 1970), p. 46.

46. Stanley Rothman, *European Society and Politics* (Indianapolis: Bobbs-Merrill, 1970).

47. Walter Kaufman, *Nietzche: Philosopher, Psychologist, Anti-Christ* (Princeton: Princeton University Press, 1951), pp. 135-136 and 172-174; Theodor Reik, *Jewish Wit* (New York: Gamut Press, 1962), pp. 226-228.

48. Victor D. Sanua, "Minority Status among Jews and Their Psychological Adjustment," *The Jewish Journal of Sociology* 4 (December 1962):242-253.

49. Mark Zborowski, "Cultural Components in Responses to Pain," in *The Study of Society*, ed. Peter Rose (New York: Random House, 1967), pp. 152-164.

50. Lowenstein, *Christians and Jews*, pp. 135-136, 172-174; Michael Argyle, *Religious Behavior* (London: Routledge and Paul, 1958), pp. 97-99; N. Goldberg, "Jews in the Police Records of Los Angeles, 1933-1947," *Yivo Annual of Jewish Social Science*, vol. 5 (1950): 266-292.

51. James Bieri, Robin Lobeck, and Harold Plotnick, "Psychosocial Factors in Differential Social Mobility," *The Journal of Social Psychology* 58 (October 1962):182-200.

52. Charles R. Snyder, "Culture and Jewish Sobriety: The Ingroup-

Outgroup Factor," in *The Jews,* ed. Marshall Sklare (Glencoe, Ill.: The Free Press, 1958).

53. David McClelland et al., *The Drinking Man* (New York: The Free Press, 1972).

54. Lowenstein, *Christians and Jews.*

55. Grete L. Bibring, "On the 'Passing of the Oedipal Complex' in a Matriarchal Family Setting," in *Drives, Affects, Behavior: Contributions to the Theory and Practice of Psychoanalysis and Its Applications,* ed. Rudolf Lowenstein (New York: International Universities Press, 1960), pp. 278-284; Martha Wolfenstein, "Two Types of Jewish Mothers," in *Childhood in Contemporary Cultures,* ed. Margaret Mead and Martha Wolfenstein (Chicago: University of Chicago Press, 1955), pp. 424-442.

56. Bibring, "Oedipal Complex"; and Wolfenstein, "Two Types."

57. Lionel Ovessy, "Pseudohomosexuality and Homosexuality in Men: Psychodynamics as a Guide to Treatment," in *Sexual Inversion,* ed. Judd Marmor (New York: Basic Books, 1965).

58. Mal Slavin, "The Myth of Feminine Evil: A Psychoanalytic Exploration" (Ph.D. dissertation, Harvard University, 1972).

59. Donald L. Gerard and Joseph Siegal, "The Family Background of Schizophrenia," *Psychoanalytic Quarterly* 24 (1950):47-73; Victor D. Sanua, "The Socio-Cultural Aspects of Schizophrenia: A Comparison of Protestant and Jewish Schizophrenics," *International Journal of Social Psychiatry* 9, no. 1 (1963):27-36.

60. Fred L. Strodtbeck, "Family Interaction, Values and Achievement," in *Talent and Society,* ed. David McClelland (New York: Van Nostrand Reinhold, 1958), pp. 135-191; Joseph Giordano, *Ethnicity and Mental Health: Research and Recommendations* (New York: Institute of Human Relations, 1973).

61. Jules Nydes, "The Paranoid-Masochistic Character," *Psychoanalytic Review* 50 (Summer 1963):215-251.

62. Defensive projection is a process whereby painful impulses or ideas which arise from internal psychic conflicts are attributed to the external world. The wish to injure others thus becomes their wish to injure you. A certain amount of defensive projection (i.e., healthy suspiciousness) can be quite adaptive. However, a high degree of projection, as in paranoia, is pathological. To note that a "paranoid-masochistic" character structure is modal among Jews is *not* to argue that Jews are more

pathological than other groups.

63. Reik, *Jewish Wit;* Lowenstein, *Christians and Jews.*

64. Andrew Greeley, "Political Attitudes among White Ethnics" (mimeographed paper presented at the Meeting of the American Political Science Association, September 1971, table 12); Melvin Kohn, *Class and Conformity* (Homewood, Ill.: Dorsey Press, 1969).

65. John W. M. Whiting and Irvin L. Child, *Child Training and Personality: A Cross-Cultural Study* (New Haven: Yale University Press, 1953).

66. Kenneth Keniston, *The Uncommitted* (New York: Harcourt Brace Jovanovich, 1960).

67. Fred Weinstein and Gerald M. Platt, *The Wish to be Free* (Berkeley: University of California Press, 1969.)

68. Dotson Rader, *Blood Dues* (New York: Knopf, 1973).

69. Tom Wolfe, "Radical Chic."

70. Rothman and Isenberg, "Politics of Marginality," and "Jewish Marginality."

71. Glantz, "New Left Radicalism."

72. T. W. Adorno et al., *The Authoritarian Personality* (New York: American Jewish Committee, 1950).

73. Nydes, "Paranoid-Masochistic Character."

74. Erik H. Erikson, *Childhood and Society* (New York: W. W. Norton and Co., 1963), pp. 326-358.

75. Dotson Rader, *I Ain't Marching Anymore* (New York: David McKay, 1969), p. 6.

76. Sale, *SDS*, p. 204.

77. Ibid., p. 206.

78. Rader, *Blood Dues,* pp. 113-114.

79. Annie Gottlieb, review of *Charlie Simpson's Apocalypse* by Joe Eszterhas, *New York Times Book Review,* 27 January 1974, pp. 4-5.

80. Alice R. Gold, Lucy N. Friedman, and Richard Christie, "The Anatomy of Revolutionists," *The Journal of Applied Social Psychology* 1 (1971):26-43.

81. As noted below, we also made a special attempt to contact additional radical students. Several of the groups we did contact were

recommended to us by academics who had been sympathetic to the student movement and who told us that these young people represented the quintessence of the humane radicalism which had characterized the earlier phase of the student movement.

82. Gold, Friedman, and Christie, "Anatomy." A detailed discussion of our sampling techniques as well as the reliability and validity of our instruments will be found in our original essay.

83. Given the universities from which we drew our sample, it contains relatively few very conservative or right wing respondents.

84. Our sample of radicals include both graduate and undergraduate students and a few who had recently graduated from college (and perhaps done some graduate work) and were at this time active in one radical group or another.

85. For example see Block, Haan, and Smith, "Socialization Correlates"; and Troll, Neugarten, and Kraines, "Similarities in Values."

86. Concerning problems of reliability see A. Anastasi, *Psychological Testing* (New York: Macmillan, 1968); O. K. Buros, ed., *Personality Tests and Reviews* (Highland Park, N.J.: Gryphon Press, 1970), pp. 615-652 and 676-698; W. Henry, "The Thematic Apperception Test," in *The Prediction of Overt Behavior through the Use of Projective Techniques*, ed. Carr et al. (Springfield, Ill.: Thomas, 1960). See also Jean N. Knutson, ed., *Handbook of Political Psychology* (San Francisco: Jossey-Bass, 1973).

87. See McClelland et al., *Drinking Man*.

88. David Rapaport, Merton M. Gill, and Roy Schafer, *Diagnostic Psychological Testing*, rev. ed., ed. Robert R. Holt (New York: International Universities Press, 1968).

89. See John W. Atkinson, ed., *Motives in Fantasy Action and Society* (New York: Van Nostrand, 1958); David C. McClelland, *The Achieving Society* (New York: Van Nostrand, 1961); McClelland et al., *Drinking Man*; and David G. Winter, *The Power Motive* (New York: The Free Press, 1973). Again a full discussion of problems and validity and reliability will be found in our original paper.

90. See David McClelland, *Power: The Inner Experience* (New York: Irvington, 1976); Atkinson, *Motives*; McClelland et al., *Drinking Man*; Winter, *Power Motive*.

91. McClelland et al., *Drinking Man*, pp. 351-356.

92. Rationalization is defined as a defense mechanism in which the individual advances rational explanations of behavior in an attempt to hide from him or herself (as well as others) the actual motives underlying his or her behavior.

93. McClelland et al., *Drinking Man.*

94. Alker, "Quasi-Paranoid Feature"; Ira S. Rohter, "The Righteous Rightists," *Transaction*, vol. 4, no. 6 (May 1967):27-35; and Stephen Joel Cummings, "Development of a New Scale for Paranoia" (Ph.D. dissertation, University of Colorado, 1972).

95. Winter, *Power Motive*, p. 143.

96. Ibid., pp. 147; 154-159.

97. A full discussion will be found in McClelland, *Power: Inner Experience*, pp. 299-303, 351-356, 278-282, 295-299.

98. Unfortunately we have not yet scored for "level of psychosexual development." Further, questions designed to measure castration anxiety were added after the study began, and we could not score as many subjects as for some of the other measures.

99. Charles E. Osgood, George J. Suci, and Percy H. Tannenbaum, *The Measurement of Meaning* (Urbana, Ill.: University of Illinois Press, 1964).

100. Fred N. Kerlinger, *Foundations of Behavioral Research*, 2d ed. (New York: Holt, Rinehart and Winston, 1973).

101. Martin A. Jacobs et al., "Perceptions of Faulty Parent-Child Relationships and Illness Behavior," *Journal of Consulting and Clinical Psychology*, vol. 39, no. 1 (August 1972):49-55.

102. Jacobs, personal communication.

103. For discussion of problems of reliability and construct validity we refer interested readers to our original essay.

104. For this preliminary analysis of our data we used planned orthogonal comparison, Hubert M. Blalock, Jr., *Social Statistics* (New York: McGraw-Hill, 1972), pp. 330-334; William L. Hays, *Statistics for the Social Sciences*, 2d ed. (New York: Holt, Rinehart and Winston, 1973), pp. 581-612. Our reasons for doing so are described in our original essay.

105. Paul Cozby, "Self-Disclosure: A Literature Review," *Psychology Bulletin* 79 (February 1973):73-91.

106. Only those items with a loading of $\geq .4$ on a particular factor were used in computing subscale means.

107. Professor S. Robert Lichter, of the University of North Carolina at Greensboro, conducted a study of German students using the same instruments we used in our investigation.

108. The Rorschach consists of a series of 10 standard cards containing inkblots. Respondents are asked to tell what they see according to certain standard procedures which involve first free association, and then an inquiry by the clinician designed to obtain certain further information. Theoretically, Rorschachs tap deeper levels of personality configurations than do the TATs because they are less structured than pictures. See Rapaport et al., *Diagnostic.*

109. Keniston, *The Uncommitted.*

Notes to Chapter 4

1. See Karl Marx, *The Poverty of Philosophy* (New York: International Publishers, 1963) for his critique of Proudhon.

2. The statement, by Angelo Tasca, is quoted without source in Giuseppe Fiori, *Antonio Gramsci: Life of a Revolutionary* (New York: Dutton, 1971), p. 126.

3. This chapter is based on two of my unpublished papers: "Sources of French Radicalism: Archaic Protest, Antibureaucratic Rebellion and Anticapitalist Revolt" (presented at the Workshop on the Sources of Radicalism and the Revolutionary Process, Columbia University Research Institute on International Change, February 5, 1975) and "Italy: Political Integration in a Fragmented Political System" (presented at the Annual Meeting of the American Political Science Association, San Francisco, California, September 2-5, 1975).

4. Although the two countries have many of the same problems, not since the 1950s, when a series of volumes appeared under Mario Einaudi's direction, have they been systematically compared. See, in particular, Einaudi, Domenach, and Garosci, *Communism in Western Europe* (Ithaca, New York: Cornell University Press, 1953). Two efforts to overcome this long hiatus are found in Donald L. M. Blackmer and Sidney Tarrow, eds., *Communism in Italy and France* (Princeton, N.J.: Princeton University Press, 1975), and Sidney Tarrow, *Between Center and Periphery: Grassroots Politics in Italy and France* (New Haven, Conn.: Yale University Press, 1977).

5. George Lichtheim, *Marxism in Modern France* (New York: Columbia University Press, 1966), p. 53.

6. Robert Wohl, *French Communism in the Making, 1914-1924* (Stanford, Calif.: Stanford University Press, 1966).

7. Gabriel Almond and G. Bingham Powell, *Comparative Politics: A Developmental Approach* (Boston: Little, Brown and Co., 1966), p. 112.

8. Ibid., p. 64.

9. Gabriel Almond, "Comparative Political Systems," *The Journal of Politics* 18 (August 1956): 308-407; reprinted in Roy Macridis and Bernard Brown, eds., *Comparative Politics: Notes and Readings* (Homewood, Ill.: The Dorsey Press, 1967), p. 48.

10. Ibid.

11. Ibid., p. 47.

12. Almond et al., *The Appeals of Communism* (Princeton, N.J.: Princeton University Press, 1954).

13. Ibid., p. 380.

14. For evidence on the relationship between political ideology and political entrepreneurship, see my "Partisanship and Political Exchange in French and Italian Local Politics: A Contribution to the Typology of Party Systems," *Sage Professional Papers in Contemporary Political Sociology* 1, no. 06-044 (1974). For an elaboration, see the evidence on Italian local elites in Tarrow, *Between Center and Periphery*, chapters 5 and 6.

15. Gunther Roth, *The Social Democrats in Imperial Germany* (Totowa, N.J.: The Bedminster Press, 1963). For an attempt to apply part of the Central European model to Italy, see Juan Linz, "La democrazia italiana di fronte al futuro," in *Il caso italiano*, ed. Fabio Luca Cavazza and Stephan Graubard (Milan: Garzanti, 1974) pp. 124-155. For a synthesis of the literature on "class-mass parties," see Sigmund Neumann, *Modern Political Parties* (Chicago: University of Chicago Press, 1956), pp. 395-421.

16. For evidence on the organization, the social heterogeneity, and the membership activism of the Italian parties, see Giacomo Sani, "Le Strutture organizzative del P.C.I. e della D.C.," in *L'organizzazione partitica del P.C.I. e della D.C.*, ed. Instituto di Studi e Ricerche Carlo

Cattaneo (Bologna: Il Mulino, 1968), pp. 23-208. For French party organization very little comparable work has been done, partly because of an absence of available data.

17. For an outline of some of the policy correlates of a "productive coalition," see my "From Center to Periphery: Alternative Models of National-Local Policy Impact and an Application to France and Italy," *Western Societies Occasional Paper No. 4*, Cornell University Center for International Studies, April 1976.

18. For the concept of a "coalition for patronage," and for the accompanying notion of a "coalition for universalism," I am indebted to my colleague Martin Shefter and to his unpublished paper, "Patronage and its Opponents: A Theory and Some European Cases" (presented at the Seminar on State and Capitalism since 1800, Center for European Studies, Harvard University, May 1976.)

19. See my concluding chapter to *Communism in Italy and France*, Blackmer and Tarrow, for an elaboration of these differences.

20. At the risk of oversimplification of what is an extremely rich and varied set of insights, my summary of Hoffmann's model is derived from its original statement in his essay "Protest in Modern France" in *The Revolution in World Politics*, ed. Morton Kaplan (New York and London: John Wiley & Sons, 1962). The essay, with recent revisions, also appears in Stanley Hoffmann, *Decline or Renewal: France Since the 1930s* (New York: Viking, 1974). Citations are from the Kaplan reader, except where revisions have been introduced in the later version. A richer and more elaborate statement can also be found in Hoffmann's "Paradoxes of French Political Community," in *In Search of France*, Stanley Hoffmann et al. (New York: Harper & Row, 1965), chapter 1.

21. Hoffmann, "Protest," pp. 74-75.

22. Ibid., pp. 79-80, and Hoffmann, "Paradoxes," pp. 14-15.

23. Hoffmann, "Protest," pp. 75-77, and "Paradoxes," pp. 13-14.

24. Hoffmann, "Protest," p. 77.

25. On the authoritarianism of the school system, see Jan Boorsch's unforgettable "Primary Education," in "Why Jeannot *can* read," *Yale French Studies* 20 (Winter-Spring 1958-59). The family and the peer group are the object of Jesse Pitts' study "Continuity and Change in Bourgeois France," in *In Search of France*, Hoffmann et al. The family is the special subject of Rhoda Metraux and Margaret Mead, *Themes in French Culture: A Preface to a Study of French Community* (Stanford, Calif.: Stanford University Press, 1954).

26. Hoffmann, "Protest," p. 73.

27. Ibid., pp. 73-74.

28. Hoffmann, "Paradoxes," p. 15.

29. Ibid., p. 18.

30. Hoffmann, "Protest," p. 78.

31. The essays by Christopher, Sawyer and Landes in *Modern France: Problems of the Third and Fourth Republics*, ed. E. M. Earle (Princeton, N.J.: Princeton University Press, 1951) are the standard sources on these problems. For a summary, see Kindleberger, "The Postwar Resurgence of the French Economy," in *In Search of France*, Hoffmann et al., pp. 118-158.

32. On the Third Republic's institutions, see David Thomson's *Democracy in France*, 4th ed. (New York and London: Oxford University Press, 1964), chapter 2. On the Fourth, see Philip Williams, *Crisis and Compromise: Parties and Politics in the Fourth French Republic* (Garden City, New York: Doubleday & Co., 1966).

33. Hoffmann, "Paradoxes," p. 17.

34. For a case study of school authority structures with conclusions along these lines, see William R. Schonfeld, "Youth and Authority in France: A Study of Secondary Schools," *Sage Professional Papers in Comparative Politics* (Beverly Hills: Sage Publications, 1971).

35. This was true of the early recruiting ground of the PCF among workers of government-owned railroads. See Annie Kriegel, *Les communistes français* (Paris: Seuil, 1968), p. 61.

36. As Hoffmann argues in "The Ruled: Protest as a Way of Life," *Decline or Renewal?*, p. 139.

37. Ibid., p. 137.

38. Ibid., p. 138.

39. Ibid., p. 139.

40. The argument is developed in both Crozier, *The Bureaucratic Phenomenon* (Chicago: University of Chicago Press, 1960), and Crozier, *The Stalled Society* (New York: Viking, 1973).

41. Crozier, *Bureaucratic Phenomenon*, chapter 7.

42. Crozier, *Stalled Society*, p. 99.

43. Ibid., p. 34.

44. Ibid., p. 96.

45. Ibid., p. 111.

46. Ibid., p. 78.

47. Ibid., p. 92.

48. Thus also Crozier's enthusiasm for the United States, where he sees the apotheosis of organizational rationality. For a penetrating critique, see Francois Bourricaud, "Michel Crozier et le syndrom de blocage," *Critique* 26 (November 1970):967-969.

49. Crozier, *Stalled Society*, p. 101.

50. Ibid.

51. See Gordon Wright, *Rural Revolution in France* (Stanford, Calif.: Stanford University Press, 1964), chapter 8.

52. Bourricaud, "Michel Crozier," pp. 968-969.

53. Crozier, *Stalled Society*, pp. 96-101.

54. Ibid., pp. 108-123.

55. The best evidence comes from a source that is far from unsympathetic to French capitalism. See John H. McArthur and Bruce R. Scott, *Industrial Planning in France* (Cambridge, Mass.: Harvard University Press, 1969). For a particular case of the merger of public and private power, see Manuel Castells and Francis Godard, *Monopolville: l'entreprise, l'état, l'urbain* (Paris: Mouton, 1974).

56. Anthony Downs, *An Economic Theory of Democracy* (New York: Harper & Row, 1957). The key assumption is that "parties will formulate policies in order to win elections, rather than win elections in order to formulate policies," p. 28.

57. Otto Kirchheimer, "The Transformation of the European Party Systems," in *Political Parties and Political Development*, ed. Joseph LaPalombara and Myron Weiner (Princeton, N.J.: Princeton University Press, 1965), chapter 6.

58. Samuel Barnes, "Left, Right and the Italian Voter," *Comparative Political Studies* 4 (July 1971):157-176.

59. Giovanni Sartori, "European Political Parties: The Case of Polarized Pluralism," in *Political Parties and Political Development*, ed. LaPalombara and Weiner.

60. Sartori, "Opposition and Control: Problems and Prospects," in *Studies in Opposition*, ed. Rodney Barker (London: Macmillan, 1971) p. 34.

61. Sartori, "Modelli spaziali di competizione tra partiti," *Rassegna Italiana di Sociologia* 6 (January-March 1965):27.

62. In LaPalombara and Weiner, *Political Parties*, p. 139.

63. Ibid., pp. 138-139.

64. For an empirical test at the local level in Italy and France, see William Ascher and Sidney Tarrow, "The Stability of Communist Electorates: Evidence from a Longitudinal Analysis of French and Italian Aggregate Data," *American Journal of Political Science* 19 (August 1975):475-499.

65. Alberto Spreafico, in "Risultati elettorali ed evoluzione del sistema partitico," in *Un sistema politico alla prova*, ed. Mario Caciagli and Alberto Spreafico (Bologna: Mulino, 1975) points out that 60 percent of the neofascist vote in 1972 came from five regions, four of them in the south, pp. 49-60.

66. From a graphic presented by Sani on the self-definition of noncommunist voters, it appears that half of them score between 50 and 60 on a 100 point scale of left-right ideological self-definition, with an additional 20 percent in the two deciles on either side: scarcely a situation in which maximizing campaign managers would choose to make an extremist appeal. See Sani's "La strategia del PCI e l'elettorato italiano," *Rivista Italiana di Scienza Politica* 3 (December 1973):568. Revised version in *Communism in Italy and France*, Blackmer and Tarrow.

67. Suzanne Berger, "Uso politico e sopravivanza dei ceti in declino," in *Il caso italiano*, Cavazza and Graubard, p. 307. Also see the chapters by Stephen Hellman on the PCI's strategy toward the middle class, and by Sidney Tarrow on PCI activists in local goverment, in *Communism in Italy and France*, Blackmer and Tarrow.

68. Sani, "La strategia del PCI," p. 558.

69. See the chapters by Donald Blackmer, Peter Lange and Peter Weitz in *Communism in Italy and France*, Blackmer and Tarrow, for supporting evidence. Also see Franco Cazzola, "Consenso e opposizione nel Parlamento italiano: il ruolo del PCI," *Rivista Italiana di Scienza Politica* 1 (April 1972):71-96, on the PCI in Parliament.

70. "Le Parti communiste italien dans le système politique italien," mimeographed (paper presented at the Colloque sur le Communisme en France et en Italie, Fondation Nationale des Sciences Politiques, Paris, 1968). A similar argument is made in my conclusion to *Communism in Italy and France*, Blackmer and Tarrow.

71. See my *Peasant Communism in Southern Italy* (New Haven: Yale University Press, 1967) for evidence of this effect.

72. See Alessandro Pizzorno's "I ceti medi nei meccanismi del consenso," in *Il caso italiano*, Cavazza and Graubard, pp. 314-337, for evidence.

73. See MacArthur and Scott, *Industrial Planning in France.*

74. See Gianfranco Pasquino, "Il sistema politico italiano tra neotrasformismo e democrazia consociativa," *Il Mulino* 12 (1973):549-566; and F. Bourricaud, "Partitocrazia: consolidamento o rottura?" in *Il caso italiano*, Cavazza and Graubard, p. 121.

75. Arend Lijphart, "Typologies of Democratic Systems," *Comparative Political Studies* 1 (April 1968):20.

Notes to Chapter 5

1. The original draft of this paper was prepared for the Workshop on Radicalism, Research Institute on International Change, Columbia University, 5 February 1975. This revised version benefited greatly from the discussion at the workshop. Professor Donald Zagoria, the principal commentator on the paper, deserves special thanks.

2. George D. Jackson, Jr., *Comintern and Peasant in East Europe, 1919-1930* (New York: Columbia University Press, 1966).

3. For a brief summary, see Fred A. Shannon, *American Farmers' Movements* (New York: Van Nostrand Reinhold, 1957).

4. Seymour Martin Lipset, *Agrarian Socialism*, rev. ed. (Berkeley: University of California, 1971). The first chapter of this famous study summarizes the U.S. experience; the remainder of the book analyzes rural "radicalism."

5. A broad definition of the term "peasant" is used in this essay, and refers to all low status rural cultivators. Included in this category are landless laborers, tenants, sharecroppers, and small landholders. Two important considerations necessitate adopting such a broad definition: (1) peasants may occupy (simultaneously or intermittently) more than one status mentioned above; and (2) only when the analyst considers the extremely complex relations between these groups can certain essential aspects of rural protest be understood. For a more detailed

definition, see Henry A. Landsberger, ed., *Latin American Peasant Movements* (Ithaca, New York: Cornell University Press, 1969) pp. 1-61.

6. Anibal O. Quijano, "Contemporary Peasant Movements," in *Elites in Latin America*, ed. Seymour Martin Lipset and Aldo Solari (New York: Oxford University Press, 1966), pp. 301-340.

7. Eric J. Hobsbawm, *Bandits* (London: Delacorte Press, 1969), p. 23.

8. Henry Ehrmann, "The French Peasant and Communism," *American Political Science Review* 46, no. 1 (March 1952):19-43.

9. Donald Zagoria, "Tenancy Systems and Peasant Communism in Asia," in *Peasant Rebellion and Communist Revolution in Asia*, ed. John Lewis (Stanford, Calif.: Stanford University Press, 1974).

10. James Petras and Maurice Zeitlin, "Agrarian Radicalism in Chile," *British Journal of Sociology* 19, no. 3 (September 1968). See also the Petras and Zeitlin essay in *Agrarian Problems and Peasant Movements in Latin America*, ed. Rodolfo Stavenhagen (Garden City, New York: Doubleday Anchor, 1970), pp. 503-531.

11. Roy Hofheinz, "The Ecology of Chinese Communist Success: Rural Influence Patterns, 1923-1945," in *Chinese Communist Politics in Action*, ed. A. Doak Barnett (Seattle: University of Washington Press, 1969), pp. 34-52.

12. George M. Foster, "Peasant Society and the Image of the Limited Good," *American Anthropologist* 67, no. 2 (April 1965): 296-303.

13. Edward C. Banfield, *The Moral Basis of a Backward Society* (Glencoe, Ill.: The Free Press, 1958).

14. Oscar Lewis, *La Vida: A Puerto Rican Family in the Culture of Poverty* (New York: Random House, 1966), pp. xliii-xlviii.

15. Gerrit Huizer, *The Revolutionary Potential of Peasants in Latin America* (Lexington, Mass.: D. C. Heath and Co., Lexington Books, 1972), pp. 21-70; and James Petras and Hugo M. Zemelman, *Peasants in Revolt: A Chilean Case Study, 1965-1971* (Austin: University of Texas Press, 1972).

16. Karl Marx, "The Eighteenth Brumaire of Louis Bonaparte," in *The Marx-Engels Reader*, ed. Robert C. Tucker (New York: W. W. Norton, 1972), pp. 517-518.

17. James C. Scott, "The Political Economy of the Peasant Subsistence Ethic in South East Asia" (manuscript prepared for the South East Asia Development Advisory Group, Asia Society, New York, 1974), p. 306.

Society, New York, 1974), p. 306.

18. Euclides da Cunha, *Rebellion in the Backlands* (Chicago: University of Chicago Press, 1944).

19. Edward Malefakis, "Peasants, Politics and Civil War in Spain, 1931-39," in *Modern European Social History*, ed. Robert J. Bezucha Lexington, Mass.: D. C. Heath, 1972), pp. 192-227.

20. For a summary of the work of Doughty, Holmberg, and Quijano on this point, see Huizer, *Revolutionary Potential.*

21. See Joel S. Migdal, *Peasants, Politics and Revolution: Pressures Toward Political and Social Change in the Third World* (Princeton: Princeton University Press, 1975), pp. 304 et seq.; and Petras and Zemelman, *Peasants in Revolt.*

22. Howard Wolpe, "Some Problems Concerning Revolutionary Consciousness," *The Socialist Register: 1970* (London: Merlin Press, 1970).

23. For example, Zagoria, "Tenancy Systems," p. 41.

24. Migdal, *Peasants, Politics, and Revolution*, p. 220.

25. Petras and Zemelman, *Peasants in Revolt*, p. 102.

26. Ibid., pp. 66-78, exp. p. 77.

27. Ibid., p. 97.

28. Robert Redfield, *Peasant Society and Culture* (Chicago: University of Chicago Press, 1956).

29. Four studies in particular reveal the inadequacy of Redfield's "integrated folk society" thesis: Barrington Moore, *Social Origins of Dictatorship and Democracy* (Boston: Beacon Press, 1966), pp. 215 and 317; Hugh Borton, *Peasant Uprisings in Japan of the Tokugawa Period* (New York: Paragon Books Reprint Corp., 1968); Samuel L. Popkin, "Corporatism and Colonialism: The Political Economy of Rural Change in Vietnam," *Comparative Politics* 8, no. 3 (1976):431-464; and Rodney H. Hilton, "Peasant Society, Peasant Movements and Feudalism in Medieval Europe," in *Rural Protest: Peasant Movements and Social Change*, ed. Henry A. Landsberger (London: Macmillan, 1974), pp. 67-94.

30. Arthur L. Stinchcombe, "Agricultural Enterprise and Rural Class Relations," *American Journal of Sociology* 67, no. 2 (1961): 165-176.

31. Julio Cotler, "The Mechanics of Internal Domination and Social Change in Peru," *Studies in Comparative International Development* 3,

no. 12 (1967-1968).

32. Eric R. Wolf, *Peasants* (Englewood Cliffs, N. J.: Prentice-Hall, 1966), pp. 3-4.

33. Moore, *Social Origins,* pp. 470-473.

34. John S. Gitlitz, "Hacienda, Communidad and Peasant Protest in Northern Peru" (Ph.D. dissertation, University of North Carolina, 1975).

35. Ernest Feder, *The Rape of the Peasantry: Latin America's Landholding System* (Garden City, N. Y.: Doubleday, 1971).

36. James C. Scott, "Patron-client Politics and Political Exchange in Southeast Asia," *American Political Science Review* 66, no. 1 (March 1972):91-113.

37. Migdal, *Peasants, Politics, and Revolution,* chapter 2.

38. Eric R. Wolf, "Types of Latin American Peasantry: A Preliminary Discussion," *American Anthropologist* 57 (June 1955):452-471; and Eric R. Wolf, "Closed Corporate Communities in Mesoamerica and Central Java," *Southwestern Journal of Anthropology* 13 (Spring 1957):1-18.

39. In Germany, for example, the entire latter half of the fifteenth century was marked by peasant unrest; the *Bundschuh* revolts, clearly the best known, are only the most notable examples and not the total picture, of this period. For detailed descriptions of peasant unrest in Europe, see Roland Mousnier, *Peasant Uprisings in Seventeenth Century France, Russia and China* (London: George Allen and Unwin, 1971); B. H. Slicher van Bath, *The Agrarian History of Europe, A.D. 500-1850* (London: Edward Arnold, 1963); and Hilton, "Peasant Society in Medieval Europe."

A study of the highlands of Peru not only touches upon the various Inca uprisings up to the Tupac Amaru Rebellion of 1780, but also cites numerous works which show that the unrest in the 1960s did not represent a sudden awakening; i.e., peasant unrest was frequent in the 1870s, episodic in the entire period 1903-1928, recurrent in 1945, and chronic from 1958 onward. See Edward Dew, *Politics in the Altiplano* (Austin: University of Texas Press, 1969).

40. Charles Tilly, Louise Tilly, and Richard Tilly, *The Rebellious Century, 1830-1930* (Cambridge: Harvard University Press, 1975).

41. Moore, *Social Origins,* p. 171; Scott, "Patron-client Politics," pp. 91-113; and Peter Lupsha, "Explanation of Political Violence: Some

Psychological Theories Versus Indignation," *Politics and Society* (Fall 1971):89-104. Lupsha stresses painstakingly that moral outrage and indignation, not merely deprivation, are important influences in the peasant's reaction. Scott suggests that the collapse of vertical ties of "loyalty"—a collapse which was precipitated by the efforts of large landlords and better-off peasants to shut out the poorer peasants from access to common land, forests, or other privileges—caused resentment among peasants not only because it deprived the poorer peasants of their livelihood, but also because it constituted offenses against ancient rights. Scott notes that this is true for peasant societies of Latin America as well as Southeast Asia.

42. The interest in the relationship between rural inequality and unrest entered the modern literature through Russett's cross-national indicator study. It had its share of logical weakness, as all pathbreaking studies are likely to have. The measured inequality was rural, but the instability was national, not rural, so that all kinds of ecological fallacies could have occurred. It should also be noted that Russett focused on "inequality" as a static concept rather than as a dynamic condition. Thus, Russett's study does not consider the effects of "increasing inequality" on "growing" peasant discontent—a primary interest of most scholars in the field. Cf. Bruce Russett, "Inequality and Instability: The Relation of Land Tenure to Politics," *World Politics* 16, no. 3 (April 1964):442-454.

43. Migdal, *Peasants, Politics, and Revolution.* See also Migdal, "Why Change? Towards a Theory of Change among Individuals in the Process of Modernization," *World Politics* 26, no. 2 (January 1974):189-206.

44. Eric R. Wolf, *Peasant Wars of the Twentieth Century* (New York: Harper & Row, 1969).

45. Zagoria, "Tenancy Systems." Zagoria places heavy emphasis on "land hunger": too many peasants faced with too little land. Zagoria is concerned to emphasize that demographic pressure is by itself insufficient to cause "land hunger." To become the source of unrest, it requires, in addition, low per capita output as well as inequitable distribution of land.

On the role of demographic pressures in peasant unrest, see also Moore, *Social Origins*, p. 367; Migdal, *Peasants, Politics, and Revolution*, chapter 6; Wolf, *Peasant Wars*, p. 281; and Eric R. Wolf, "Peasant Rebellion and Revolution," in *National Liberation: Revolution in the Third World*, ed. Norman Miller and Roderick Aya (New York: The Free Press, 1971), p. 50. Moore refers to demographic pressure in connection with India, even though it did not lead to an outbreak of peasant revolts there. Wolf makes "rapid acceleration of population growth" one of the three "major crises" which have caused peasant revolutions in the twentieth century. Migdal, in his sophisticated attempt to integrate research findings from all geographic areas in which "peasant revolutions" have occurred, likewise mentions population growth as one of four major factors which place the village under such stress that customary mechanisms for containing tension and preserving isolation from a destabilizing larger environment break down.

46. Clifford Geertz, *Agricultural Involution* (Berkeley: University of California Press, 1971).

47. Wilbert Moore, *Economic Demography of Eastern and Southern Europe* (Geneva: League of Nations, 1945).

48. Thus, the better educated peasant is often the same peasant who utilizes mass media, and who comes from a somewhat better-off family in which the father was himself perhaps quite militant. This makes extremely difficult the task of isolating which of these factors contributed most to the heightened militancy of a particular peasant society. Notable examples of leaders of peasant uprisings whose backgrounds suggest a combination of "radicalizing factors" are Mexico's Emiliano Zapata and Bolivia's Juan Rojas.

49. Strangely enough, only Marx's famous comment about the conservatism of small, property-owning French peasants is widely known. For various reasons—such as geographic dispersal and the absence of a division of labor—Marx thought them "incapable of enforcing their class interest." What is rarely cited is that some two years earlier, in their "Address of the Central Committee to the Communist League," Marx and Engels had indicated that the rural proletariat (i.e., landless laborers) could be the allies of workers: "Just as the democrats combine with the peasants so must the workers combine with the rural proletariat." Engels, in "The Tactics of Social Democracy," written in the last year of his life, emphasized both the need for and the possibility of "conquering" (in this context: convincing) the "small peasant." And some paragraphs earlier, he had not even used the qualifier "small." In these two brief but to him apparently important references, Engels seems to have reached the now classical position of Lenin and Mao, and thereby reversed Marx's earlier position. In the context in which Engels wrote, he was referring specifically to voting for the German Socialist Party. Lenin and Mao referred, of course, to more direct revolutionary action. Cf. Karl Marx and Friedrich Engels, "Address

of the Central Committee to the Communist League," in Tucker, *Marx-Engels Reader*, p. 371; and Friedrich Engels, "The Tactics of Social Democracy," ibid., pp. 420-421.

50. Wolf, *Peasant Wars*, pp. 291-293. See also Landsberger, *Latin American Peasant Movements*, pp. 1-61, esp. p. 39.

51. Malefakis, "Civil War in Spain"; for a more detailed account see Edward Malefakis, *Agrarian Reform and Peasant Revolution in Spain* (New Haven: Yale University Press, 1970).

52. Zagoria, "Tenancy Systems."

53. Hofheinz, "Ecology," p. 77.

54. Wolf, *Peasant Wars*, pp. 291 and 293; and Wolf, "Peasant Rebellion," pp. 57-58.

55. Malefakis, "Civil War in Spain," p. 220.

56. Eric J. Hobsbawm and George Rude, *Captain Swing* (London: Lawrence and Wishart, 1969).

57. After initial mistakes in both China and Vietnam, the communist parties in both countries (and Lenin's in Russia, for that matter) realized that reliance on the revolutionary potential of the poor peasantry would be counterproductive in the early stages of the revolution if *sustained* action was needed.

58. Jeffrey M. Paige, *Agrarian Revolution: Social Movements and Export Agriculture in the Underdeveloped World* (New York: The Free Press, 1975).

59. Stinchcombe, "Agricultural Enterprise"; Julian Steward et al., *The People of Puerto Rico: A Study in Social Anthropology* (Urbana, Ill.: University of Illinois Press, 1956); and Wolf, *Peasant Wars*.

60. Paige, *Agrarian Revolution*, p. 208.

61. La Mond F. Tullis, *Lord and Peasant in Peru: A Paradigm of Political and Social Change* (Cambridge: Harvard University Press, 1970), p. 142; Howard Handleman, *Struggle in the Andes* (Austin, Texas: University of Texas Press, 1974), pp. 97-98; and Gitlitz, "Hacienda."

62. Hamza Alavi, "Peasants and Revolution," in *Socialist Register: 1965*, eds. Ralph Miliband and John Saville (London: Merlin Press, 1965), pp. 244-277.

63. Juan J. Linz, "Patterns of Land Tenure, Division of Labor, and Voting Behavior in Europe," *Comparative Politics*, Special Issue on

"Peasants and Revolution," vol. 8, no. 3 (April 1976):365-430. See also Malefakis, "Civil War in Spain."

64. Jackson, *Comintern and Peasant*, p. 40.

65. See, for example, the studies of Lipset and Linz on Canada and France, respectively, which clearly allow for historical particulars: Lipset, *Agrarian Socialism;* and Linz, "Patterns of Land Tenure."

66. Clark Kerr et al., *Industrialism and Industrial Man* (Cambridge: Harvard University Press, 1960).

67. For a summary see Huizer, *Revolutionary Potential.* See also Jerome Blum, *Lord and Peasant in Russia from the Ninth to the Nineteenth Century* (New York: Atheneum, 1968). For the U.S. South, a poignant picture was recently drawn by Theodore Rosengarten, *All God's Dangers: The Life of Nate Shaw* (New York: Alfred A. Knopf, 1975).

68. Eric J. Hobsbawm, *Primitive Rebels* (New York: W. W. Norton, 1959); and Hobsbawm, *Bandits.*

69. Scott, "Political Economy."

70. See, for example, Philip Longworth, "The Pugachev Revolt," in Landsberger, *Rural Protest,* pp. 194-256.

71. Quijano, "Contemporary Peasant Movements."

72. Gil Carl AlRoy, "The Peasantry in the Cuban Revolution," *The Review of Politics* 29, no. 1 (January 1967):87-99.

73. See, for example, Antonio Gramsci, *The Modern Prince and Other Writings* (New York: International Publishers, 1972).

74. Teodor Shanin, "Peasantry as a Political Factor," in *Peasants and Peasant Societies,* ed. Teodor Shanin (Baltimore: Penguin Books, 1971), p. 256.

75. Peter P. Lord, "The Peasantry as an Emerging Political Factor in Mexico, Bolivia and Venezuela" (paper prepared for the Land Tenure Center, University of Wisconsin, LTC no. 35, Madison, Wisconsin, May 1965), p. 94.

76. V. G. Kiernan, "The Peasant Revolution: Some Questions," *Socialist Register: 1970* (London: Merlin Press, 1970), pp. 9-35.

77. Alavi, "Peasants and Revolution."

78. For an obviously poor fusion between urban radicals and peasants, see John Badgley, "Burmese Communist Schisms," in Lewis, *Peasant*

Rebellion, pp. 151-168.

79. Chalmers A. Johnson, *Peasant Nationalism and Communist Power* (Stanford: Stanford University Press, 1962).

80. Christine Pelzer White, "The Vietnamese Revolutionary Alliance: Intellectuals, Workers, Peasants," in Lewis, *Peasant Rebellion,* p. 95.

81. Chinese communist tactics have been well described and analyzed. Three fine examples are Mark Seldon, "The Yenan Legacy: The Mass Line," in Barnett, *Chinese Communist Politics in Action,* pp. 99-151; Seldon, "Revolution and Third World Development: People's War and the Transformation of Peasant Society," in Miller and Aya, *National Liberation,* pp. 214-248; and Ilpyong J. Kim, "Mass Mobilization Policies and Techniques Developed in the Period of the Chinese Soviet Republic," in Barnett, *Chinese Communist Politics in Action,* pp. 78-98.

82. White, "Vietnamese Revolutionary Alliance," p. 95.

83. Kim, "Mass Mobilization."

84. Seldon, "Yenan Legacy," pp. 121-126.

85. Seldon, "Revolution and Third World," p. 226.

86. White, "Vietnamese Revolutionary Alliance," p. 93.

87. AlRoy, "Peasantry in Cuban Revolution."

88. Ibid., pp. 98-99.

89. Similar to Hobsbawm's and Rude's general treatment in *Captain Swing,* although there is no special reference to Cuba.

90. William Overholt, "Martial Law, Revolution and Democracy in the Philippines," *Southeast Asia* 2, no. 2 (Spring 1973); and William J. Pomeroy, "Participation by the Philippine Peasantry in Revolutionary Struggles," mimeographed (paper presented at the Seminar on Peasants, University of London, 1972-73).

91. Scott, "Political Economy," p. 349.

92. Ibid., p. 347.

93. Friedrich Engels, "The Tactics of Social Democracy" (1895), in Tucker, *Marx-Engels Reader,* pp. 406-423.

94. Richard Gott, *Guerrilla Movements in Latin America* (London: Nelson, 1970).

Notes to Chapter 6

1. For a comprehensive synthesis of the literature on revolution, see William H. Overholt, *Political Revolution* (Boulder, Colo.: Westview Press, forthcoming). For the ways in which theories of revolution are embedded in the larger literature of political sociology, see my "Organization, Revolution and Democracy: Toward a Sociology of Politics" (Ph.D. dissertation, Yale University, 1972).

2. Daniel Bell, ed., *The Radical Right* (Garden City, N.Y.: Doubleday-Anchor Books, 1963).

3. David M. Gordon, *Theories of Poverty and Unemployment* (Lexington, Mass.: Lexington Books, 1972).

4. Egon Bittner, "Radicalism and the Organization of Radical Movements," *American Sociological Review* 27 (December 1963):928-940; Max Weber, "Politics as a Vocation," in *From Max Weber,* ed. Hans H. Gerth and C. Wright Mills (New York: Oxford University Press, 1946); and Egon Bittner, "Radicalism," *International Encyclopedia of the Social Sciences* (New York: Macmillan and The Free Press, 1968).

5. I am indebted to Herman Kahn for remarks on this point.

6. Samuel P. Huntington, *Political Order in Changing Societies* (New Haven: Yale University Press, 1968), p. 264.

7. Wilbert E. Moore, "Predicting Discontinuities in Social Change," *American Sociological Review* 29, no. 3 (June 1964):337, defines revolution as "fundamental change in the normative order, notably the forms of legality and, crucially, the basis of legitimacy for the state itself." Rex D. Hopper, "The Revolutionary Process," *Social Forces* 28, no. 3 (March 1950):271, defines it as "social change which occurs when the basic institutional (i.e., legally enforced) values of a social order are rejected and new values are accepted."

8. Crane Brinton, *The Anatomy of Revolution* (New York: Random House, 1965), identifies "skullduggery" as an essential element of revolution.

9. Anthony F. C. Wallace, "Revitalization Movements," in *Studies in Social Movements,* ed. Barry McLaughlin (New York: The Free Press, 1969), pp. 30-52.

10. On this extended revolution, see Edwin O. Reischauer and John K. Fairbank, *East Asia: The Great Tradition* (Boston: Houghton Mifflin,

1960), pp. 123-170. Franz Schurmann, *Ideology and Organization in Communist China* (Berkeley: University of California Press, 1966), p. xl, calls attention to the Ch'in social revolution in the third century B.C. Since the Ch'in dynasty first unified the Chinese state, their coming to power does not constitute a revolution in our terms. But that event involved destruction of an aristocracy, creation of powerful new central institutions, a new ideology called legalism, and a sweeping land reform. This should give pause to those who believe revolutions are modern phenomena and yet employ fairly inclusive definitions of revolution.

11. Marion J. Levy, *Modernization and the Structure of Societies* (Princeton: Princeton University Press, 1969), pp. 479-487, defines revolution as any form of general change, including nineteenth century British political changes and the leisure revolution.

12. Samuel P. Huntington, *Political Order,* uses speed as one criterion.

13. Rosenau and Eckstein employ typologies of war which subsume revolution. James Rosenau, ed., *International Aspects of Civil Strife* (Princeton: Princeton University Press, 1964), pp. 63-64; and Harry Eckstein, ed., *Internal War* (New York: The Free Press, 1964), p. 12.

14. Violence is perhaps the most common theme used to define revolution. See, for example, Huntington, *Political Order,* p. 264; Eckstein, *Internal War,* pp. 63-64; Andrew C. Janos, "Authority and Violence: The Political Framework of Internal War," in *Internal War,* ed. Harry Eckstein, p. 133; Ted Robert Gurr, *Why Men Rebel* (Princeton: Princeton University Press, 1970), pp. 5 and 9; Brinton, *Anatomy of Revolution,* p. 4; and Ted Robert Gurr, "Psychological Factors in Civil Strife," *World Politics* 20, no. 2 (January 1966):246; Chalmers Johnson, *Revolutionary Change* (Boston: Little, Brown, 1966), pp. 1, 8, and 13, defines revolution as violent social change and violence as disorienting behavior. Peter Amman, "Revolution: A Redefinition," *Political Science Quarterly* 79, no. 1 (March 1962):36-53, defines revolution as an effective challenge to a state's monopoly of power, a definition based on a misunderstanding of Weber and a false assumption that any state can exercise a monopoly of all power. In response to arguments like Gurr's *(Why Men Rebel,* p. 5) that definitions in terms of violence are useful because violence is a central theme of political science, Henry Bienen, *Violence and Social Change* (Chicago: University of Chicago Press, 1966), p. 66, retorts that most thinkers who define revolution in this way neglect violence in their analyses of revolution.

15. Chalmers Johnson, *Revolution and the Social System* (Stanford: Hoover Institution Press, 1964), uses this factor in the construction

of a typology.

16. Johnson, *Revolutionary Change*, pp. 146-147, argues that revolutions should be so classified, but does not provide a typology of societies.

17. Hannah Arendt, *On Revolution* (New York: Viking, 1965), pp. 30, 36; Huntington, *Political Order*, p. 265, does not define revolution in terms of progressiveness, but does maintain that "revolution is the ultimate expression of the modernizing outlook, the belief that it is within the power of man to control and to change his environment," a judgment which seems to me to neglect innumerable peasant revolts which were confident of ability to create heaven on earth. Arendt's position (*On Revolution*, p. 15) is similar to Huntington's.

18. Arendt, *On Revolution*, pp. 21-22: "Crucial, then to an understanding of revolutions in the modern age is that the idea of freedom and the experience of a new beginning should coincide."

19. Huntington takes the position that revolutions are transitional phenomena (*Political Order*, p. 265), and Johnson that they are modern phenomena (*Revolutionary Change*, p. 14).

20. Arendt, *On Revolution*, pp. 30 and 36.

21. Eric Hoffer, *The True Believer* (New York: Time Inc., 1963), p. 32.

22. For example, in Moore, "Predicting Discontinuities."

23. Disequilibrium is the central concept characterizing revolution in Johnson, *Revolutionary Change*.

24. For alternative structural definitions see Brinton, *Anatomy of Revolution*, p. 5; Louis Gottschalk, "Causes of Revolution," *American Journal of Sociology* 50, no. 1 (July 1944):4; Carl J. Friedrich, "An Introductory Note on Revolution," in *Revolution*, ed. Carl J. Friedrich (New York: Lieber-Atherton, 1969), p. 5; Huntington's definition previously cited; Sigmund Neumann, "The International Civil War," *World Politics* 1, no. 3 (April 1949):33; Harold Lasswell, *Politics: Who Gets What, When, How* (New York: World Publishing Co., 1965), p. 113; and James Burnham, *The Machiavellians* (Chicago: Gateway, 1943), p. 257.

25. Jules Michelet, *History of the Revolution*, quoted in Edmund Wilson, *To the Finland Station: A Study in the Writing and Acting of History* (Garden City, N.Y.: Doubleday, 1953), p. 17.

26. Karl Marx, "Wage Labor and Capital," in Karl Marx and Friedrich Engels, *Selected Works* (Moscow: Foreign Languages Publishing House, 1962), p. 94; Karl Marx, "The Class Struggles in France, 1848-1850," in Marx and Engels, *Selected Works*, p. 231; Karl Marx, *Capital* (New

York: Modern Library, n.d.), pp. 708-709. Cf. also the commentary on this point in Reinhard Bendix and Seymour Martin Lipset, eds., *Class, Status and Power* (New York: The Free Press, 1966), p. 10; Erich Fromm, *Escape From Freedom* (New York: Discus Books, 1967); David Reisman, et al., *The Lonely Crowd* (New Haven: Yale University Press, 1969), esp. p. 242; C. Wright Mills, *White Collar* (New York: Oxford University Press, 1956); Robert K. Merton, *Social Theory and Social Structure* (New York: The Free Press, 1968), chapter 6; Emile Durkheim, *Suicide* (New York: The Free Press, 1951); Paul Goodman, *Growing Up Absurd* (New York: Random House, 1960). On peasants, cf. James C. Scott, "Explorations in Rural Class Relations: A Victim's Perspective," *Comparative Politics* 7, no. 4 (July 1975):489-532. See also my "Revolution," fn. 118, 199, and 120.

27. Ted Robert Gurr, *Why Men Rebel*; Ivo K. Feierabend, Rosalind L. Feierabend, and Betty A. Nesvold, "Social Change and Political Violence: Cross-National Patterns," in *Violence in America: Historical and Comparative Perspectives*, ed. Hugh Davis Graham and Ted Robert Gurr (Washington, D.C.: National Commission on the Causes and Prevention of Violence, 1969).

28. For a recent example, see Harry J. Benda, "Reflections on Asian Communism," *Yale Review* 56, no. 1 (September 1966):1-16.

29. Kurt Riezler, "On the Psychology of the Modern Revolution," *Social Research* 10 (September 1963):320-336.

30. Frantz Fanon, *The Wretched of the Earth* (New York: Grove Press, 1968).

31. Fromm, *Escape from Freedom*, pp. 96-97.

32. Chalmers Johnson, *Revolutionary Change*, pp. 84-85; Hoffer, *True Believer*, chapter 1.

33. Bittner, "The Organization of Radical Movements."

34. Ibid.

35. Johnson, *Revolutionary Change*, as previously noted.

36. Barrington Moore, *Political Power and Social Theory* (New York: Harper & Row, 1968), p. 7. For the concept "Western revolution," see Huntington, *Political Order*, chapter 5.

37. V. I. Lenin, *What Is To Be Done?* (New York: International Publishers, 1943), p. 40.

38. Mao Tse-tung, "The Struggle in the Chingkang Mountains," *Selected Works* (New York: International Publishers, 1954), vol. 1, p. 99.

39. James Petras and Maurice Zeitlin, "Miners and Agrarian Radicalism," *American Sociological Review* 32, no. 4 (August 1967):578-586.

40. Donald von Eschen, "The Politics of Factories in the Field" (paper for American Sociological Association Annual Meeting, Montreal, August 1974).

41. Barrington Moore, *Political Power*, p. 7.

42. Peter A. Lupsha, "Explanation of Political Violence: Some Psychological Theories Versus Indignation," *Politics and Society* 2, no. 1 (Fall 1971):89-104.

43. Fromm, *Escape from Freedom*; T. W. Adorno, Else Frenkel-Brunswick, D. J. Levinson, and R. N. Sanford, *The Authoritarian Personality* (New York: Harper, 1950).

44. Milton Rokeach, *The Open and Closed Mind* (New York: Basic Books, 1960).

45. Leon Festinger, *A Theory of Cognitive Dissonance* (Stanford, Calif.: Stanford University Press, 1957).

46. Conrad Morrow, "Aggression toward Whom: A Psychological Model of Aggressive Political Behavior" (Ph.D. dissertation, Yale University, 1973).

47. E. Victor Wolfenstein, *Revolutionary Personality: Lenin, Trotsky, Gandhi* (Princeton, N.J.: Princeton University Press, 1967).

48. Edgar Snow, *Red Star over China* (New York: Grove Press, 1961), p. 123ff.

49. E. Victor Wolfenstein, *Violence or Nonviolence: A Psychoanalytic Exploration of the Choice of Political Means in Social Change* (Princeton, N.J.: Center of International Studies, 1966).

50. Cf. Wilson, *Finland Station*, pp. 266, 232, and 446-447.

51. Erik H. Erikson, *Gandhi's Truth* (New York: Norton, 1969); and *Young Man Luther* (New York: Norton, 1958).

52. Fromm, *Escape from Freedom*, p. 83.

53. Feierabend et al., "Social Change and Political Violence."

54. James C. Davies, "The J-Curve of Rising and Declining Satisfactions as a Cause of some Great Revolutions and a Contained Rebellion," in *Violence in America*, ed. Graham and Gurr.

55. Roy Hofheinz, Jr., "The Ecology of Chinese Communist Success: Rural Influence Patterns, 1923-45," in *Chinese Communist Politics in Action*, ed. A. Doak Barnett (Seattle: University of Washington Press,

1969), pp. 3-77; Ted R. Gurr, "Psychological Factors in Civil Strife," *World Politics* 20, no. 2 (January 1968):245-278; Gurr, *Why Men Rebel*; Edward J. Mitchell, "Inequality and Insurgency: A Statistical Study of South Vietnam," *World Politics* 20, no 3 (April 1968):421-438. Mitchell's work on the Huks has proved to be unreproducible, according to H. A. Averch, F. H. Denton, and J. E. Koehler, *A Crisis of Ambiguity: Political and Economic Development in the Philippines* (Santa Monica: RAND, 1970), 207n; and Mitchell's work on Vietnam has been effectively challenged by Jeffrey M. Paige, "Inequality and Insurgency in Vietnam: A Re-analysis," *World Politics* 23, no. 1 (October 1970):24-37. See also Bruce M. Russett, "Inequality and Instability: The Relation of Land Tenure to Politics," *World Politics* 16, no. 3 (April 1964):442-454; Donald S. Zagoria, "Kerala and West Bengal," *Problems of Communism* 22, no. 1 (January-February 1973):16-27; Donald S. Zagoria, "A Note on Landlessness, Literacy and Agrarian Communism in India," *European Journal of Sociology* 12 (1972):326-334; and Donald S. Zagoria, "The Ecology of Peasant Communism in India," *American Political Science Review* 65, no. 1 (March 1971).

56. The contradiction is resolved by treating discontent as one requisite frequently absent. Cf. Overholt, "Revolution," pp. 18-20.

57. David E. Apter, *The Politics of Modernization* (Chicago: University of Chicago Press, 1967), pp. 12-22, provides a simpler division of theories into normative, behavioral, and structural.

58. On dysfunctions in a theory of revolution, see Chalmers Johnson, *Revolution and the Social System*; on disequilibrium, see his *Revolutionary Change*; on strain, see Neil J. Smelser, *Theory of Collective Behavior* (New York: The Free Press, 1962); on incongruence between values and environment as a source of political instability, see Johnson, *Revolutionary Change*; on incongruence of authority patterns as a source of instability in democracy, see Harry Eckstein, *Division and Cohesion in a Democracy* (Princeton, N.J.: Princeton University Press, 1966); on stress, see Wallace, "Revitalization Movements"; on tension management, see Arnold S. Feldman, "Violence and Volatility: The Likelihood of Revolution," in *Internal War*, ed. Eckstein, pp. 11-29. The concept of contradictions is familiar from Marx and Mao.

59. Arthur O. Lovejoy, *The Great Chain of Being: A Study in the History of an Idea* (Cambridge, Mass.: Harvard University Press, 1936).

60. For a discussion of Marx's theory of revolution at this level of generality, see Robert C. Tucker, *The Marxian Revolutionary Idea* (New York: Norton, 1969), chapter 1.

61. Karl Marx, "Wage Labor and Capital," in Marx and Engels, *Selected Works*, p. 94.

62. Karl Marx, "The Class Struggles in France," in *Selected Works*, p. 231.

63. Karl Marx, *Capital*, pp. 708-709.

64. Johnson, *Revolutionary Change*, p. 3.

65. Johnson, *Revolution and the Social System*.

66. Johnson, *Revolutionary Change*.

67. Ibid., p. 13.

68. Ibid., pp. 92 and 99.

69. For instance, Smelser, *Collective Behavior*, p. 352.

70. Lyford P. Edwards, *The Natural History of Revolution* (New York: Russell and Russell, 1965).

71. For the relevant discussion of precipitants, see Marx, "Class Struggles in France," in *Selected Works*, p. 98ff.

72. Johnson, *Revolutionary Change*, p. 99.

73. Feldman, "Violence and Volatility."

74. Bienen, *Violence and Social Change*, p. 69.

75. Philip Selznick, *The Organizational Weapon: A Study of Bolshevik Strategy and Tactics* (New York: McGraw-Hill, 1952).

76. Franz Schurmann, *Ideology and Organization in Communist China* (Berkeley and Los Angeles: University of California Press, 1966).

77. Ibid., pp. 69-73.

78. Huntington, *Political Order*. See also John R. Gillis, "Political Decay and the European Revolutions," *World Politics* 22, no. 3 (April 1970):344-370.

79. Stanley H. Kochanek, "Perspectives on the Study of Revolution and Social Change," *Comparative Politics* 5, no. 3 (April 1973):318.

80. Janos, "Authority and Violence."

81. Brinton, *Anatomy of Revolution*.

82. Wallace, "Revitalization Movements."

83. Huntington, *Political Order*, pp. 266-274.

84. Hopper, "The Revolutionary Process."

85. Hans Toch, *The Psychology of Social Movements* (New York: Bobbs-Merrill, 1965).

86. Gurr, *Why Men Rebel*, p. 13.

87. Smelser, *Collective Behavior*, p. 14ff, for the basic sequence. For his discussion of conduciveness in a revolutionary context, cf. pp. 319-338.

88. Huntington, *Political Order*.

89. Barrington Moore, *Political Power*, chapter 1.

90. Ibid., p. 2.

91. Ibid., p. 3.

92. Ibid., p. 4.

93. Ibid., p. 26.

94. Nathan Leites and C. Wolf, Jr., *Rebellion and Authority* (Chicago: Markham, 1970).

95. Ibid., p. 3.

96. Cf. n. 1 of this chapter.

97. Charles Tilly, "Does Modernization Breed Revolution?" *Comparative Politics* 5, no. 3 (April 1973):425-447.

98. Wilson, *Finland Station*, p. 482-483.

99. Nathan Glazer and Daniel Moynihan, "Why Ethnicity?" *Commentary* 58, no. 4 (October 1974):33-39.

100. For further discussion, see William H. Overholt and Herman Kahn, "Perceptions of Quality of Life: Some Effects of Social Strata and Social Change," in *Qualities of Life*, Commission on Critical Choices for Americans (Lexington, Mass.: Lexington Books, 1976).

101. Cf. William H. Overholt, "Martial Law, Revolution and Democracy in the Philippines," *Southeast Asia Quarterly* 2, no. 2 (Spring 1972).

102. Sheldon S. Wolin, "The Politics of the Study of Revolution," *Comparative Politics* 5, no. 3 (April 1973):343-358.

103. Ibid., p. 354.